Guerrilla Marketing

Chicago Studies in Practices of Meaning

A series edited by Andreas Glaeser, William Mazzarella, William H. Sewell Jr., Kaushik Sunder Rajan, and Lisa Wedeen

Published in collaboration with the Chicago Center for Contemporary Theory
http://ccct.uchicago.edu

Recent books in the series

WHAT NOSTALGIA WAS: WAR, EMPIRE, AND THE TIME OF A DEADLY EMOTION *by Thomas Dodman*

THE MANA OF MASS SOCIETY *by William Mazzarella*

THE SINS OF THE FATHER: GERMANY, MEMORY, METHOD *by Jeffrey K. Olick*

THE POLITICS OF DIALOGIC IMAGINATION: POWER AND POPULAR CULTURE IN EARLY MODERN JAPAN *by Katsuya Hirano*

AMERICAN VALUE: MIGRANTS, MONEY, AND MEANING IN EL SALVADOR AND THE UNITED STATES *by David Pedersen*

QUESTIONING SECULARISM: ISLAM, SOVEREIGNTY, AND THE RULE OF LAW IN MODERN EGYPT *by Hussein Ali Agrama*

THE MAKING OF ROMANTIC LOVE: LONGING AND SEXUALITY IN EUROPE, SOUTH ASIA, AND JAPAN, 900–1200 CE *by William M. Reddy*

THE MORAL NEOLIBERAL: WELFARE AND CITIZENSHIP IN ITALY *by Andrea Muehlebach*

THE GENEALOGICAL SCIENCE: THE SEARCH FOR JEWISH ORIGINS AND THE POLITICS OF EPISTEMOLOGY *by Nadia Abu El-Haj*

LAUGHING AT LEVIATHAN: SOVEREIGNTY AND AUDIENCE IN WEST PAPUA *by Danilyn Rutherford*

Guerrilla Marketing

Counterinsurgency and Capitalism in Colombia

ALEXANDER L. FATTAL

THE UNIVERSITY OF CHICAGO PRESS   CHICAGO AND LONDON

The University of Chicago Press, Chicago 60637
The University of Chicago Press, Ltd., London
© 2018 by The University of Chicago
Published 2018
Printed in the United States of America

27 26 25 24 23 22 21 20 19   2 3 4 5

ISBN-13: 978-0-226-59050-9 (cloth)
ISBN-13: 978-0-226-59064-6 (paper)
ISBN-13: 978-0-226-59078-3 (e-book)
DOI: https://doi.org/10.7208/chicago/9780226590783.001.0001

Library of Congress Cataloging-in-Publication Data

Names: Fattal, Alexander L., author.
Title: Guerrilla marketing : counterinsurgency and capitalism in Colombia /
    Alexander L. Fattal.
Other titles: Chicago studies in practices of meaning.
Description: Chicago ; London : The University of Chicago Press, 2018. | Series: Chicago
    studies in practices of meaning | Includes bibliographical references and index.
Identifiers: LCCN 2018019138 | ISBN 9780226590509 (cloth : alk. paper) |
    ISBN 9780226590646 (pbk. : alk. paper) | ISBN 9780226590783 (e-book)
Subjects: LCSH: Colombia—Politics and government—1974– | Propaganda—Colombia. |
    Counterinsurgency—Colombia. | Mass media and peace—Colombia. | Mass media
    and war—Colombia. | Insurgency—Colombia. | Fuerzas Armadas Revolucionarias
    de Colombia.
Classification: LCC F2279 .F387 2018 | DDC 986.106/34—dc23
LC record available at https://lccn.loc.gov/2018019138

FOR MOM, DAD, JOSH, AND OUR FAMILIES—
MORE AND LESS NUCLEAR

Contents

Preface   ix

Introduction: Guerrilla Marketing   1
          Omar   34

CHAPTER 1.   An Archaeology of Media Spectacle, 1974–2008   41
          Juana   69

CHAPTER 2.   Operation Christmas   79
          Gabriel   111

CHAPTER 3.   Operation Genuine   125
          Claudia   155

CHAPTER 4.   The Good Life Deferred and Risks of
          Remobilization   163
          Sergio   198

Conclusion: The Colombian Model   205
          Diego   222

Epilogue: Target Intimacy   229

          Acknowledgments   247
          Notes   253
          Bibliography   285
          Index   301

Preface

B efore Being a Guerrilla, You Are My Child.
Paid for by the Colombian Ministry of Defense and expertly crafted by the consumer marketing firm Lowe/SSP3, this campaign used personal photographs, the kind that mothers store in shoeboxes and tape into family albums. One picture features a puffy-cheeked toddler primly dressed in white. A second picture, of a boy posing in pants two years too big, is washed out in a sepia tone. In a third photo, grainy and poorly focused, a mother holds an excitable infant in her arms. From the mother's gaze, it seems like she is collaborating to produce a memory with the photographer (the baby's father?). In the ventriloquism so central to their trade, the marketers behind the campaign created a disembodied voice—that of a guerrilla fighter's mother who calls to her daughter or son to abandon the insurgency and return home for the Christmas holidays.

Every Christmas season between 2010 and 2014, the Ministry of Defense and Lowe/SSP3 would work together to release a new emotionally charged multimedia onslaught.[1] Here, in the 2013 campaign, "You Are My Child," soldiers stand in formation and hold the posters bearing childhood photographs for the camera, pinching their fingers on command (figure P.1). There will be much by way of contextualization in the following pages, but now I want to rip this image from its context, for it condenses the themes of this book: the convergence of consumer marketing and counterinsurgency; intimacy as a target of both spheres of expertise; how the shifting grounds of kinship, gender, social relations, and cultural production condition the way antiguerrilla warfare is waged; and the belief in branding's ability to reconcile the irreconcilable, such as the idea of a humanitarian counterinsurgency.

FIGURE P.I. Still photograph from "You Are My Child" campaign of Christmas 2013. Photo courtesy of Colombian Ministry of National Defense.

The message of "You Are My Child" is misleadingly simple. It only skims the surface. But the point of this book is to go deep beneath the surface, to untangle a web of images, affects, and ideologies that this carefully composed photograph with its militarized formation of other photographs can only wink at. What follows is not a systematic study of how these campaigns were received by audiences. I am interested in affects more than effects, though clearly the two are intertwined. Consider, for example, the affective response to "You Are My Child" of Lara Logan, a reporter for *60 Minutes*. She arrived to Bogotá one week after Colombia signed a historic peace accord with the Revolutionary Armed Forces of Colombia (FARC). The American television newsmagazine had come to feature the work of Lowe/SSP3 in Colombia, not its stewardship of brands like Mazda and Red Bull, but its ten-year effort to lure fighters out of the FARC and ELN, two Marxist insurgencies that date back to the mid-1960s.[2] *60 Minutes'* report, "Advertising to Sell Peace Not Products," is fawning. Miguel Sokoloff, the most prominent partner of Lowe/SSP3, gave Logan a multimedia presentation of the company's work on the Ministry of Defense account. When he presented the videos from "You Are My Child," he gave the tag line "Before being a guerrilla, you are my child," and added, "So come home, I will always be waiting for you at Christmastime."

Her eyes wet with emotion, Logan said, "We call that going for the jugular Jose, because . . . wow."

The segment's producer, Alan Goldberg, was also impressed. CBS posted an interview with him on its webpage as a supplement to its coverage; he concluded by saying, "Who knows what will happen after our report airs. Maybe Sokoloff's phone will be ringing off the hook from other governments looking for a way to solve their wars."[3]

The slick advertising spots derive their force from surprise—surprise at their unlikely creativity, humanism, and intelligence. Those associations—surprise, creativity, humanism, intelligence—had been antithetical to the image of the Colombian military. Lowe/SSP3's task was not only to lure people out of the guerrilla but also to reorient the public's affective disposition toward the armed forces.

Logan and Goldberg's enchantment with Sokoloff's story was no accident. For years Sokoloff had promoted his firm's work to international audiences in particular. In 2014 he gave a TED talk in Rio de Janeiro titled "How Christmas Lights Helped Guerrillas Put Down Their Guns." His story was so compelling that it induced CBS's flagship news program to forget the most basic principle of journalism: do not rely on only one source. *60 Minutes'* reporting did not include the voices of any former guerrillas and relied exclusively on materials and representations provided by the marketers. Even one of my favorite shows, the quirky and inquisitive radio magazine *This American Life*, fell into the same trap, creating a segment that did not deviate from the marketers' perspective.

The idea that marketing had the power to debilitate one of the world's largest and most formidable insurgencies and precipitate peace seduced distinguished US media programs and Colombia's mass media, as well as policy elites in Washington and Bogotá. Behind the unexpected creativity of campaigns such as "You Are My Child" lies an ideological axis ready to embrace the idea that the world's most intractable problems can be branded away. Lowe/SSP3 is both the vanguard and the poster child for this idea.

In this book I examine what is at stake in the confluence of marketing and counterinsurgency in Colombia. Through ethnographic analysis I raise questions beyond the scope of *60 Minutes'* coverage. Questions like *What does it mean to weaponize advertising, the crux of late capitalism, in a bid to vanquish armed Marxism from the Americas? How has branding emerged as a central battleground in wars of the twenty-first century? To what extent do people who desert leave war behind, and to what extent are they remobilized in another? What might it mean to cast the marketization of counterinsurgency as a model to be replicated internationally?* The answers that I have found in my research, however fragmentary, paint a much more complex picture than the triumphalist narrative that Lowe/SSP3 and the Colombian Ministry of Defense skillfully pitched to news outlets and their audiences.

Another glaring absence from the *60 Minutes* segment is discussion of the plebiscite on an initial peace agreement between the Colombian government and the FARC in 2016. In that referendum held on October 2, 2016, the No vote carried the day, winning with a margin of 0.4 percent. The narrow victory of the No campaign sent the government and the FARC back to the negotiating table. On November 30, 2016, the Colombian Congress approved a slightly modified version of the accord. The 310-page agreement outlined a formidable list of transitional and transcendental reforms. A few of the pillars of the peace accord are redistributing land; forging a more inclusive democracy; creating a transitional justice framework to balance the demands of truth, justice, and punishment; and designing a framework for demobilizing and reintegrating the FARC's fighters. While the announcement of negotiations in 2012 created widespread excitement in Colombia, by the time the two parties emerged with the document four years later that excitement was long gone. Right-wing politicians systematically attacked the agreement throughout the negotiating period, in the campaign leading up to the plebiscite, and in the implementation of the final accord—effectively fulfilling their promise to shred the accord.[4]

Why the plebiscite failed is a question deserving of a book of its own. For the purposes of this one, however, it is important to note that Lowe/SSP3 played a role in that too. Unlike its work with for the Ministry of Defense however, the firm's efforts here had intense competition. Lowe/SSP3 was essentially outmarketed. Whereas the Yes campaign relied primarily on television and radio advertisements to spread its universal message of peace, the No campaign sowed division with different messages that micro-targeted demographic subgroups via social media. Led by former president Álvaro Uribe, the No campaign used disinformation and conservative wedge issues to fracture the Yes campaign's invocation of peace as a magical transformation on the horizon. Uribe and his followers mobilized against issues as diverse and divisive as the prospect of former FARC fighters receiving welfare and the incremental progress on expanding rights to people of all sexual orientations. The campaign played upon deep-seated fears of communist subversion from within the political system and reinvigorated a long-standing alliance between the interests of the religious right, conservative political factions, and the Colombian military, sectors of society threatened by the changes written into the accord.

As the post–peace accord political system in Colombia absorbs the intensity of the war, the battles over Colombia's future will be fought with the changing arsenal of consumer marketing. The story that unfolds in these pages is of a particular moment in the mutating assemblage of war and marketing, the period between 2003 and 2016, when sixteen thousand guerrilla fighters deserted from the FARC and joined the government's individual demobilization program. Note that the number of FARC fighters who disarmed and demobilized individually is nearly double the number of those who disarmed and began their demobilization and reintegration process in 2017 after the peace agreement. The demobilizations of 2003–16 have been largely eclipsed by the political and historical significance of the 2016 accord, yet it was during the first years of the third millennium when marketing emerged as a central strategy of antiguerrilla warfare in Colombia, and it was also when the postconflict state was born.

Guerrilla Marketing

When I began my research I ventured into the library's stacks to review the academic literature on the Colombian conflict. I spent the afternoon gradually zigzagging between rows of shelves, down one aisle and over to the next. The density and intensity of the conflict, dizzying in its complexity, leapt off the page. It felt like the war's many mutations, over generations, had been analyzed from every angle. Did libraries need another book about political violence in Colombia? I left that first foray into scholarly production about Colombia's war with a sense that the conflict was overdiagnosed and that my multiyear project—which might one day become another book on those shelves—was futile.

Fieldwork cured my doubts. In Colombia's individual demobilization program I found a subject rich in contradictions and ripe for ethnographic analysis. The Program for Humanitarian Attention to the Demobilized, or PAHD, is a special unit within the Colombian Ministry of Defense dedicated to demobilizing individual FARC fighters.[1] I learned that the PAHD embodied a larger process: the state's striving for postconflict status. The program expressed the government's dual aspirations, to defeat its Marxist challengers and to prove—to itself and to the world—that it had consolidated its historically fragmented sovereignty and overcome the invisible forces pulling the country, time and again, toward political violence. The postconflict state is built upon images that stimulate imaginaries of this continually deferred future, on the one hand, and an agenda for reforms, on the other.

Those reforms moved in two competing directions, paring down the funds for social welfare in neoliberal fashion while bloating the budget of the country's armed forces. This double movement aligned Colombia's form of neoliberalism with that of the United States. What is unique to Colombia, however, is its massive allocation of targeted welfare for the war's victims and perpetrators. The government would, in essence, purchase the complacency of the populations most affected by the war—the forcibly displaced and demobilized members of the groups that displaced them—rather than address the social and economic conditions that have historically fueled the conflict. The contradictory process began in the early 1990s when the country started a process of *apertura* (opening) that would liberalize trade and shear spending on health and education.[2] In the early 2000s, rather than question the organization of the economy in which expenditure on social programs decreased while military budgets expanded, the government began to pay the displaced and the demobilized, as archetypal victims and perpetrators, in elaborate welfare schemes. As we will see, branding as a neoliberal technology for managing the visible and invisible dimensions of global capitalism served the purposes of the Colombian government uncannily well. Through brand management, Colombian policy elites could highlight the robust facets of the state—military modernization and postconflict social welfare—while hiding the hollowing out of other state institutions such as the ministries of health and education.

The circumstances that would give rise to the postconflict state started to come together in 2002, after the failure of the Caguán peace negotiations (named after the southern city where they were held). In the three-year period of the Caguán peace talks (1999–2002), the FARC had grown stronger and wealthier, taking advantage of President Andrés Pastrana's order for the military to withdraw from five municipalities, an area the size of Maryland, to facilitate the talks. The military referred to the zone derisively as "FARC-landia" for the way in which it gave the national map a black eye of sorts and became a place where the Marxist group openly enacted its own sovereign imaginary. When negotiations broke down in February 2002, the military fought to reclaim the territory.

As peace by violent pacification replaced peace by negotiation, the Colombian government, paradoxically, proceeded to create a series of policies typically reserved for a post–peace accord moment. Congress passed laws and invented agencies to design and implement programs *as if* an accord had been struck. The individual demobilization of guerrilla fighters was only one of the policies put into place in the early 2000s to perform postconflictness. The government also negotiated an agreement with its paramilitary allies and proceeded to demobilize their rank and file. It created a commission to compensate victims of the conflict, most notably those who had been displaced from their homes, and to write definitive reports about historical memory. An alphabet soup of government agencies implemented this bundle of postconflict policies. Since 2003 those agencies have changed their names and reshuffled their portfolios, all the while expanding their scope and digging roots deeper into state structures. Anthropologist Kimberly Theidon has aptly termed this temporal jumble of enacting transitional policies in the midst of a war "pre-post conflict."[3] By focusing on the PAHD, I have chosen to zoom in on one pillar of Colombia's (pre-)postconflict state, and by analyzing marketing's prominent role in the individual demobilization program, I elucidate how marketing and militarism work together to conjure a future mission-accomplished moment.

I will turn to marketing, specifically branding, in the next section, but first I want to place the PAHD in political context. The first step in the daunting task of providing a synopsis of Colombia's seemingly endless war is to make a simple point: a singular Colombian conflict does not exist. What Colombians refer to casually as "the conflict" is really an overlapping and interrelated set of different conflicts staggered through history. This has not stopped think tanks and government agencies from aggregating statistics about *the* Colombian conflict. The Center for National Memory (heir to the National Commission for Reparation and Reconciliation, created in 2005) is one of Colombia's premier prepostconflict agencies, and in 2013 it issued its definitive report on *the* Colombian armed conflict. It concluded that the war killed "at least 220,000 people" between 1958 and 2012.[4] The report goes on to document various types of atrocities—massacres, kidnappings, forced disappearances, displacement of the civilian population—and to apportion, in mathematical fashion, the responsibility of guerrillas, paramilitaries, government forces, and "unknown groups" for each of these tragic categories.

For those unfamiliar with these various groups, allow me to sketch in the main actors in Colombia's layered conflicts. By the 2010s, when I conducted the research for this book, the FARC and the ELN were the only remaining guerrilla groups. Founded in the mid-1960s, both espoused Marxism. The ELN drew inspiration from the Cuban Revolution, especially Che Guevara's tactical doctrine of swarming small guerrilla nuclei (*focos*), and later liberation theology, an interpretation of Christian teaching that takes the religion's commitment to the downtrodden seriously, to the point that it condones taking up arms on their behalf. The FARC, for its part, has been inextricably linked to the Colombian Communist Party. A confluence of communist guerrillas and militant liberals, both of whom had gone to war with the conservative governments of the late 1940s and early 1950s, gave birth to the FARC. That period, known simply as La Violencia in Colombia, was a time when the country split into regional conflicts. Elites from the two principal political parties mobilized their bases in a partisan bloodletting. The Conservative Party brought together the powerful institutions of the church and the military in a traditionalist platform, whereas the Liberal Party held together a fissile coalition of party elites, social democrats, marginalized ethnic groups, and an array of more militant leftist movements.

In 1958 a bipartisan power-sharing agreement precipitated a period of relative calm that preceded the mobilization of the FARC and the ELN, which were by no means the only guerrilla groups founded in the 1960s.[5] (The power-sharing agreement struck between Liberals and Conservatives in 1958 is known as the National Front. It lasted until 1974 and underlined the exclusionary nature of Colombian politics.) As in many countries in Latin America, revolutionary fervor boiled after the Cuban Revolution.[6] Of the myriad other revolutionary groups spawned between the mid-1960s and early 1980s, the most prominent were the Popular Liberation Army (EPL), Maoist in inspiration; the M19, a nationalist, more urban guerrilla organization; and the Quintín Lame Armed Movement, a group committed to the rights and liberation of indigenous people, especially of Cauca Department.[7]

For the FARC, which always stood out for its capacity to resist the military's aggressive efforts to hunt it down, land was the principal issue. Agrarian reform and redistribution of land to the peasants is a potent platform in a country that has the most unequal distribution of land in Latin America, the world's least equitable region.[8] To what extent ideology has remained a driving force in Colombia's wars is hotly debated. With the influx of billions of dollars in drug profits in the late 1970s and 1980s, narcomafias and paramilitary groups proliferated.[9] Colombian cocaine dominated the world market. It still does. The largesse created by this illicit economy helped to pad the coffers of all of the country's armed groups.[10] By the 1990s, when many civil wars in the region were coming to political resolution in the twilight of the Cold War, the FARC enmeshed itself in the supply chain of cocaine. Its adversaries have used its decision to finance its operations by taxing the drug trade to argue that the FARC abandoned its ideological program and devolved into just another armed actor profiting on the authority of its weapons. Though the contradiction of Marxist insurgents acting as savvy capitalists is undeniable, the conclusion that the group's turn to drug trafficking for funds voided its political project is specious. That is not to say that the 1990s were not a period of ideological challenges for the FARC— they were, but rather for a series of other reasons. For starters, its historical ideologue Jacobo Arenas died in 1990. That happened in the midst of a fierce debate in the Colombian left about the merits and demerits of electoral versus armed struggle. A coterie of guerrilla groups chose to transform into political parties, while members of the Patriotic Union, a FARC-affiliated party, were systematically assassinated, retrenching the FARC's commitment to armed insurrection. Internationally, the left reeled from the implosion of the Soviet Union. This is all to say that the 1990s were a period of ideological flux, even crisis, for the FARC, but not because of its decision to involve itself in the drug trade.

Despite the challenge posed through the late 1980s and 1990s, the FARC expanded exponentially, growing each front until it could spin off into two, three, or four new fronts.[11] This growth was due, in no small measure, to a crisis of legitimacy in the state paired with economic devastation in the countryside where 90 percent of FARC combatants hail from. From the vantage of the peasantry, soaring rural poverty and a threadbare safety net spurred by neoliberal reforms at the beginning of the 1990s pushed people to join the FARC. The FARC's recruitment practices are the flip side of PAHD's efforts to demobilize guerrilla fighters.

The FARC takes a wide-ranging approach to recruitment. As one former midlevel FARC guerrilla told me, "Ask ten people why they joined, and you will get ten different answers." Parents volunteer their children in some cases; more commonly, kids flee home to escape abusive parents or stepparents. Siblings or cousins recruit their kin, while some orphans who want a change from the hard labor of pulling coca leaves opt for three meals a day. Some join because they had a teenage crush on a guerrilla fighter; others enlist out of a deep ideological commitment to social change. Some revere the authority of guns, while the cars and motorcycles on which guerrillas roll through town enchant others. Some make the decision to join when they are drunk or barely adolescents, or both. Some decide to avenge the death of a relative at the hands of the paramilitaries; others defect from the military, where they felt humiliated by a commanding officer.[12] Though many factors pushed people to join the insurgency, neoliberal economic reforms and a crisis of state legitimacy were two central circumstances operating in the background.

The influence of drug money in politics fueled the Colombian state's legitimacy crisis. A high-profile scandal in which the Cali cartel had funded the winning presidential campaign of Ernesto Samper in 1994 illustrated the reach of Colombia's narco-economy ("narco-democracy," according to DEA agent Joe Toft). By the end of the 1990s the FARC had encroached on Bogotá's southern and eastern perimeter. The CIA, in 1994, concluded that without decisive action the group had a 50 percent chance of taking power within ten years.[13] Rebel victories at military bases such as Las Delicias (1996) and Patascoy (1997) further sounded this alarm. As the guerrilla threat grew, so did the paramilitary response.

In 1996 regional paramilitary groups syndicated as the United Self-Defense Forces of Colombia, or AUC. Who are the paramilitaries? "The term itself," writes anthropologist Michael Taussig, "is as elusive as what it points to, namely soldiers who are not really soldiers but more like ghosts flitting between the visible and the invisible, between the regular army and the criminal underworld of killers and torturers that all states seem to have no trouble recruiting when their backs are up against the wall."[14] A plethora of studies have investigated this ghastly world. Report after report has shown that a mixture of regional elites, corporations, and Colombian military officers have sponsored and supported these right-wing henchmen.[15] As the mercenary monster of paramilitarism roared militarily, it also seeped deeper into Colombian government and society. In 2010, Colombian political scientist Francisco Gutiérrez Sanin wrote, "When a paramilitary leader claimed that 35 percent of the Congress was in his hands, many thought it was an exaggeration. Judicial processes presently suggest that it was rather an understatement."[16]

Thanks to the fearless work of human rights defenders, the AUC's macabre tactics—for instance, playing soccer with the heads of its victims and dismembering corpses with chainsaws—became an unbearable stigma on the state.[17] By the early 2000s, the government could no longer look the other way as its paramilitary ally carried out massacre after massacre. The cost to the state's legitimacy had grown too great. The administration of President Álvaro Uribe struck a deal with the AUC's leadership that ended in the group's demobilization between 2003 and 2006. National television broadcast ceremonies of camouflage-clad fighters handing over their weapons created the impression that the plague of paramilitarism had magically disappeared. The problems with the de-mobilization and reintegration of the AUC—especially fraud and lack of justice for victims—have been the subject of other books, and are too elaborate to recount here.[18] Human Rights Watch decried the process as "smoke and mirrors."[19] What is most disconcerting about the demo-bilization of the AUC is that it failed to contain the paramilitary threat. Shortly after the elaborate disarmament ceremonies, regional groups known in Colombia alternatively as neoparamilitaries or criminal gangs sprouted up. These new groups combined a new generation of mercenar-ies with *re*mobilized members of the AUC. Regional groups—the Black Eagles, the Remains, the Gaintanist Association of Colombia, the Ura-beños, and the Paisas, among others—did not need to report to a na-tional command structure. They violently asserted their dominance over a territory to profit from the illegal economies in that area (drugs, extor-tion, mining). These groups have kept intact a long-standing tradition of killing leftist political activists and community leaders. By the late 2000s and 2010s, neoparamilitary groups began striking up precarious nonag-gression pacts among themselves and with the armed left—agreements that gave civilian populations minimal respite from the intensity of liv-ing in a contested territory. Although neoparamilitaries and guerrillas both found themselves subject to the state's coercive apparatus, the mili-tary prioritized the guerrilla threat despite the fact that neoparamilitary violence proved more pervasive.

Even in this short historical overview, one can begin to see how Co-lombia's armed conflict is an open-ended, recombinatory system of ac-tors, interests, and ideologies. The constellation of guerrilla groups, paramilitaries, criminal networks, and militarized responses is never static. Strategies, tactics, and discourses of each actor are utterly mod-ular, reappearing in different guises across ideological divides and tra-versing cracks in the fragile logic of alliance and rivalry. What I want to suggest is that peace policy helps to spur the mutations in this sys-tem.[20] Political scientists have taken great interest in how states develop through the act of making war, often unpacking Charles Tilly's adage that "war made the state, and the state made war."[21] Yet state making in Colombia was tied not only to waging war but also to the attempts to achieve a state of affairs that might resemble peace. Through the de-cades in which the open-ended system of Colombia's wars has spiraled along, the triangulation of peace policy, demobilization, and remobiliza-tion has shaped the Colombian state's modernizing project.

In the early 2000s the government of President Álvaro Uribe moved to co-opt the historical cycle of demobilization and remobilization, making it a matter of government policy. Through the PAHD, the Ministry of Defense not only plied former rebels for information but also, in many cases, armed them as combatants in military operations against their former comrades and used them as guides in rebel-held territory, chipping into the FARC's and ELN's greatest advantage: knowledge of the terrain.[22] (I have also heard of instances in which the military lent demobilized guerrillas to the paramilitaries to identify guerrilla collaborators to be killed.) Through these practices, the government *re*mobilized former guerrillas upon *de*mobilizing them. What I want to underline here is that this policy has strategically conflated attacking morale through psychological warfare, fomenting desertion, and flipping enemies into informants—all standard strategies of war going back millennia—and the technocratic peace-building initiatives of the United Nations. In 2006 the UN codified its policy on DDR, short for disarmament, demobilization, and reintegration, in a document called the Integrated Disarmament, Demobilization and Reintegration Standards, which states: "There are certain preconditions for DDR to take place, including: the signing of a negotiated peace agreement that provides a legal framework for DDR; trust in the peace process; willingness of the parties to the conflict to engage in DDR; and a minimum guarantee of security."[23] In Colombia in 2003, when the government created the PAHD, none of those preconditions had been met. DDR, according to the UN, is an instrument of peace by negotiation, not peace by military imposition.

Contra UN convention, Colombia has redefined demobilization policy as a counterinsurgency strategy, and in the process folded counterinsurgency, policing, and peacemaking in on each other.[24] Colombia, in essence, has upended the United Nations' definition of demobilization as a collective exercise to be undertaken after a peace agreement, and transformed it into a program to fragment guerrilla units by fomenting desertion through appeals to an individual's desires.[25] The story of Colombia's postconflict state relies on the government's ability to create and erase categories and boundaries as it sees fit in an impossible bid to manage the recombinatory system that is the country's armed conflict.[26]

The origin of the pre-postconflict state was on January 7, 1999, and was televised live from the main plaza of San Vicente del Caguán, a town in Caquetá Department. Audiences in the plaza and across the country watched President Andrés Pastrana sitting on a dais next to a conspicu-

FIGURE O.1. Colombian President Andrés Pastrana waits for FARC leader Manuel Marulanda, a no-show, at the opening of peace talks on January 7, 1999. State television and a FARC videographer record the scene. Photo by Marcelo Salinas/AFP.

ously empty white plastic chair. Foreboding the peace process's failure, Manuel Marulanda, the FARC's founder and patriarch, never showed (see figure O.1).[27]

President Pastrana may not have anticipated Marulanda's snub, but he did anticipate the possibility of failure. Days before his inauguration, he had sat in the Oval Office of the White House and appealed to US president Bill Clinton for a "Marshall Plan for Colombia." One month earlier, socialist firebrand Hugo Chávez had been elected president of neighboring Venezuela. Pastrana's appeal fell on receptive ears. "Plan Colombia" funneled more than $2 billion in US aid to Bogotá between 2000 and 2004, the vast majority of it dedicated to boosting the capacity of the armed forces. These upgrades outfitted mobile brigades and provided game-changing military hardware, such as Black Hawk helicopters that enabled night assaults. Although that type of assistance is what is most commonly associated with Plan Colombia, the United States also helped with two other crucial aspects of the counterinsurgency: professionalizing the propaganda effort and improving intelligence gathering.[28] This surge in military aid at the turn of the millennium often came in the form of subcontracts to US advisers. That is when iconic Madison

Avenue companies such as McCann-Erickson helped the Ministry of Defense craft institutional campaigns such as "In Colombia Heroes Exist" and "Faith in the Cause," which bear strong echoes of campaigns for the US Marines that featured choreographed action scenes with tanks, fighters jets, and resolute soldiers.[29] At the same time, global propaganda mercenaries such as John Rendon (who is most famous for helping stage the scene of American troops liberating Kuwait in the first Gulf War) began advising the Colombian military.[30] Rendon's overarching counsel was that the military needed to communicate offensively and not allow others, such as journalists or human rights activists, to define their actions and intentions. When I interviewed him in 2013 in an upscale Bogotá hotel, Rendon described how he pitched his message to the military in a language they could understand, saying, "If you view information as terrain, you only want to fight for the ground once—establish (the high ground) both with favorability and credibility."

In 2002 the Colombian people elected President Álvaro Uribe, who set a high bar when it came to communicating offensively.[31] The demagoguery sustained his popularity. If the Constitutional Court had not intervened, Colombian voters would likely have elected Uribe to a third term. Uribe labeled his cluster of war and peace policies "Democratic Security," a term that in practice meant subsuming democracy to security. The underlying goal, as stated in the government's 2003 "Democratic Security" policy paper, was to rectify "the historical inability of Colombian democracy to affirm the authority of its institutions over the entirety of the territory."[32] The document's authors reasoned that if people began to view the state as legitimate, they would then cooperate with the counterinsurgency, creating a "virtuous circle." Israeli security consultants helped flesh out the idea of the virtuous circle, which appears in a Democratic Security policy document as a diagrammed circle in which "investment in security" points to "trust and stability" (presumably of the civilian population), which points to "investment in security," which points to "economic growth," which points to "taxes and social investment," which points to "social welfare and satisfying needs," which points back to "investing in security" (figure 0.2).[33] Marxist geographer David Harvey has label this securitized iteration of trickle-down economics "armed neoliberalism."[34] The PAHD was but one cog in the state's infrastructure designed to spin this virtuous circle, a mechanism to both debilitate the FARC and project an aspirational image of the country's postconflict future. To render the counterinsurgency virtuous,

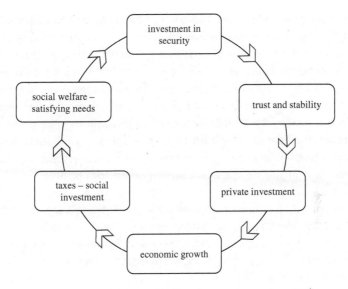

FIGURE 0.2. The virtuous circle, a pillar of Uribe's democratic security policies.

policy elites in the ministry of defense turned to their corporate counterparts, specifically marketers, experts in imbuing commodities with virtues.

Brand Warfare

We took the position that we can't let the media just talk, we need to be on the air all the time. It's a constant war. — Juan Pablo, manager of the PAHD account at Lowe/SSP3

Ernst Jünger rose to prominence as an intellectual of Weimar Germany for his poetic, highly aestheticized account of the First World War. ("He rests at the dark door of death like a bullet that has reached its goal. And the purple waves dash over him.")[35] In a short essay, "Total Mobilization," published in 1932, Jünger offered a rationale for Germany's loss in the war and a blueprint for its fascistic turn. He argued that Germany had failed to mobilize the entirety of the nation's industrial and human capacity, and lamented the leadership's inability to recognize that defending the state "is no longer the prerogative of the professional soldier, but the responsibility of everyone who can bear arms."[36] Similarly, he wanted to keep the war machine in perpetual motion and urged "a stretching of all possible credit" rather than relying on a fixed war budget. Even more than a matter of industry and finance, total mobilization was about labor. Jünger envisioned a world in which the division between workers and soldiers melted away, where "armed combat merges into the more extended image of the gigantic labor process."[37] He looked with envy toward the United States and its institutions, such as the merchant marine, that enabled a seamless transition from economic to military missions. Jünger's dream was tantamount to the inversion of Eisenhower's warning to beware of the military industrial complex.

In provisioning for World War II, both Allied and Axis powers strove to achieve the total mobilization that Jünger had called for. A Volkswagen factory, which Hitler had laid the cornerstone of, produced not only consumer vehicles such as the Beetle but also its amphibious military derivative, the VW type 128. In the United States the sale of war bonds, promoted in advertising schemes that rode patriotic sentiment, enabled the "stretching of all possible credit" for the war effort.[38] Provisioning for World War II proved a global exercise in total mobilization. Yet as the United States would find out in Vietnam, such a materially oriented total mobilization was not total at all.

The United States' defeat in Vietnam introduced the need for an *affective* total mobilization that could help win hearts and minds in the theater of operation and back at home. "Vietnam syndrome" became shorthand for withering political support for a war effort.[39] Through the 1980s the United States tried to vanquish the specter of Vietnam by exercising its political will in Central American conflicts, mostly covert affairs. The real reckoning with the legacy of Southeast Asia came in the First Gulf War. On March 1, 1991, George H. W. Bush declared victory and exulted, "By God, we've kicked the Vietnam syndrome once and for all."[40] Scholars look to the ousting of Saddam Hussein from Kuwait in 1991 as a watershed moment for the mediation of warfare and the rise of what media studies scholar Roger Stahl has called "militainment."[41] Militainment, Stahl explains, is the marriage of media interests with those of the Pentagon, enabling mutual gains through the production of cheap, entertaining, and sanitized representations of war. The public relations aspect of Operation Desert Storm, as the US military dubbed it, had proven potent. The Pentagon wrangled journalists with embedding programs and fed the press video-game-like scenes of buildings and enemy tanks in pilots' crosshairs suddenly obliterated by an explosion. Approval ratings for the president and top generals soared, as did the viewership of cable television, especially a then-upstart cable station, CNN. Writing about CNN's live coverage, which had been facilitated by the new technologies of broadcast satellites and fiber optic cable, cultural theorist Paul Virilio wrote, "Live television is a veritable injunction. One does not discuss a live image, one undergoes it."[42] Virilio's moderately technophobic analysis and the interpretations of other scholars interested in the hypermediation of Operation Desert Storm focused on questions of spectatorship and government efforts to curate a deluge of images.

In the first decade of the 2000s the academic literature on the cultural dimensions of militarism began to explicate what political scientist James Der Derian labeled the military-industrial-media-entertainment complex, or MIME, which had become an increasingly interactive system. For instance, in 2002 the US military began recruiting soldiers through the interactive video game America's Army. Unlike recruiting posters of a finger-pointing Uncle Sam, the video game lacked a direct appeal. Casey Wardynski, a colonel who designed the game, said, "It's kind of, try it on for size and see if you like it and, if you do, the logical action will arise."[43] This experiential marketing as a form of recruitment had a parallel in training exercises set in virtual Afghan, Iraqi, or Somali villages.[44] Der Derian argues that the production of high-tech, low-risk wars that fetishize virtual worlds play an important role in constructing the mythos of war as virtuous and therefore justifiable.[45]

Although Der Derian's analysis is insightful and compelling, his emphasis on technologies of virtuality—like Virilio's focus on cable news a decade earlier—renders his project a reactive, amazement-laden lament of techno-fetishism and militarism run amok. But what are the forces driving the MIME complex? How might the cultural and economic logics of late capitalism give us analytical tools to understand and anticipate the ways in which cultural production and warfare are remaking each other in the twenty-first century? What I want to suggest is that marketing's political economy, emergent forms, and cultural dimensions are fueling a new mode of total mobilization in which an affective infrastructure is coproduced and managed across military and civilian spheres. In short, the marketing is the message. By adapting Marshall McLuhan's famous aphorism, I am intentionally changing the focus from medium to marketing, because the former is ultimately shaped by the latter. The opaque algorithmic process by which advertising is sold, the corporate digital surveillance of our online activity, and the sly ways in which branding slips into our daily lives are not merely trends in the advertising industry, but they structure the media we consume and have profound cultural and political consequences.[46] Those consequences cluster around the erasure of distinctions central to modernism, such as the scientific delineation of fact from fiction.[47] Within this larger frame of indistinction, I will focus on one in particular, the increasingly hazy boundary between peace and war.

Total mobilization is no longer a matter of a fluid transition from peace to war, but a matter of the continual co-presence of the two in a hot peace in which everywhere is always a potential scene of violence.[48] As commentators frequently note, the Global War on Terror is unbounded in scope and duration, an unending concatenation of episodes that render the world a battlefield from Waziristan, which has borne the brunt of drone warfare, to suburban Watertown, Massachusetts, in the wake of the Boston Marathon bomb attacks of 2013.[49] What connects sites as disparate as Waziristan and Watertown is not only the War on Terror but marketing as a system of global provisioning that is productive of affective attachments.[50] I borrow the idea of affect as a form of infrastructure from anthropologist Joseph Masco, who deftly teases out continuities between the Cold War and the War on Terror. For Masco, this affective infrastructure is built by the national security state, expansive in the wake of the "ongoing injury" of the September 11 attacks. "Affect," Masco writes, "becomes a kind of infrastructure for the security state, creating the collective intensities of feeling necessary to produce individual commitments, remake ethical standards, and energize modes of personal, and collective, sacrifice."[51]

The layering of national security affect, primarily paranoia and fear, I argue, cannot be separated from the aspirational affect of consumer culture, for the two have coevolved. At the height of the Cold War, for instance, advertisements pitched "Luxury Fall-Out Shelters" to people who would prefer to wait out a nuclear apocalypse in comfort.[52] Such advertisements normalized the very idea of nuclear warfare and the paranoia it generated. Similarly, George W. Bush's call on Americans to go shopping one week after September 11, 2001, mobilized consumption as a means of coping with the Global War on Terror. I take as given the idea, demonstrated by historical accounts of the coevolution of marketing and warfare in the twentieth century, that marketization and militarization are deeply interpenetrated.[53] I am fascinated by how their convergence shapes an affective mode of governance in the early twenty-first century, a moment when simmering fears of an everywhere war and the rising aspirations of the global middle classes expand in tandem. It is more than a little curious that in the 2000s, just as war diffused further into everyday life, everything—nations, militaries, cities, universities, individual selves—became brands.[54]

The language of the convergence of marketing and militarism is revealing. *Targeting*, for example, serves as a switch that connects the marketing nation and the security state. As marketers study, segment, and create new publics to target, the military compiles lists of targets to monitor and, at the right moment, destroy.[55] A drive toward ever-greater precision unites both practices of targeting. Each year marketers improve their ability to micro-target tightly defined demographic groups by tracking users across the internet with algorithmic intelligence.[56] Similarly the military, through the use of special forces and drone warfare, creates micro-kill zones. In the words of Grégoire Chamayou, a French theorist of drone warfare, "The zone of armed conflict, having been fragmented into miniaturizable kill boxes, tends *ideally* to be reduced to the single body of the enemy-prey"—modern warfare as hunting.[57] Whether it's data capitalism's drive to psychologically profile individual consumers or the whack-a-mole logic of twenty-first-century counterinsurgency, this scaling down to the individual approaches a vanishing point: advertising as nonadvertising, war as nonwar. Neither negation is neutral, nor is their entanglement haphazard. To the contrary, I would like to suggest that in this double negation there lies a key to understanding the state of the relationship between war and capitalism in the early twenty-first century.

Enter the double meaning of this book's title, guerrilla marketing, which in business parlance is code for a bundle of tactics, most of which seek to invisibilize the sales pitch.[58] Tom Himpe, an advertising intellectual, describes this tendency as "advertising that blends in seamlessly with real entertainment, real events or real life to the extent that it is not possible to tell what is advertising and what is not."[59] Drawing upon the legacy of guerrilla warfare as articulated by Che Guevara and Mao Zedong, guerrilla marketing draws its strength from camouflage.[60] But marketing's camouflage aspires not merely to blend into the background but to act upon it. Branding, I argue, operates as an activist form of camouflage that seeks to subtly transform the environment. As an instrument of total mobilization, brands have proved to be modular weapons of productive persuasion, from the black flag of ISIS and its calls to mobilize individuals alienated from the West to a real estate mogul's use of brand strategies to bluster his way to the White House. As an emergent phenomenon of extraordinary political consequence, brand warfare is ripe for critical analysis.

The appropriation of brands for military confrontation is a logical consequence of their role in the increasingly bellicose competition for market share. Brands exist to protect companies from the damaging effects of war—price war. As the law of supply and demand dictates, competition drives down price in a process known as commoditization. In the face of aggressive competition, companies construct brand personas to create an affective connection with consumers to induce them to pay a premium for their product, rather than purchase a cheaper, similar, if not identical alternative. It was only a matter of time until the military paid attention to the affective force of branding. In 2007 the Rand Corporation published a report for the US Joint Forces Command titled *Enlisting Madison Avenue: The Marketing Approach to Earning Popular Support in Theaters of Operation*. The document passed almost entirely unnoticed by scholarly communities and the media, even as the revision of the *U.S. Army / Marine Corps Counterinsurgency Field Manual* generated widespread publicity and controversy. The authors of *Enlisting Madison Avenue* write, "Like commercial firms that must update unattractive brand identities, so too should the United States consider updating its military's brand identity to suit current and future operational environments."[61] Whereas the US military was theorizing about how to rebrand itself in the mid-2000s, the Colombian military was doing it. While the US military was reinventing its doctrine on population-centric warfare and employing anthropologists, sociologists, and psychologists as part of an ill-fated cultural (re)turn in counterinsurgency strategy, the Colombian government was deploying marketers who have assumed the roles of amateur social scientists–cum–public intellectuals to great fanfare.[62]

But what is the appeal of brand expertise to militaries? In the corporate realm brands have become extremely valuable assets and are an ascendant mode of generating surplus value in contemporary capitalism. Coca-Cola's estimated brand value in 2016 was $73.1 billion, almost 40 percent of its market capitalization.[63] Brand value is predicated on the cultivation of trust, loyalty, even love—affective investments that promise future returns by differentiating themselves from the competition. Brands have displaced sales as companies' strategic advantage, leading

Phil Knight, founder and CEO of Nike, to refer to his company as a marketing and design company that just happens to sell specific objects like basketball sneakers. Stated otherwise, "value does not reside in the merchandise, but in the mind of the customer," according to marketing theorist Paul Wesley Ivey.[64] It is precisely the belief that marketing can operate on individual minds and collective perceptions that has attracted the attention of militaries and militants alike.

Marketing, capitalism's meaning-making system, has an impressive track record in helping to co-opt and control entire populations by promoting consumerism at the expense of citizenship. (It is all too appropriate that a Los Angeles–based brand marketing consultancy with clients that included Microsoft and General Electric named itself Culture Industry, after the concept of mass distraction articulated by Theodor Adorno and Max Horkheimer.)[65] By reifying commodities, brands give hygienic singular personas to objects that emerge from messy, sometimes violent processes of production in multiple parts of the world. Increasingly, brands not only distract from the often sordid conditions of supply chains but also instill commodities with liberal values such as "environmentally friendly" or "fair trade." Sanitizing warfare and rendering it righteous is the logical extension of marketing's herculean feat of resignifying capitalism as ethical.

What undergirds the Colombian government's deployment of brand warfare through the partnership between the PAHD and Lowe/SSP3 is the construction of a humanitarian counterinsurgency. The idea that the military is defined no longer through combat but rather by saving the human beings it targets, guerrilla combatants, contributes to the Colombian government's projection of postconflict status. A central ideologue of the postconflict state in Colombia is a man named Sergio Jaramillo. In the early years of the Uribe administration, Jaramillo helped draft key documents laying out the president's democratic security doctrine and conceptualize the PAHD. A few years later he worked in the Ministry of Defense under then Minister Juan Manuel Santos. It was at that point, in late 2006, when he approached Lowe/SSP3 to publicize the individual demobilization program.

In Lowe/SSP3's chic northern Bogotá headquarters I interviewed Juan Pablo, the manager who handled the PAHD account. He explained the initial exchange between the two organizations: "The condition we set before accepting the [demobilization] program was that we manage it like a brand, not like a program or project. And what are the conditions of a brand? That it be consistent through time, that it be coherent with what it says, and third, that it has financial backing to stay on stage." Lowe/SSP3 was clear with its government interlocutors: it was not interested in crafting a one-off campaign. Over time, the idea of building a brand rippled through the armed forces to the point that marketers have gradually convinced the national security apparatus to reconceive itself as a constellation of brands. Juan Pablo laid out this vision:

> JP: Here I have a brand that's called the demobilization program. I have another brand that's called the military. I have another brand that's called the police. I have another brand that's called the Ministry of Defense. Each one is fulfilling a role in the same strategy.
>
> AF: What's that?
>
> JP: In the end, to debilitate to the maximum those people [in the guerrilla]. The objective in the end is peace and all that stuff, but from a defense point of view, each one has different strengths. So I have a brand that's demobilization and that hits him emotionally, appealing to the human being, the core of the person. I have another brand that's called the military that also debilitates him emotionally but appeals to the guerrilla, the delinquent, the terrorist, the enemy.

"Peace and all that stuff" is indeed the end goal; however, in the meantime brands facilitate a multifaceted attack on the guerrilla. Before moving on to how the PAHD helps the military construct the paradoxical notion of a humanitarian counterinsurgency, let's turn back to Jaramillo's perspective on the program.

In the beginning of the Santos administration, from 2010 to 2012, Jaramillo served as the national security adviser *and* the high commissioner for peace, one more indication of just how imbricated counterinsurgency and peace policy had become. I spoke with him over lunch after he lectured at Harvard's John F. Kennedy School of Government. In the British accent acquired during his studies at Oxford and Cambridge, he laid out the impact of the individual demobilization program: "Mono Jojoy [a notorious military commander for the FARC] was much more worried about demobilization than kills in combat. If you kill somebody in an operation, you make people angry. If you demobilize someone, you leave a huge question mark. Where did they go? Why did they leave? Why are they there, and why am I here?"

Jaramillo went on: "This program opened up the FARC. It allowed us to understand how the organization thinks—its commanders." He described himself as "an addict" of the interviews that state agents conduct with former rebels. The counterinsurgency value of the former rebels, whether from a perspective of psychological warfare, military strategy, or combat tactics, is difficult to overstate. As the program operated on FARC and ELN militants in this classified realm, its advertising campaigns saturated the Colombian public sphere in prime media slots: soccer games, news programming, and among the trailers in movie theaters. Through one program, the PAHD, the government managed to debilitate its enemy and remake its image—two crucial interventions rarely so closely correlated.

Branding's strength as a vehicle of total mobilization in Colombia is its capacity to articulate and manage not only the public and secret facets of the war but also the relationship between the conflict's material and immaterial dimensions. Take figure 0.3. The military spent tens (if not hundreds) of thousands of dollars' worth of hardware and logistics to stage this image at Tres Esquinas Air Base. President Juan Manuel Santos is promoting "Operation Rivers of Light," an aggressive advertis-

FIGURE 0.3. President Juan Manuel Santos, first lady María Clemencía Rodríguez, and Defense Minister Juan Carlos Pinzón place glowing plastic balls in the Orteguaza River in Caquetá Department. Photo by author, December 2011.

ing campaign that calls upon rebels to abandon the armed struggle and reunite with their families (see chapter 2). The night before this photograph was taken fighter jets shot red streams of tracer bullets, strafing the shore behind the president in an assault on nobody that lasted until dawn. In the words of the colonel commanding the base, the jets were "sending a message" in case the FARC had any ideas of disrupting the public relations show scheduled for the next day. Given the effort that went into staging this image for live television and its extensive media coverage, it is worth pausing to reflect on the image itself and the two applications of pixelated camouflage on these gunships.

As a means of expressing the militaristic populism he embodied, former president Álvaro Uribe liked to say that underneath his suit he wore a soldier's uniform. Here President Santos embodies a different form of militarism, dressed in a camouflaged life preserver. Perhaps the literal translation of the Colombian Spanish, "life savior" (*salvavidas*), is more fitting in light of the parable of military humanism into which the president has been cast. His life preserver is layered over the PAHD's white T-shirt, which announces the program's slogan, "There's another life, demobilization is the way out," and logo, a red heart clasping a white flag. The life preservers and T-shirts combine to project a vision of the military as peace-loving savior. Unlike the camouflage worn by the rifle-toting soldiers in the boat ahead, the president's camouflage is easy to shed. He embodies a rebranded militarism, enlightened by the conciliatory message of his T-shirt. Thanks to consumer marketing, the state naturalizes the paradox of fighting while demobilizing, and in the process projects an image of itself as a powerful, benevolent, and coherent entity. In the battle of images, sensations, and psychology, marketers have become field marshals.

As branding became the terrain of warfare in the 2000s, even the FARC's revolutionary project was lured onto it. Systematically denied political and media space at the national level, the FARC sought to complement its regional radio stations, newsletters, and other mediated efforts for winning over community members where it operated with online platforms. It created news websites such as New Colombian News Agency (ANNCOL), and its former militants and sympathizers ran an affiliated radio program, Café Estereo—both incorporated in Sweden because of its liberal freedom-of-speech laws. For five months in 2009 I traveled through Sweden and Denmark to research the radical left's use of the internet to claim media space it had been denied in Colombia. I attended a recording of Café Estereo in a Stockholm basement and marveled at how the group, which was frequently hacked by the Colombian military, needed six thousand miles of distance to produce its programming.[66] Overall, I found a legal battle playing out in the Colombian government's favor. For example, Fighters and Lovers, a Danish collective, had openly defied European Union antiterror legislation by sending the proceeds of the sale of CDs, lighters, perfumes, and T-shirts—approximately $5,000—to the Popular Front for the Liberation of Palestine, or PFLP, and to the FARC (organizations listed on the EU's list of terrorist organizations). In March 2009 I sat in the gallery of the Danish Supreme Court in Copenhagen as a judge read the verdict in a case that had wound its way through Denmark's lower courts. He ruled that the fundraising was indeed a material support for terrorism and definitively illegal.

When I interviewed one of the defendants a few days before the ruling, he explained the group's marketing this way: "We are talking about principles, values which are very fundamental, but it's important for us that it doesn't get very airy and remote from the daily life of our own people, Danish people, Europeans more generally. We try to connect the political message to items that people use in their daily life, like a T-shirt, like a cap, like a lighter."

He reached into his left pocket and pulled out a lighter. "You can have this one," he said, weaving it into the discussion naturally:

> You have the opportunity with this lighter, the next time you are with somebody who smokes and asks you for a light—you can start a conversation about this issue. If you wear the T-shirt you can't avoid this kind of discussion, especially these days, when it has been a very controversial issue here in Denmark. By producing music created by FARC musicians and Copenhagen DJs, we create a possibility for raising these issues in another environment, because it's music. Is music also a kind of terrorist propaganda? Is this illegal?

Within a week of our interview, I watched disappointment wash over his face as a judge read the finding of the Danish Supreme Court. It upheld a lower court's ruling against him and six other defendants. Fighters and Lovers' brand-based resistance to EU antiterror legislation was definitively illegal. The website soon disappeared, and so did the FARC merchandise. I draw attention to the truncated campaign of Fighters and Lovers to show how marketing has become the inescapable ground of proguerrilla as well as antiguerrilla politics. That ground has been inherently uneven. On the run from the coercive apparatus of the state, legally outlawed in Colombia, and marginalized internationally, the FARC struggled unsuccessfully to brand itself as a legitimate resistance movement.[67]

The brand war between the Colombian government and the FARC must be understood within a larger branding project: the Colombian nation-state. As Colombia sought to carve out its own space in the neoliberal world order, it resorted to nation branding to attract tourists and foreign investment. In a global marketplace of nations vying for the same with slogans, such as "Po-Land of Opportunities" and "Brand India," Colombia offered cheap skilled labor and the promise of an economic boom on the horizon once the nation achieved its always deferred postconflict status. In the mid-2000s the government began to run campaigns such as "Colombia, the only risk is wanting to stay" and "Colombia, land of magical realism." Three decades earlier artist Antonio Caro had intuited this turn, making one of the emblematic works of contemporary Colombian art, both prescient and elegant in its simplicity.

FIGURE 0.4. Painting by Colombian artist Antonio Caro, 1977. Reproduced with artist's permission.

Access and Ethics

I first arrived in Colombia in August 2001 when the war was at full boil (a point I did not fully appreciate at the time). As a recent graduate of Duke University on a Fulbright scholarship, I spent that year researching the politics of photojournalistic images of the armed conflict. But my youthful desire to *do something* about mass media practices that skewed and manipulated the voices of the war's victims overtook that research project. I began teaching photography to children and youth who, with their families, had fled violence raging in the countryside and then found themselves at risk of recruitment by the same armed groups that had displaced them.[68] The participatory photography project I founded, Shooting Cameras for Peace, struck a chord in the community and became an NGO, which kept me coming back to Colombia. In 2006 I began my graduate studies, and over time my interest in the mediation of the armed conflict expanded beyond documentary photography to the broader media ecology in which images and messages fluidly traverse platforms and formats. I focused my attention on the mass media demobilization campaigns that began in 2003, which the Ministry of Defense outsourced to Lowe/SSP3 in 2007.

If you are a journalist or researcher in Colombia and want to learn about the country's disarmament, demobilization, and reintegration programs (DDR), your first stop would be the Colombian Agency for Reintegration (ACR), an agency that has been alternatively affiliated with the president's office and the Ministry of the Interior, often changing its name through bureaucratic reshuffling. (After the peace agreement of 2016 it changed its name yet again, to the Agency for Reincorporation and Normalization.) Its headquarters is staffed by highly educated Colombians and has protocols for dealing with a steady stream of journalists and academics. It is a "jealous" entity, as one might say in Colombia, in that it strives to shape all representations of the reintegration process.[69] I chose to approach the government through the Ministry of Defense rather than the ACR in order to focus on the military dimension of Colombia's DDR program. Although the literature on DDR is packed with articles that focus on the challenges of social and economic reintegration, little ethnographic work has been done on the formative early stages of the process.[70] This is the most sensitive moment when the military is cross-examining the former combatants and plying them for information, and in Colombia access is almost entirely restricted. My US citizenship, my position at a prestigious university, and the PAHD's investment in public relations—the very object of my research—all conspired to provide me rare access.

My first contact with the PAHD was accidental. Thanks to a linguistic confusion between *desplazado* (displaced) and *desmovilizado* (demobilized), Abbey, a friend of mine researching forced displacement, was referred to the wrong person at the US embassy in Bogotá. Back then, in 2007, the issue du jour in the NGO offices of northern Bogotá was shifting from the displacement crisis that had peaked in the first years of the millennium to the Uribe government's strategic repurposing of demobilization policy in the mid-2000s. The ceremonies prematurely feting the demobilization of paramilitaries (2003–6) had recently concluded, and the nonprofit sector was adapting its programming accordingly. The change in emphasis from victim to perpetrator, blurry as those categories can be, required some rewiring in the country's humanitarian apparatus.[71] Abbey had been mistakenly referred to Alfonso (who specialized in *desmovilizados*, not *desplazados*) and passed me his contact information.[72]

To meet Alfonso I cleared three rings of security at the US embassy compound. As I approached a maze of felt cubicles, a barrel-chested Puerto Rican fellow stood up and greeted me with a firm handshake. With a blend of machismo and a desire to educate the Harvard PhD student, Alfonso boastfully described his portfolios. After the meeting he handed me his business card with Narcotic Affairs Section (NAS) embossed on it. NAS was a lead organization in coordinating Plan Colombia, the earlier-mentioned multibillion-dollar aid program to upgrade the Colombian armed forces and law enforcement. Although NAS is formally located in the Department of State, it works across agencies with the Department of Defense, US intelligence agencies, and the DEA. When I expressed interest in the demobilization program and its media dimensions, Alfonso responded energetically. He knew just the person: Marcela (who features in chapter 2).

Alfonso had convinced Marcela to resign as the director of RCN's midday television news broadcast, a position of extraordinary media influence, to take on an important role in the government's communications. (In the PAHD, Marcela received a salary through NAS, which paid on a US diplomatic pay scale.) From 2005 to 2012, Marcela shaped the PAHD's every media decision. I initially shadowed her in the summers of 2007 and 2008, when the program demobilized, on average, thirty-three hundred individual guerrillas per year—more than any other year before or after. At six feet two inches tall, she towers over most Colombian men and practically all Colombian women. She speaks quickly, works her phone deftly, and exudes competence, confidence, and professionalism. From my first summer following the PAHD's communications team in 2007 until halfway through my long-term fieldwork in 2011–13, she was generous with her time and introductions. In the summers of 2007 and 2008 I traveled with PAHD staff in military aircraft to cultural events they cosponsored, including a concert in El Banco, Magdalena, and a propaganda theater performance in Puerto Leguízamo, Putumayo, building rapport with Marcela's communications team.

When I returned to Bogotá from these trips, I gradually learned the full dimensions of the PAHD as members of her team introduced me to a mix of active military, retired military, and skilled civilians working in the individual demobilization program.[73] I began to familiarize myself with the financial incentives unit (which offers rewards for collaboration); the halfway houses where the demobilized live after their time with a local military unit, but before certification as demobilized; and the "strategic area" team, a group of military intelligence analysts who work in collaboration with their colleagues on brigades throughout the country to extract information from the demobilized and try to persuade high-ranking FARC rebels to demobilize.

In the strategic area unit I met Nicolás (who features in chapter 3), a major at the time and head of the unit. With his permission I sat in his office and wrote in my notebook as intelligence agents and former rebels funneled in the door. As I witnessed the exchanges and asked follow-up questions, I glimpsed aspects of the PAHD that are meticulously kept out of public view. Four years later, as a lieutenant colonel and commander of a regional intelligence unit, Nicolás would wring an imaginary washcloth to illustrate his job: to squeeze the demobilized for every last drop of information. When he was a major in the PAHD, his mission had been the same.

My rapport with Marcela, Nicolás, and other members of the PAHD would eventually shift from warm to strained (though it has cautiously warmed again since). They invited me into their world, but in retrospect it is clear that they understood my presence through the lens of their experiences handling journalists and shaping their stories. They did not expect me to dig around for so long, or so deeply, despite my best efforts to describe the scope of my project. Perhaps they misconceived my study as a vehicle for generating favorable coverage in elite circles in the United States. Another possibility is that they deduced that I was part of some secret US support unit despite my declarations to the contrary. I suspect they understood my presence through the subject that motivated my research: their aggressive stance toward generating publicity.

At a certain point, however, it became clear that my research was not going in that direction. "You've spoken to too many people," Marcela once told me with frustration in her voice. My refusal to be photographed by Nicolás while out drinking one night provoked this gem of a drunken utterance: "If I wanted to take a picture of you, I could take thirty different pictures in my office and you wouldn't even know it." While anthropologists commonly become their subjects' object of study, I was clearly being observed more closely than most.

My position as a gringo had helped to get me behind the electronically secured doors of the PAHD's headquarters. US patronage and personnel are part of the institutional landscape, and in the eyes of the PAHD staff, my citizenship positioned me as sympathetic to the program, perhaps even an undercover agent supporting it. Some lower-ranking officials grew disappointed when they learned that unlike the NAS officer who replaced Alfonso, I did not have a slush fund for pet projects.

After the first eight months of fieldwork, my access to the PAHD began to diminish, in part because I did not prove useful. Spy or anthropologist, what the PAHD wanted from me was feedback. Here lies the crux of the ethical challenge presented by this research. In response to the fallout of the Human Terrain Systems project in which the US military recruited social scientists as counterinsurgency specialists, I, along with the other members of the Network of Concerned Anthropologists, vowed not to give private briefings to the military. This became an axis of contention. Nicolás would ask me for opinions as I peered over his shoulder at PowerPoint presentations to be delivered to top generals. When I declined, he would accuse me of taking without giving. "He's a sponge that absorbs and absorbs, but who knows where he squeezes out" was one colorful expression. I could understand his position. I traveled inside military vehicles, slept on military bases, consumed officers' time with endless questions, but other than buying an odd meal I gave very little in return. This prompted "jokes," and sometimes explicit concern that I was somebody's agent.

An unforeseen event conspired to close doors that had opened for me within the PAHD. My good friend and roommate Roméo Langlois is a French journalist who had embedded with the Colombian military to cover an antinarcotics mission in southern Colombia for France 24, a French cable news station. The FARC ambushed the operation, killing five soldiers, including the soldier charged with protecting Langlois. As the FARC closed in on the military's position, one of its combatants shot Langlois in the left elbow. He continued filming for a moment and then turned himself over to the FARC's Fifteenth Front.[74] The FARC seized the media spotlight and—ignoring the fact that Langlois had embedded with FARC fronts on multiple occasions—cried media bias on account of reporters accompanying the military.

I called Marcela during the first moments after Langlois walked through the crossfire with his hands up to turn himself in to the FARC, before anyone in Bogotá or Paris knew his fate. She was traveling with the minister of defense and fed me updates on the unfolding events. The first assessment she shared was that the FARC had killed Langlois in combat. Suddenly I found myself lobbying Marcela to use her influence to have the military scale back operations. Marcela made a comment illustrative of her zeal for the media war she was directing: "The most important thing is that the FARC not put on any shows." I corrected her, saying that what was most important was that Langlois return to his family in good health as soon as possible.[75]

The FARC released Langlois thirty-three days after his capture in a ceremony that included a hog roast and speeches by FARC commanders. During a press conference before he flew back to Paris, Langlois said, "When the military is in certain areas, peasants stay at home and consider the army a terrorist." The comment, though not inaccurate, defied a long-standing taboo against highlighting the crimes of the military. Langlois ignited the ire of the right-wing Twitterverse led by former president Uribe.

Unsurprisingly, my access to the PAHD began to wane. Knowing the rhythms of academic publication, I had assured my interlocutors that the results of my study would emerge only years later. The untimeliness of my project allayed fears of PAHD personnel that I was looking for some investigative scoop, and indeed the temporality of academic production proved an important condition of access. But when the FARC captured Langlois, that promise to remain out of sync with the rhythm of the news cycle was violated. I had already learned a great deal from the state's perspective, so I decided to refocus my ethnography on former guerrillas struggling to eke out a living and avoid being drawn back into a war they had fled.

With former rebels, time was the most important element in forging relationships of trust. They have an amazing ability to size people up. After quickly studying my gait, my accent, and any number of signs, they surmised that I was not affiliated with the FARC, but only time and interest in their lives made clear that I did not work for the Colombian or US government. I built trust by coming to their neighborhoods, meeting their families, and accompanying them in the chores of everyday life. Like any researcher, I had to learn what *not* to ask, and when. Again, familiarity and the situational awareness that it bestowed was key. Conversations about their past needed to take place in privacy. In settings with multiple former guerrillas, it was crucial to know the level of trust between them, their shared histories, and their trajectories within *la organización*, the term they used to refer to the FARC. Most sensitive of all was the question of collaboration with the military. Every former rebel I spoke with about the first days, weeks, and months following his or her disarmament recounted visceral memories of navigating an unknown system and vacillating between collaborating and withholding information. Long-term ethnographic research enabled me to access these stories, which cast shadows over the reintegration process.

The depth of my relationships with the demobilized varied. Sometimes I interviewed a former rebel only once or twice; in other cases I struck up lasting friendships. Some preferred not to venture beyond the interview setting lest I spoil the secret identity they keep hidden in their daily lives. Others saw in me the chance to cultivate an ally in the hope that it might bestow benefits. Having a friend, especially an American researcher friend, is a weak but valued protection against attacks that might come from the political right. Such a connection also bolsters the position of former rebels in discussions with state agents, closing the power differential ever so slightly. The association is both a form of protection and capital; two things the demobilized desperately lack. This utilitarian view was notable among politically active former combatants; especially those who had formed their own community-based organizations. Narcoparamilitarism had such organizations and their members in its crosshairs, which meant that the demobilized who had turned to activism stood to benefit the most from associating with a privileged outsider. These dynamics were part of the structural challenge of conducting this research, and I did my best to fulfill the unspoken obligations that I assumed. I made introductions and accompanied ex-combatants in their interactions with government officials, NGO workers, and community partners. Where possible I tried to channel some of my social capital for my interlocutors' benefit. Over time, inevitably, certain relationships flourished, growing into genuine friendships, while others failed to transcend a transactional dynamic.

I have taken standard measures to protect the identities of the people in this book, such as giving them pseudonyms. With the exception of people who are public figures or have given their permission to use their real names—Carlos, Arjaid, Marcela, Juan Pablo, Ciro—all the names are fake.[76] When interviewing then-active guerrillas, I have used their chosen alias by which they are publicly known. For the community of former rebels I studied, I falsified other details of no analytic significance, such as the name or number of the front that they fought with and other geographic references and place-names. (This may cause confusion for experts who know that certain fronts did not operate in the given areas.) In chapter 4 I invented the name of a city, "Raconto," to discuss an urban community in which many former guerrillas have settled, and in many narratives I created new, nonexistent names for rivers, towns, and companies. In a few instances (though not in the profiles of former guerrillas that separate the chapters), I have divided the narrative of one person and attributed parts of it to more than one name, or attributed anecdotes from two different people to the same name. Although this bundle of protective strategies is not as hermetic as the creation of full-on composite characters or declaring the book a work of ethno-fiction, it provides my interlocutors with important safeguards while being clear that the representations contained in these pages are factual, not fictional.

Though I have researched this book intermittently from 2007 to 2016, my fieldwork was most concentrated in a twenty-two-month period from November 2011 to August 2013. (To avoid confusion for non-Colombian readers, the monetary values used in the book are in US dollars. I have used the average exchange rate for that period, 1,800 Colombian pesos per US dollar for the vast majority of conversions, and 2,800 COP/USD when converting values from the years 2015 and 2016.) The research consisted of more than two hundred interviews with former combatants, military officers, and the publicists they hire; two dozen life-history interviews; a half-dozen focus groups; participatory observation in demobilized communities and government institutions; archival work on Colombia's propaganda war; and five months of research with political exiles from the militant left who fled Colombia for Sweden in the late 1980s and early 1990s, many of whom engage in internet-based media activism. This mixed-method, multisited approach befits a program that has outdone the Marxist left at its own game of "combining all of the forms of struggle."[77]

To minimize risks to my subjects and myself, I began to do research with active FARC members and the group's leadership only once the 2012–16 negotiations had reached an advanced stage. The idea that neutrality was not an option hounded me. When I arrived in Havana in March 2016 to interview FARC and government negotiators, the two sides were locked in a standoff on the last major unresolved point on their agenda: the FARC's potential disarmament and reintegration into civilian life. Each side asked me to develop documents to give them ammunition at the negotiating table. I respectfully declined each invitation, but later wrote one email to both sides, copying the Norwegian diplomat helping to shepherd the talks along, to offer my services to the negotiating table rather than to either side. Unsurprisingly, my note went unanswered. The zero-sum logic of the war had translated to the negotiating table in Cuba. In September 2016 I traveled to the FARC's final guerrilla conference, an extraordinary display of the group's media ambitions. I have included some material from that trip at the end of this book; however, the subject of the FARC's mediated transition to a political movement, another form of guerrilla marketing, will have to wait for another book.

Readers might rightfully wonder how I identify politically. It's a fair question. What I will say, in a paragraph, is this. Through the course of my research, I have done my best to downplay my own opinions, not out of any antiquated notion of apolitical objectivity but so as not to jeopardize access in the various milieus through which I circulated. My own affinity is with Colombia's democratic left. The Colombian government bears the brunt of my criticism in this book, but that is because one of its programs is my main subject. I am also very critical of the FARC for its hardheaded insistence on the armed struggle, decades after it became clear that politics was a much more effective and less damaging means of effecting change. As the war degenerated through the 1990s and 2000s, the FARC lost its ability to differentiate clearly between means and ends. Its standards for recruitment and kidnapping fell, making broad swaths of the population targets of one or the other. Also, its concern for collateral damage inflicted on the civilian population waned as the war intensified. Yes, the FARC also became more deeply enmeshed with drug trafficking during this period, but the suggestion that this meant that the group had lost its political orientation was often overstated for propagandistic effect. Throughout its ups and downs, the group has maintained deep ideological commitments to redistributive politics and social justice in a Marxist-Leninist key. The ideological problem with the FARC is not that it abandoned its political commitments but that it was slow to appreciate changes happening outside its insular world. What plagued the group more than anything else, I would argue, was an aging vanguard that had honed the FARC's ability to resist at the expense of allowing it to adapt. I pin my own hopes for Colombia's future on a new generation of the democratic left who are clear-eyed about the structural problems facing the nation and pragmatic about reform. The ultimate barometer of the success of the peace agreement of 2016 will be its ability to make space for the democratic left to flourish so that it can rejuvenate a political system that has insisted on recycling itself and its exclusionary practices generation after generation.

The Terrain, Chapter by Chapter

In chapter 1, "An Archaeology of Media Spectacle, 1974–2008," I trace a history of spectacle through the dramatic antics of the M19 rebel group that began in 1974, Pablo Escobar's bid to promote his agenda through kidnapping, branding, and bravado in the early 1990s, and the FARC's counterproductive efforts to intervene in a hostile media ecology with the high-visibility tactic of kidnapping. I parse the resonances between the media strategies of the country's various armed groups, while highlighting inflection points in the country's propaganda war.

In chapter 2, "Operation Christmas," I examine the partnership of the PAHD and Lowe/SSP3 through a campaign that urges rebels to desert during the Christmas season. I follow the Christmas campaign, which has won awards in Cannes and New York, from drawing board to focus group to presidential launch. This paradigmatic act of brand warfare simultaneously targets national and international publics with its message of a kinder, smarter, more modern, and more humane form of counterinsurgency.

Chapter 3, "Operation Genuine," focuses on a yearlong intelligence operation to demobilize a rising star in the FARC's Caribbean Bloc.

Embedded in a military intelligence unit, I follow the operation to reveal the demobilization program's unstated objective: to gain the intelligence that former rebels provide. This type of targeting depends on intimate knowledge of a given rebel's life and the strategic use of messages
via carefully selected messengers and media forms. The chapter teases
apart the paradox of humanitarian counterinsurgency.

Based on an ethnography of a community of former rebels from
southern Colombia who have settled in the *barrios* that ring a city I call
Raconto, chapter 4, "The Good Life Deferred and Risks of Remobilization," shows the struggles attending social and economic reintegration,
especially the variety promoted by the Colombian government, which
focuses on transforming former combatants into entrepreneurs. As the
promise of the good life based on inclusion in the formal economy with-
ers, former guerrillas find themselves tempted by lucrative offers to rearm with neoparamilitary groups.

Between the chapters I have interspersed excerpts from life-history
interviews with former guerrillas. These are lightly edited transcripts
that add a testimonial dimension to the book and give relief to the analysis in the chapters. With dialectical aspirations, this juxtaposition of registers is intended to entice readers to make thematic and contextual
connections, opening both the analysis and the biographies to new readings and interpretations. As compared with other books that also use
first-person narratives as a structuring device, I have deliberately chosen to leave these profiles in a longer form because they open a window into the lived experiences of former rebels and the social dynamics of the armed conflict in ways that can be fully appreciated only over
a wider trajectory. Most often the material for these lives came from a
single life-history interview, but in a few instances the profiles combine
two or three interviews with the same person and are stitched together
as a single narrative. Accompanying the testimonials are drawings by
Colombian artist Lucas Ospina. The sketches are not intended as literal
renderings of the story but poetic figurations intended to enliven the testimonials and stir an empathic engagement with the stories. The same
intentions undergird this book's accompanying documentary, installation, and transmedia project *Dreams from the Mountain*.[78]

In the conclusion, "The Colombian Model," I focus on the transnational dimensions of Colombia's DDR programs and the government's
elaborate diplomatic offensive to propagate the idea of a "Colombian
model" of militarized peacebuilding. This Colombian model, I argue,

contributes to a US-aligned geopolitical project that seeks to overtake the United Nations' leadership in postconflict policy.

In the epilogue I reflect on the implications of this book for the post-peace-accord moment in Colombia and the process of the FARC's *collective* reintegration that began in 2017. Based on an ethnography of the FARC's tenth and final guerrilla conference deep in guerrilla territory, I explore Colombia's prospects for fulfilling its continually deferred dream of genuine postconflict status. I pay special attention to Lowe/SSP3's role in the failed plebiscite to approve an initial peace accord, and reflect on the limitations of brand warfare.

Omar

A dozen former guerrillas stood on the grass by the sidewalk, taking turns tossing a 100-peso coin toward a small ditch burrowed in the dirt, a game akin to a miniaturized version of horseshoes. The PAHD had chosen a purposefully nondescript building that it named New Day to serve as an all-male halfway house where thirty to forty rebels waited to be officially certified as demobilized. Omar and I sat in a side room as his peers played "little coin" outside. Omar adjusted the baseball cap covering his shaved head and launched into his story.

o: *I am going to tell it to you from the beginning.*

The paramilitaries had killed a cousin of mine. We were like brothers. When the paramilitaries killed him I was offended, hurt.

When I spoke with my friends we all agreed, it wasn't right what the paramilitaries did, and that's when Commander Victor arrived. He came to hold a meeting and afterward he said, "I need to talk with you."

He took me to a school and told me why the paras killed my cousin. There was a firefight between the guerrilla and the paramilitaries. My cousin had a bus [una chiva]. The guerrilla had a few dead and injured, and the guerrilla forced the people off the bus so they could carry their dead to throw them in the San Miguel River, on the border [with Ecuador]. What could [my cousin] do? If an armed group comes and orders, well, you have to obey, no? So he helped load the dead and throw them in the San Miguel River. But an informant for the military, or maybe the paras, was there. When he got back to Puerto Asís they caught him and tortured him for being a guerrilla collaborator; but they knew it wasn't like that, that he had [actually] been ordered.

Commander Victor told me all of this and then immediately got into the politics. "Are you just going to sit there with your arms crossed? You need to confront the state because they're the ones who killed him—the paras are the military."

I told him that I wasn't in a position to help them.

He said, "It's simple, you only need to come and give us information and, for the moment, just do an errand in town. Go to the market and get us some supplies."

I asked if it would be dangerous.

He said, "No, just go to the supermarket and buy us this, that, and the other. Then get a car and bring it here."

I said okay. That's how I joined.

When Victor left [the area], then Paolo arrived looking for me. He asked me for the same favor. Then came the Costeño, then came another they called the Horse. They would be around for a while and another would come. They had me that way until Miguel arrived with someone that they called Cocaine, the other commander. That's when they told me that the military was looking for me, that it would be better for me to enter [the FARC].

They gave me a rifle, a pistol, a [military] vest, grenades, and they took me to the camp and taught me how to shoot . . . I marched with them, but they would let me leave with my rifle and told me to stash coca paste, money, munitions. When they would go into town they would give me their rifles, vests, and everything to hold on to.

A: To hold on to for two or three days?

O: *No, for whenever they would say. When I got injured by a bullet, they told me that they wouldn't pick up the material for a while.*

A: Did you get shot in combat?

O: *No, that was during a festival. The community asked for guerrilla presence so there wouldn't be problems, but a bullet-fest started for who knows what reason, and they got me. The man that shot me was some guy [named] Charo. They say that they had sent him to kill me.*

A: Who?

O: *The paramilitaries, the paras. At that time I didn't leave the town because the military and the paras were looking for me. So the paras paid Charo to kill me. . . . The guy gave me up for dead. He was with six others, but nobody has figured out who they were. The guerrilla gave me $110 while I recovered, but that doesn't do anything.*

That was when the military caught me in the area of Wutoyo. They had sent me to that area to do intelligence. But I wasn't hot, not yet burned.

They caught me like this: I was drinking beers in a small house and they took me out and said, "We need to verify a few things." I said okay and went, very tipsy.

They didn't ask me anything. They tied me up by the hands and feet and started hitting me, throwing me four meters downhill and insulting me: "Son-of-a-bitch guerrilla, we've been needing you. You work with the guerrilla."

I told them no, that I was a campesino, *that I didn't have anything to do with the guerrilla. They tied me to a tree and kept me there until about one in the morning. Because of the drinks that I had taken, I had a nasty thirst. I asked, "Mr. Agent, why don't you do me a favor and give me a little water. I'm thirsty."*

He said, "Sure, son of a bitch," and he went and brought a bucket of water and poom—*he threw it at me. He brought ten buckets and threw them on me.*

A: While you were tied to the tree?

O: *Yes, and then he came back and said, "Easy, son of a bitch, in a little bit we'll let you go." And at about three in the morning a man came up to me and said, "You know what, son of a bitch, get out of here. And if you start talking about the army, you have no idea what we are going to do to you. This was nothing."*

I left the road and started running once I heard shots. They shot at me four or five times. I ran toward a guy herding his cattle. I asked him to help me.

"What happened?" he asked.

I told him, "The army caught me while I was in the cantina drinking, and look at how they left me."

He asked why.

"They're accusing me, saying I work with the guerrilla," is what I told him. I denied it to the man. I didn't tell the truth.

He asked what I was going to do.

I said, "Well, help me."

He said, "I can't. Because if you work with the guerrilla—that could be true—I can't do anything. If they hear about it they'll come and kill me. I can't do anything."

So I kept running through all the fields and by the road. I found a car and got out of there.

A: And how did you get over the fear to turn yourself in to those same people?

O: *To the army? Well, because my woman started to pressure me. I had her*

pregnant. I kept saying to her, "How can I? They might do the same thing."
So I told a friend, "I am tired of working with these guys, they don't give
you any options. And now my woman is pregnant."

He came out and said, "Run away, my child."

Omar overcame his fear of the military to turn himself in, heeding
the advice of a friend who insisted that he do so with villagers from the
Communal Action Board as witnesses. He did so after barely escaping
an army ambush.

The guys who fought in the operation, those were the ones I turned my-
self in to. When I arrived, I started talking with them, and that's how they
proved that I was a member of the [guerrilla] front.

They said, "You're the one who got away running in that direction."

I said yes.

The guy said, "You know what? Be grateful I didn't shoot you, but
I had you in the sights of my machine gun. I didn't shoot, but you gave
me a moment to in the beginning. Then you disappeared into the forest. I
couldn't shoot without an order." . . .

A: How did the army respond when you turned yourself in?

O: *They had like eight motorcycles and came with a pickup truck with the col-*
onel inside. I arrived and introduced myself.

The colonel said, "Nice to meet you. You made a good decision; it was
the best thing you could do." He asked why I hadn't done it earlier, and
said, "We've been looking for you for so long."

I said, "Fear."

"Fear of what?"

I told him about what had happened in Wutoyo.

He said, "We're not all the same. Here the army is good. There's also
part of the army that does things that aren't right, but it's not all of us."

They received me well.

I told him, "My woman is pregnant."

He said, "We know. We all know your wife is pregnant." And then he
said, "Where is she?"

"She's at home."

"Far from here?"

"No, about a half hour by car."

He said, "Don't worry, get in and we'll go get her. [Otherwise] the guer-
rilla will kill her."

I said, "Yes, of course, let's go."

She was at the house and I told her to get her suitcase ready, and we left for the battalion.

At the battalion they were good to us. If the army were like them, there wouldn't be any more guerrilla, because there are a lot of stories of the army mistreating the people. Over there the police have roadside checks and put their hands in women's intimate parts looking for coca. And they look for coca, and if they find it, they take it, stealing the merchandise to sell it. . . . The women have denounced this, but the state doesn't do anything.

A: And did you hear any of the advertisements the government circulates for the [demobilization] program?

O: *Of course, but it's not like they say. The advertisements on the army radio stations say, "Hi, I'm this guy and I turned myself in. Now I am working, they gave me a job, they're helping me to pay for a house." But here there aren't any of those benefits. Nope, I've spoken with the* señores *and no, here the only thing they give you is $150 and you have to find your way with that. . . . In two or three years they might give you $4,440—that's all they'll guarantee. Here they give you the CODA (official disarmament certificate) and you have to leave [the halfway house]. So it's very hard. Imagine, you don't have a bed, not even a pot to cook with, no stove, nothing.*

A: How do you feel about having changed sides?

O: *It's a radical change. How do I feel? Well, nervous, because as soon as [the guerrilla] realizes where you are, they'll send someone to kill you. There's no way out. That's why I've thought about staying here in the city, because it's big—so they don't find you. But in any case I can't stay here. I haven't had much schooling, so I can't get a job. I have to go to a small town and find a job, picking coffee or whatever, because $150 will only get you so far. What I gave [the army], they should pay me for it, no? So I can get a bed at least, which is what I think about the most. My baby, where is it going to rest? They'll pay you, but you have to stay in the city [to get the money]. In the meantime you look for work, but that all takes time. That's why I need to go.*

A: Do you worry about your parents who are still in the area?

O: *Of course, but we're poor. We have no place to go.*

FIGURE INT.1. Drawing by Lucas Ospina.

CHAPTER ONE

An Archaeology of Media Spectacle, 1974–2008

How did the state come to believe that branding could help defeat the FARC? What I will argue in this chapter is that the government's marketing campaigns to demobilize individual guerrillas emerges from a layered history of the Colombian armed conflict's mediatization. By *mediatization* I mean the increasingly central role of the media in the war as it wore on. The chronicle starts in the early 1970s and ends in the mid-2000s, when the PAHD began to outsource its campaigns to Lowe/SSP3. Until the turn of the millennium, the state's media operations had largely acted defensively, responding to provocations from guerrilla groups, drug cartels, and paramilitary forces. Locked in a spiral of crisis and response, the state tumbled along in a multifront propaganda battle with a mutating cohort of violent groups. For most of this history, illegal armed actors proved more agile than the state in adapting to a changing media environment. Each armed group adopted the others' media tactics and adapted them in a process of multiparty mirroring. Faced with the impossible task of tracing all of the feedback of media tactics among the multiplicity of armed actors in the late twentieth century, I have chosen to highlight a few of the strategic adaptations of one group's tactics by another. Taken together, the transitions I expand upon below provide crucial context for the emergence of the PAHD's brand of brand warfare.

The M19: From Agitprop to Armed Propaganda

Since its beginnings in the mid-1960s, the FARC has drawn upon the communist tradition of agitprop, a portmanteau of agitation and propaganda, which emerged in the Soviet Union after the Bolshevik Revolution of 1917. The theoretical distinction between agitation and propaganda was precisely that: theoretical. In *What Is to Be Done?* Vladimir Lenin validated Russian Marxist Georgi Plekhanov's idea that agitation strategically simplifies and repeats a message to the masses, while propaganda is a matter of contextual critique that targets elites. Peter Kenez, historian of the early Soviet Union, maintains that "the distinction between agitation and propaganda is not a helpful one. One suspects it became part of Soviet parlance only because of Lenin's endorsement."[1]

As a practice, agitprop emerged from the Russian Civil War that followed the October Revolution of 1917, when the Red Army traveled with mobile propaganda theaters to build support for socialist ideals as it contended with defenders of the old regime. In the 1920s the Soviets drew upon their experience with propaganda theater to deploy agitprop brigades to factories and rural areas. The hallmark of agitprop was its highly materialist focus. For example, the agitprop brigades enlisted workers to contribute financially to the operation of the plant and, like sales managers, set benchmarks in their efforts to bolster collectivization in the rural areas. These roving troupes used satirical songs, tongue twisters, literary montages, and short skits to try to instill a sense of responsibility for collective production among factory workers and peasants.[2] The agitprop brigades complemented the ideological work of state-produced newspapers, books, films, and posters. Kenez compellingly argues that this early period laid the foundation of the Soviet propaganda state.

Between the 1930s and early 1970s, the Soviets exported their propaganda techniques through international communist parties and their youth leagues. Agitprop focused on local, often nonliterate publics, which meant that it translated easily to Latin American contexts. Promising youth leaders from across the region traveled to ideological meetings with their Latin American peers in Moscow. The meetings included discussion of the principles of agitprop and training in the technologies of the day. In Colombia, these young men (they were almost always men) were drawn from the Communist Youth League, or JUCO, and

fast-tracked into the FARC's leadership upon their return. Heavily influ-
enced by the Soviet Union and the Communist Party since its inception,
the FARC has retained a materialist disposition toward propaganda and
a primarily rural vision of the revolution (postures that after the mid-
1980s it would cautiously reform).

By the end of the 1960s, in the midst of expanding urbanization, a
new branch of revolutionary fervor was growing in Latin America that
argued for the need to bring the struggle to the cities. The first groups
of this new wave were National Liberation Action in Brazil (1967–74),
Tupamaros in Uruguay (1967–72), and Montoneros in Argentina (1970–
79).[3] The idea of an urban guerrilla came to Colombia a bit later. In 1972
a group of young people, many of whom had been alienated by the Communist Party, and some of whom had attended ideological trainings
in Moscow, began to challenge central assumptions of the Colombian
left. They questioned the utility of importing ideologies from the Soviet
Union, China, or Cuba, as well as the rural bias of revolutionary struggle. By February 1974 they would break off and begin their own group,
the Movimiento 19 de Abril, or M19.[4]

The M19 became famous for its signature strategy, *propaganda armada*, or armed propaganda. Most definitions I gathered from former
militants track closely with that of Carlos, an early member of the M19,
who said: "*Propaganda armada* is a military action whose fundamental objective is to disseminate a message, an ideological message. It is a
propaganda action that's done with the help of arms." In essence, *propaganda armada* privileges political message over military force, in actions that tend to render weaponry stage props first and deadly arma-
ment second. The M19's theatrical acts resignified symbols to engage
in a mediated dialogue with politics at the national level, as opposed to
more localized communication. *Propaganda armada* is best explained
by example, which is why I focus on the event that served as the M19's
dramatic launch: the theft of the sword of Simon Bolívar, independence
hero of northern South America. But first let's back up and meet the
story's protagonist.

Jaime Bateman defied stereotypes of disciplined revolutionaries. His
curly afro and gregarious style marked him as a *costeño* (someone from
Colombia's Caribbean coast). He carried himself with an air of informality and irreverence, and would liken the revolution to a party to which
Colombians of all types were invited. He rose quickly through the ranks
of the Communist Youth League, or JUCO. On multiple occasions the

Communist Party selected him for ideological training in Moscow and Havana. In Bogotá, Bateman excelled at agitprop, a skill that launched him into the group's national leadership. He visited FARC camps to deliver supplies and lecture the rank and file about Marxism. His charisma and dedication earned him the trust of Jacobo Arenas, the FARC's ideologue and second in command.[5]

Even as he ascended in the FARC, Bateman maintained his strongest relationships with his Bogotá-based comrades in the JUCO. When the Communist Party tasked Bateman with creating a military structure to oversee logistics in the cities, he turned to friends from the JUCO, many of whom had dramatic ideas for urban operations. Luis Otero, a zealous member of the JUCO, recalled one conversation with Bateman about Simon Bolívar's sword:

> The original idea came from reading a book by the Tupamaros [urban guerrilla group in Montevideo, Uruguay] where they talked about how they recuperated the flag of Artigas. I told El Flaco [Bateman's nickname, "Skinny"], "The Tupamaros stole the flag of Artigas—why don't we steal Bolívar's sword?" He answered, "Propose it to the military commission [of the FARC]."[6]

Otero recalled that when Bateman proposed the idea to the leadership of the Communist Party, "they responded that it was foolish because the sword is just an object in a museum."[7]

Feeling restricted by party discipline, Bateman and his friends began to gather informally. The Communist Party accused Bateman of being a "fractionalist" and engaging in "parallelism" for meeting with people who had been banned from the party, and in 1972 the party expelled him. The secretary general implored members of the party to avoid contact with Bateman's growing clique: "We have to guard against . . . those who are singing to the young communists with a siren's voice about the 'urban guerrilla.' Its adventurist ideas are out of sync with the reality of our country."[8] Though the accusation of adventurism proved prescient, thousands of people were flooding the cities to look for work. In that sense the FARC and the Communist Party were the ones out of sync with Colombia reality.

For a short year Bateman and a group of friends and conspirators met. They talked about transcending the "ideological cannibalism of the left" and creating an urban guerrilla that could embody an appealing and nondogmatic style.[9] In October 1973 the group held what is now considered the M19's foundational meeting. As Arjaid, one of the twenty-two people present that day, told me, "We didn't want to talk about the huge socialist debates of Hegel, Marx, Engels, Lenin. No, here we needed to interpret ourselves, to build socialism the Colombian way."

In preparing for the group's dramatic launch, Bateman, thirty-four years old at the time, would rely not only on a group of twentysomethings but also on the friendships he cultivated among the intelligentsia. In designing the propaganda strategy for the operation to "recuperate" Bolívar's sword, Bateman relied on his friend Nelson Osorio, a poet and singer-songwriter who earned a living in consumer marketing. Carlos, who played a key role in the M19's early media operations, described Osorio as the M19's closest collaborator. Carlos had sought asylum in Sweden in 1986, and in one of our interviews in Stockholm's Culture House, he described to me Osorio's role in the M19's early propaganda operations:[10] "Anything that had to do with propaganda strategy, he was the man. [The M19 leadership] had total confidence in him."

Osorio died of cancer in the early 2000s. I located his son Orlando, a *telenovela* producer in Bogotá. Orlando and I spoke in Bogotá's Commerce Club. He was surprised that I had sought him out but pleased at the chance to reflect on his father's life. "He was a salesman for Cabot. He never spoke about it—he hated it. He traveled to different parts of the country selling drugs from laboratories," he said.

"What kind of drugs?" I asked.

"Alercet and Bayer, all the labs that are here. For [artists], they were annoying jobs. Though they were the kind of people who never get bored. In the 1970s, intellectuals started going into publicity [*publicidad*]. . . . Television was coming to the country, and all of a sudden there were a lot of jobs in publicity."

Carlos recounted one of the campaigns that Nelson Osorio crafted.

He told me, "I need to do something to bring a new refrigerator to the Colombian market. I have an idea, but it's going to be pretty expensive."

"What's the idea?"

"I think I need to put a small animal from the arctic, Antarctica, inside the refrigerator, and when the owner opens it the animal comes out—to give an idea of the natural cold."

"A penguin," I said.

"That's it!" he said."

In designing the advertising campaign to build expectation for the theft of Bolívar's sword, Osorio combined the element of surprise he had used in the penguin commercial with his experience selling over-the-counter drugs.

On January 12, 1974, the M19 placed its first advertisement in *El Tiempo*, Colombia's largest daily paper. "Parasites . . . worms? Wait—M19." The advertisement was simple in its design, with white block letters on a black background and two equilateral triangles connected at a point, like a bowtie. Iterations of the ad appeared in the Colombian press with increasing frequency over the following week: "Aging . . . lack of memory? Wait—M19"; "Low on energy . . . bored? Wait—M19" (figure 1.1). The advertisements ran in the major newspapers of Colombia's most populous cities, often displayed prominently at the foot of a page dedicated to movie listings and graphic advertisements—a dense semiotic space. Carlos paraphrased the advertising campaign for me: "Insomnia, anxiety, stomach problems? Wait—M19." Smirking, he said, "People were expecting a new medicine."

On January 17, 1974, the day of the operation, *El Tiempo* carried a simple text box on the top left corner on its front page that read, "It's coming . . . today the M19 arrives."

Between 4:30 and 5:00 p.m., when most tourists were leaving, six militants trickled into the Quinta de Bolívar, the liberator's last Bogotá residence, which the government had transformed into a museum. Álvaro Fayad, known as "the Turk" (an oblique reference to his Lebanese heritage), commanded the operation. On cue, the group tied up the security guards and stormed into Bolívar's bedroom. Fayad shattered the crystalline casing, grabbed the sword's handle, and tucked its 85-centimeter blade under his full-length ruana. Other militants scattered copies of the M19's first public declaration—"Bolívar, Your Sword has Returned to the Struggle"—throughout the museum. Here is an excerpt from that statement:

> Bolívar has not died. His sword breaks through the cobwebs of the museum to the battles of the present. And now it points its tip at those who exploit the people. Against those who, with foreigners, own the country. Against those who shuttered it in a museum to rust. Those who distort the idea of the liberator.

When the getaway car passed the agreed-upon spot, Carlos Pizarro (who would go on to become the M19's last commander) alerted the media:

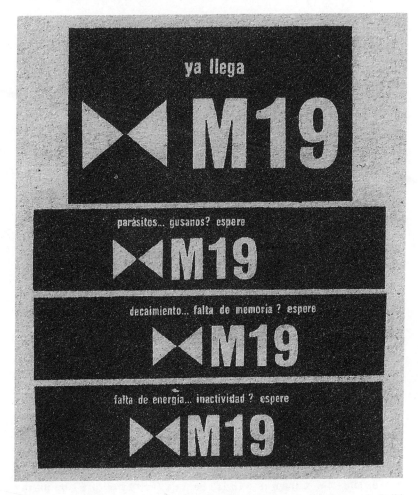

FIGURE 1.1. Advertisements that the M19 placed in newspapers in January 1974 to build expectation before its launch: "It's coming: M19," "Parasites, worms? wait for M19," "feeling down . . . lack of memory? wait for M19," "Low on energy . . . bored? wait for M19." Image courtesy of Darío Villamizar Herrera.

"Go to the Quinta de Bolívar. It's the M19."[11] Within three hours the radio was reporting the news.

Alternativa magazine, Latin America's most exciting literary project of the 1970s, launched one month after the M19 stole Bolívar's sword, and the magazine lavished coverage on the event in its inaugural issue. The news dominated its cover. Atop page 24 the magazine pub-

Aparecíó la espada de Bolívar. Está en América Latina!

FIGURE 1.2. Photograph featured in *Alternativa*, February 15–28, first issue, page 24. The caption reads, "Bolívar's sword appeared. It is in Latin America!" Image scanned from print edition.

lished a photograph of the sword lying diagonally on top of a map of South America, in front of an M19 banner, the barrel of a rifle jutting into the frame (figure 1.2). Bateman frequented the offices of *Alternativa*, which is where he recruited Carlos. *Alternativa* grew out of a collaboration between Gabriel García Márquez, the country's most famous journalist-turned-novelist and 1982 Nobel laureate in literature; Enrique Santos Calderón, scion of a family that produces presidents and has owned *El Tiempo*, who, in a betrayal of his class, tacked to the left; and Orlando Fals Borda, the renowned sociologist of the Colombian conflict.[12]

The media played a pivotal role at every stage of the operation. The M19 managed to create a media event through its savvy use of adver-

tising, not only resignifying the sword and shifting the ideological justification of guerrilla struggle from a menu of international leftist doc-
trines to a more nationalist key, but also transforming media spectacle
into a central dimension of Colombia's guerrilla wars. Without firing a
shot or injuring a human being, the M19 had managed to take a sacred
object from the state and activate its dormant political potency.[13] Bateman aptly described the sword as "a symbol worth more than a thousand
rifles."[14]

Throughout the fifteen years of the group's existence, the military
tried in vain to recapture the sword, detaining and torturing many M19
members and sympathizers. In the process, the military studied the M19
and its acts of *propaganda armada*. These armed antics entertained
middle-class Colombian audiences and won the group unprecedented
sympathy in the cities by confounding expectations of the militant left.
The group's political currency rose with its media profile.

As Bateman's growing clique experimented with its novel form of
armed media politics, it found that its most successful acts did not end
with the loss of life. In 1976, two years after the M19 stole Bolívar's
sword, it kidnapped José Raquel Mercado, a union boss that it accused
of betraying his base by secretly colluding with the aristocracy. The M19
called for a public "trial" and asked people to opine on whether Mercado was guilty. The M19 circulated photographs of Mercado held in a
"people's jail" and printed the "charges" leveled against him, threatening to kill him on their namesake day, April 19. The M19 demanded four
significant pro-labor reforms in exchange for Mercado's life. The government refused to negotiate, sweeping up members of the M19 (and nearly
capturing Bolívar's sword in the process). The rebel group decided to
kill Mercado, and left his body on a sidewalk alongside a busy public
square in Bogotá, with two bullet wounds in its chest. Darío Villamizar
Herrera, a former member of the M19 and its official historian, wrote
that the kidnapping, "trial," and death of Mercado "placed the M19 before the country no longer as a group of audacious and cool young people, but as a guerrilla movement." Bateman himself came to lament the
episode, insinuating that he had hoped the government would negotiate
and that the result would have been different. Villamizar Herrera writes,
"For many people, even with all of the charges [against Mercado] and
people shouting from every corner 'Yes, guilty,' extinguishing a life that
way was an inhumane resolution."[15]

The M19 learned its lesson. When the group tunneled into a military weapons depot in northern Bogotá in 1978, only military pride was injured. That injury, however, prompted the military to lash out at the M19, rounding up and torturing many of its militants. Few civilians, however, were affected.[16] In 1980 the M19 stormed the embassy of the Dominican Republic in Bogotá and held sixteen ambassadors (including those from the United States and the Vatican) hostage for two months. After a dramatic negotiation, the rebels secured safe passage for themselves and their hostages to Cuba, and a ransom of $1 million (but not the freedom of their imprisoned comrades). When the group returned to kidnapping as public theater, it made sure its victims walked free afterward. In 1981 the M19 kidnapped the country's most prominent television star, Fernando González Pacheco, along with journalist Alexandra Pineda, only to grant the two an exclusive interview over whiskey with Bateman and release them the next day. The stunt was a publicity ploy tied to an amnesty proposal being debated at the time.[17] In the broader context of political violence in Colombia, these dramatic media-oriented events caused minimal suffering, and even that was often overlooked on account of the entertainment value of the M19's unpredictable style. Its most frequent act of *propaganda armada* was hijacking milk trucks and distributing their contents freely in impoverished neighborhoods. The group played the roles of trickster and Robin Hood more effectively than that of guerrilla army.

In the early 1980s the Colombian government embarked on its first effort to reach a political solution to the armed conflict since the emergence of the FARC and ELN in the mid-1960s. The government held parallel negotiations with the FARC and the M19, which culminated in the Uribe Accords with the FARC and the Corinto Accords with the M19—both signed in 1984. During precarious ceasefires that followed, elite sectors of the military and the state helped to unleash right-wing groups that assassinated guerrilla leaders and ordinary citizens affiliated with left-wing political movements, notably the Patriotic Union (UP), a FARC-affiliated political party that arose from the Uribe Peace Accords.[18] Sixteen hundred members of the UP were killed between 1984 and 1997.[19] This violence prompted the FARC to withdraw from its experiment in electoral politics and fortify its military project. The M19 also suffered from paramilitary violence targeting its leadership and membership. As the accords unraveled, the M19 began to discuss the need for a revolutionary publicity coup (*golpe revolucionario publicita-rio*). The plan it ultimately settled upon, seizing the Palace of Justice, would prove a traumatic event in Colombia's recent history and precipitate the M19's demobilization.

On November 6, 1985, the M19 stormed the Palace of Justice in the Plaza de Bolívar, Bogotá's seat of government and the nation's central political stage. The ensuing siege and standoff lasted twenty-six hours and led to the deaths of ninety-eight people, including eleven Supreme Court justices and all thirty-three guerrillas involved in the action.

The M19's expressed purpose in seizing the Palace of Justice was to present an "armed petition" to Colombia's highest court. That petition insisted that Colombian president Belisario Betancur stand trial for violating the Corinto Accords. The M19 took cumbersome video cameras into the building to film the "trial," imagining that the event would be a media phenomenon of the highest order. The operation was grandiose to the point of megalomaniacal, and named accordingly: Operation Antonio Nariño for the Rights of Man.[20]

After tanks breached the front door of the palace, commandos rappelled from hovering helicopters onto its roof. As flames engulfed the building, Alfonso Reyes Echandía, chief justice of the Supreme Court, spoke by telephone to a Caracol Radio reporter who broadcast the conversation live. In her book about the event, journalist Ana Carrigan describes that conversation: "His voice at times drowned out by other desperate voices, screaming orders and obscenities in the immediate vicinity, the Chief Justice now tells his fellow citizens that from where he sits, at the very center of the battle raging between the army and the guerrillas, something is horrendously out of control."[21]

The reporter interjected, "But Judge, Chief Justice Reyes, what should we do?"

Reyes responded, "The details are not important. What is important is that the order finally be given, here within the building, for a ceasefire. Help us, please. The situation is dramatic. There must be an immediate ceasefire."[22]

Inside the court complex, the military pressed ahead, eager to retake the palace before public support for a negotiated solution could swell.[23] The interview with Justice Reyes had defied an order by the minister of communications "to abstain from broadcasting, by radio or television, any information regarding the operations of the military, directly or through interviews or press releases."[24] Having learned by now that the M19's strongest weapon was the media, the government did its best to blunt it. The minister of communication rushed to cut off any further broadcasts from the palace. Within minutes of Justice Reyes's interview, Caracol Radio announced, "Attention Colombians! We have news of the utmost importance for the entire nation! The soccer matches scheduled for tonight between Millonarios and Unión Magdalena here in the nation's capital, and between America and Nacional in Medellín, *will* take place as planned. Kickoff in the Campín de Bogotá at 8 p.m. Be there!"[25] But the tactics of mass distraction, often so effective, revealed rather than obscured the fact that a dark chapter of Colombian history was about to get even darker.

Luis Otero, the same militant who had conceived of the theft of Bolívar's sword, directed the takeover of the Palace of Justice. Otero and the M19 leadership calculated that the government would negotiate and that in the decisive moment it would not allow its top magistrates to die. The M19 believed that the event would resolve similarly to the storming of the Dominican Embassy, as a highly mediated, high-stakes story of audacity, compromise, and relief, which the M19 could claim as a victory.[26] As journalists and historians pore back over the event, it is clear that had a few things gone differently, the M19 might have been correct. Many tragedies in Colombia are foretold; the bloody end of the Palace of Justice siege was not one of them. History has judged the state harshly for its intransigence, excessive force, and what amounted to a momentary military imposition over the state's civilian leadership.[27] In the end, it is but another blemish on the government's legitimacy. The M19, however, never recovered from the fiasco.

Propaganda armada had enabled the M19 to stand out in a crowded field of guerrilla groups that sprang up in the revolutionary fervor of the 1960s and 1970s. Other non-state actors took note. In 1993, four years after the M19's collective demobilization, members of the FARC would rebrand themselves as "Bolivarians," usurping the M19's call to nationalism (and echoing the discourse of Venezuelan president Hugo Chávez, who had also studied the M19's discourse). Before then, an entrepreneurial drug trafficker recognized in the M19's antics a way of manipulating the public, not for ideological purposes but for personal interest. Pablo Escobar, the leader of the Medellín cartel, intensified what the M19 began, operating in cities and using media spectacle to attack the state at its symbolic core.[28] He similarly used mass mediation to drive a national political agenda. This is the story to which we now turn.

Pablo Escobar, the Brand of the Extraditables, and Violence as Spectacle

We need to create total chaos so they call us to discuss peace. . . . If we start harassing the politicians, burning down their houses, unleashing a disastrous civil war, they'll have to call for dialogue, get on good terms with everyone, and fix our problems. There is no other solution. — Pablo Escobar[29]

No Colombian in history ever possessed or exercised a talent like [Pablo Escobar's] for shaping public opinion. — Gabriel García Márquez[30]

Pablo Escobar is arguably the most famous Colombian of the late twentieth century. If he lived in the 2010s, he would be considered not only a narcoterrorist outlaw but also a guru of self-branding.[31] I turn to the well-worn story of Pablo Escobar and the Medellín cartel in this section to show how he adapted the *propaganda armada* of the M19 and developed a prototype of brand warfare in Colombia.

The drug baron cultivated fame. When the adulatory variety was no longer possible, he settled for infamy. The story of his personal rise through the underworld of Medellín to become the world's most wanted man has become an epic tale that has been told, embellished, and retold in books, television series, and movies. That Caracol TV, Netflix, and Hollywood would focus on Escobar's story is not surprising, considering how he carefully crafted his larger-than-life persona at a time when TV series such as *Miami Vice* and blockbuster films like *Scarface* glorified the battle between US law enforcement and Latin American narcos. Those representations heaped backhanded admiration on their villains, a practice that drew from and spilled back into the real world as narco-culture and popular culture became increasingly interwoven through the 1980s.

The 1980s also saw branding emerge as a powerful economic phenomenon. It was then that the discourse and quasi-scientific practice of branding emerged from a blitz of mergers and acquisitions in the United States. In the Wall Street–brokered deals of the time, sellers insisted that they be compensated for their intangible assets. The brand became the solution to the problem of ascribing value to the affective connection that companies fostered, through advertising, with their customers. Although I am not positing a direct or causal link between New York deal making and the drug business of Medellín (though cocaine certainly connected the two entrepreneurial milieus), branding was creeping into the globalized *Geist* of the moment. The Medellín cartel's experience with *la merca*, short in narco-slang for "the merchandise" or "the goods," helped cultivate its savvy about *la marca*, or the brand. García Márquez wrote that the Medellín cartel "was a true shadow-force with a business brand—the Extraditables."[32] Escobar and company branded themselves the Extraditables and coined a slogan: "We prefer a grave in Colombia to a jail cell in the United States."[33]

The Medellín cartel trafficked not only in cocaine but also in televised images of horror, bodies of prominent people, and dramatically written communiqués. The Extraditables did not need to buy advertising; the press reproduced their communiqués in an ongoing telenovela of violence, which seemed to air almost daily. Like the M19, Escobar selected his targets with a semiotic sensibility—but with important differences. Whereas the M19's operations echoed those of the French Situationists with their commitment to playful resignification, or *détournement*, the semiotics of Escobar's violence operated on a different plane: brute intimidation.[34] The terror that Escobar unleashed used bodies as a medium: kidnapped bodies; bodies buried beneath buildings crumpled by dynamite explosions; bodies left to die in public spaces; bodies of politicians, government agents, rivals, and critics shot at close range. The very public exhibition of these cadavers made clear that Escobar's targets were both the victim and the public.[35] While the M19 came to lament its assassination of union boss José Raquel Mercado, Escobar never showed remorse. He toyed with the drama that even the innocent might die, leveraging this fatal uncertainty for even more media coverage. Yet at the same time, he sought to evoke the Robin Hood–like narrative that the guerrillas projected, by financing public housing and soccer courts in downtrodden Medellín neighborhoods, especially the cramped *comunas* of the city's northeastern hills, the same sectors whence he recruited his assassins.

Here I scrutinize a particular moment in Escobar's biography, from 1990 to 1993. But to set the stage it's important to review some of the backstory. The three-year period in question comes after his rise through the underworld of contraband in Medellín (1971–74); after he coordinated cocaine production from Peru to Panama (1974–76); after he banded together with a group of elites and gangsters in the department of Antioquia to build the Medellín cartel (1974–76). It is also after he participated in the proto-paramilitary group Muerte a Secuestradores (Death to Kidnappers; 1981) and after he mobilized his networks of patronage to win a congressional seat in 1982 with the Liberal Party. In 1984 Escobar had a showdown with Rodrigo Lara Bonilla, the minister of justice in the Betancur administration, which changed his trajectory. Lara Bonilla had ordered a raid on Tranquilandia (Land of Tranquility), a sprawling farm that served as Escobar's largest drug depot. The police confiscated twelve airplanes and helicopters and more than $1 billion dollars' worth of cocaine. At that point Escobar, unmasked as a drug kingpin, resigned from Congress. The United States revoked his visa. In an interview years later for the documentary film *Sins of My Father*, his son Juan Pablo—by then living in Buenos Aires under an assumed name—said, "I think at that point he lost it, he was completely out of control."[36]

With Escobar's political aspirations thwarted and his attempts to threaten Lara Bonilla into silence ineffective, he retreated into the world of assassins.[37] In his final statement before resigning from Congress, he threatened once more: "The minister of justice lied when he said he would not resign. We'll see what happens in the next few days." Either Lara Bonilla and the criminal justice system he represented would be cowed, or Escobar would begin a war on the Colombian state. The bloody path of the latter began on the night of April 30, 1984, when Escobar sent an assassin to rip a lethal burst of automatic gunfire from the back of a motorcycle into Lara Bonilla's car.

To show its resolve in the fight against narcotraffic, the government passed a law permitting the extradition of Colombians to the United States, setting the stage for a frontal confrontation with the Medellín cartel. In my focus on the last three years of Escobar's life, I zoom in on a spate of kidnappings of prominent journalists, many of whom hailed from families of the political elite.[38] Escobar selected his hostages to maximize the fear the kidnappings would strike in the ruling class and the media storm they would generate. In holding these high-profile figures, Escobar toyed with the question, will they die?

By the mid-1980s television had displaced radio as Colombia's most influential mass medium.[39] Although political violence in Colombia has been mediated since Simon Bolívar carted around a printing press during the battles for independence, the saturation of television added a newfound impact.[40] As W. J. T. Mitchell has noted, live television of un-folding events has "the terrifying *immediacy* of viscerally intimate vio-lence portrayed in real time" (italics in the original).[41] That immediacy amplified Escobar's gruesome acts and abetted his project of bending the Colombian state to his demands.

What could make for more immediate news than snatching journal-ists whose colleagues would be committed to covering the story in fine-grained detail? Escobar's macabre twist on the M19's habit of kidnap-ping journalists to grant them exclusive interviews and then releasing them proved to be a potent tactic. First came Diana Turbay, daughter of President Julio César Turbay (1978–82) and director of the television news program *Criptón* and the magazine *Hoy x Hoy*. Escobar's men kid-napped Turbay and five members of her staff in August 1990. Then the Extraditables kidnapped Francisco "Pacho" Santos, editor of *El Tiempo* and member of the powerful Santos family. Two months later Escobar's henchmen captured Maruja Pachón and her sister-in-law Beatriz Villa-mizar. Pachón was an award-winning journalist, and Villamizar worked as her assistant. In a period of four months in 1990, Escobar collected a fistful of aces that he would play in his bid to avoid extradition.

Frustrated by the hands-off approach of César Gaviria's administra-tion (1990–94) to the plight of her daughter, Nydia Quintero, the mother of Diana Turbay and former first lady, hit the airwaves with determina-tion. In a testament to the dramatic absurdity of Colombian politics, Ga-briel García Márquez returned to writing nonfiction to recount the story of Escobar's high-profile kidnappings. In *Noticias de un secuestro* (*News of a Kidnapping*) he wrote:

[Quintero] had planned the appearance of groups of children on radio and television newscasts all over the country to read a plea for the release of the hostages. On October 19, the "Day of National Reconciliation," she had ar-ranged for simultaneous noon masses in various cities and towns to pray for goodwill among Colombians. In Bogotá, while crowds waving white hand-kerchiefs gathered in many neighborhoods to demonstrate for peace, the cer-emony took place on the Plaza de Bolívar, where a torch was lit, the flame to burn until the safe return of the captives. Through her efforts, television newscasts began each program with photographs of all the hostages, kept a tally of the days they had been held captive, and removed the correspond-ing picture as each prisoner was freed. It was on her initiative that soccer matches throughout the country opened with a call for the release of the hostages. Maribel Gutiérrez, Colombia's beauty queen for 1990, began her acceptance speech with a call for their freedom.[42]

Thanks to Nydia Quintero, kidnapping went primetime.

As Escobar's prospects of repealing Colombia's extradition treaty ebbed and flowed, he killed and released hostages. He killed Marina Montoya, daughter of Germán Montoya, who was an adviser to President Barco (1986–90). Diana Turbay died in a rescue operation that took place despite President Gaviria's assurances to her family that he would not attempt such a mission without its consent. To show goodwill, Escobar then released Beatriz Villamizar on February 6, 1991, two weeks after Turbay's death. But he held tightly to his two most valuable hostages: Pacho Santos and Maruja Pachón. The media profile of their plight ballooned as the possibility that Escobar would execute them loomed.

In the first few months of 1991, Escobar's band of hired assassins killed approximately five hundred police officers—the result of his "bribes or bullets" (*plata o plomo*) policy. With the bombing of the Hilton hotel in Cartagena in 1989, the Extraditables initiated a campaign of massive explosions. They proceeded to detonate large explosives in the bullfighting ring in Medellín, the headquarters of DAS (Colombia's equivalent of the FBI) in Bogotá, and the main building of *El Espectador*, Colombia's second-largest newspaper. Perhaps Escobar's most terrifying attack was a botched attempt to kill presidential candidate César Gaviria in 1989. That bombing sent Avianca flight 203 plunging to the ground southwest of Bogotá.[43]

The government began to show flexibility toward the Medellín cartel. In 1991 the government passed Decree 3030, which stipulated the conditions under which the Colombian justice system, rather than that of the United States, would prosecute mafia bosses. Decree 3030, however, did not outlaw extradition. On January 7, 1991, the Extraditables published a letter explaining why the decree did not go far enough, leaving the government and its criminal antagonists at an impasse. Then, in a surprise move, the Colombian Supreme Court ruled that no topic could be excluded from the Constitutional Assembly of 1991, which had been tasked with drafting a new constitution. The Supreme Court's decision revived Escobar's hopes that by influencing the politicians participating in the Constitutional Assembly, thereby bypassing the legislative and executive branches, he could strike down extradition.

As the Constitutional Assembly approached, Escobar decided to release hostages as a public relations strategy. The press camped outside the homes of Pacho Santos and Maruja Pachón and had a field day with the liberation. In announcing their decision to free the hostages, the Extraditables claimed they wanted to "erase any doubt that we are pressuring the National Constitutional Assembly."[44] The statement was transparent in its dishonesty. In a more candid moment Escobar penned a handwritten letter to Pachón apologizing for the ordeal: "Don't pay attention to my press releases, they're only to apply pressure."[45] Escobar turned himself over to the Colombian authorities the day after he freed Pachón and Santos. He had obtained his goal, although the country did not yet know it. Escobar's public pressure, private threats, and handsome bribes worked in concert.

A special commission departed in two helicopters to apprehend Escobar for his long-awaited "subjugation." García Márquez described the scene: "He raised the pant-leg of his left leg and pulled out the pistol he carried in a harness tied to his ankle. A magnificent gem: Sig Sauer 9, with a gold monogram on the plates of the handles. Escobar didn't take out the clip but rather he removed the bullets one by one and dropped them on the ground. It was a theatrical gesture that seemed practiced."[46] Almost simultaneously, news that the Constitutional Assembly had eliminated the legal provision allowing for the extradition of Colombian citizens blared from radio speakers throughout the country.

Though Escobar abandoned his famous Hacienda Nápoles, a seven-thousand-acre estate with six swimming pools, twenty artificial lakes, a bullfighting ring, a raceway, and a zoo stocked with camels, flamingos, giraffes, and hippopotami (which have since reproduced and become an invasive species), he did not intend to live in the austerity of a jail cell. He converted his detention center outside Medellín into luxurious quarters with large-screen televisions, imported furniture, a pool, a bar, and a waterfall. This "prison" served as the site of licentious parties and as the new headquarters of Escobar's drug business. After thirteen months he fled his luxury incarceration in the middle of the day with nine of his closest associates. His disappearance set off a fifteen-month manhunt led by a special Colombian police unit that received DEA support and collaborated with a cadre of Escobar's rivals, a group known as Los Pepes. The Pepes acted like Escobar, killing and kidnapping in brazen waves of violence. The effort culminated in the Colombian police shooting the mafia boss as he ran across a Medellín rooftop (a scene depicted by Colombia's most famous painter, Fernando Botero).

The Medellín cartel adopted the media-oriented tactics of the M19 in a way that leveraged the news media's bias for sensationalism and emphasis on powerful families and personal dramas. In the end, Escobar's spectacular violence undermined the sovereign authority of the state to such a degree that there could be no negotiation—only death would do. Films and television programs that work loosely from Escobar's life story, such as *Narcos, The Father of Evil*, and *Surviving Pablo Escobar*, are driven by drama and conflict. They have ample material to work with. Those two criteria for good television, drama and conflict, defined Escobar's modus operandi.

Each kidnapping, each bombing, each assassination was intended not only to do harm but also to communicate a message to his targets. The war Escobar waged on his enemies could not be disentangled from a broader war to control the narrative of the moment. This lent his violence a mediatic dimension that ensnared the media in the conflict in unprecedented ways. Take Escobar's clash with the country's second-largest newspaper, *El Espectador*. Escobar deemed assassinating Guillermo Cano, its award-winning editor, insufficient punishment for the paper's investigative reporting and critical editorial line. When the municipality of Medellín erected a bust in Cano's honor, Escobar ordered the bust pulverized by dynamite. Shortly thereafter his cronies planted a car bomb outside *El Espectador*'s headquarters in Bogotá that ripped through the building. The Medellín cartel treated the country's second-largest newspaper as one of its rivals in the cocaine business. How many exclamation points did the cartel need to convey its chilling message to the country's journalistic community?

The Extraditables set themselves apart in a crowded field of armed actors in the 1980s and early 1990s through the spectacularization of violence. They transformed the fear and notoriety they generated into a productive form of publicity.

Escobar's ability to drive the circulation of media images shocked the state into realizing the importance of monopolizing the media narrative surrounding violence. After his death the state moved quickly to paper over the cracks in its sovereignty that Escobar had exposed. President Gaviria created an advertising campaign to mend the country's image abroad and stoke a sense of nationalism at home through Colombia's participation in the 1994 World Cup. The Colombian team featured the dynamic duo of Carlos Valderrama, a flamboyant striker with a mop of curly yellow hair, and Andrés Escobar, a clean-cut sweeper (no relation to Pablo). No public relations campaign, however, could hide a country in crisis. The script of national redemption through soccer did not go as planned. On the field Colombia lost its first two games, exiting the tournament and puncturing expectations. In the second game, against the United States, star defender Escobar inadvertently scored on his own goal. Within a week of the team's return to Colombia, Escobar was killed in a Medellín nightclub. International headlines such as "A Fatal Goal for Colombia" and "Colombia: The Kosovo Next Door" compounded the shame of the team's elimination. In an interview conducted from prison for the ESPN documentary *The Two Escobars*, Popeye, one of Escobar's closest lieutenants, summed up the situation in the crass argot of Medellín street talk: "President Gaviria paid a ton of money to clean Colombia's image. Back then cleaning Colombia's image was like when you have gonorrhea and throw alcohol on your cock, but the gonorrhea is strong and it's inside. . . . President Gaviria threw his money away. Back then, *nobody* could fix Colombia's image."[47]

Whereas the M19 made advertising and mass publicity a feature of Colombia's armed conflict, Escobar and the Extraditables refashioned the guerrilla groups' tactics of *propaganda armada* to wage what amounted to a beta version of brand warfare, one that relied on spectacular violence. Although the Gaviria administration failed at its first attempt to harness advertising to upgrade the government's reactive and bumbling propaganda operations, that failure would motivate the government to seek support from Madison Avenue in New York and the Washington Beltway. Under the overlapping categories of marketing and information warfare, US-based consultants coached the Colombian government, and especially the military, on how to take the offensive in the country's media war.

Through the 1990s the FARC intensified its relationship with drug traffickers, taking a tax on coca cultivation and processing.[48] In the next section I turn to another of the FARC's principal fundraising strategies: kidnapping. The insurgency iterated upon Escobar's use of kidnapping as spectacle. Whereas Escobar engendered terror but also a degree of veneration, like a proper antihero, the FARC's use of kidnapping provoked outrage and hatred across a vast swath of Colombia's political spectrum.

The FARC: Kidnapping and Political Isolation

One day when I was conducting research in a military intelligence battalion (chapter 3), Nicolás, the commander of the unit, handed me a book. Its black cover and stylish design gave it the authoritative feel of a publication produced by a Bogotá think tank or a European NGO. The cover lacked an author's name, but the title left no doubt about the book's editorial approach: *FARC: Guerrilla, Infamy and Suffering.*[49] I leafed through the photographs, long captions, and press reports that the book compiled. As I turned the pages, I marveled at the idea of the military writing the FARC's history.

Absent a negotiating process or the implementation of a peace agreement, the FARC cannot brand itself, though it can be branded by others—including its sworn enemy. The Colombian government has intermittently declared the Communist Party, which has been closely affiliated with the FARC since its inception, illegal. Antiterror legislation has shuttered expressions of international solidarity, like Fighters and Lovers' sale of T-shirts and CDs in Denmark. The Cold War, the War on Terror, and military persecution have conspired to inhibit the FARC's ability to speak for itself.

On the run and underground, the FARC has been forced to deprioritize propaganda. In my 2016 interview in Havana with Sergio Marín, the FARC's director of propaganda and communication (*propaganda y divulgación*), he conceded that "from a military standpoint we were able to resist, but politically and ideologically we have to recognize that they hit us hard, because we had no way of answering the state's propaganda. They had an open field when it came to political and ideological issues, because they could give a one-sided portrayal." The FARC maintained a webpage and a bulletin, both titled *Resistance*, and a regional radio program called *Voice of Resistance*, while also managing a basic, unstable web presence. During the Caguán peace negotiations (1999–2002) and the Havana peace talks (2012–16), the FARC worked to make up for lost ground in the propaganda war, but always found that its adversaries far outmatched its own media capacity.

Facing this scenario, the FARC during the 1990s and 2000s highlighted its military strength and belligerent status in the vast majority of its communications. The videos it uploaded to YouTube documented its successful assaults (such as those in Mitú, Vaupes [1998], and Mira-

flores, Guaviare [1999]). FARC videographers and their military counterparts documented each armed confrontation—not unlike the way professional sports teams record their matches for postgame analysis. The
combat images taken by the FARC and posted online became contested
texts, used by the government to argue for an investment in the Colombian military and to vilify the FARC. A similar dynamic played out even
more dramatically in the context of the FARC's practice of kidnapping.
Scenes of hostages marching in shackles and images of men and women
held in barbed-wire pens that evoked cages or even concentration camps
haunted the group's efforts to achieve political legitimacy.

In the late 1990s and early 2000s, the FARC's acts of kidnapping became the most visible and disdained dimension of the armed conflict,
much more so than the exponential growth of paramilitary massacres
that were taking place at the same time. For years, coverage of the human rights abuses of the armed left eclipsed media representations of
the even more pervasive abuses of the armed right, a tendency has as
much to with class as with politics. On average, the paramilitaries' victims were poorer than those of the FARC. The FARC had little recourse
to control the narrative of the conflict. Its cynical use of hostages to
fundraise for the revolution and apply pressure on the political class inspired fear and anger, but without the quiet admiration engendered by
the M19's playful audacity or Escobar's antiheroism. Like the Extraditables, the FARC kidnapped key government figures. It snatched presidential candidates, ministers, governors, members of congress, mayors,
and local councilors. Like the Extraditables, the FARC released communiqués, though the press did not reproduce them at the same length
as those of the flamboyant drug traffickers. In 2000 the group justified
its practice of kidnapping by decreeing a "law" defining kidnapping as
a tax on people or companies worth more than $1 million. But whatever
Robin Hood effect it tried to conjure proved empty when the group began "the miraculous catch." This religiously loaded euphemism meant
pulling people off buses at random to extort ransoms from their families. Carla, a leftist activist close to the FARC's leadership who was living in exile in rural Sweden, reflected with sardonic frustration, "The
miraculous catch must have been the idea of someone who infiltrated."
Kidnapping, she concluded, has been devastating to the FARC's legitimacy, expanding the affliction of the upper classes to the wider public.
Although kidnapping allowed the FARC to intervene in a hostile media

environment that did not allow it to speak for itself, it paid a heavy political price for the publicity.

What Nydia Quintero, the mother of Diana Turbay, had started in the days of Pablo Escobar—building public sympathy for hostages through media activism—expanded exponentially in the late 1990s as more and more family members faced the nightmare of trying to free a loved one held captive. As the visibility of kidnapping rose through the 1990s and early 2000s, so did public outrage toward the FARC. A radio program in which family members could send messages to kidnapped loved ones became not only a lifeline for the hostages and their families but also a way of generalizing their suffering to the nation. The dramas of kidnapping laid bare the depravity of a war that had degenerated through many mutations to unthinkable depths.

The fledgling Caguán peace negotiations imploded in 2002. President Pastrana went on television showing satellite imagery to prove that the FARC was using the demilitarized zone that the government had ceded for peace talks to run drugs, hold hostages, and fortify itself militarily. The president dispatched the military to retake the zone. In retaliation, the guerrillas collected more high-profile hostages and angled for prisoner exchanges with the government.

On February 23, 2002, the FARC kidnapped Íngrid Betancourt, a presidential candidate and French-Colombian dual citizen, along with members of her campaign staff. A year later the FARC captured three American contractors working for Northrop Grumman, a US military contractor tasked with surveillance of FARC territory, after their single-engine plane crashed. Betancourt and the three US contractors all but fell into the FARC's arms. In other instances, however, the FARC played the trickster in a way that was not dissimilar to the M19's imagination or Escobar's emphasis on drama and conflict. These cases reveal the FARC's unsuccessful attempts to brand itself as not only a belligerent force but also modern and media savvy.

The event I home in on is the FARC's 2002 kidnapping of twelve council members from the Valle de Cauca's departmental assembly. The FARC plucked these regional representatives from the assembly building in the middle of Cali, Colombia's third-largest city, at 11 a.m. The event is perhaps best conveyed by the video that the FARC produced of its duplicitous operation, in which guerrillas pose as members of the Colombian military and storm into the building warning of a bomb attack.

The fourteen-minute video begins with the dramatic moment of the kidnapping, flashes back to the preparations, and then tells the story of the operation from beginning to end. It makes a mockery of the state, especially the government's security forces, while highlighting the FARC's audacity, cunning, and media prowess.

In the opening scene, people scramble through the portico of a colonial building while an off-screen voice, amplified by a megaphone, directs the chaos. The FARC logo hangs in the upper left corner of the screen as the slow gait and unsteady hand of the videographer guide the viewer onto a bus. "FARC-EP Productions" bisects the screen as the voice behind the megaphone announces, "For the parliamentarians, there's a special vehicle." The title card, "For an Exchange"—of hostages—sits over a still image of suited parliamentarians seated on the bus, staring blankly at the camera. The video then flashes back to preparations for their kidnapping. The scenes toggle between bootcamp drills and rebels in formation responding to staccato orders. The videographer zooms in on a German shepherd that will act as a bomb-sniffing dog during the operation, a shrewd detail in the performance of authenticity on which it will hinge. In another scene the FARC choreographs logistics, using black plastic sheeting to create a blueprint of the parliament building.

Over a quiet nightscape, the female videographer's voice whispers to a colleague that the cluster of lights in the distance is a base from which the FARC fears a military response will come. Cut to the morning, good-luck handshakes, and a shaky recording of the bus's descent along a switchback. The date-time stamp reads "April 11, 9:05:23 a.m." Walkie-talkie static interrupts birds' chirping. Then the scene shifts to a second camera looking through the windshield of the bus, commercial radio blaring. Motorcycles lead the bus into the outskirts of Cali, its wealthy suburbs, and finally the city center. The scene suddenly cuts back to the pandemonium in the portico. After a few moments of unsteadily recorded images, we are back on the bus, this time with the parliamentarians. Sigifredo López, the only hostage who would survive, responds to a question from the guerrilla videographer posing as a local journalist—a poignant example of how the media itself had become a tactical weapon in the armed conflict. "The army says there's a gas cylinder [a crude bomb used by the FARC] and made us evacuate the building," López says.

When I interviewed López in a Bogotá café in 2012, he recalled that the videographer was wearing a T-shirt with the logo of TelePacífico, the regional state-sponsored television station. He reflected, "In that moment of the video, we didn't yet know we were kidnapped. I interpret the video as a joke the FARC made, not only at our expense but also making fun of the state's security apparatus, because of the form of the kidnapping itself, the spectacle of it. To come into downtown Cali, the third-largest city in Colombia, and take us like sheep to slaughter."

On screen, as the bus revs up a hill, the parliamentarians clamor, "Where are we heading, boss?" The question is received in silence. Then, a belated reply: "Ladies and gentlemen, we are the FARC. We are taking you from downtown Cali." The motor roars as the bus speeds off toward the Farallones Mountains. As the insurgents, now wearing FARC armbands, move their hostages from the bus to a cattle truck, the captives recognize the gravity of their situation and look at one another in disbelief. When the truck pulls into a rebel-controlled area, a passenger in the cab gives a thumbs-up. A salsa ballad composed for the occasion fills the audio track. Its refrain, "Listen up, generals," plays as the rebels embrace, and the video flashes back to previous scenes. The prankish braggadocio then shifts to an ideological key as the video ends with a series of leftist critiques denouncing an exclusive political elite, state terrorism, and US intervention. Finally, the credits:

- FARC-EP Productions, February 2004, Edited in the Mountains of Colombia
- All of the images in this video have been made by camera people of the FARC-EP during the preparation and execution phases of the operation that culminated in the detention of the 12 parliamentarians of the Assembly of Valle de Cauca

In splashing "Edited in the Mountains of Colombia" across the screen, as well as crediting the "camera people of the FARC-EP," the video conjures a parallel, occult universe of media production capable of documenting and promoting the FARC's operations.

In a halfway house for former guerrillas, I spoke to Roberto, a demobilized rebel from the FARC's Sixth Front, which operates in the region where the kidnapping took place. He recalled watching the video projected onto a screen in a rebel camp. "At the time I thought it was the best thing the movement could do," he said. "They told us these were the kind of operations we needed to do, that we should take notes."

For a decade the video failed to circulate in an unadulterated form. The media hegemony of Colombian mass media was effectively transferred into the online sphere. When the FARC video appeared on streaming sites like YouTube or Daily Motion, it would be promptly removed.[50] Videos that remained online and circulated in its stead remixed raw footage from the FARC's original as evidence that the guerrillas deserve their terrorist distinction, and, according to many of those who commented anonymously beneath those remixed videos, also an ignominious death. The video's recombinatory circulation—by which I mean its fragmentation into derivative videos that displaced the original— muted the FARC's ability to speak online, leaving others to shout at them.[51]

Throughout its history the FARC has done its public image no favors. Its most astounding act of self-sabotage occurred on June 28, 2007, more than five years after the Cali kidnapping. That is when a laconic *comunicado* announced the deaths of eleven of the twelve hostages.[52] Their lives ended more abruptly than their abduction. Sigifredo López, chained to a tree eighty meters from the main FARC camp—punishment for leaving a red shirt out to dry while the military was flying overhead—heard barrages of gunfire and the cry "Don't let them go!" After the incident, the Sixtieth Front, the custodian of the hostages, kept López isolated. He sensed the import of the exchange only days later when one of the rebels confided to him, "Some idiots from the Twenty-Ninth Front came in without warning. We fucked it up."[53] While 6,723 people were kidnapped in Colombia between 1996 and 2006, it was the parliamentarians' deaths that sparked a massive Facebook campaign, "A Million Voices against the FARC." The online mobilization, stoked by mass media and the Colombian government, tapped into outrage at the FARC and a general disgust with the macabre absurdity of the war, and culminated in a global mobilization denouncing the FARC in more than two hundred cities—a defining moment in the group's political isolation.[54]

The FARC, like the Medellín cartel and the M19, transformed kidnapping into a form of spectacle. But unlike those groups, its practice of hostage taking provoked an unambiguous rejection in Colombian civil society. That rejection—born of the FARC's own hubris, avarice, and ideological inconsistency, and also of the structural conditions of the Cold War and the War on Terror—left the group little space to communicate beyond its ranks. As the FARC insisted upon using kidnapping as a means of financing the revolution and achieving a threatening vis-

ibility in the media, it abetted its own political marginalization. As the
military tide began to turn on the FARC in the 2000s, the FARC's insistence on kidnapping (a practice it abandoned at the outset of the Havana peace negotiations) enabled the military to claim the humanitarian
high ground.

In 2008, one year after the death of the parliamentarians, the Colombian military, in a dialogical response to the FARC kidnapping in
Cali, liberated Íngrid Betancourt, the three Northrop Grumman contractors, and eleven other long-term hostages in a dramatic ruse. The
military created a hoax in which an international humanitarian commission was to check up on the hostages. A white helicopter carried intelligence agents posing as FARC envoys (in Che Guevara T-shirts), international observers, aid workers (their foreign accents picked up in acting
lessons), a journalist, and a cameraman. When the helicopter took off
again, it carried the hostages to freedom.[55] The commanding officer
told the hostages that their new captors were really their saviors: "We're
from the national army, and you're free!" Those words, the inverse of the
FARC's announcement while abducting the parliamentarians from Cali,
exacted the revenge hailed by the recombinatory circulation pattern of
the FARC's video, surprisingly bloodlessly. The government had finally
adapted the M19's method of *propaganda armada*, resignified Escobar's
usage of kidnapping as spectacle, and outmatched the FARC's duplicitous tactics. The footage was compelling, the news was excellent, and the
political stakes were high. So images from Operation Check flowed from
a fake reporter's camera to audiences around the world, with barely a
trace of antagonistic recombination—only quibbles about members of
"the humanitarian commission" wearing the logo of the International
Red Cross in violation of the Geneva Conventions.

A Layered History of Brand Warfare

The genealogy of historical precedents for the PAHD's turn toward
brand warfare in the late 2000s that I have laid out above is at once
extraordinarily dense and terribly incomplete. This piecemeal history
does not pretend to be a comprehensive account of media warfare over
the three dozen years it spans.[56] Rather, it illuminates the way in which
a multiplicity of armed actors adopted media strategies and tactics from
each other, a process that drove the mediatization and spectaculariza-

tion of the armed conflict through the late twentieth and early twenty-first centuries. This intensive borrowing between the conflict's armed actors has further blurred the boundaries between politics, business, crime, revolution, and counterrevolution, attenuating the conflict's earlier ideological framing in the face of a sweeping and popularly held idea that the war, in its later iterations, had become nothing but a business. One corollary of this logic is that if war can be reduced to business, the victor will be the party with either the best product or the best marketing. It was to the realm of business that the government turned to compensate for its late arrival to a mode of warfare in which propaganda was no longer an ancillary dimension to the armed conflict but rather a central axis.

Juana

J: *Back then, they didn't let themselves be seen. If you saw them, they were dressed like anybody else, so you couldn't recognize them. But then they started to declare who they were. They weren't called guerrillas but rather* compañeros. *When I was like nine years old an uncle joined the guerrilla. My mom said, "Don't talk to those people, because they take children with them." My mom would lie to us so we wouldn't hang out with them.*

In our house there were lots of problems, and sometimes they affect you. There were problems between my dad and my mom. At ten you start to feel big. I said to myself, "The best option is to leave," but I couldn't find a place to go. When I turned eleven I took the decision. Because when I was ten [the guerrilla] said, "No, we can't take you yet, because you're a small girl." When I turned eleven I was a little bigger and they said, "If you want to join you can, it's no problem." I left by running away at night so [my parents] wouldn't know.

A: What was your first reaction, joining as an eleven-year-old?

J: *Well, you join as a little grasshopper. When you arrive, someone orients you and tells you what you have to do and what you can't do. They read you the rules, the laws. Every day they tell you what you can and can't do. Ayyyy no, after three days I wanted to go back.*

I said, "I am sick of this, I want to go home."

Then they told me I couldn't, that when you come in, you join forever [tiempo indefinido].

My dad found out and went to talk to the commander so they would send me home. They moved me to a different front so my dad wouldn't bother them and so I wouldn't think about where I lived so much. That's when I started to adapt to the good things and bad things, catching the rhythm of living there. What else was I going to do?

A: What was the hardest part of adapting to life over there?

J: *Walking at night in the dark is very hard.*

A: Can you describe it for someone who hasn't had that experience?

J: *At midnight or one in the morning [someone says,] "Stand up, we're going!" What a pain! They'd say, "We need to move to a different hamlet. To get there we need to cross some pastures, but we can't be seen so we're going at night."*

During the day we would be still, quietly waiting for night to come. At six in the afternoon you have your pack ready. At six-thirty, seven, they start numbering you one, two; one, two; one, two. Ones will cover the left, twos the right. Before leaving, they give everyone two code words in case you get lost and have to meet up later. When you are walking you can smash into someone else in the darkness, because the night is very dark.

Sometimes you rest for an hour or so, depending on how much weight you are carrying. One time we were trekking at night and I sat and fell asleep. When I woke up—my God!—there wasn't anyone around, and I didn't know the area. I thought, "What am I going to do?" Thank good-ness they had counted off and realized I was missing. The guide came looking for me, saying "psst, psst" and whistling.

You have to find a place to stay by five a.m., before it gets light out. You stay there until going out at night again.

A: When was your first combat experience?

J: *I was fourteen. At the end of the day I was lucky, because I joined as a lit-tle girl, and they didn't make me carry a heavy pack. Then they put me in a unit called Finances where we only ate, slept, and accompanied those who carried the money.*

When I was thirteen and a half, they put me in a six-month course to be able to fight. They left us for three days to suffer from hunger so we would have to survive off of the mountain. I didn't know how. I was scared to climb the trees, but the boys weren't. In the mountain there are many seeds to eat, but I didn't know about them.

They trained us for six months, they took us [to fight]. It went so badly. We got caught in a counterambush. Do you know what a counterambush is? You are waiting for the enemy and the enemy gives it to you! [Laughs] We were going to take a police station. [The commanders] showed us a model, and everything looked good. But the people who did the intelli-gence didn't realize that the police had underground tunnels outside the base. When [the guerrilla] entered there was a big bloodbath.

A: What happened?

J: *We were leaving the páramo* (highlands) *to go to Tolima. We saw [the military] coming along the road; they were below us and it looked easy to ambush them. But as they were coming along the road, there was another patrol that came this way, and we were between them. Then we heard branches breaking. That's when we knew they were above us.*

We went down to warn the others that the army was above us. Since we were kids they didn't believe us. They killed twenty-four of ours.

The fear, my God! We hid in the ferns and covered ourselves up. We heard the military saying, "We got this guy and that guy." There were five of us hidden in those ferns. They said, "What happened to those who went down through this pasture?" . . .

A: When did you first meet the father of your daughter?

J: *When I was almost fifteen years old. I was one of the troops of Marulanda [the FARC's founder and patriarch] for three years, and that's where I first saw the father of my girl. It was a special unit. You need to be well behaved, be someone who is very correct and studious. If you're not disciplined they'll kick you out of there quickly. We always had to be the example. We went to bed at eight o'clock at night. There couldn't be any noise, no talking or gossiping. In class he would tell lots of stories and we could ask him questions. He was a very simple but strict man.*

I lasted until I was sixteen with him. Marulanda kicked us out of there. He said, "You are all getting old over here. You have to go to a front with all of the experience you've had with me." That's when they brought us to the páramo. I went with the father of my children.

A: Were you a couple in the guerrilla?

J: *Yes. Over there, if you like someone and there's no reason why not, you can couple up. But, for example, if you're irresponsible—like a woman that jumps from one to another, they don't let her be in a couple. It's very strict. But when the woman and the man are responsible, they say, "You want to live together, go for it." They let you live together until the two decide to separate.*

When I was sixteen, I lived with the father of my daughter. We would fight side by side and do everything side by side. They always sent us together. I had lived with him for ten years.

A: What was it like to have a daughter and be a guerrilla? I thought there was mandatory family planning and they didn't allow women to have children.

J: *It's prohibited. There you can't have children. The story of my daughter is a long story. I think God let me have her. My daughter was going to be aborted. You see, when I was fifteen they were going to take all of the chil-dren out [of their mothers' stomachs].*

When they were going to take the girl out I was approximately three and a half months, going on four. They took fifteen girls out of the camp. Of the fifteen, my daughter was the only one who was saved.

As luck had it, my husband had to leave to receive some personnel. We went to collect them but couldn't arrive that day. The next morning an op-eration fell on us and we scattered.

When we came back to the group, they had already taken the babies out of the others. The (military) operation is what saved my daughter. I con-sider that operation something from God. I don't know.

A: How did you feel through all of that?

J: *When they tell you that they're going to take out the children, it's very ugly. I cried. I told my husband that we should run away.*

My husband said, "I can't. You know we can't. If we desert, we'll have enemies outside and here inside." He was already a recognized com-mander. If he were to desert they would catch him and put him in jail. He said, "Let's not run away. Let's see how we can solve things."

I said, "But how are we going to solve things? You know what the rules say: nothing else matters, here you have to follow the laws, that's it."

He said, "No, let's wait."

He spoke [with the leadership] and the order was to abort. In the end you resign yourself—what else are you going to do? But then that opera-tion happened, and when it was over I was more than six months along, the baby was big. They transferred [my husband] to another front to fight, and I was alone. I thought, "My God, now what am I going to do?"

He said, "If they're going to send me somewhere else to fight and get killed, I don't want them to take out her baby."

So they sanctioned him. They said, "Your punishment is to lose your command."

He said, "It doesn't matter, what's important is the baby."

They asked me what I thought. I said, "I also want the baby."

They said to me, "Under the condition that you go, have the baby, and come back."

I said yes, I would go, have the baby, and come back.

A: Is it that they don't abort after so much time?

J: *No. They make you abort even if you have [been pregnant] a long time. My*

sister was at seven months. She used a device called the T, but she got preg-
nant. She was poorly disciplined; [the guerrilla] forced her to abort.

They let me have the baby, but they took my gun away. I only carried a
pistol. They left me in a finance commission until I had the girl. I had the
girl in La Promesa, and they almost caught me.

A: In the hospital?

J: *Yes, in the hospital, where I got a tremendous fright. I wasn't registered any-*
where, so they called the attorney general's office [because unregistered
patients are often affiliated with armed groups]. I said [to myself], "No!"

A nurse came in and said, "Look, we are going to do something. Give
each of us $110 and you can go. We'll throw out all the papers and every-
thing, and we'll say we don't know that patient.

That's when the odontologist [who works with the guerrilla] arrived,
and I told him, "We need $220. The attorney general's office is coming and
they are going to catch me."

He said, "No, no way, they're not going to catch you." Immediately he
took out $110, and then another $110.

They put me on a bed with the baby and took us out the back door. The
odontologist was there in a taxi and we disappeared. If not, they would
have caught me. That's how I became the lost patient [laughing].

A: Where did you go?

J: *To the odontologist's house. I stayed there for two weeks and went back to*
the páramo.

A: Where did you leave the baby?

J: *With my aunt. Ayyy, I didn't want to go. I said, "No, I am not going. I want*
to stay with the baby."

Juana, however, fulfilled her end of the bargain and returned to the
FARC. She helped defend the highlands of Sumapaz, where the military
was in the midst of an offensive. The area is of strategic importance not
only because it is the high ground above Bogotá but because it serves as
a geographic axis connecting the southeastern region, where the FARC
has been strongest, with the country's Andean center. By the early 2000s
the guerrilla was backpedaling from Sumapaz.

J: *Sometimes the dead warn the living.*

My husband said, "Babe, if something happens to me, you know that if
you ask for permission to go home, they won't send you. It's better that one

*day you just don't come back. You know they won't let you go so easily.
You have to be really sick and messed up for them to let you leave."*

That was just before they sent him to fight and he fell into an ambush
and they killed him.

A: How did you respond?

J: *A difficult situation. Difficult because I was suffering from gallstones that
kept me sick. That day he said, "Don't come, because you are very sick. If
we have to run, they might catch you."*

I said, "Okay, I'll stay back."

*It was like one in the afternoon when he called me and said, "We're
coming home."*

I said, "Oh, good."

*A little later it started to drizzle. It was quiet and then we heard a lead
storm. I said, "My God, they are in a fight."*

*I started to call but he didn't respond. Twenty minutes later I called
again. When you are a leader you get a radio to communicate. I called, and
a man with a deep voice responded and said, "Don't call them again, forget it."*

*I thought, "They caught him." I called again and they said outright that
they were from such and such brigade. It was so hard to get news like that.*

A: How did you decide to leave the guerrilla?

J: *I reflected a lot when they killed the father of my daughter. I felt a huge
emptiness.*

A: In what year did they kill him?

J: *They killed him in 2004.*

A: And when did you demobilize?

J: *In 2008.*

A: During those four years, what were you doing in the guerrilla?

J: *They sent me to work with finances. When you have many years [in the
FARC], they start to trust you. They also realize who is good at what. They
sent me to pick up drugs, things that people carried from one place to another. There are lots of people who work with the guerrilla bringing in provisions, gas, drugs, clothes. You pick them up and pay them. You have a
little notebook and write, "This guy brought so much."*

*Later they started saying that Operation Pistol was coming, that they
were killing everyone who worked with that stuff, even just receiving it.
When they said Operation Pistol was coming, I said to myself, "I am not
going to wait for Operation Pistol to kill me."*

A: What was Operation Pistol?

J: *When the paramilitaries came in, practically the military itself, but dressed in civilian clothes and on motorcycles, and—*pam pam*—they kill you.*

A: And these paramilitaries were killing people who were with the guerrillas in the cities?

J: *Yes, everyone that worked with that stuff. That's when I told them, "I don't want to be here anymore. Transfer me."*

They said, "No, if you don't like the good life, we'll send you back to a combat unit."

That's what they did; they sent me to one of those units. That's when I said, "I am done with this type of life."

I asked for permission to do the child's paperwork, because she wasn't registered or anything. They said yes and I came to where the girl was. That's when they caught me coming from Villao after visiting my mom.

A: I don't understand. You asked for permission to get the papers for the girl and . . .

J: *What happened was they caught me, because I went to visit my mom without authorization [from the guerrilla] and the military caught me in Villao. There they took me off the bus. That was another fright.*

A: They took you off the bus?

J: *I demobilized by force* [a la fuerza]. *[Laughing] When the bus stopped, I turned around to look and saw the military. One came aboard and said, "Everyone get down. ID cards please".*

My God, I thought, I am going to jail. I got very scared. Now what are [the FARC] going to say since they gave me permission to do paperwork for the child but I got caught in Villao?

They threw me in a car. I said, "They disappeared me!" [Laughter]

I said [to myself], "Either they'll kill me or they'll give me who knows how many years." I thought so many things.

They said, "Were you in the guerrilla?"

I said, "The truth is, yes. Why am I going to deny it?" I said, "They gave me permission to take a month off."

"For what?"

"I have a daughter, and a month ago I came for the girl, but I also came to visit my mom."

"You were on the list of those to be captured. But look, we are going to give you an option: go to jail or demobilize."

I said, "What's demobilization?"

He said, "Demobilizing is where you get help. You go for a few days to a halfway house. You are still free, but you can't go back to the guerrilla anymore, no more guns." He started explaining things.

I said, "Well, I don't have any option other than that one."

That's where I decided and said, "Yes, I'll demobilize. What do I have to do?"

I think if I hadn't gone over [to my mom's house], I wouldn't have demobilized. I'd still be there, or who knows what would have come of my life.

A: How have things gone for you in civilian life?

J: *Good. My husband works every day and almost doesn't let me work. He says, "Go study," and I've studied.*

A: And you have a child with him?

J: *Yes. I didn't want to have more kids. He was the one who kept talking about babies. I wanted to keep it to the girl that I had.*

A: How old is she?

J: *She's eighteen.*

A: Does she know your story?

J: *Yes, because every once in a while—ayyy, poor thing!—they would bring her to visit me. She would say, "Mommy, let's go, come with me." [The military] killed her dad when she was six, and a six-year-old remembers well.*

If you have a good commander and you ask permission, they let you bring the baby or the family. You have to make the case and say, "I want to see this member of my family for that reason." If you are someone who is disciplined, they'll let you bring them.

A: So she came to visit when you were . . .

J: *When I was in Caquetá.*

A: That's a long trip for a six-year-old kid.

J: *Yes. Before she traveled with my aunt she would get happy and say, "We're going to bring Mommy home."*

It was terrible; I don't want to remember it. I said to myself, "I would love to, but what if I die [trying to escape]? What will happen to her life?"

My aunt would say [to me], "Look for someone else to take care of the girl, because she's growing and needs schooling. Who is going to pay for her studies? I am very poor and can't give her everything that she wants."

I started thinking, "It's true. What is my daughter going to do in her life?"

Eventually I said to her, "Sweetie, don't worry, one day I'll make the decision and go, even if that means doing whatever it takes."

She said, "I am holding on to hope, Mommy, I am holding on." My daughter was so small yet so insistent, saying, "Mommy what are you doing here? Let's go, Mommy. You don't have my dad—what are you doing here? Come stay with me."

Thank God things worked out the way they did.

FIGURE INT.2. Drawing by Lucas Ospina.

CHAPTER TWO

Operation Christmas

Lowe/SSP3

Giant patina-chic metal doors lead to a cheerful receptionist. She distributes infrared cards to visitors, like me, allowed to pass through the turnstile threshold of Lowe/SSP3's headquarters. The offices of this elite Colombian consumer marketing firm have the playful feel of a Palo Alto tech company and the curated cool of a Lower Manhattan ad agency. The foosball, the gourmet coffee, the young, hip employees—it all contrasted with the spartan cubicles of the Colombian Ministry of Defense, Lowe/SSP3's most high-profile client. Lowe/SSP3 has built a reputation for creativity thanks to its work for the ministry of defense's Program for Humanitarian Attention to the Demobilized (PAHD). The PAHD disarms and demobilizes guerrilla fighters, wringing them for intelligence before passing them off to the civilian side of the bureaucracy, the Colombian Agency for Reintegration, or ACR, charged with socioeconomic reintegration.

Lowe/SSP3's work for the PAHD models a new form of warfare, one that deploys sensations and soldiers in an ever more intricate and coordinated effort. Take this scene. You (the viewer) are seated across from and bouncing along with a solider in a military jeep. His face, which has been painted black, part of his evening camouflage, reflects the greenyellow glow of the camera's night vision mode. He says, "I want to wish a merry Christmas to everyone in the guerrilla." After a pause, he adds, "And for your own good, demobilize. It's your only way out."

Soldierly scenes such as these, conceived in the stylish offices of Lowe/SSP3, exemplify "brand warfare." By using the term here I mean the conjunction of military power and marketing expertise that takes as its object of intervention not just the hearts and minds of FARC fighters but also categories as amorphous as the national mood, the cultural atmosphere, and the international imagination. The PAHD's mobilization of consumer marketing serves the dual purpose of deploying an aggressive mode of psychological warfare, sowing doubts and paranoia among guerrilla fighters, while also rebranding the military by building a narrative about the armed forces' sophistication and benevolence. What is fascinating is how military propaganda, a state function, is refracted through the commodity form. Since the 1980s, the apparatus of marketing has emerged as a privileged producer of what Raymond Williams has called the "structure of feeling" of our age.[1] In the 2000s and 2010s the apparatus of marketing expanded beyond global provisioning and into spheres of governance. This chapter peels back the film that advertising layers onto statecraft, a film that colors structures of feeling in a global moment marked by boundless faith in brands and festering fears of lurking enemies.

Lowe/SSP3 is a hybrid: part local Colombian outfit, part global conglomerate. SSP3 is an acronym for the last names of the Colombian partners, while Lowe references Lowe and Partners, a global network of marketing agencies from which the Colombian office draws resources and to which it contributes a percentage of its earnings. On its website Lowe and Partners describes its approach as using "laser-like analysis of the core problem and brilliant insight into contemporary culture, to create enduring ideas that change behavior on and offline." London-based Lowe and Partners is part of the public relations conglomerate Interpublic Group, or IPG, its abbreviation on the New York Stock Exchange. Lowe and Partners and IPG have represented a vast portfolio of clients including Volkswagen, Microsoft, and the United Nations. In Colombia, Lowe/SSP3 has represented, among others, Mazda, Red Bull, SAB Miller, and, since 2007, the PAHD.

The idea that a sustained barrage of well-targeted emotional messages can influence decisions is what connects the ads Lowe/SSP3 produces for the PAHD and those it crafts for its corporate clients. At the same time that Lowe/SSP3 designed the Christmas campaign of 2010 for the PAHD, it finished a new advertisement for the Mazda 3, a compact sedan. That commercial stitches together scenes in which a young boy rides a go-cart downhill, a teenager roller-skates off a ramp, and two teenagers trick a skateboard and then a BMX bike off a larger ramp. The bicycle appears in the side-view mirror of the blue sedan as a young man shifts the car into gear. An inspirational soundtrack plays over shots of the car's exterior as it swerves in city driving. The deep, raspy voiceover concludes: "Mazda 3, all new [in English]. The emotion is born with you [in Spanish]."[2] The montage insinuates that the car represents the ideal next transportation toy for a male twentysomething reluctant to let go of his adolescence. A consumption pattern—go-cart, roller skates, skate-board, bicycle, car—replaces ritual in marking a boy's transition to man-hood. The car in question is positioned as the ideal vehicle for navigating the obstacle-laden passage.

In both the Mazda commercial and Lowe/SSP3's work for the PAHD, the thirty-second advertisements offer a developmentalist narrative that periodizes lives amidst a transition, boy to man, combatant to civilian. One depicts coming of age through consumption, while the other cre-ates a vision for the transformation of a politicized subject into a docile economic one. When I interviewed Miguel Sokoloff, the most prominent partner of Lowe/SSP3, he made the comparison between car sales and demobilization explicit. He swiveled slightly in his chair as he likened the decision to defect from the FARC to deciding to purchase a new car. Buying a car, he said, is a decision that can percolate for ten years, and during those ten years the best thing a car company can do is keep its car in potential customers' minds. Sokoloff understood both demobilization and buying a car as "life changes" and used the metaphor of pinball to explain the role of his agency.

> Publicity today is like a pinball machine. Once you release the ball it's go-ing to bounce around and you don't know what it's going to do. What you *can* do as a publicist, as the government, in this case, is to keep the ball up there. These life-changing decisions that [the demobilized] took meant risking their lives. You need to keep [people in the guerrilla] thinking about it. You're not going to change their mentality, but you have to keep the ball in play.

Lowe/SSP3, like military planners, plays the long game. (Periods lon-ger than electoral cycles, at least.) To focus too tightly on any single ad-vertisement would miss the strategic intentions of multiyear brand plans. Since 2007 the PAHD-Lowe/SSP3 partnership has deployed television commercials, radio spots, leaflets, YouTube videos, Facebook posts, loudspeakers fastened to helicopters, anti-aircraft spotlights, plastic balls with LED lights that float down rivers, soccer balls stickered with messages and thrown from helicopters, faux lipstick advertisements, giant posters with childhood photographs of guerrilla fighters, and banners next to trees illuminated with Christmas lights—all to keep the ball in play. This variety of formats and props constitutes a cluttered semiotic field in which the campaign, and ultimately the brand it strives to embody, is the medium. According to marketing doctrine, beneath the dizzying array of elements used to construct a brand should lie a simple, unwavering, and relentlessly repeated message.

In 2006 when Sergio Jaramillo, then vice minister of defense for human rights and international relations, approached the partners of Lowe/SSP3, he made clear that the government could not afford to pay the agency the same rates as its corporate clients, but assured Lowe/SSP3 it would win industry awards for its work with the PAHD. His vision would be fulfilled four years later—after Operation Christmas. When I went to interview Miguel Sokoloff in early 2012, he was basking in the recent success of the Christmas campaigns. "[The Ministry of Defense] gave us something they never gave before: access to the demobilized," he said. In a warm and enthusiastic manner he described the company's quasi-ethnographic market research method: "We listened to their life stories and asked them, What do you do for fun? . . . The people on the creative side started to build personal relationships with the demobilized. They talked to them about life, and ended up talking about publicity: Have you seen the government's propaganda? What's going on in your life? How often are you exposed to the media? What are you feeling?"

These interviews and focus groups led to a piercing *insight*. (Lowe/SSP3 employees use the word in English as part of transnational public relations lingo.) Juan Pablo, a young account manager, summarized the conclusion of their research: "Before being guerrillas, they're people. For them it's not a terrorist group but a life choice." He continued: "We use the anguish they feel while being in the guerrilla and show them a way out, tell them that there are other options." When Lowe/SSP3 creates ads for consumers considering a new car, they suggestively present a different lifestyle; but its campaigns for the PAHD offer a new life altogether.

Lowe/SSP3 imposed a condition before accepting the PAHD account. The agency would *not* create a series of one-off campaigns for the military. The company would accept the Ministry of Defense's business only if it could transform the program into a brand. Juan Pablo explained: "We decided to treat the [demobilization] program as a brand and define a posture and start to build a simple and poignant message,

easy to understand and remember, respectful of the enemy, without tri-
umphalism, and without questioning the validity of the armed struggle."

Their research led to a new slogan: "There's another life, demobilization is the way out" (it rhymes in Spanish: "Hay otra vida, la desmovilización es la salida"). Juan Pablo likened this message to Nike's "Just do
it," in that the slogan was a container that could be filled with different
contents: basketball, tennis, golf, in Nike's case; Christmas, soccer, family togetherness, for the PAHD.

The FARC's statutes state clearly that joining the revolution is a commitment for life. It doesn't matter if you joined when you were fifteen, as
many do. Once you've enlisted, there is, with rare exception, no door to
leave from. By creating the PAHD, the government built a back door.
Military force pushes people toward that door. While Lowe/SSP3 stokes
rebels' desire to desert, battalions of the Colombian army, navy, and
air force hunt the FARC and work to dismantle its military structures.
The line between being captured and demobilizing is often difficult to
discern.

Juan Pablo, the young sophisticate charged with managing the PAHD
account, understood the importance of military pressure through the
theory of the "hierarchy of needs" developed by Abraham Maslow, a
mid-twentieth-century American psychologist. Maslow's tiered system,
extraordinarily influential in consumer marketing, establishes a pyramid
of human needs that, when fulfilled, enable what Maslow called "self-
actualization." The hierarchy goes from the basic physiological needs
of eating, sleeping, and breathing, at the bottom, to creativity, morality, and problem solving at the top.[3] Juan Pablo explained: "When a helicopter is bombing every three days, your survival is in question. You
don't have food, it's always wet, you can't sleep, you're sick." Lowe/
SSP3's strategy was to complement the military's assault by attacking the
third rung of Maslow's ladder, "love and belonging," understood as family and other close relationships. "After we"—note his identification with
the military—"sufficiently attacked the base of the pyramid we jumped
and attacked the third level. That's what we did with Operation Christmas." Clicking to a PowerPoint presentation the company had prepared
for a US-funded trip to Afghanistan for PAHD personnel, he continued:
"It was done with an utterly emotional tone, it was a way of attacking the
heart. It was to say, 'You stopped living. If you demobilize you can feel
again.'"

The phrase "attacking the heart" made me think: what kind of variation on the goal of counterinsurgency operations vis-à-vis civilian populations, so often rendered "winning hearts and minds," was this? Whereas "winning hearts and minds" is often code for the soft power of persuasion as opposed to coercion, Juan Pablo's phrase "attacking the heart" is a tacit acknowledgment that persuasion and coercion are inseparable. What better time to send a message that attacks the heart and promises regeneration through reconnection with loved ones than Christmas?

Operation Christmas (2010)

The pulsing music of the song "Deserter" by American pop musician Matthew Dear provides a catchy introduction to the title card: "Operation Christmas, November 2010." The first image is a soft-focus shot of blue Christmas lights. The beat accelerates as the captions that provide the video's narrative structure read, "December, the most moving part of the year. When many rebels take the decision to demobilize. They're far from their home, their parents, their children, their friends." English lyrics come onto the track as Dear's deep voice sings, "What was that. You sound deserted. Lost and alone." The captions continue:

"In the middle of the jungle, unable to spend Christmas together."

"We took this opportunity to show them that during Christmas anything is possible." The video shifts to a daylight scene of soldiers trekking through the forest and gesturing in silent coordination, simulating combat conditions. The captions continue:

"We invited them to demobilize, by bringing Christmas to the jungle."

"From a military base in La Macarena, Meta. With the help of the Rapid Response Force, FUDRA."

The images shift again to preparations on the base and a commander explaining the mission in front of a giant map.

"We prepared a special operation that lasted 4 days."

"Two counterguerrilla units, two Black Hawk helicopters, 2,000 Christmas lights." Images illustrate the list. A shot from above records a Black Hawk helicopter flying over forest canopy as the subtitles explain: "We arrived to one of the principal supply lines for the guerrilla." Cut to a shot of soldiers looking up a tree trunk. "We chose a 25-meter-tall tree and decorated it with lights." Images show a soldier climbing the tree and wrapping it in blue Christmas lights.

Cut to a night scene rendered in the yellow-green hue of night-vision goggles. "We used a military activation device that would light up when rebels passed by." On screen, a soldier backpedals while laying a wire. The camera tilts up the tree, now glowing with blue Christmas lights. The caption reads: "Thousands of lights will help them remember that Christmas is the best part of the year to start their lives again." The words "Like this tree, many others are being illuminated to promote demobilizations" are imposed over images of a helicopter flying over the canopy. Cut to a view from above, the lights pulsating like a heart. It is a sublime image, and cues the campaign's tag line: "Because during Christmas, anything is possible."[4]

The video ends with soldiers turned amateur actors sending messages to rebels.

SOLDIER I, GLEEFULLY: We just left the jungle in the Macarena and successfully completed Operation Christmas.

SOLDIER 2: We hope that by giving this Christmas message to the guerrilla, they'll demobilize.

SOLDIER 3: I want to wish a merry Christmas to everyone in the guerrilla. And for your own good, demobilize. It's your only way out.

SOLDIER 4: Señor guerrillero, if we could bring Christmas to the jungle, you can celebrate it at home. Demobilize already.

Fade to black.

This Christmas commercial retains but resignifies the threat of war machines and soldiers, classic fare of military propaganda, while adding traits such as intelligence, creativity, and benevolence to the military's identity. The Black Hawk helicopters, the FUDRA (the army's elite rapid-response unit), and the large map are meant to invoke a modernized, more agile, and more precise military. The implicit visual argument of Operation Christmas, named to sound like a military action, is that the counterinsurgency is not only a set of well oiled, highly coordinated war machines but also humane and magnanimous, as evidenced by the offer extended to its mortal enemy. The lights connect the armed forces with the intimate space of people's homes. In offering the gift of demobilization, the commercial implicitly equates the ministry of defense with Santa Claus. By refashioning the military's image, Lowe/SSP3 manages to show a new side to an old institution, updating the military's brand while retaining the bellicose core of its identity.

Operation Christmas benefited from its ideological affinity with Colombian and Western media outlets, an advantage Lowe/SSP3 exploited relentlessly by publicizing its own work (and building Lowe/SSP3's own brand in the process). The lyrics in English and the constant descriptions of the "operation" are two indicators of how Lowe/SSP3 staged the campaign as a media event in its own right, rolling out different pieces to different audiences so as to maximize the campaign's visibility. First it launched the thirty-second commercial. Then it released longer videos, like the three-minute video from 2010 described above, often with behind-the-scenes footage. These longer pieces target elite audiences in and beyond Colombia as part of its offensive effort to accumulate prestige through media coverage and award ceremonies. (My Facebook feed is a continuing reminder of the agency's ongoing success. My interlocutors in Lowe/SSP3 post photos of themselves receiving awards, posing in glossy magazine spreads, and even presenting their work to Pope Francis in the Vatican.)

The Lowe/SSP3–Ministry of Defense partnership flooded the Colombian airwaves with a thirty-second commercial that ran on both television and radio. It lacks the three-minute video's international pretensions (no English lyrics) and uses shorter cuts of many of the same images. The use of captions is limited to setting the scene: "Rapid Response Force—FUDRA, December 2010; Strategic supply line, Colombian jungle." Rather than having soldiers deliver the message to the rebels, the thirty-second commercial's slogan is delivered in the deep timbre of a narrator: "If we could bring Christmas to the jungle, we can help you come home. Guerrilla, demobilize. During Christmas, anything is possible."

Lighting the tree in rebel territory was an assertion of authority over guerrilla-controlled territory. On one level, it signals the military's ability to launch an operation "anywhere in the national territory," a phrase often repeated in military leaders' public remarks that speaks to the state's sovereignty anxieties. Motion sensors spark the tree's illumination, turning the relationship of camouflage and surprise in guerrilla warfare inside out by remediating guerrilla surprises such as ambushes and land mines. In the process, the Lowe/SSP3–Ministry of Defense partnership claims the humane high ground in Colombia's information war. With undertones of the burning bush, this symbolic conquest evokes the miraculous and the possibility of redemption.[5]

The efficacy of Operation Christmas's evocations depend upon the campaign's ability to move seamlessly between three sets of publics: active guerrillas, Colombians not affiliated with the guerrillas, and non-Colombian audiences. Each public brings its own sets of interpretive dispositions to the various texts in circulation. I delineate between these three sets of publics—though I in no way mean to imply that there is any homogeneity within them—to highlight how in targeting each audience, the PAHD–Lowe/SSP3 alliance is concerned with the prevalence and prominence of the message rather than its reception. Recall Sokoloff's metaphor of pinball.

When targeting guerrilla fighters, the campaign's planners operated under the valid assumption that many people in the guerrilla want to leave but do not know how, given the guerrilla's internal controls. When the PAHD surveys those who have recently demobilized about the conditions under which its messages percolate through to FARC rebels and how those messages are interpreted, it devotes more questions to the mode of transmission than to any other issue. The PAHD's internal 2011 survey found that only 15 percent of respondents learned about the demobilization program through television, while 42 percent heard about it on the radio.

Whereas the PAHD's is most keenly interested in targeting guerrillas, Lowe/SSP3 emphasizes the impact of its work on the "national mood," a term that recurs in the company's assessments of its work for the PAHD. To target the mood is to target the atmosphere—the aim is omnipresence. The best way to be everywhere is through television and radio, and Lowe/SSP3 has put its emphasis on the former believing in the potency of visual images to build a narrative of the military as a generous, humanitarian actor, and therefore the war's righteous party. The limited resistance to such a simplistic line of argumentation, often expressed in muted academic forums and in the marginalized spaces where left politics have been confined, is overwhelmed by spectacular visuals and the sheer repetition of the message. The thirty-second commercial for the 2010 campaign ran throughout December and much of January in some of the most valuable television and radio slots in the country, such as the 7 p.m. network news and nationally broadcast soccer matches.[6]

Lowe/SSP3's obsession with affecting the national mood, by which it means inculcating a sense of optimism that the military is winning the war, is closely interwoven with its emphasis in courting international audiences. By actively seeking out recognition abroad, Lowe/SSP3 taps into nationalistic impulses, which paradoxically thrive upon international recognition. The Christmas campaign of 2010 succeeded in re-branding the armed forces abroad. It went on to win more than forty awards in industry competitions from Cannes to Buenos Aires, Madrid to New York. News stories that latched on to the media hook of the campaign—"fighting with Christmas trees"—appeared in *Wired* magazine and on CNN. Those stories then prompted the national press to report on the campaigns in a fawning tone. Lowe/SSP3 managed to cast its work with the Ministry of Defense as an example of the power of advertising in a righteous struggle against violent extremists, which has been key to its celebratory reception. Without ever claiming to promote the Ministry of Defense, the contrived scene of Operation Christmas equated the armed forces with a constellation of positive associations, feelings, and affects in Colombia and abroad. The expressed purpose of the campaign, ratcheting up psychological and emotional pressure on guerrilla fighters to desert, was really but one of two prongs; the other was to rebrand the military and control the narrative surrounding the conflict. The military-marketing partnership looked to replicate its success the following year.

Operation Rivers of Light (Christmas 2011)

Marcela passed her Blackberry around the table during a working brunch in early November 2011. The image on the small screen was of a dead man, Guillermo León Sáenz Vargas, alias Alfonso Cano, the FARC's top commander. Eight days earlier, on November 4, 2011, the Colombian military had killed Cano after its tightening cordon found him trying to escape through the forest after a series of aerial bombardments. A photograph of Cano's slain body had already been published on the front pages of Colombian newspapers. Marcela's photo showed the same corpse but at night, only hours after Cano had been killed. He had shaved his signature beard in a bid to slip from the siege, and in the photo his jaw was exposed—locked and contorted to the left.

In addition to directing the PAHD's communications team, Marcela led a rapid-response propaganda unit that traveled to the site of recent events to conduct radio programs and issue calls for demobilization from speakers affixed to helicopters and printed on leaflets sent fluttering to the ground. As part of this "shock plan," as she called it, Marcela and two members of her team were on the ground where Cano was killed within hours. She coordinated the arrival of President Santos, who called on rebel fighters to demobilize via a giant speaker affixed to the undercarriage of the military helicopter in which he was flying. Marcela wrangled more than thirty journalists to report on the propaganda outing, a recursive move she had honed in the PAHD.

Cano had been an anthropology student at the National University in the 1960s, at the height of its revolutionary ferment. He broke away from his middle-class roots in Bogotá to join the Communist Party. In the 1970s he rose through its ranks to serve as right-hand man to the FARC's principal ideologue, Jacobo Arenas. After Manuel Marulanda died of natural causes in 2008, Cano became the FARC's top commander. His assassination was the latest blow to the FARC's leadership. In March 2008 the military killed Raúl Reyes, the FARC's spokesman and then No. 2, in a trans-border raid in Ecuador. That same month a subordinate of secretariat member Iván Ríos killed his boss to claim reward money (he cut off Ríos's right hand as proof). In September 2010 the Colombian air force killed Mono Jojoy, the FARC's leading military commander in the southeastern department of Meta. Prior to 2008 the military had not managed to kill a single member of the FARC's seven-member secretariat. Between 2008 and 2011 it slayed four leaders in the secretariat. President Santos characterized Cano's death as "the most significant blow to the FARC in its entire history," and indeed Cano was the first FARC commander to be killed in combat.

Promoting demobilization in the wake of Cano's death was the backdrop to the brunch strategy session that brisk November morning. Maintaining the drumbeat for demobilization leading into the Christmas season was the challenge of the moment. The first order of business was to agree on the parameters of a commercial that would amplify President Santos's call for demobilization in the wake of Cano's death while morale in the insurgency was imagined to be in free fall.

Marcela represented the Ministry of Defense and came to the brunch meeting with Juana, her subordinate, who had recently transferred to the PAHD from the communications section of the Omega Task Force, a joint initiative (air force, navy, army) designed to take the offensive in Colombia's Amazonian south, a FARC stronghold. Eduardo, a bald thirtysomething who produces the commercials, joined Juan Pablo in representing Lowe/SSP3. We ate gourmet omelets on the back patio of an upscale restaurant in north Bogotá. The radiant warmth of a gas heater shielded us from the nip of the morning while classical music played in the background. Eduardo regaled the group with stories from his trip to London to accept an award for the 2010 Christmas commercial. According to Eduardo, during the black-tie ceremony the audience was moved to tears by the commercial. After chitchat about how wonderful the news from London was, the group got down to planning for Christmas 2011.

The Christmas campaign of 2011 would be the second major campaign of the year. A bureaucratic problem in the public contracting process had left the PAHD unable to create any of its propaganda from January to June. The first major campaign of the year, Come Back and Play (Vuelve a Jugar), had been recently launched and was on the minds of everyone at the table that morning. Although it was not winning international awards, colonels on military bases throughout the country were raving about it. Intelligence officials reported that it was creating buzz within the guerrilla. Inspired by the commercial, General Pérez Guarnizo, who commands the army's Third Division, sent helicopters over FARC territory and had his troops throw soccer balls stickered with the PAHD logo out the windows, replicating a scene in the commercial. The soccer campaign was designed to piggyback on the buzz surrounding the under-twenty World Cup that Colombia hosted in 2011 and to tap into the country's obsession with soccer and pride in hosting an international event.

The PAHD/Lowe-SSP3 partnership was promulgating a vision of a socially connected and recreation-filled life. By associating demobilization with Christmas and soccer, Lowe/SSP3 substitutes one set of experiences—collaborating with the military, coping with the legacies of trauma, worrying about persecution from the FARC, struggling to eke out a living—with another: eating Christmas pastries, exchanging gifts with family, setting off fireworks, dancing during alcohol-infused parties, scoring goals, and drinking with friends after the match.

The drive to influence the imaginaries of rebel, national, and international publics pushes the military and its brand managers toward increasingly extreme forms of spectacle. When Miguel Sokoloff clicked to the slides about Come Back and Play in his presentation, he told me how his firm wanted to fly military planes over the stadium and for the teams to play with soccer balls stamped with the demobilization logo and slogan. He lamented, "FIFA didn't allow it," adding, "Sometimes we have things under control, other times we don't." The publicist's fantasy of the world as his stage had bumped against its limits. Despite the soccer campaign's success in creating buzz within the guerrilla, Sokoloff's disappointment at not making a bigger splash demonstrates the degree to which Lowe/SSP3 and the Ministry of Defense prioritize branding the program nationally and internationally. In that regard neither Come Back and Play nor any of the PAHD's other campaigns could compete with Operation Christmas.

In the focus groups that Lowe/SSP3 organized to help plan the soccer campaign, one former rebel urged them to put soccer balls in rivers, because "rivers are the highways of the jungle." That comment provided the underpinning of the next Christmas campaign. Focus groups have proved a powerful mechanism for the publicists at Lowe/SSP3 to learn about guerrilla culture and media-consumption practices in the FARC. Focus groups have taught Lowe/SSP3 that rebels retire to their huts of plastic sheeting or camouflage nylon (*caletas*) at 8 p.m. and listen to their personal radios as they fall asleep. The PAHD began to air its commercials on radio stations between 8 and 9 p.m., the only window in which individual insurgents could turn the dial to prohibited stations without others hearing. Many rebel fronts adjusted by restricting personal radios to senior commanders (damaging morale in the process). The key comment in designing Operation Rivers of Light, "Rivers are the highways of the jungle," provided a metaphoric translation between the marketers' urban world and the rebels' jungle environment. In 2011 Lowe/SSP3 repeated its luminous intervention from 2010, transforming the rebel landscape with light and thereby reinforcing the imaginary of rebel territories as shadowy, dangerous, underdeveloped places that require penetration and taming by the military and the market.

At brunch, Lowe/SSP3 and the PAHD quickly agreed on the idea of sending messages to the guerrilla in floating plastic balls that glow at night. (This prop was meant to represent Christmas tree decorations.) The questions on the table that morning were, What messages? Who would send them? And how to frame Operation Rivers of Light? Marcela drew inspiration from a recent statement by the Basque separatist group Euskadi Ta Askatasuna (ETA) justifying its decision to end decades of armed struggle for autonomy in Spain. She had seen an online video of a masked ETA spokesman saying, "Bravery is knowing when to withdraw." (In retrospect, I suspect that her invocation of this reference was connected to highly classified information she had about the then secretive preliminary peace negotiations with the FARC.) The publicists politely brushed her suggestion aside. Everyone agreed that given the timing of Cano's death, the Christmas campaign of 2011 needed to strike a more political note than that of 2010. Marcela's desire for an explicitly political message made Lowe/SSP3's assignment more difficult, because political conditions across the country varied widely. Marcela was acutely aware of the strategic areas in which the military was concentrating: Nudo de Paramillo, a northern corridor connecting the Atlantic, Andean, and Pacific regions; Catatumbo, a volatile portion of the Venezuelan border wracked by drug traffic, where insurgents, paramilitaries, and criminal gangs were forging alliances; the Ecuadoran border used by traffickers to import and export drug and arms; and the mountainous region where the Cauca, Huila, and Tolima Departments converge. Ideally the demobilization message would resonate across these contexts where the military was rolling out new joint task forces to bring coordinated offensives to bear on the FARC.

Beyond more political content, Marcela had additional requests: she wanted to give roles to "family members" of guerrilla fighters; she wanted "a symbol in every scene." This request stuck me as the most curious. Why was she so focused on symbols? To what extent was she aware of the symbolic order that she was participating in and reproducing? She fetishized national symbols, believing in their intrinsic communicative power.[7] Marcela wanted images that communicated meaning—to her and, via her own expert divination, to the unwieldy aggregate of *los colombianos*.

To keep Marcela happy, Lowe/SSP3 included a handshake between an indigenous person and a soldier in the final cut. That image would clash with reality less than two weeks after the brunch. Security concerns scuttled the PAHD's attempt to launch Operation Rivers of Light with an event in Cauca Department, where the armed conflict is inflected by a long history of indigenous political organizing.[8] I chose to continue with my research in the PAHD's halfway houses for the recently demobilized rather than travel to Cauca. I missed the action. The FARC launched two crude projectiles from a hilltop adjacent to the event, and Marcela convinced Minister of Defense Juan Carlos Pinzón to abort his visit at the last minute. Canceling the event would have been seen as conceding a propaganda victory to the FARC, so the PAHD and a government-aligned indigenous group held a quick closed-door event. Marcela postponed the media launch of Operation Rivers of Light to the following week in Tibú, Catatumbo.

The marketers at Lowe/SSP3 used the interim to tweak the commercial, especially the role that family would play in the campaign. At the planning brunch, Marcela had articulated a vision for the Operation Rivers of Light commercial that began with President Santos writing a letter to an imaginary rebel and urging him to demobilize. That image would dissolve into a mother writing to her child, as if it were part of the same letter the president had started, and then handing that message to the military, which would place it in a floating plastic sphere to send downriver.[9] The imagined montage would express a seamless synchronicity between the paternal state and the private, presumably maternal sphere of domestic life.

Such a scene is consistent with how the state has conceived of the demobilized as prodigal sons who return home broken and repentant. Colombian anthropologist Juan Felipe Hoyos García writes, "The moral of the story is not only that the demobilized is a lost son who is accepted upon his return, but that his return reinforces the paternal relationship between the State and its subject."[10] The dozens of campaigns produced by Lowe/SSP3 for the PAHD bear out Hoyos García's analysis, but none so blatantly as its 2013 Christmas campaign, You Are My Child. That campaign interpellates guerrilla fighters by reactivating the affective bonds of kinship that the FARC and ELN have sought to displace with the ties of camaraderie. The soldiers in the image from the You Are My Child campaign—with which I began this book—stand in for fathers presumed to be missing. The commercial casts the military into a relationship of proxy intimacy with mothers from the peasantry and working classes, from which the vast majority of guerrillas are recruited. The government's appeal to demobilize is a call to return to the domestic space of a mother's love, protected by the father figure of the militarized state.

What is at stake in the prodigal son's return is not only the restoration of the patriarchal authority of the state but also social reproduction and domestic patriarchy.[11] As we see in the leaflet reproduced in figure 2.1, the PAHD's call for the prodigal sons of the nation to resubject themselves to the state is nested within another call: to remake themselves as domestic subjects, fathers.

The family is ground zero for the PAHD and the FARC. Gustavo, a former FARC combatant, described to me how FARC leaders "explain why you don't have to cry the day your mother or father dies." The FARC seeks to control not only affective ties to family but also the emotional and sexual life of its combatants. Many commanders regu-

Su familia lo sigue esperando para celebrar la Navidad.

FIGURE 2.1. PAHD flyer distributed during Christmas 2012. The text reads: "Your family is still waiting for you to celebrate Christmas." Image courtesy of Colombian Ministry of National Defense.

late sex by requiring lovers to register their relations in advance in the unit's logbook (*el minuto*).[12] When it comes to sanctioning relationships, the FARC is wary, concerned that they will lead to desertion, especially in the event of pregnancy, when fighters might reevaluate their life trajectory. (The nurse of each front is responsible for administering birth control, via injection, to all women guerrillas.) The Lowe/SSP3-PAHD partnership seeks to activate the affective relations that the FARC suppresses, urging rebels to think about nuclear family life and childrearing as opposed to the camaraderie within its ranks and the collective political project of revolution.

The finalized commercial of Operation Rivers of Light contained three parts: (1) a disc jockey at a military radio station speaking rapidly and calling on people with relatives in the insurgency to send them a message; (2) images of villagers placing personal items into the plastic balls and writing letters; and (3) military officers filling duffel bags with plastic balls to send downstream at night. Operation Rivers of Light lacked the narrative coherence, documentary feel, and impact of the 2010 campaign, leaving viewers with unanswered questions. What are plastic balls resembling tree ornaments doing floating down the river? Are the messages really expected to reach the rebels?

But the commercial itself is only one element of a sophisticated public relations assault. In Lowe/SSP3's high-end cafeteria, Juan Pablo explained: "One thing is what we tell the public [*la opinión pública*] we
did; the other thing is the commercial itself. The commercial is just a
piece." He quickened his speech. "The story we tell is that we've done
this in different parts of the country, which is what needs to go to the
media, needs to be told." The Colombian government as a whole produced elaborate events to tell that story, and they managed to grab headlines from Bogotá to Tokyo. The launch event featuring the minister of
defense ultimately took place in Tibú, Catatumbo.

Tibú, Catatumbo: Launching Operation Rivers of Light

I arrived at the checkpoint outside the Catam airbase at 4:30 a.m. Four
trucks were waiting to enter. When I asked Francisco from the PAHD's
communications team what was inside the trucks, he responded, "Humanitarian aid, stuff like that." Hours later, on the C-130 Hercules heading east toward the Venezuelan border, I realized that the "humanitarian aid" was mostly staging for a concert starring Peter Manjarrés, a
popular vallenato singer.[13]

After we waited for more than four hours at the austere departure
gate, the transport plane was ready to board. Inside, a crew member
strapped down the cargo, which included plastic balls with LED lights,
reams of PAHD literature, and hats and T-shirts emblazoned with
"Enough, here I'm free," the slogan for the PAHD's highly ineffective
effort to curb recruitment into the FARC and the ELN. We latched ourselves into red cargo nets held taut with metal poles, rigging that served
as bench seating. Two young men from the event coordination company
shared earbuds and bopped their heads to music while the rest of us let
our ears adapt to the loud hum of the engine reverberating in the plane's
cavernous interior. A crew member signaled thumbs-up from the back,
and five minutes later we were hurtling down the runway, our torsos
slanting to the left, shoulders pressing into shoulders.

As we descended, the pilot bobbed the plane up and down to throw
off anyone below who might be taking aim. Olive green open-air vehicles pulled up behind the Hercules as its hatch lowered to the ground.
Marcela's colleague Hugo, whose silvery hair and symmetrical facial features have earned him comparisons to Richard Gere, began to give in-

structions to the local military officers—"T-shirts over here, brochures over there"—while Marcela went straight to the commanding colonel, her partner in executing the complex event plan.

The PAHD team, the staging company staff, and I piled into the back of police pickups as dozens of people stared from behind a fence. It felt like we were a circus that had just arrived, only nobody was smiling. As I absorbed the scene, Marcela came up to me and said, "Let's go, we're heading to the hotel." After a silent beat she smiled wryly and added, "Where the only star is you." (It took me a moment to get the joke about the hotel's less than four-star quality.) The army's Thirtieth Brigade had come from Cúcuta to provide security; its heavily armed soldiers trailed us, even along the three-block walk between the mayor's office and the hotel. During the event, the military positioned snipers on rooftops. A friend who worked with Doctors Without Borders and was living in Tibú later told me that the organization had instructed its employees not to leave their houses that day, in part for security reasons and in part to avoid compromising their relative neutrality.

Marcela called a meeting of her ten-person team and began assigning tasks: spread the word about the concert via motorcycle taxis carrying passengers with megaphones; ensure that local radio stations promoted its demobilization message; figure out how to sew together strips of red, blue, and yellow into a thirty-meter Colombian flag. In arguing with Hugo about the need for the giant flag, Marcela emphasized, "It's a huge visual show, you need to think about television," and "We're five kilometers from the border, and you know what happens on the other side." The latter statement referred to FARC camps on the Venezuelan side of the border used to launch hit-and-run attacks, camps where the military believed the FARC's top commander, Timochenko, to be based.[14]

In organizing the event, Marcela sought to evoke the same associations as the Operation Rivers of Light commercial: family and the benevolence of the military. She asked her staff, "Can a mother from the community get up and say something about how important the [flood-relief kits] are?" The answer was yes, but as Marcela would find out in the coming hours, the staging for the concert had taken up the majority of the plane's 6.5-ton cargo capacity, displacing the flood-relief kits. The other military plane that was supposed to deliver additional cargo, including the kits, had been rerouted (likely for a military operation).

The Ministry of Defense hoped to distribute the flood-relief kits to the residents of La Gabarra, a small town fifty kilometers north of Tibú on a road that is all but impassable amid a downpour. Marcela explained Plan B, in case of rain, to her team: "We give a symbolic aid package and tell the journalists that there is four tons of aid"—presumably on its way. The Tibú–La Gabarra corridor—and the Catatumbo region as a whole—could use some nonfictitious aid from the Colombian state. It's not that the region does not produce wealth; it does. Colombia's first golf course, built for oil executives, is located in Tibú's outskirts. Catatumbo has suffered not only from unequal development but also from a history of confrontation between armed groups. In the 1990s the FARC and the ELN vied for territory (despite their ideological affinity). Just as the FARC emerged victorious from that confrontation, the security situation deteriorated further. In May 1999, the United Self-Defense Forces of Colombia (AUC), paramilitaries, arrived. Salvatore Mancuso, one of the AUC's top leaders, came to the region to create the Catatumbo Bloc, which would violently usurp the rebels' primary source of financing, cocaine production and distribution. As was common, the AUC punctuated its arrival with massacres while the armed forces looked the other way.[15] Within four months of its arrival, the AUC had killed approximately one hundred civilians, about half of whom were from the small town of La Gabarra, where the minister of defense was now slated to deliver a handful of flood-relief kits.[16]

The Catatumbo Bloc of the AUC collectively demobilized in 2004 and 2005 in a pair of staged disarmament events.[17] The bloc's leaders provided two lists of approximately fifteen hundred paramilitary combatants each, and the government doled out benefits on the basis of those lists. Mancuso was extradited to the US in 2008 on drug-trafficking charges, leaving his victims with more questions than answers, a void he has slowly been filling via videoconferences from a Virginia jail. Paramilitaries under Mancuso's command took advantage of the demobilization program's legal benefits while rearming as new paramilitary groups that continue to traffic drugs and terrorize the population. By 2011 these new groups in Catatumbo—known as Los Rastrojos and Las Águilas Negras—had profited handsomely from the drug trade and had worked out a fragile truce with the FARC's Thirty-Third Front. Many of the paramilitaries that had demobilized in the early 2000s lived freely in Catatumbo communities, and many others ruled the region through familiar, if less spectacular, practices of intimidation and violence while profiting from the drug trade and extortion. In Catatumbo, as in other parts of the country scarred by paramilitarism, the demobilization of the

AUC, and the swift remobilization of their successor groups, the word *demobilization* carried a negative connotation and engendered great skepticism.

Aside from a euphemism repeated twice by Minister of Defense Pinzón in his speech—"you've had a hard time" (*les ha tocado duro*)—the festivities to promote demobilizations from the FARC and ELN made no mention of recent events. Instead of addressing the latent history, the PAHD provided the people of Tibú and surrounding areas an elaborate show that included a parade, a performance by the local police salsa band "They're from the Law" (Son de la Ley), and a gift-giving ceremony in which a general gave the town's soccer champions and a cooperative of single mothers a flat-screen television and a microwave oven, respectively.

To inaugurate Operation Rivers of Light in Tibú, the PAHD projected the commercial onto giant screens behind the stage. The faces in the audience ranged between bored and annoyed. Then came the critical act, according to Marcela: the unfurling the thirty-meter-long flag by passing it hand to hand over the heads of the crowd while the television cameras rolled (figure 2.2). Finally, vallenato star Peter Manjarrés took the stage and the crowd gave its first genuine applause.

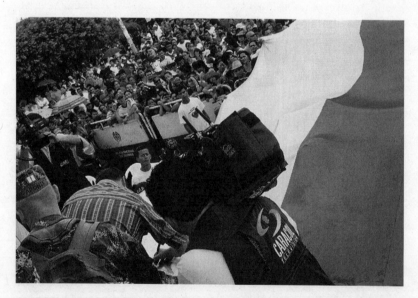

FIGURE 2.2. Minister of Defense Juan Carlos Pinzón signs a giant flag that unfurls across the crowd as broadcast television giant Caracol records. Photo by author, 2011.

As the concert began, the minister of defense boarded a helicopter to La Gabarra to deliver the symbolic humanitarian aid. Citing lack of space in the helicopter, Marcela explained to the journalists that only one photographer could travel with him. The flood assistance was reduced to a photo op, raising the question: who is assisting whom in this "humanitarian" exchange? The more substantive exchange during the minister's brief appearance in La Gabarra was of bullets. As his helicopter elevated to return to Tibú, the local police station took fire from the FARC's Thirty-Third Front. Nobody was injured, but the skirmish left a few more pockmarks in the building's facade. The FARC was sending its own message.

Marcel Mauss's classic book on the gift and the literature it has spawned have provided anthropologists with an analytic framework for understanding humanitarian aid as an expression of power relations.[18] In this line of critique, gifts given in the wake of an emergency or during or after a military confrontation assert a soft form domination over the receiver of the aid (be it a person, organization, or institution). Such a critique could be applied to the military's distribution of token flood-relief kits. The act places the military in the position of ameliorating the effects of recent inundations of roadways that have left the residents cut off from critical markets and struggling to access basic provisions. By showing its disposition to combat natural disaster, the military seeks to articulate its primary war-waging function with its ancillary role as an armed relief agency. One logical conclusion of this armed humanitarianism is that the FARC is but another disaster and the local population, which is receiving the ministry's flood-relief kits, is symbolically subordinated to the military and interpellated as military collaborators.

On an interpretive level this critique makes sense, however; the highly mediated tokenism of the minister's gift to the residents of La Gabarra raises a set of different and more interesting concerns. Primarily, what, if any, reciprocity can be expected for a gift that is so transparently self-interested? Mariella Pandolfi writes that "the haze of humanitarianism hides the implication of its actions behind the immediate moral camouflage of saving lives."[19] Paradoxically, the ministry's reduction of aid to a photo op strips away that haze, moving the power play of the humanitarian gift into plain sight and therefore attenuating whatever efficacy it may have. There can be no clearer indication that the photo op was a failed exchange than Marcela's decision not to provide the journalists present with a photograph of the minister giving the "humanitarian aid" to residents of La Gabarra. She had enough elements to sate the journalists and their editors; this one image could be buried without consequence.

Back in Tibú, print and radio journalists were on deadline and upset that they had not been granted interviews with the minister. Marcela dispatched the colonel directing the PAHD. The journalists pounced.

JOURNALIST: Why don't you tell us a little bit more about the rivers?

COLONEL: What we want to do is send a message—especially in December—to say that all Colombians are part of this light. These capsules that you saw carry messages to the FARC, messages written by the community, messages written by family members, messages written by children asking them to think about what they're doing, and how demobilization is their way out.

JOURNALIST: In which rivers did you do this?

COLONEL: In the Omega Joint Task Force.

JOURNALIST: In the Macarena . . .

COLONEL: All over the Macarena is where the military is doing this the most.

In producing the commercial, one military radio station *did* collect messages from family members, and in producing the commercial the military *did* send the plastic capsules down a river in La Mácarena; however, I never heard of the exercise being repeated as anything other than a media stunt. While not surprised by the tenuous veracity of the colonel's claims, I was amazed that the journalists did not subject his answer to any critical follow-up questions. Staging an extravaganza and dripping out details through often specious statements were only two pieces in Marcela's arsenal. She also anticipated the rhythms of journalistic production, the predictable criteria of editors and reporters, and their workflow. Crucially, she gave the journalists more angles than they could handle—the demobilization appeal, the minister's statements, the vallenato concert, the creativity of the campaign, images of Christmas and the war. The journalists could focus on any or all of those elements— thereby maintaining the illusion of reporters' choice—but given constraints on airtime and word counts, critical analysis lay definitively beyond the scope of the coverage.

Though the event in Catatumbo generated favorable press nationally, what, if any, impact did it have on the population of Tibú and its surroundings? To answer that question the PAHD turned to Vanera, one of Colombia's largest market research firms. In a gesture toward the scientific method, Vanera conducted a baseline study two weeks before the event and a follow-up study two weeks afterward, mixing surveys and semi-structured interviews. I spoke with Juan Carlos, the young anthropologist Vanera dispatched to Tibú for four days to conduct the post-event analysis. We spoke over a glass of tea in his mother's middle-class living room.

"The people don't believe in demobilization. What they say is "Demobilization is a farce." I put this in my report and explained the reasons, but I don't think [the company] showed it to the ministry; it probably showed them what it wanted to hear." Juan Carlos had struggled to solicit opinions about the demobilization program during his time in Tibú. Facing an entrenched code of silence, he resorted to paying people $28 per interview. He explained: "When people spoke about demobilization in Tibú, it generated feelings, sadness, worry. I had a hard time achieving my objective because people were very affected not only by the war but also by the peace." Summarizing public sentiment about the deeply problematic demobilization of paramilitaries in Catatumbo (2004–5), Juan Carlos said, "The *paras* were given welfare, were given awards, were given presents. They rewarded the violent ones, the assassins." As Juan Carlos said, "[Local people] perceive [demobilization] as a political strategy, the government of the moment trying to show success, not a form of reparation or justice."

Perhaps Vanera did submit Juan Carlos's report undoctored. The Ministry of Defense did not renew Vanera's contract. Juan Carlos, who bemoaned the lack of research opportunities for anthropologists, had already begun looking for another job.[20]

Statecraft and Stagecraft in Tres Esquinas, Caquetá

The Christmas campaign of 2010 reinvigorated high government officials' interest in the individual demobilization program. Back in 2008, 2,791 people demobilized from the FARC, more than in any subsequent year.[21] Not coincidentally, 2008 was the worst year for the FARC in its history. Two of its top leaders were killed and fourteen of its most valuable hostages, including presidential candidate Íngrid Betancourt, were freed in a cinematic liberation. The success of that operation consummated the shift in momentum that had begun to swing in the govern-

ment's favor in 2003. But since the heady months of 2008, demobilization statistics had dropped, and as they did, so too fell the PAHD's
profile. The publicity success of the 2010 Christmas campaign buttressed
the PAHD's status in the government. By 2011 it was again commanding
presidential attention.

Only days before Christmas 2011, President Santos, his cabinet (with
two exceptions), and the majority of the military's high command descended on the Tres Esquinas air force base in southern Colombia to
promote Operation Rivers of Light.[22] The stagecraft exceeded that of
previous minister-level events by an order of magnitude. The military
would mobilize multiple aircraft and a half-dozen *pirañas*, heavily
armed speedboats designed for river combat.

As with the event in Tibú, I traveled with the PAHD team in the belly
of a Hercules cargo plane. When we arrived at Tres Esquinas, military
operations were already under way to secure the base. Those operations
intensified after dark. Planes circled above and strafed the other side of
the Orteguaza River. The first time I heard the crackle of aerial gunfire, I instinctively squatted in the bed of the pickup we were traveling in.
That reflex prompted a round of anxious laughter. After the giggles sub-
sided, Marcela explained that the exercise was "just in case" the rebels
had any ideas about disrupting the event the next day. Orders that night
were to sleep with clothes and shoes on. "With everything going on to-
morrow, we can't let our guard down," one military officer explained. I
bunked in an empty hospital room at the far end of the base, shoes on,
with four members of the PAHD's communications team, three of them
soldiers. The aerial assault on nobody continued until dawn.

The next day Marcela engaged in a tug-of-war with the president's
media coordinator. Younger, two heads shorter, and lacking Marcela's
confidence, she struggled to formulate arguments for her staging pref-
erences. Marcela got her way in every instance. The two bickered about
how to facilitate the live television transmission via satellite, when each
minister would speak, where the military officers would stand, and
where to film the president's remarks. The only concern that rivaled how
the event should look on television was the president's security. At one
point I overheard Marcela's rival relay a note of caution from the president's security detail: "If a grenade goes off here, we can't guarantee the
president's life." Marcela's preferred site for President Santos's address,
with the backdrop of the river, happened to be adjacent to a munitions
depot. After some back and forth, Marcela won the argument by saying

that if they recorded the event in the officers' cafeteria, the whole thing might as well take place in Paris.

The exact source of Marcela's authority is hard to pinpoint. She makes all the right facial responses and inflects her voice deftly to embody a form of female command that is nonthreatening, sometimes harried, but always respectful. When the intensity of a situation mounts, she speaks more quickly and presses her thumbs harder into her Blackberry. The fact that she is paid by the United States as part of an elite group of professional advisers also bestows status, as does her prior experience.[23] As a journalist, she worked her way up from a field reporter to become the director of the midday news for RCN Television. She held that extraordinarily influential position for seven years before beginning to work for the government. What was clear from watching the event unfold in Tres Esquinas was that Marcela's authority, for a moment, trumped that of the country's top military brass, the cabinet members, and even the president. She was directing the show (figure 2.3).

What is a show without lights? Lowe/SSP3 brought two hundred plastic light capsules from Bogotá, the military brought the three hun-

FIGURE 2.3. Marcela coaching President Santos on the logistics for the river outing, while first lady María Clemencía Rodríguez, Lowe/SSP3 partner Francisco Samper (background, center), and national security adviser Sergio Jaramillo (far left) look on. Photo by author, 2011.

dred used to film the commercial in La Macarena, and another hundred fifty were ordered from Bogotá. Marcela kept repeating to the Lowe/ SSP3 staff, "The president wants the rivers to be *really* full of light." She planned the event to culminate with President Santos placing a glowing plastic ball in the river. Dogs trained to sniff out explosives delved their noses into the piles of plastic spheres while soldiers tucked leaflets into individual balls. Unlike in the commercial, these leaflets did not contain loving messages from family members urging sons, daughters, and siblings to demobilize. Rather, they were fake $20,000 peso bills (US$11) with messages urging rebels to demobilize on the flip side (figure 2.4). Those messages called on rebels to join "the democracy" or, for a monetary reward, to inform on a regional commander (figure 2.5). The logic of disguising the flyer as currency is simple: to entice rebels to pick it up and to sidestep the FARC's ban against carrying enemy propaganda.

The use of currency as a medium of propaganda is fitting on multiple levels. First, as Virginia Hewitt, a curator at the British Museum, has noted, money serves as "officially sanctioned propaganda."[24] The reason it exists as a substrate for national propaganda is that currency undergirds not only economic contracts but also the social contracts that lie beneath them. The efficacy of propaganda hinges on credibility; and the efficacy of money depends upon trust. The two are closely related. What then does it mean for the state to counterfeit its own bill? What message stews beneath the literal call to demobilize printed on the fake currency's flip side? I would argue that this curious counterfeit exposes how the state's self-defense function, when unchecked by robust public

FIGURE 2.4. A fake 20,000 peso bill distributed in western Caquetá as part of Operation Rivers of Light, 2011. Image scanned from flyer collected during campaign event.

FIGURE 2.5. Text reads: "Earn up to $670,000 for information that locates 'Romaña,' [call] 312.432.0355; total confidentiality, we'll protect your life." Distributed in western Caquetá as part of Operation Rivers of Light, 2011. Image scanned from flyer collected during campaign event.

scrutiny, expands to capture the state from within. What else could explain why the government is willing to counterfeit itself and undermine the trust that sits at the heart of the social and economic contract that is the lifeblood of body politic?

The PAHD's use of such fake currency (which dates back to 2003, four years before it contracted Lowe/SSP3) toys not only with trust but also with desire. What might the Marxist-Leninist guerrilla who bends down to pick up a bill stranded in a muddy patch after it has fluttered down from the open window of a helicopter be thinking the moment before he realizes it is fake? What will he imagine buying? Currency stokes desires that can quickly concatenate in visions of accumulating more currency—a prospect clearly signaled by the bags of money depicted in figure 2.5. The two sides to this counterfeit bill are suggestive of the type of subjects the PAHD interpolates: avaricious and disposed to turn against their comrades.

As the bomb-sniffing dogs inspected the plastic capsules, I spoke with Federico, the "creative" behind the Christmas campaigns of 2010 and 2011. A creative, in public-relations lingo, is a person who translates research into campaign ideas and, in coordination with an account manager, pitches those ideas to clients. Their aesthetic sensibilities shape advertising. Unconvinced about the overall coherence of the Operation Rivers of Light campaign, I asked Federico, "Why did you design the

campaign around sending plastic balls of light down the river?" He answered, "The rivers are beautiful. Publicity is an art, and creatives always want the spectacle to make an impact."[25] As opposed to Juan
Pablo, who justified the aesthetic decisions of the campaign by connecting them to the company's research, Federico reverted to an argument
familiar to propagandists going back to Joseph Goebbels: the primacy
of visual impact. Earlier that day my minder, a lieutenant whom I occasionally found peering over my shoulder and into my notebook, offered a different inspiration for Operation Rivers of Light. He pointed
to Federico and said, "The original idea is from China, where they
have something in their culture with candles that float down the rivers."
(Federico denied drawing any inspiration from Chinese rituals.) These
variant creation stories positioned the publicity campaign along different narratives: *we are artists*; *we are diligent researchers*; *we are global*.
The common thread is how these framings highlight the marketers' skill
and savvy, traits the PAHD seeks to align itself with through its relationship with Lowe/SSP3.

In the hangar a special lunch was organized for the troops who also
needed some Christmas cheer. I approached a pair of air force colonels
and asked about the crackle of gunfire the night before. The first colonel replied tersely, "Communication," and the second, following the lead
of the first and added, "To send a message." Both looked at the camera strapped around my neck, then at each other. They made no further
comment.

Normally Tres Esquinas Air Base provides a staging ground for military operations, not propaganda shows. In 2008, jets blasted down the
runway on their way to bomb a camp in Ecuador, killing Raúl Reyes, the
FARC's No. 2 commander. The base has also been a focal point for US
support. In 2009 the US air force donated six TPS-70 long-range radar
systems to the Colombian air force to interdict planes ferrying refined
cocaine. During Operation Rivers of Light, Tres Esquinas provided a
different type of theater of operations. Down on the dock, Marcela and
her team prepared for a trial run of the choreography of six *piraña* gun-
boats with the general. Marcela explained the importance of keeping
the boats in tight formation to facilitate clear images of President Santos
placing his plastic capsule in the river at dusk.

By midafternoon the show was under way. When President Santos arrived (on the same plane as Francisco Samper, a partner in Lowe/
SSP3), he proceeded to a religious service presided over by the base's

priest, who connected the themes of light and reconciliation in a prayer for Colombia. By 4 p.m., members of the cabinet wearing white PAHD T-shirts had settled in rows of plastic chairs arranged near a microphone. The thirty-meter flag sewn in Tibú was draped over a defensive wall of green sandbags. Marcela coached President Santos on the order of the show and demonstrated to the ministers how to write their messages to the rebels and place them in the plastic balls. One by one, the ministers wrote messages to the rebels. Minster of the Interior Germán Vargas Lleras concluded his note with a threat: "Demobilize—you don't have much time." Minister of Labor Rafael Pardo had a more nuanced message:

> Twenty years ago, a little more, I had the opportunity to dialogue on behalf of the government with two people. . . . One didn't demobilize. His name was Alfonso Cano, and you know what happened to him. The other did demobilize; his name is Gustavo Petro [a former member of the M19], the mayor of Bogotá. If you demobilize you have opportunities, and you'll find a country that lends you a hand; and you don't have to change your ideas.

Two former rebels delivered remarks from behind oversized sunglasses and hats pulled down over their brows, visibly worried about the consequences of making public statements in support of the government.

After the speeches, the president, ministers, and journalists walked down to the dock for the nautical choreography. CNN en Español and every major Colombian broadcaster filmed the scene. The journalists playfully shouted to President Santos's boat to come closer. After four takes of the president putting a plastic capsule of light in the water, the photographers were satisfied. Even I snapped the image that all of the media and military preparations were designed to disseminate (figure 0.3 on page 19).

When the show was over, the journalists trod up the ramp from the dock to the cafeteria and filed their stories. The military and media logistics had worked as Marcela envisioned, and the government's message of creativity and benevolence would resound not only in the often-repeated commercial but also in the news stories generated by the event. Marcela had bent the news media to her will, promoting the PAHD and its vision of a humanitarian counterinsurgency. This extreme form of stagecraft-cum-statecraft is predicated on media manipulation. Witness Marcela and Juan Pablo's obsession with portraying the Christmas campaigns to the media, if not outright staging them for the media. International coverage is particularly important because it confers validation that has a ripple effect. When London's *The Telegraph* publishes a story with the headline "Colombian Army Gives Militants Giant Jungle Christmas Tree," or CNN publishes "Colombian Military's New Weapon against Rebels: Christmas Trees," it signals to Colombia's national press to write similar stories. The commercial and its accompanying videos, government statements, and staged events combine to provide media outlets with visually rich, politically relevant coverage—two central criteria for editors.

To focus on any one element of the Christmas campaigns would be misguided. The five Christmas "operations" that ran annually from 2010 to 2014 moved promiscuously across different media platforms and formats, deploying a range of artifacts, from military objects to consumer merchandise to fake currency, in a symbolic blitzkrieg. (In 2012 the theme of the campaign was the Star of Bethlehem, portrayed as an antiaircraft spotlight that would guide deserters to the city.) The organizing principle behind the offensive is the brand. At the heart of the PAHD's brand is the contradictory notion of a humanitarian counterinsurgency. Although Operation Christmas and Operation Rivers of Light are ostensibly about demobilization, they became a potent way for the armed forces to represent themselves to national and international audiences. This rebranding effort is nestled within a larger rebranding of the nation that is stunning in its coordination. Marcela left the PAHD in late 2012 to work as the media strategist for the Colombian government's team of negotiators during peace talks with the FARC while also working to sync the communications divisions across all government ministries, a career move that shows just how central she had become to the government's communication strategy. The Christmas campaigns that she coordinated cannot be divorced from the concerted government-led effort to tell "success stories" that seek to derail reflexive associations of the country's name with guerrilla war, massacres, kidnapping, paramilitaries, and drug violence. Whether highlighting a tourist boom, a military success, a cultural event, a positive economic indicator, or international recognition of any sort, government officials and communications professionals have partnered to present a collage of stories about national improvement while suppressing anything that does not fit that narrative.

Branding, which became big business in the 1980s, has emerged as big governance in the early twenty-first century. Countries increasingly look to secure their position in a global hierarchy structured by capital flows by crafting and managing their national identity as a brand.[26] A nation's apparent trajectory—emergent, stagnant, in decline—can make a crucial difference in investors' decisions. In Colombia the phenomenon has played out in dramatic fashion, motivating the country to position itself as a "postconflict" nation-state. At the crux of this renarration of the nation is the idea of a country that has stepped back from the brink of "failed state" status and is now secure and ripe for investment. Foreign direct investment in Colombia skyrocketed through the 2000s, going from $1.5 billion in 1999 to nearly $16 billion in 2013. Similarly, the arrival of foreign tourists more than quintupled between 2001 and 2016, with more than five million international visitors arriving in 2016. Fueling and celebrating this Colombian "success story" are national tourism campaigns such as "Colombia Is Passion," "Colombia: Land of Magical Realism," and "Colombia, the only risk is wanting to stay."[27] The latter campaign provides a visual tour of beautiful landscapes coupled with a voiceover that says, in English purposely accented to sound *auténtico*, "A place where the past lives harmoniously with the future and the word *infinite* is written on the colors of the beach, the mountains, the jungle, and the sky." As one official document lauding the "only risk is that you'll want to stay" campaign explained, its goal was to "convert risk into an opportunity"—speculative capitalism pure and simple.[28]

This offensive mode of nation branding is not without its defensive dimensions. During the 2012 Christmas season I was sitting in the PAHD's offices while the lawyer for the program and two other officials riffed on one of the program's buzzwords that year, *blindar*, which means "to shield" or "to armor." Such shielding is a defensive posture that anticipates scandal, controversy, and unwelcome elements of reality that percolate through the elaborate systems of information control and brand management.[29] Opportunistic parodies of the PAHD's marketing exist but are rare, appearing on graffiti-scrawled walls and protest signs that read "Uribe Demobilize," referring to the former president's alleged ties to paramilitaries, or "Soldier Demobilize" (figure 2.6). These occasional apparitions, however, have not flourished, since they would quickly attract a punitive response. "To shield" is to remain vigilant about possible counterattacks in the brand war that has become an increasingly thick thread running through Colombia's armed conflict. Through its commit-

FIGURE 2.6. "Soldier, Demobilize" graffiti in central Bogotá. Photo courtesy of Yanilda González, 2012.

ment to branding, the PAHD plays offense and defense simultaneously. Its offensive dimensions, which I have highlighted in this chapter, have the invisible consequence of infusing military propaganda into the cultural atmosphere. In the case of Operation Christmas, this has meant militarizing the very spirit of Christmas.

Gabriel

W e walk up to my office, conveniently tucked in a side corner of a university building. I close the door, and Gabriel unzips his jacket, revealing a black bulletproof vest. He rips the Velcro open and tucks the vest under the desk. I lift it off the ground and am surprised by how light it is. "Will that protect you?" I ask. He replies, "So they say." He takes in the scenery of the green hills through the large window behind me before launching into his story.

G: *As a kid I always walked at my father's side. I stuck to him, and he stuck to me.*

   When I was small my dad had another farm, a cattle ranch, and he sent me to take care of it. I had twelve workers. I grazed twenty-seven Holstein cows in Huila. It was very cold over there. At that age I had big responsibilities. I managed workers, planted beans.

A: How old were you?

G: *I was thirteen, fourteen years old.*

A: How did your dad get so much land and resources?

G: *Through coffee. He would go to Cauca and bring indigenous people to Huila and put them to work. Not like a slave owner—he paid them. Back then the [workers] in Huila were lazier than the indigenous from Cauca, who were more grateful.*

   I was on that farm for a while until I got tired of it. I went back to picking coffee on my dad's other farm. I was like fifteen. Then one day when I was picking coffee with a bunch of other workers, I told him, "Dad, I am going." It was 1979, the height of the coca.

   My uncle had said to me, "Let's go to San José del Guaviare and make some money."

A: Were you close to that uncle?

G: *Of course. He loved me a lot. He said, "I like Gabriel because Gabriel is responsible and a badass worker* [berraco para el trabajo]. *I am going to take him." He was already a cocaine chemist.*

    He taught me everything about chemistry in San José del Guaviare. I had never been up a river, and he took me up the Aremaca and Forobero Rivers. We had come to San José from Villavicencio in a small plane. It was the biggest boom time. When I got there, there was prostitution. God damn. I was healthy though. There were drugs like you can't imagine, but me—nothing. I didn't yet know much about the coca. I didn't know the Peruvian [coca]; I knew the other one, La Pringa María, the wild kind.

    They would say, "Come on, white guy [mono], *let's do such and such." I started to get involved that way. They had me manage a house of prostitutes with some guy. [They would say,] "Gabriel is responsible, let him store the weapons, the money." My uncle left me stranded there, I didn't have anyone—imagine.*

    He told me, "You are going to stay with this guy, and we'll see each other upriver in two weeks. I am going to cut some merchandise. Here you have everything, money, girls."

    That was bullshit. In a few weeks everyone had disappeared. I went to help a guy selling gas. Milicianos [guerrilla informants and clandestine supporter structures] controlled the area. I would wake up to nasty firefights—I had never seen that. In the morning people were hanging from the hooks in the butchery. Groups were trying to take over the narcotraffic.

A: Who was the FARC fighting?

G: *With the military that has a base there. They were there with others called The Black Hand.*

    Then a man called Romero came and said, "Man, what's going on? Do you want to come with me up[river]?"

    I said, "Let's go."

A: At that time you were fourteen or fifteen?

G: *I was fifteen. We went up and I had everything. I tried whiskey and it seemed like the best thing. I started going around like a bum. God damn, women all over the place. Back then I was with a girl who was worth $22. A lot of money! In the beginning the river was wide, from like here to the highway [pointing through the window, across the hill to a roadway in the distance], but in the end the canoe could barely enter. I shook with fear. The driver, Raul, said, "This is scary, have a drink."*

    It took us eight days to arrive by canoe. The canoe was filled with per-

manganate, sulfur, ammonium, and provisions. We unloaded because the
military was upriver, and God damn, the mosquitoes. What was my role?
To shovel water out of the canoe.

When we got to the site they said, "Gabriel, here's your farm."

I said, "What farm?"

"Look, son, we are going to get provisions. Take an ax, and here are
two kilos of coca seed."

When they left, tears came from the shock. . . . I got a nasty bout of ma-
laria, you can't imagine. I couldn't walk. Those were the conditions over
there for about a year.

Then the guerrilla came, and my uncle too. He taught me how to be a
chemist, and people started looking for me. "Gabriel, come cut cocaine
with such-and-such a percentage [of purity]."

So the guerrilla would come and say, "Look, since you're a chemist,
help us with the percentage." Back then you had to give them 20 grams per
kilo. A big soup spoon was about 20 grams.

My lot was filled with coca, only four plantain trees. I had my gun in
my belt and everyone respected me. "He is the chemist, son of so-and-so,
nephew of so-and-so, he's a badass."

A: So your uncle was already involved with the FARC?

G: *Of course he had a relationship with the FARC, but he was a bandit. He*
scored goals on the FARC because he was supposed to give them the quota
[but didn't]. I saved him on like three occasions, since he didn't pay the
vaccination [a guerrilla tax]. I had become the chemist for that whole re-
gion. They respected me. I made my house and brought a girl there. She
left after a little while.

The guerrilla celebrated my sixteenth birthday by killing a heifer for
everyone.

Over there I learned that I had a few uncles who had been part of the
revolution. So I entered.

At the time that Gabriel entered the FARC, the military had cut its
supply lines, forcing the guerrilla's combatants to live off the jungle. To
break the siege, the FARC ambushed the military with an M60 machine
gun, killing several soldiers. By joining the FARC, Gabriel forfeited his
cocaine-chemistry business, but he applied his skills by working for the
front's finance unit, collecting the guerrilla's tax on cocaine from the local coca settlers.

When he turned eighteen, the commanders ordered him to do his

obligatory military service with the Colombian air force. After living on
the base for a year, Gabriel stole nine G3 rifles. He followed the FARC's
instructions, which he received on folded paper notes passed by young
women or elderly men working as *milicianos* outside of the base. He fled
south and gave the stolen rifles to the FARC.

G: *I said to the FARC, "I delivered the weapons, now leave me in peace."*

A: You didn't want to continue?

G: *No, I wanted to lay low, so I got a girl and got married.*

A: But you couldn't leave that easily, right?

G: *Well, I thought that I could withdraw.*

A: You were like nineteen then?

G: *I think so, nineteen about to turn twenty. I received a farm over there. The*
whole area was guerrilla territory, on both sides. They knew who I was.

    See how nasty the situation got for Gabriel.

    I trained horses and mules and would ride up and down. The military
was here [diagramming on the palm of his hand]. They saw me go in and
out on the horses. The military came to the farm, but—tran—I fled.

    They caught my woman and started grilling her—"Where is that son of
a . . ."—in front of the two kids.

A: You had kids at that point?

G: *She had a boy [from a previous relationship] and we had a girl.*

    She lived in Mosquera and I stayed on the other side, alone. When I
went to visit Mosquera it was militarized, but there's the back way. I went
down on a good young mare, at night. I took the girl and put her on the
saddle; she was barely four years old.

    As we were traveling the next day, going to meet her mom, the army
came out. "Be still!"

    The girl asked, "What happened?"

    "Dismount, you big son of a bitch. We know who you are," they said.

    I said, "Let me go home, just up the way. Come with me, I have to drop
off the girl."

    The captain and his squadron came to the house. I dismounted and
they took the girl. My wife began to cry.

    "Where are your comrades, those sons of bitches?"

    "I don't know what you are saying. Ask in the village: I am only a wran-
gler, and I am on this farm training the horses and mules."

    There were cement pools filled with water, a water tank with foam from
being so cold. They tied me up, picked me up, and threw me in. When I

went to get out, they pushed their hands against me. That was a bitch of a torture. Why? Because of the fucking cold. It gives you hypothermia, a headache, everything hurts. They took the mother of the girl and abused her. There wasn't anyone who could speak up for me, nobody. I don't like to remember that day. I couldn't do anything.

I said, "If you want to capture me, well, capture me and put me in jail, but don't do that to them."

I looked like a piece in the slaughterhouse, streaming blood. They broke my head with their clubs, kicked like a son of a bitch. They put the bag on me. Do you know what a bag with Fab soap on the head, tightened, feels like? A bunch of peasants showed up, and they left me alone.

A: What did they gain from all of that?

G: *Nothing, I didn't say anything. The only thing they gained was raping my woman in front of everyone, in front of our daughter. They humiliated me like a son of a bitch. Nothing came out of me.*

A: I can't imagine being in a situation like that. Was there a moment when you said to yourself, "I am going to inform so they stop"?

G: *No, because of the girl and the woman, my family.*

A: Because if you speak . . .

G: *[The FARC] would kill my family. They'd kill my old man where they had given us a place to stay. They would even burn the doghouse, because that's the way it is.*

When [the military] withdrew a kilometer, poom—[the guerrilla] came. "Hey comrade, are you okay?" One guy started warming me up. Guerrilla women took my woman to a nurse to bathe her.

I told one of them, "Give me my equipment." That's when they gave it back to me and I got back with them.

"Comrade, we're proud of you," one said. They gave me a leadership position.

He said that the incident made him "very bloodthirsty" (*muy sangriente*), motivating him to join the FARC's special forces, known by the military as "eggshell walkers" for their ability to silently sneak up on small groups of soldiers. Gabriel rose through the ranks, working simultaneously on military and political aspects of the revolution. His daughter, who witnessed her mother's rape, grew up to join an elite unit of the FARC.

One day military helicopters dropped leaflets on his camp. He picked one up and saw that the government was offering a reward of $278,000.

He grew paranoid and did not let his comrades know which hut he slept in, among other security measures. In 2002 the Caguán peace process fell apart and combat engulfed the area. His unit was the object of a twenty-seven-day operation by the Colombian military.

G: *They sent me to be in charge of the radio station Voice of Resistance, and that's where they captured me. They had already captured some and killed others—even the Red Beret specialists. I thought they were still alive, but they had been dead for a week.*

I didn't know because I had gone with four squadrons to a different area. That's when the military caught me. I had gone to see if the military was there, but I put on civilian clothes, like I am here.

Back then I was with the woman who I am with now. She was also in the organization, and I sent a message for her to get out, to go to the road and catch a car. When she got out, the military asked her, "Ma'am, where are you going?" She was with the little child. [She said,] "I am from that farm there on the other side of that one."

Then they said, "Have you seen this guerrilla around here?"

She said, "No, I don't know that guy." [Laughs] It was her husband!

I went to scout out the area in civilian clothes. I had already gotten my wife and the child out, so I went up to the military to try to get information. The captain looked at me and said, "Take off your boots." I took my boots off, no problem; but then—shit—the green sock that said FARC.

"This son of a bitch is a miliciano," *said the captain.*

I said, "Here everyone shares clothes and I just put this on." I was cool, very cool. I had a big machete tied to my belt and—proom—they took it from me.

I looked to the road and saw a comrade that was coming, talking on the radio, telling the others that I was with the military, saying "The Stone [Gabriel's alias] is over there, the military has him." The captain had his radio on, and they were scanning everything. The Virgin was smiling on me, because in a moment pam pam pam—*those guys came to get me out and I escaped.*

A: Without boots?

G: *No boots, clean footed [laughs]. When I ran off, the Black Hawk helicopter was firing M60 rounds.*

I arrived at a school, exhausted. It was raining like a son of a bitch. It got cloudy and the helicopter couldn't land. So I got to the school and a teacher was there, a woman. I took my green underwear and green T-shirt off and threw them in the fire. My feet were cut, and she gave me some socks and her sweatshirt. My arrival scared her. Then proom—*the army came and found me there. Those badasses had followed me.*

"Come here, we know who you are, you beautiful son of a bitch."

Immediately the place filled with peasants and the army. They said, "Put on your military uniform so we can take the photo of you captured."

Then the helicopter came from over there, it was like 5 p.m. and getting dark. When I turned around to sit down, proom—*the media had arrived, RCN and Caracol, [saying,] "So-and-so has been captured" [laughing]— the whole show.*

If they had caught me in uniform they would have killed me for the reward.

They didn't know who I was. They knew I was a guerrilla but didn't know who. I stayed quiet. Then they caught a kid and made him sing everything, including the national anthem.

I told the kid, "You're not going to say shit—shut your face, because you know how things work."

But the kid was like thirteen years old. When we got [to the combat zone] there were those vultures that eat whatever smells bad, a ton of vultures, and I thought, "Shit, what happened here?"

There were troops everywhere. They said, "Come here, look at your friends." When I went to look they were all dead. They had been dead for one week, two weeks, because they were exploding from the worms—you can't imagine.

The kid had probably never seen anyone dead, and he immediately started to scream, he went into shock, and right there he said, "He's done everything, he's the commander here."

I had to pick up the dead, throw them on my shoulder, and put them in the helicopter. The skin was falling off all of them. They killed fifteen, including two journalists from the radio station.

Gabriel knew about the demobilization program, and he convinced the military to register him as a deserter, an agreement that would benefit both sides. The military kept him at a battalion headquarters in a locked room without windows for eight months. The FARC considered him a political prisoner and gave him a lawyer. When Gabriel met his lawyer, the lawyer said, "You smell like formaldehyde." Once it was clear to the FARC that Gabriel had begun to work with the military, the commanders took action and confiscated the farm they had placed his father on. Gabriel relocated his dad, putting him on a farm five hours from Bogotá.

A: When you were running the radio station, what did you do to push back against the messages on the pamphlets that said "Demobilize"?

G: *When they started to send those messages, we told ourselves, "We are stronger. They want us to disintegrate because they have planes. We have the people, which is different. They are caring for an empire, for eighteen families [FARC shorthand for the Colombian ultra-elite]. We are caring for the Colombian people." We would sing revolutionary hymns.*

A: But did you have specific countercampaigns so people wouldn't desert?

G: *Of course, we had our revolutionary lessons. We had campaigns. We said, "If a guerrilla deserts, if you realize he's been one of ours, inform. Tell the closest* miliciano.*"*

A: So you can take measures?

G: *Yeah, so we can capture him again. If that person deserts, he can turn us in, turn in [the location] of our camps, get comrades killed, their families too. We also motivate: "Join Colombia's revolutionary movement. FARC is waiting for you with open arms, a revolutionary hug to welcome you to the revolutionary ranks of Colombia. FARC-EP, the people's army. Peasant, join the PCCC [Partido Comunista Clandestino Colombiano].*

A: Those were the slogans?

G: *Yeah, among others. "Friendly teacher, join the Partido Revolucionario de Colombia and motivate your students for the PCC, Partido Comunista Clandestino." We would say those [slogans] between revolutionary songs.*

A: Shortwave?

G: *Yes, of course.*

A: How much territory does shortwave cover?

G: *Two departments. Sometimes they heard us in Huila, Caquetá, Meta. [We would send] "regards to the Jacobo Arenas [Mobile Column] from so-and-so" between revolutionary poems. Or we would send regards to this commander and the mother of the commander. It was really beautiful.*

   I turned the radio station in [to the military], but they didn't pay me.

A: Why did you turn it in?

G: *Because they sentenced me to forty-five years in prison—an entire life. They knew what I had [done].*

Gabriel went through the reintegration program, denying any involvement in crimes against humanity such as kidnapping and recruiting minors. The state has selectively ignored Gabriel's actions that exceed the legal limits of forgiveness written into the demobilization program in exchange for his close collaboration in fighting the insurgency. Though I do not know the scope of his collaboration, he has spoken of helping the government locate hostages and unearthing a large stash of the guerrilla's money. He moved to a farm with his wife and kids. The paramilitaries paid him a visit.

G: *I was tired of the city, so I went to get an agrarian credit to buy a farm that had been all but abandoned. I started working it with my kids. One was fourteen, the other was eight, the other four years old. I started working with the Communal Action Board. We went to the municipality with a teacher and asked for lime to paint the school, got a scythe to cut the grass.*

One Sunday I went to the village to buy supplies, grain. When I left I saw some guys in civilian clothes, but armed. They looked at me and said hi. I walked by calmly. I thought, "Shit, this thing is getting heavy."

Later they came and offered me a beer. We had a beer and nothing else happened. I didn't ask them anything. A week later I went out and saw two soldiers, supposedly soldiers. But since I know about weapons, I realized their guns weren't what the military uses—they had a different caliber. I said to myself, "They're paramilitaries."

They said, "Are you Gabriel?"

I said, "Yes. How can I help you, soldier?"

He said, "My commander needs you."

When I heard that, "My commander," I knew they were paramilitaries. I went over there and they said, "Give me your CODA [official certification card for the demobilized]."

I said to them, "Why do you want the CODA?"

He said, "We know who you are."

I said to them, "Are you going to kill me?"

He said, "No, no. We need a favor from you."

One said to the other, "Bring me the bag."

Tan, tan, tan—they put $3,300 on the table.

He said, "I need a favor. I have two G3 rifles that are jammed. I need you to fix them. I know you know how to fix [guns]."

I said, "Pass them over," but I was shaking so hard that I could hardly grasp them. I imagined that they were going to kill me. The kids wouldn't leave my side. My children were my angels.

They said, "Get the kids out of here."

I said, "No, they're my kids, they need to be here. They've been here in good times, why shouldn't they be here in bad times?"

I started working on a G3. The firing pin had flipped, causing the jam. I undid it and said, "Look, the firing pin is damaged near the dock. Same thing with the other one."

They said, "You're the one we need." As we were walking, one of them said, "Comrade, at your command." At that moment, proom—son of a bitch, I saw their move. They thought that I had accepted the $3,300, but no.

"Give me a week to think about it," I said.

They said, "Come on, take the money."

I said, "I am not taking any money."

Taking one peso of that money would have been a commitment—so I went home.

Two, three, four days went by and I kept thinking. At the end of the week they were all over the place. On Friday they were looking at my kids, at my wife. I was working and they were keeping an eye on me.

Finally they said, "Hey, what's going on?"

I said, "All right, tell me the truth. What happens if I don't accept?"

He said, "That's your choice. But what will happen to your kids and your woman?"

I sent my wife to Bogotá to sell an apartment I had gotten from my dad.

The next day two of them came, a couple. "Hey Gabriel, how are you? We came to see if you would give us some milk."

I said, "Of course, whatever you want. If you want, I'll give you sugarcane too. Here's the milk."

I finished milking and gave it to them. One of them kept looking at me, and then he said, "You know what, you're cool. Brother, leave here tonight, because they are going to kill you."

We escaped at two in the morning when it was raining, with the little kid (the four-year-old), but we left the other one [the eight-year-old] there. We got to Bogotá and were in shock, without the kid. I wouldn't wish it on anyone.

A: I am not sure I understand the logic of leaving the kid.

G: If I left with everyone, they would follow us and kill us. The guarantee was that I would return for him. But I wasn't going back, because they would kill me. I left him with some old people who have died by now. The fourteen-year-old could defend himself, so I sent him one way and we went another. I arrived at four in the morning to a milk distributor, and a truck *was passing by loaded with milk. I made him stop and said, "I need you to take me out of town."*

    He said, "No, I can't do that."

    I put a pistol to his head and said, "You'll take me because this is a matter of life and death. Should I drive?"

    He said, "No, no, let's go."

A: I am trying to imagine things from the kid's perspective, in the hands of the paramilitaries. Wow. What were you thinking at that point?

G: *What was I thinking? That I should go back so they would give me the kid, but I knew they would kill me. They wanted me to teach them everything about the PCCC, how the FARC manages its troops, how you work the masses, cells.*

A: What year was this?

G: *2007.*

A: And what happened to the kid?

G: *La Defensoría [del Pueblo, the government institution dedicated to protecting human rights] got him out.*

A: How did the Defensoría get the kid out?

G: *Talk.*

A: They came and talked to the paras?

G: *They spoke with the paras, but the paras wouldn't accept anything. The kid had hepatitis, so eleven months later they left him in a school. Dr. Pérez from the Defensoria del Pueblo told us where the kid was and took $560 out of his own pocket. We contracted a motorcycle, and my wife went to the village herself to pick up the kid. The kid didn't believe it was his mom, or he thought he was dreaming. We had to stay quiet and hide the kid because maybe they were using the kid to figure out where we were. . . . I had to get a psychologist for the kid. They raped him, did everything to him.*

Gabriel moved his family to a shantytown outside Bogotá. The paramilitaries came looking for him.

G: *They asked me, "Are you Gabriel?" [I said,] "No, look, it's that guy there." They were in a [Isuzu] Trooper. They got out quickly and pam pam pam— and I got out of there. They killed the other guy. A few months later they killed my father. I don't really want to talk about that.*

A: Have you thought about leaving the country?

G: *But to where?*

A: I don't know. Ecuador?

G: *My sister said, "Gabriel, if you come to Mexico you'll do well."*

I say, "Yeah, doing what?"

She said, "Join the Zapatistas, you like that shit."

I said, "No, to go from some crap to another, no. The paramilitaries killed my father. I couldn't even go to my father's funeral. I want to make my life, have my family, a little farm, work there, see the kids grow—that's it."

FIGURE INT.3. Drawing by Lucas Ospina.

CHAPTER THREE

Operation Genuine

Operations deceiving the adversary cause imbalance, confusion, panic, disquiet and in-conformity inside the rival's system. — footnote in PowerPoint about Operation Genuine

Nicolás took a liking to me. When he saw me he would enthusiasti-cally intone, "Alis Fataleh"—struggling with the *x* of my first name and riffing on my last name's menacing connotation in Colombian Span-ish: *deadly.* The gringos that visited him tend to work for the CIA. I, on the other hand, was different and difficult to place, an unarmed gringo from Harvard. His "joking" doubts about my real identity expressed a simmering concern that I might actually be an adversarial agent. Nico-lás deduced otherwise and took pride in selectively schooling me in his craft.

We met for the first time in 2007, after I had returned from a trip with Marcela's communications team. He allowed me to loiter in his of-fice, observe, absorb, and scribble in my notebook. His office was tucked behind a blackened glass door in an out-of-the-way corner of a central shopping complex in downtown Bogotá. A brass handle jutting out of the black glass door opened onto a phalanx of closed-circuit security cameras and split-screen surveillance monitors. The corridor leading to his office cut through eight interview stations, each no larger than two phone booths joined together. In the space surrounding his office, agents worked phones and Excel spreadsheets in cubicles. The PAHD had plucked these intelligence agents from the Ministry of Defense's four ar-eas (army, navy, air force, police). They would burst through his door in-forming Nicolás of problems: A former rebel is receiving death threats via text message—*tap the line that sent it.* Somebody is suspected of ly-ing in interrogation—*remind him that perjury is punishable by prison.*

The vice minister for political and international affairs (responsible for the PAHD) needs to be briefed in preparation for his trip abroad—*stay up all night and refine the PowerPoint*. As I sat and jotted notes, a window opened onto the demobilization program's covert side, a view very different from, but dialectically related to, the mass-media campaigns designed by Lowe/SSP3. Each time I approached the brass handle, I was struck by how this secretive world existed amid shopping arcades, only one floor above primly dressed male mannequins posed in business suits.

In 2007 Nicolás held the rank of major and led the coterie of intelligence agents that constituted the "strategic area" of the PAHD. The agents under his command served as points of contact between the PAHD and military brigades across Colombia. The team's primary objective was to persuade midlevel FARC commanders to abandon the struggle. By targeting the insurgency's upper-middle rungs, the intelligence officers sought to breach command-and-control structures and collect high-quality intelligence. This information then fed back to the military's brigades, leading to more-effective offensives, which in turn would prompt more demobilizations. The strategic area team connected the three sides of a triangle at the heart of the counterinsurgency: desertion, intelligence collection, and military operations.

Marcela's world of media campaigns cannot be understood independently from Nicolás's world of military intelligence. The PAHD's publicity campaigns obscure the information war at the root of Colombia's demobilization program. The human intelligence, or HUMINT in military lingo, that former combatants provide is a key ingredient in what Nicolás and his colleagues call "results." This is the military's most prominent euphemism; it can mean kills in combat, seized drug stashes, or demobilized rebels—anything that officers can tally toward the goal of ascending the ranks.

Within Colombia's demobilization program, Nicolás's intelligence world is "publicity's secret," to borrow a term from cultural theorist Jodi Dean, who argues that secrecy is publicity's other. "Disclosure may really be concealments," Dean warns.[1] What I would like to suggest is that the simultaneous impulse to show while hiding and hide while showing defines the parameters of politics. Critical interrogation of that dialectical movement can serve as a diagnostic of political power.[2] Secrecy, as anthropological studies have shown, binds together those who share the hidden knowledge, and in the process inflates their power in the eyes of those excluded.[3] Declaring that a secret exists, let alone an entire secretive sphere of governance, is also a way of projecting an image. Concealment may really be disclosure, to flip Dean's adage. Image managers, like Marcela, and intelligence officers, like Nicolás, operate across intertwining structures of visibility and invisibility. Marcela, for instance, has high-level security clearance and receives and interacts with intelligence reports, while Nicolás pens ghostwritten op-eds in regional and national newspapers. The PAHD has enabled a gradual melding of these two worlds.

The ethnography in this chapter focuses on the PAHD's unspoken objective: gathering strategic and tactical intelligence from former combatants. My goal in this chapter is not merely to explore the invisible dimension of the Colombian government's individual demobilization program but to illuminate how it exists in a muted dialogue with the program's public persona. An ethnography of warfare that flips between both sides of counterinsurgency's coin, public and private, propels a central claim of this book: that branding has emerged as a mode of governance in the early twenty-first century because of its perceived ability to shape the relationship between visibility and invisibility, thereby operating effectively in a world in which contrary categories—counterinsurgency and humanitarianism, military and civilian, and conflict and postconflict— dissolve into each other. Branding, through its rootedness in the malleability of signification, offers a schema for controlling messages and managing meaning in an era of indistinction.[4]

Chapter 2 showed how Marcela and Lowe/SSP3 produced the contradictory category of a humanitarian counterinsurgency; in this chapter the ethnography explores how humanitarian impulses—expressions of love and care—are mobilized to render the counterinsurgency more effective. What is important to keep in mind is how the two processes exist in a mutually reinforcing relationship to project the idea of a humanitarian counterinsurgency across audiences, from the mass of viewers of Colombian television news to the micro-targeted public of a specific FARC leader. In what follows I focus on the micro-targeting of a midlevel FARC commander considered to be of "strategic value."

When I sought out Nicolás during my extended field research in 2011–12, he had risen to the rank of lieutenant colonel and commanded a regional intelligence battalion in the Caribbean region for one of the army's seven divisions. Our relationship swung from warm to acrimonious to cordial. At times Nicolás grew frustrated with my refusal to provide feedback on his PowerPoint presentations, known as "products" in the businesslike argot of the military. Despite my initial insistence that I could in no way contribute to the counterinsurgency, my refusals to make myself useful made the relationship a one-way street. He was helping me with my work, but I would not help him with his. In moments of frustration he would sneer to his subordinates, "He writes down everything," or provoke me with slurs. These exchanges highlighted the structural challenge of conducting this embedded ethnography: finding ways to reciprocate in my relationship with Nicolás without collaborating with the counterinsurgency.

My position was quite different from that of other anthropologists who draw upon split professional identities and assume institutional roles as an investment banker–researcher, or policy wonk–anthropologist, for example. As Winifred Tate notes, often this style of gaining deep institutional knowledge is born of a political affinity with the organization in which one embeds.[5] In my case there was no such affinity. Although my hosts had read me as an elite North American and supporter of the PAHD's project, they gradually realized that my critical and progressive positions were at odds with the narrative they sought to promulgate.

My embeddedness, rather, was more akin to that of critical investigative journalists who resist the message-control that the embedding system is designed for. The problem with embedded journalism, in my view, is when journalists report from only a single perspective. Monogamy when it comes to embedding is not a virtue. Yet anything other than monogamy gets tricky. Institutions hosting an embedded anthropologist can come to see the visitor as *their* anthropologist (an inversion of anthropologists' historical practice of referring to *their* tribe) and expect reciprocity for the access they provide—some political solidarity at least. Such was the dynamic I had to navigate in my research. Though I avoided reciprocating on work-related matters, I forged empathic, respectful relationships that over time transcended institutional positionality. I kept my promise not to publish my findings for years. Ultimately my interlocutors came to understand my purpose through the ebb and flow of the research more than any of my repeated efforts to describe it.

When I arrived at Nicolás's new office on the Caribbean coast in 2011, the impression that he had ascended in the army's hierarchy struck me as immediately as the chill blasting from the air conditioner above his desk. The large sliding door of his office offered a panorama of the countryside, a region that was both a tourist destination and wracked by neoparamilitary groups. Although a secretary tried to act as his gatekeeper, Nicolás's subordinates poured through the door with problems to solve, documents to sign, and breaking intelligence to appraise. This stream of personnel coming for counsel and authorization made his office feel strikingly familiar to me. I recognized the décor from his Bogotá office: the large diplomas from the Colombian Military Academy, the certificate from National Defense University in Washington, DC, and a postgraduate certificate from an elite Bogotá university, declaring him a specialist in conflict resolution.[6] During his studies Nicolás read the works of scholars such as Mark Duffield and Mary Kaldor who theorize "new wars," asymmetrical conflicts, and the convergence of militarism, development, and humanitarianism.[7] While our professional training and personal perspective could not have been more different, we both, in our respective professions, were grappling with the transformations of militarism in the late twentieth and early twenty-first centuries.

Above the doorway of Nicolás's office is a vow he signed: "The army will never be ashamed of me." He is proud not to be under investigation for human rights abuses. His rise through the officer corps has corresponded with what policy analysts call security sector reform. In the late 1990s and the 2000s the Ministry of Defense set out to create a cadre of counterinsurgency warriors with unblemished records, so as to avoid endangering the supply of US military aid over pesky human rights concerns.[8] Nicolás, who has risen to colonel and has good prospects of ascending to general, was a member of this cohort.

His leadership style was based upon an impetuous charisma. He swung from dour and demanding to warm and affectionate, skillfully performing these swings while gauging people's reactions. Punctilious about PowerPoints for the generals, he would demand that a map, slide, or chart be reworked repeatedly, to the chagrin of the subordinates whose weekends these tasks consumed. Nicolás could also be generous with his praise. When an analyst placed arrows on an aerial photograph showing the most likely transit corridor for rebels in a planned operation, Nicolás erupted in congratulatory high-fives and backslapping. On his iPad he studied the layout of *Semana.com*, the website of Colombia's principal newsweekly, for visual ideas to use in his PowerPoints, which he viewed as expressions of his professionalism to his superiors.

In step with military doctrine, Nicolás maintained his appearance meticulously. "At the first sign of a hole, I throw the shirt out," he once declared.[9] Like many Colombian colonels and generals who seek status in brand-name goods, he is fixated on Levi jeans, Oakley sunglasses, and Tommy Hilfiger clothing. This obsession became apparent as we walked around one of the battalion leadership's favorite places to socialize out of uniform: the mall. The brands and the mall both indexed a worldview in which status markers travel from north to south. But nothing signaled this mental hierarchy as strongly as Nicolás's repeated questions about the housing market in Orlando, Florida. While he had previously mused about getting out of the war and retiring somewhere on Colombia's Caribbean coast, at a certain point he began to pin his hopes on Florida. Like the rebels he tries to lure into the demobilization process, Nicolás knows that escaping his past will not be easy. The three years since we had seen each other (2008–11) had taken a toll on him. His boyishness had slipped away, his gaze had grown more cautious, and a belly popped beneath his shirts. Politically, I would label Nicolás right wing. He pumped his fist in the air while listening to the radio program of conservative politician Fernando Londoño (President Uribe's minister of the interior and justice) as Londoño listed the FARC's abuses of the civilian population. In hushed tones, however, he also confessed that he agrees with rebel critiques of economic inequality.

When we met again in 2011, I explained that I was still interested in the process of convincing mid-ranking rebels to abandon the insurgency. Could he help me? He perked up and reminded me that in 2007 and 2008, when he led the PAHD's strategic area team, more rebels had demobilized than in any other year. He assured me that militarized persuasion was still very much his business.

I arrived unaware of my good timing. Two weeks earlier Nicolás's unit had demobilized the third in command of the FARC's Twelfth Front, Pablo. I wanted to follow a case as it progressed, but given the sensitivity of such operations it was easier to learn about a past case. Nicolás instructed José, a young intelligence officer with carefully parted black hair, to talk me through the PowerPoint presentation about Operación Genuino, or Operation Genuine, a curious name, as we will see. José is Nicolás's right-hand man. Together they had presented the PowerPoint to President Juan Manuel Santos and Minister of Defense Juan Carlos Pinzón and received their personal congratulations. José clicked on the PowerPoint on his laptop, and fifty thumbnails populated the left side of the screen.

Operation Genuine

"We learned they were going to have a meeting of all of the front commanders from the bloc," José said. It was a *pleno* in the FARC's terminology, and it would be held in Colombian territory. The bloc in question is the Martín Caballero Bloc, which operated in Colombia's northeastern Caribbean region.[10] Militarily it was the weakest of the FARC's seven blocs, though arguably the guerrilla's most strategic in that it included a disproportionate number of the FARC's top ideologues, propagandists, and international spokespeople. Those big fish—or, in military lingo, OMAVEs (the acronym for "military targets of high strategic value")— camped on the Venezuelan side of the border. The Regional Military Intelligence unit, or RIME, which Nicolás commanded, learned about the regional meeting, but only three weeks before it took place. The RIME did not have time to spy on it, so Nicolás set out to figure out what happened after the fact. He learned about the bloc's annual plan for 2011: how many ambushes, how many acts of sabotage, and how much extortion, per front.

Within the FARC, blocs were subunits that covered territories too vast to oversee carefully. This means that fronts were the most salient units of command at a tactical level. Three commanders and three replacements composed a front's leadership. Bloc leaders were the equivalent of generals and front leaders the equivalent of colonels. The leadership of the Martín Caballero Bloc was composed largely of aging veterans; however, a few young stars were emerging as charismatic front leaders. None of those stars were rising as quickly as Pablo. One leader of the Martín Caballero Bloc, who was instrumental in the FARC's expansion into the Caribbean region in the late 1980s saw the politically persuasive and militarily assertive young commander as a son. According to the file the military kept on Pablo, he is purported to have led small FARC units that ambushed an army patrol, blew up railroad tracks and gas pipelines, erected roadblocks, and kidnapped people for ransom, a rap sheet that could earn him approximately thirty-five years in prison if convicted in the criminal justice system. Like much of the Martín Caballero Bloc, Pablo retreated toward Venezuela in 2003 when the military intensified its offensive in the Caribbean region, particularly in the Sierra Nevada de Santa Marta.[11]

Pablo's defection would deprive the bloc of an emerging leader, demoralize his subordinates, yield intelligence on the bloc's leadership,

and perhaps help to demobilize or kill an OMAVE. For Nicolás, demobilizing Pablo would lead to a cascade of "results." José had only begun clicking through the PowerPoint of Operation Genuine when Nicolás came over to ask me, "What do you think?"

"Very interesting, very rigorous," I said.

"Rigorous and with good results," Nicolás added.

The intelligence unit set out to determine the best messenger to pitch
demobilization to Pablo. Two informants that had infiltrated the Twelfth
Front provided photographs and short videos of Pablo that they had
taken surreptitiously with cell phone cameras in a camp on the Venezuelan side of the border. The photos looked like images that rebels
might upload to their Facebook pages. (Some rebels based in Venezuela
had Facebook profiles, and the percentage of guerrillas online surged in
2015 as peace negotiations intensified.) The photos are casual portraits
of guerrillas in candid poses, often proudly displaying their rifles. In one
of the videos Pablo interrupts a comrade listening to vallenato music
and orders him to prepare a meal.[12] When I expressed surprise that the
FARC allowed so many casual photographs to be taken, José responded,
"Between them it's OK," and then made a comparison that reminded me
that we were sitting in a hotbed of espionage and counterintelligence:
"It's like here, nobody knows who is taking photos for the other side."

The two spies concurred that Pablo's sister was the family member
closest to Pablo. Nicolás and his team reasoned that Pablo's sister had
direct access, "level 1," to Pablo, that he trusted her more than anyone
else. After weighing their options, they set out to recruit Pablo's sister,
who had demobilized from the FARC in the mid-2000s. They gave her a
code name, Abraham, and began an in-depth study of her life.

The RIME organized its study of Abraham into five categories: location and access, customs and routines, contacts, weaknesses and opportunities, strengths and threats. Posing at various times as public health
officials conducting a survey, representatives of the local housing authority, and market researchers for a cable television company, intelligence agents collected gossip from Abraham's neighbors. Curious about
this method, I prodded José for more details. The most common ruse, he
said, was to pose as market researchers for cell phone carriers and begin with questions such as "Which promotion do you like more, ten free
minutes, or call for less than five minutes as much as you like?" and then
shift the conversation.

"How do you get people talking?" I asked.

"They're very chatty, and we give a prize to the most helpful," José said. He returned to the story, forwarding to the next slide in the Power-Point:

Findings
- She has debts
- She almost lost her job, which pays poorly
- She works ten hours per day, six days a week
- She is easily persuaded by small favors
- Her mother is very ill
- She abandoned her studies in 9th grade

The slide describing her strengths and the liabilities of contacting her listed the following:

Strengths
- Suspicious of strangers
- Was part of the FARC
- Comes from a FARC family
- Has a good memory

Liabilities
- In contact with the Martín Caballero Bloc
- From a neighborhood with subversive elements
- Unstable personality
- Undefined politics

In designing an approach to Abraham, Nicolás's RIME decided to emphasize the opportunity to make money to pay her debts and support her mother. To "win her affection and willingness to work," as one sub-title in the PowerPoint read, they sent an agent to seduce her, or, in the literal translation of the Colombian Spanish, "to conquer her" (*conquistarla*). The conquest began on her long bus ride to work. The agent listened to her gripe about her boss and built rapport through casual conversation. I asked José if the agent and Abraham had slept together. He almost spat up the ice-pop he was sucking on. With a mixture of surprise and embarrassment he said, "I don't know. What's important is the work." After a pause he answered obliquely: "In some cases they stay together." Clearly, "conquest" is a common tactic.

While Nicolás's RIME conducted its research, the FARC's Fortieth Front, a close ally of Pablo's Twelfth Front, burned two tractor-trailers and a soda distribution truck and tagged them with FARC graffiti. The act sparked news stories expressing concern about the FARC's return to Cesar Department, where the military had supposedly vanquished it. The Fortieth and the Fifty-First Fronts proceeded toward the goals that the bloc leadership had set for them at the beginning of the year. The Twelfth Front lagged behind its two siblings in the northern Colombo-Venezuelan borderland. Operation Genuine progressed against a clock ticking at an unknown pace. In October 2011, technical intelligence revealed that Pablo was preparing to lead a commission of insurgents into Colombia. In early December 2011, the agent that Nicolás had sent to take Abraham dancing and "win her affection" invited her to lunch at a busy restaurant—"the most important moment of the operation," according to José. "If his voice quivers, everything is lost." At lunch, the agent slid a folder across the table. "Open it," he said. Inside were photos: Abraham at work, her son, Pablo. Between surprise and shock, she asked, "How do you know so much about me?" The agent asked about Pablo. She initially denied staying in touch with him but later conceded that they communicated regularly. Visibly distressed, she asked, "Are you going to kill him?" José paraphrased the agent's response: "No, we want him here like you, free."

Abraham agreed to help the RIME demobilize her brother. Agents met her the next day, and they agreed on a course of action: she would travel to her brother's camp when he was in Colombia; Christmas festivities provided a perfect opportunity. She carried whiskey, meat, and other gifts. Unbeknownst to her, the military hid a tracking device among the presents. What the RIME gained from this treacherous gift exchange was Pablo's exact location—a Christmas present to itself. On December 24 she hiked into the temporary camp where Pablo and his group of fifteen rebels were celebrating Christmas in the Sierra Nevada de Santa Marta mountain range. In a private moment, she appealed to her brother to demobilize and gave him a phone number to call.

At this point it is important to note that the FARC had a long-standing tradition of bolstering its troops' morale during the holiday season by throwing parties. I pause the story about Operation Genuine to quote from a conversation about Christmas in the insurgency with two former FARC combatants who are now married to each other.

FREDDY: [Christmas in the guerrilla] is tough because of the sadness of not
being able to be with family, but it's cool because you know, as of November, all of the units from the front start coming together. You know you're
going to go someplace and have the party—you make your bunk nice.

ALEJANDRA: A dance floor . . .

FREDDY: You know you are going to see people you haven't seen in months,
the happiness in seeing them is always with hugs and kisses. It's an awesome feeling.

ALEJANDRA: It's such a beautiful feeling it would make me want to cry.

FREDDY: Because when you go out on a commission, you say goodbye to
everyone as if . . .

ALEJANDRA: As if you weren't coming back.

The conversation returned to the party. I asked if it was not a security
risk to have the entire front in one place.

FREDDY: Of course, the commanders divide the front in two; half are put on
guard and the other half dance. The next day the other half stand guard
while the others dance.

ALEJANDRA: When they throw these parties there's lots of security in advance, and alcohol is very controlled. If there's going to be one hundred
people they calculate how many bottles and divide by the number of people so there are only two or three shots of aguardiente (an alcoholic beverage made of sugar cane that has an anise flavor) per person and nobody
gets drunk. Can you imagine the chaos if everyone was drinking and nobody was standing guard?

Pablo's commission of fifteen rebels was not able to be with their
families for Christmas, and neither could they celebrate with the rest of
their front in Venezuela. Pablo organized a small party to ease the isolation. After Abraham left the rebel camp the next day, December 25, she
called the intelligence agent who had seduced her and reported on the
encounter.

The optimal scenario for Nicolás and his RIME was to convince
Pablo to demobilize with his entire commission. José's eyes widened
with possibility as he said, "He was only the third commander [of the
front,] but he was the leader in Colombia." The goal of demobilizing
Pablo, and possibly his comrades, toward which Nicolás's RIME had

worked diligently for a year, was within reach. The military, however, is a hydra. Two different tactical intelligence teams working for antiguerrilla battalions in the mountain range had also located Pablo's commission. That information quickly made its way to the general commanding the Division. The general convened a meeting in which he decided to bomb Pablo's commission on December 25. Nicolás claimed he had opposed that decision to bomb. José, like Nicolás, disagreed with the decision but would express his disagreement only obliquely, insinuating that the generals were overzealous. He recalled how they would eagerly ask the RIME, "What is there to do?" Abraham knew none of this.

A female rebel in Pablo's commission died in the bombardment. The rest of the commission scattered and trekked back to Venezuela.

On December 26 Abraham called the intelligence agent. She was furious. "You tricked me! You made me kill my brother!" Almost simultaneously, Pablo called the number his sister had given him—he wanted to turn himself in.

Pablo had one condition: that his sister and her son be present as witnesses. This request, which the RIME honored, served as insurance against the military killing Pablo.

In a video that is the highlight of the PowerPoint, Nicolás wears no shirt but a bulletproof vest, and is illuminated only by the small light of the video camera. As he walks toward Pablo, he shouts, "Welcome to freedom!" Pablo emerges from the darkness stumbling down the mountainside, whimpering in an emotional overload.

Hoping to find other members of Pablo's commission and convince them to demobilize as well, José and other members of the RIME returned the next day to the site of the bombardment with Pablo, troops, and a megaphone. The sound of their voices calling after survivors of the attack drifted up the mountain. Only chirping birds responded. Then an officer in the RIME began to call the cell phones of members of Pablo's front. José re-created the ensuing conversation.

OFFICER: I'm going to pass you to a friend of yours.
PABLO: What's going on, *compañero*?
REBEL X: What? I thought the military killed you!
PABLO: No, I'm here doing well. You should come too.

Two members of Pablo's commission demobilized the following week.

José recited from memory the official one-sentence summary the

RIME gave the operation after its completion: "Operation Guenuine caused a series of voluntary presentations [demobilizations] that won the hearts and will of members of the Martín Caballero Bloc."

The PowerPoint ends with images of Pablo eating a *sancocho* soup with his mother and other family members. Knowing the backstory does not make the scene of Pablo's mother embracing him and beaming with joy any less heartwarming. Nicolás looked over our shoulders and said, "Look at that, the love of his mother. He was her lost son."

I met Pablo on my next trip to the coast, months after José gave me the PowerPoint briefing. Pablo wore charcoal-colored jeans, a striped shirt, and large bee-eyed sunglasses. We sat in the RIME's air-conditioned library. He had come to the RIME to pick up a check, one large enough to pay for a small plot of land. After explaining my research, I asked if he would grant me an interview. He asked a few questions, a quick cross-examination to ensure I was not affiliated with the guerrilla, and removed his sunglasses—a sign that I could proceed. He explained his precaution: "The FARC is offering $56,000 to whoever kills me."

Reflecting on his decision to join the FARC, Pablo described the two-day journey by donkey to transport coffee and vegetables from his family's farm to market, traveling unpaved roads and sleeping overnight on mountainsides. He then switched subjects to speak about the paramilitary incursion into Cesar Department. "They killed many people, people that didn't know anything about the guerrilla." He recited these stories and their implications confidently, and as he did I imagined him in camouflage "engaging the masses," the FARC's phrase for conducting politics through community relations. I could see him rousing an audience with the guerrilla's messages about the state's abandonment of rural areas and how the paramilitaries are merely an extension of an exclusive oligarchy. Pablo joined the FARC at the age of fifteen and deserted at thirty-six. He has fifteen siblings, six of whom joined the FARC. Of those six, five demobilized successfully, and one fled from a rebel camp in Venezuela only for the FARC to hunt him down in Venezuelan territory and execute him.

Pablo described the night after Christmas stoically: "They assaulted, shooting and bombarding. A girl was killed, and I was alone." In the moment that Pablo turned himself in, he had visions of his own death at the hands of the military. What happened was something else entirely. "They took me to the mall, the beach, things I never saw before," Pablo said. "Imagine, I never saw the ocean, and they were saying, 'Go in.'"

At the age of thirty-six, having lived in the Caribbean region his entire life, Pablo waded into the ocean and submerged himself in its salty water for the first time. If his voice was any indication, what most shocked him about his military handlers was "They asked me how I was feeling."

The RIME set out to seduce him, more figuratively than the agency had seduced his sister. They treated him to dinner in a fancy restaurant, let him climb into a helicopter, and gave him a turkey on December 31. Nicolás acknowledged that his colleagues' treatment of the demobilized is not always so kind. He contorted his face in mock anger and said, "Come here you son of a bitch, give me the information," to illustrate his point.

For Nicolás, the key to the process is spoiling (*consintiendo*) deserters from the moment of first contact and, in a Machiavellian sense, *caring* for the demobilized. When Juana, Marcela's assistant from the PAHD's communications team, came to visit Nicolás's RIME, he tried to convince her to lobby for a pilot program that would pay for a full-time psychologist at his base. The psychologist would profile FARC leaders and attend to former combatants. Nicolás wanted "someone who is humble and wants to solve the problems of the demobilized, not someone who only wants a salary." Though they agreed it was a good idea, neither Nicolás nor Juana—each schooled in the bureaucracy of the Ministry of Defense—had any expectation that the idea would come to fruition. In the three-part trajectory that former combatants must pass through, humanitarian considerations are left for the last stage.

The ideal institutional trajectory for former rebels upon turning themselves in goes as follows:

1. Disarmament. Former combatants should spend no more than two weeks on a base being interrogated. Any work they do with or for the military is voluntary.
2. Demobilization. The demobilized should live for no more than two months in a halfway house while awaiting certification and keeping up a highly regimented daily routine with other former combatants.
3. Reintegration. Upon receiving certification, the Ministry of Defense passes former guerrillas to the Colombian Reintegration Agency (ACR). At this point, the military should no longer contact them. The demobilized receive basic welfare and are encouraged to create businesses or find work (see chapter 4).

In practice, these periods often extend far beyond the allotted time frames. What is more, the military deftly manipulates categories such as "voluntary" and coaxes former guerrillas into active collaboration, especially during the first two phases, by playing on their legally precarious status and promising financial rewards. Officers frequently ignore prohibitions on contacting the demobilized after they enter the reintegration phrase.

After a brief period living on Nicolás's base and working with the RIME, Pablo went to a PAHD halfway house in Bogotá, where he stayed for two and a half months. At the time of our interview, after his certification, he was working construction in a small town while continuing to collaborate with the military. Nicolás boasted to Juana that the operation to demobilize Pablo had been "so effective that he still helps us, still advises us." José made a comment that reverberated through my research: "The demobilized keep a sense of connection to two or three officials they meet upon demobilizing." He paused and then continued, "Everyone wants to take from the demobilized; few want to give."

During his time working in the PAHD headquarters in 2007 and 2008, Nicolás realized the importance of winning trust. He learned the power of the gift, even if the gift was only a cell phone minute or a cigarette. Operation Genuine combined the exploitation of emotional bonds between guerrillas and their families, the seductiveness of gifts, and the crass persuasion of cash—the three axes of Nicolás's demobilization strategy. Over the years I have seen his perspective gradually ripple through the military. It did not surprise me when José said that the war college in Bogotá uses Operation Genuine as a case study.

I have heard rumors of what one former official in the reintegration program referred to as a "cartel" within the Ministry of Defense that steals the financial rewards to be paid to the demobilized. Allegations of such corruption rarely spill into the national press.[13] During my fieldwork, the PAHD's central office struggled to track down and pay reward money it owed to former rebels from as many as nine years earlier. When I asked why, the former sergeant charged with wading through the morass of paperwork assured me it was simply bureaucratic dysfunction. Although I was unconvinced that this was true at the national level, and have interviewed many former rebels who complained that military units did not fulfill their side of the mercenary bargain, from what I can tell, Nicolás's RIME paid the demobilized promptly for their collaboration.

An internal decree of the Ministry of Defense, Directive 22 of 2011, governs transactions between the military and former rebels. That document specifies how much the military will pay for weapons, equipment, or chemicals that the demobilized bring with them, or help to locate, as well as the amount to be paid for information leading to various "results." Directive 22 of 2011 sheds light on the material foundation of Colombia's armed conflict. Here are some of the prices listed in the eighteen-page document:

- .50 caliber machine gun—$5,550
- hand grenade—$1,110
- a dozen camouflaged pants—$14
- surface-to-air missile—$16,600
- satellite telephone—$556
- cell phone with SIM card—$11
- laptop, hard drive, CPU, USB drive, or iPod with information of interest for military intelligence—$830
- detonator cord—$0.56 per meter
- laboratory for transforming hydrochloride into cocaine—up to $3,300
- mule—$28
- testifying against leaders—$1,110
- locating mass graves—$560
- locating a minefield (five mines or more)—$133
- demobilization of a rank-and-file guerrilla—$278; of a front leader—$27,800; of a bloc leader—$83,300

These figures represent the military's best approximation of the war's political economy.

I do not know how much money Pablo has received for his work with the military, but at one point Nicolás urged a member of his unit to present him with an oversized check and take a photograph of him holding it, remediating images of lottery winners. Monetary awards, gifts of strategic compassion, and the emotional exploitation of family connection work together—and in conjunction with the PAHD's sophisticated consumer-marketing campaigns—to fuel a cycle of demobilization, intelligence gathering, military operations, and more demobilizations.

I was amazed, but not surprised, that the same institution that organized Pablo's family reunion had tried to ensure his violent death. In thinking about the way Nicolás's RIME cared for Pablo and the military's instrumentalization of compassion, I continued to stew over the decision to bomb Pablo's camp. On a subsequent trip to the RIME, I asked José and Nicolás, again, "Why did the military decide to bomb?" José exclaimed, "We didn't," and deflected responsibility for the decision to the brigade and division leadership (all generals). He repeated the RIME's preference to demobilize the entire commission. The idea of a group demobilizing seemed implausible to me. It is one thing for an individual to desert, but for someone to reveal their treacherous intentions to fourteen of their comrades is something else entirely. Leadingly, I said, "But that was unlikely." José responded immediately: "No, we did a psychological study of the others and they also wanted to see their families." Independently, Nicolás said the same thing. The RIME's focus on demobilizing a small unit of guerrilla fighters made sense—it would have been national news and earned Nicolás high praise within the army, all but assuring his ascent to full colonel and putting him on track for promotion to brigadier general. (A previous group demobilization in 2006 turned out to be a staged event designed to create the impression that the FARC was imploding. The revelation became a major scandal.)[14] Bombardment, with its promise of rebel deaths, would have benefited the commanding generals, not Nicolás.

By my third trip to the coast I had learned enough to know that while Nicolás might not have had the rank to make the decision to bomb, he must have been involved in the final discussion. I pressed my question: "Why did they decide to bomb?" Nicolás responded tersely, "He had a chance to leave but didn't," and walked away. I sensed he knew this was a fraught answer. The military had bombed less than twenty-four hours after Pablo's sister made the offer. Could Pablo really have acted on the offer that quickly? What the series of events illustrates is that the military's long-standing emphasis on combat kills trumped demobilization, despite official declarations to the contrary.

The Ministry of Defense's Directive 300-28 of 2007 purports to reassess the value of various "results" within the military. Article 3B reads, "From this date onward, when measuring operational results, collective and individual demobilizations will be privileged above captures, and captures above kills in combat." The directive goes on to conclude that the goal of the reform is to ensure "the defense, protection and guarantee of human rights and the application and respect of humanitarian law." If the language of human rights seems forced, that's because it is. This decree, which made demobilizing guerrillas more important in rising through the military ranks than killing guerrillas in combat, was an anticipatory parry of a brewing but not yet public scandal that would shake the Ministry of Defense for more than a decade.

Lip service to humanitarian law aside, Directive 300-28 responded to the tragedies put in motion by another directive, number 29 of 2005, which had institutionalized a bounty of approximately $2,000 to be paid to soldiers for each guerrilla fighter they killed.[15] The perverse incentive motivated military officers to pose as recruiters and kidnap young men from the shantytowns of southwest Bogotá, transferred them halfway across the country to the department of North Santander, and dressed them in fatigues before murdering them and presenting their corpses as combat kills. They then claimed reward money for their *bajas*, literally "downings," a military euphemism for kills.[16] The scandal came to be known by another euphemism, "false positives," and was the most sordid human-rights violation committed by the Colombian military in recent history. The United Nations sent a special rapporteur to investigate how widespread the extrajudicial killings had been.[17] He concluded that the incidents were endemic in a military culture saturated with the logic of financial incentives—a finding later corroborated by Human Rights Watch.[18]

Read with the advantage of hindsight, Directive 300-28 of 2007, which changed the hierarchy of value for military promotions—making demobilizations worth more than kills—takes on additional meanings. I reasoned that its language of human rights, its promise that demobilizations would be valued over captures and kills, and its pledge to safeguard the "legitimacy that is considered the center of gravity of the military forces" were intended to preempt a scandal in waiting. I suggested this hypothesis to James, a lawyer and the formal liaison between the PAHD and the president's office, as well as Nicolás's close collaborator in 2007 and 2008. He urged me to sit down so he could convince me otherwise, but offered no facts to contradict my hypothesis. When I interviewed his boss, Sergio Jaramillo, who served as the national security adviser and high peace commissioner in the Santos administration, I asked if Directive 300-28 of 2007 had been an attempt to parry the coming false positives scandal. Jaramillo was more honest, if understated. "It would be naive to think there was no connection," he said. Jaramillo conceded that despite the ministerial directive, kills still trumped demobilizations and captures within the institutional culture of the Ministry of Defense. He insisted, however, that Directive 300-28 raised the importance of demobilization within the armed forces. When I invoked Directive 300-28 in one of my discussions with Nicolás, he simply rolled his eyes to indicate the persistent breach between the document and reality.

In the economy of military honor, Nicolás won out over the general who ordered the air strike against Pablo's camp. As José explained, the brigade commander's "result" was one kill of someone insignificant in the FARC hierarchy, while the RIME's "result" was the demobilization of a front leader and subsequent demobilizations, including a ranking member of the Martín Caballero Bloc, which led to other "results." A slide in the PowerPoint of Operation Genuine attributed seventeen demobilizations and four kills to Pablo's demobilization. Seven months after Pablo staggered down the mountainside to turn himself in, Brigadier General Jorge Eliecer Suárez Ortiz, who commanded the division, called a press conference to boast of the forty demobilizations in his region that year: twenty-nine from the FARC and eleven from the ELN. At the press conference, Suaréz arrayed many of those ex-combatants behind him like human trophies and declared, "We will continue conducting operations throughout the Caribbean region with the objective of defeating the guerrilla."[19] Dressed in white shirts with the PAHD's logo, the former combatants sat with their chins tucked to their chests and baseball caps pulled down over their eyes.

The formation refashioned scenes of captured criminals, seized drugs, or confiscated weapons marshaled for the cameras, a recursive trope (and arguably an organizing principle) of the television news that captivates audiences throughout the country at noon and 7 p.m. every day. As Pablo's case illustrates, the line between capture in combat and demobilization can be thin. For the military, capturing rebels involves not only paperwork with the police to process former combatants in the criminal system but also the risk of accusations of human rights abuses by the detainees and their families. Crucially, captured rebels are less likely to collaborate than those who demobilize.

Peace and Sadness

The timing of my research coincided with secretive meetings between the Colombian government and the FARC, encounters that would evolve into full-fledged negotiations and ultimately a peace agreement in November 2016. Former Venezuelan president Hugo Chávez helped to persuade senior FARC leaders that armed struggle had become an antiquated way of effecting change.[20] Many of Chávez's closest contacts in the FARC came from the top rung of the Caribbean Bloc, making Nicolás's work all the more "strategic." In my interviews with Pablo and Vladimir, another FARC front leader who demobilized shortly after Pablo, both mentioned having witnessed furtive arrangements for meetings between FARC leaders and senior Venezuelan officials. Only months after their demobilization, news of the clandestine negotiations became public and the possibility of peace gripped the country for the first time in ten years. On August 27, 2012, President Santos announced that the Colombian government and the FARC had agreed upon a five-point agenda for negotiations to take place in Havana, Cuba.

The effect of the peace process on the individual demobilization program became a subject of speculation within the Ministry of Defense. PAHD officials in Bogotá blamed the negotiations for falling demobilization statistics. Fewer people demobilized in 2012 than in any prior year. Many PAHD staff reasoned that guerrillas would not risk their lives to desert, knowing it involved informing on former comrades, when the same benefits, or more generous ones, might be available a few years later without the risks.

Yet three weeks after Pablo turned himself in, Vladimir did the same. After twenty-eight years of fighting the Colombian government—twelve in the ELN and then sixteen in the FARC—Vladimir decided that armed struggle was anachronistic. Members of the PAHD in Bogotá boasted about Vladimir's demobilization. He was not only part of the command of a front in the Martín Caballero Bloc but also close to Iván Márquez, the FARC's No. 2 who would be the group's lead negotiator in Havana. Within the FARC Vladimir was considered an ideologue, a skilled orator who forged political alliances with individuals, communities, and civil society groups. I accompanied Vladimir and his reticent wife, also a longtime militant in the FARC, to an interview they gave to military radio in northwestern Bogotá. In that interview, he said: "For a year I have been analyzing the political situation in Colombia. . . . I saw that in Colombia changes were happening, small as they were. I also looked at how violence as a form of struggle was wearing thin. I felt the struggle to change Colombian institutions was possible in a different way." The Santos administration could not have asked for a more convenient message. (It may have cajoled Vladimir into delivering exactly that message.)

I happened to be living on Nicolás's military base when former President Uribe leaked news of the peace talks via his Twitter account, prompting President Santos to publicly disclose the negotiations. The country buzzed with the news. Many people allowed themselves to indulge in a rare moment of hope that *maybe this time* peace might be possible. But in the two-story building of the RIME's headquarters the mood was so somber that Nicolás called a full-team meeting. He gathered the fifty people in the building and gave them a pep talk. His message was simple: "We have to support the president, he is a former minister of defense, he knows what he's doing." I don't think Nicolás believed what he was saying; rather, he was performing his loyalty to the chain of command.

If there was a president that the agents in the RIME supported, it was former president Álvaro Uribe. When his name came up in conversation that day, I asked Nicolás if the generals liked him. He pressed his hands together and bowed to indicate that I had made an understatement. Nicolás kept a photograph on his desk of himself as a younger man in uniform meeting President Uribe. In my informal survey of the intelligence officers in the RIME, "trick" (*trampa*) was the word most commonly used to express their skepticism about the peace process. They reasoned that the FARC had no intention of demobilizing as a group: it only needed a breather from the war and a microphone to claim the political legitimacy that the Colombian government, and especially its intelligence apparatus, had worked so diligently to diminish.

There was something personal about the pessimism that day. The officers felt that their hard, dangerous work weakening the FARC militarily and politically was being undone. As far as Nicolás and his unit were concerned, no ceasefire had been announced. Until further notice, work meant war as usual. A stream of agents came to Nicolás's office to plan for an operation in the Perijá mountain range along the Venezuelan border. The military planned to attack a rebel camp located eight thousand feet above sea level with Black Hawk helicopters. With a trio of agents looking over his shoulder, Nicolás inspected aerial photographs and mused aloud: "If the commander doesn't move his troops soon, they're in trouble."

A Targeted Video

In 2012 the PAHD began to send personalized video appeals directly to FARC leaders. The first came from Nicolás and his team. Ambitiously, the video targeted Julián, a bloc leader, a member of the old guard who had joined the FARC in 1970, one of the FARC's first generation of commanders. The video that the RIME sent Julián comprised five talking-head interviews with his daughter; his ex-wife; Karina, a former high-ranking FARC rebel who has been collaborating with the government since 2008; a PAHD lawyer who explained the commander's eligibility to have a forty-year sentence reduced to five to eight years under the Justice and Peace Law of 2005; and a different PAHD official who listed the financial rewards for collaborating. The PAHD's communications team recorded the sections of the video in which the bureaucrats spoke; the RIME focused on his family.

At the RIME I saw the final version of the video that the military sent to Julián. Interestingly, the final cut did not include the lawyer mentioning the five-to-eight-year jail sentence. It relied primarily on the emotional punch of the daughter's appeal. Lowe/SSP3 "attacks the heart" with its Christmas commercials, and this video did the same thing in a much more targeted form. Sitting atop a bed in a plush hotel with an imitation Jackson Pollock painting behind her, the commander's daughter, a university student, begins to cry as she recalls that her father was not present for her coming-of-age party, her fifteenth birthday. Wiping tears from her cheeks, she says, "It doesn't matter that you're a guerrilla. To me you're the best father in the world."

The FARC commander's ex-wife follows the daughter's appeal. She stoically reminds him, "There's an opportunity for you to demobilize. Once you mentioned it, but couldn't." Then she tries a different tack, invoking Julián's mother: "She thinks about you all the time. She wants to spend her last moments with you and her grandchildren." The ex-wife continues, "You always wanted to have a farm. We'll buy it for you, and there you are. If you want to be a professional in the city, close to us, we know people who can help." Finally she adds, "The government is trying to solve things." *Things* refers to Julián's legal situation. The demobilization program does not forgive breaches of international humanitarian law or crimes against humanity—a detail edited out of the video. Since he is a bloc leader who has spent more than forty years in the insurgency, the attorney general's dossier on Julián includes a litany of crimes, including kidnapping and recruiting children.

Karina, the former rebel turned government collaborator, concludes: "My message is that you make the decision and demobilize." The last person to appear in the video is the least convincing, a bureaucrat who presses his hands together when he says, "There are financial rewards for bringing people with you."

I turned to Verónica, the woman charged with showing me the video, and asked, "Do you think he'll come?"

"I think so. His daughter has the power to move him," she said.

"But he barely leaves the neighboring country," I said, intentionally using the military euphemism for Venezuela.

"We'll have to find the opportunity," she said, taking a pause.

I turned to Verónica's boss, who came over to the computer screen and was conspicuously peering into my notebook. "What do you think?" I asked.

"He's someone who is very radical, *very* radical. But everyone's weak spot is the family," he said.

This last phrase—"everyone's weak spot is the family"—was one that Nicolás repeated regularly. When Juana, Marcela's assistant from the communications team in Bogotá, visited Nicolás's unit to coordinate national and regional propaganda efforts, he spoke proudly of the video featuring the commander's daughter. Nicolás recounted how he had made the daughter cry when he asked if she knew where the money for her college education was coming from. He put his finger to the inside corner of his right eye and wiped away an imaginary tear to emphasize the point. "Their soft spot is the family, especially here on the coast," he said. "Even Alex Fattal calls his family," he said, referencing a call I had received from my brother the day before.

Nicolás suggested that Juana and her team in Bogotá start a campaign with the message "Whoever demobilizes now will receive the benefits of the peace process." I interjected, "Can you promise that? Legally it's not clear." The question prompted an immediate and emphatic response from Nicolás: "Legally, everything is messed up. Do you think it's OK that someone who has killed three hundred peasants only gets eight years of jail?" He paused to let the question linger before repeating, "Legally, everything is messed up." Nicolás transformed the sacrifice of punitive justice for political accommodation at the heart of transitional justice into a justification for dismissing the law. Upon reflection, it made sense. Nicolás's work, which included creating NGOs secretly under military control as means of waging what he called "political warfare," continuously flitted between the legal and the illegal. The law in his world was malleable if not outright dismissible. Secrecy shrouds transgressions he may commit; what is important is that he show "results." The law of results, the one that most immediately binds Nicolás, is the murk-iest of all.[21]

The legal gray zone of the demobilization program concentrates on questions of crimes against humanity and war crimes. Those who have committed such crimes should submit to the Justice and Peace Law of 2005, the transitional justice program that offers reduced sentences of five to eight years in exchange for the unabridged truth about their crimes. In practice, however, many guerrillas responsible for crimes against humanity and war crimes join the PAHD. The state turns a blind eye to these cases because of the counterinsurgency benefits it reaps from individual demobilization. The majority of former guerrillas who submitted to Justice and Peace have waited eight years without being formally convicted. They leave jail after that period but without the legal process running its course. This is but one instance of a wider phenom-enon in which the legal architecture created by the historical sedimenta-tion of transitional justice laws crumples under the weight of legal ambi-guities, heavy caseloads, and bureaucratic ineptitude.[22]

The question for Nicolás, in his "results"-dominated world, was, would Julián demobilize? "He is too ideologically committed to the FARC" was José's appraisal. Pablo, who knows Julián personally, claimed he wanted to demobilize but could not show it. (This opinion could be tinged by Pablo's desire to continue to make himself valuable to the RIME.) For Nicolás, the $12,000 that he estimated passed through the command-er's hands weekly was the strongest magnet keeping him from leaving the guerrilla. Nicolás pinned his hopes for Julián's defection on the com-mander's love for his daughter. "He calls her 'my sweet,'" Nicolás told Juana. The counterweight to that hope was the fact that the commander had a son with him in Venezuela who was also a member of the FARC. The intelligence officer who monitors the son's hacked Facebook account opined, "He is going to be badass [berraco], like his father." The com-mander never deserted.

A "Humanitarian" Counterinsurgency and the Militarization of Social Life

The stories of Nicolás's effort to demobilize Pablo and Julián are sto-ries about how the military exploits intimacy, gaming an affective matrix of allegiance, paranoia, emotional bonds, compassion, and seduction to prompt the desired betrayal.[23] For those outside of Colombia's demobilization program, this complex matrix is hidden beneath the dual cloaks of humanitarian/postconflict discourse and corporatized propaganda. But for those spies and former rebels at the center of this classified realm, the battle to turn members of the insurgency into informants injects the war further into family life and other intimate spheres. Che Guevara famously claimed that love is the spirit of revolutionary praxis. [24] In Colombia, however, it is the state's counterrevolutionary project that has converted love into a central axis of targeted persuasion. It is a move that turns love of the revolution inside out and seeks to displace it with the love of family, lovers, and close friends. This plays out in the way Nicolás's RIME depends upon a sister's love for her brother or a daughter's love for her long-lost father.

Love is also the most coveted means for accruing brand value. As anthropologists of advertising have shown, marketing seeks to guide consumers into funneling their affective investments back into products. This in turn deepens the commodification of daily life long lamented by Max Horkheimer, Theodor Adorno, and their colleagues in the Frankfurt school. Like data-driven emergent marketing tactics that seek to create new markets by insinuating themselves into increasingly intimate spheres, wars waged principally through human intelligence operate on ever more personal levels. In Colombia the PAHD, through its dialectics of secrecy and spectacle, serves as a vehicle for their convergence, which drives the double movement of the commodification and militarization of daily life.

Responses to the militarization of intimacy pass unrecognized by those outside the classified world of the PAHD's intelligence operations.[25] Instead of a public reckoning with the muddled moral matrix of Nicolás's RIME, the Colombian state offers a symbolic onslaught in propaganda campaigns such as Operation Christmas. The synthesis of these two Christmas stories illuminates the contradictory assemblage of humanitarian and counterinsurgency discourses and practices. The "humanitarian" offer to reunite Pablo with his family cannot be separated from the military prerogative to rain bombs on his encampment. Would Pablo have demobilized if not for the fright of the aerial assault? Would the military have been able to hit its target so precisely if not for its intelligence work to demobilize Pablo? The counterinsurgency is rendered more effective by its humanitarian pretensions, to the point that military intelligence officers care for and even spoil deserters. Nicolás's plea for a psychologist on the base is not motivated by concern for the mental health of the demobilized but by a desire to win trust in order to extract information. In the argot of public policy in which punishment and inducement operate together, sticks and carrots, the stick and the carrot have melded into each other. The sensitive information that former rebels provide is the reciprocity expected (and often demanded) for the legal forgiveness, personal gifts, monetary rewards, and basic welfare provided by the state.

Sometimes this exchange is felicitous, such as when Pablo's handlers won his active collaboration, prompting a cascade of other demobilizations and leaving Pablo satisfied to the point that he says with sincerity, "We are all brothers and sisters, we are all Colombians." But it does not always work that way. For instance, Nicolás's intelligence unit located an alleged member of the Martín Caballero Bloc who was visiting his family. The major left in charge of the RIME while Nicolás attended a three-day Central Military Intelligence meeting in Bogotá planned an "operation of confrontation" to demobilize the alleged FARC member. Having overheard a conversation about the case, I interjected, "How can you demobilize somebody if you have no proof he's a member of the FARC?" The major responded smugly: "I'm going to arrive with someone who is demobilized who will say, 'You did this and that and this.'" The accusation, he hoped, would lead the alleged guerrilla to incriminate himself and then accept the demobilization offer when facing the prospect of jail. I repeated, somewhat confused, "But there's no arrest warrant for this guy." The major's face brightened, indicating he had planned for that: "If he says no, I'll take a picture of him with the troops and send it to the [FARC]." I raised my eyebrows, struggling to contain my shock. The major added, "The guy will be burned." If the "operation of confrontation" didn't yield a demobilization, it would sow divisions in the guerrilla and potentially spur the FARC to kill its own troops, which would drive down morale and potentially lead to more demobilizations. The confrontation never happened. The alleged guerrilla fled the area, leaving only beer bottles as a trace.

Demobilization added new layers to the covert war against the FARC. For example, the military extricated some of its spies from risky situations under the cover of demobilization. The halfway houses, where the demobilized waited to be certified, were dens of intelligence and counterintelligence. While I was researching in one of those homes, the PAHD's strategic area team began interviewing the demobilized in the houses as well as in the program's offices to weed out FARC spies. I spoke with Marta, a demobilized rebel who had been sexually abused by a FARC commander. When the commander found out she was pregnant with his child, he sent two rebels to "demobilize" and gather intelligence about her. Marta observed that her former comrades "were very stiff, like they had orders." She asked to be transferred to a different halfway house. They soon abandoned the demobilization program and returned to southern Colombia, where they were promptly assassinated. Marta speculated that the FARC killed them because they had not completed their mission and therefore might have switched sides.

Simply put, the demobilization program had become a new front in the war, and as with other fronts, death surrounded it. The dead include those who tried to desert but were caught and faced the FARC's firing squad, as well as family members of former rebels who had nothing to do with the war but were the only people available to be punished for the transgressions of a deserter. In one of the focus groups led by Lowe/SSP3 that I attended, one former guerrilla put it bluntly: "Before, the FARC didn't mess with the family. Not anymore." As the deceptions of war became more intricate, the demobilized and their kin were nudged into its invisible front lines.

In contrast to the United Nations' vision of demobilization policy as a means of separating people from armed conflict, the intelligence emphasis of the Colombian government's individual demobilization program keeps combatants linked to the war and prompts acts of blowback. As anthropologist Joseph Masco has noted, blowback—the reaction to a covert operation—is rendered unintelligible to publics unaware of the classified act to which the blowback responds.[26] With the covert war hidden from public view, the compassionate, conciliatory, "humanitarian" image of the demobilization program as established in mass-media campaigns such as Operation Christmas was left unchallenged. Blowback from the PAHD's classified actions, an unknown quantity of death and displacement, was considered acceptable collateral damage for a *seemingly* more humane and an increasingly effective counterinsurgency. Between 2003 and 2016, the FARC's military influence waned in all but a few regions where the group had historically served as the de facto authority. The military's battlefield success was due, in part, to the demobilization program that picks apart entire military structures from within. After Pablo demobilized, the Twelfth Front went into receivership of the larger and more cohesive Fortieth Front.

If my framing of Colombia's individual demobilization program sounds like a diagnosis of schizophrenia, allow me to complicate the judgment underlying such a diagnosis. The deeper I have gone in my research, the further I myself am stuck in a moral spiderweb. Here is an excerpt from a field note I wrote on August 25, 2012. Nicolás had invited me into his home on the base after a long day in the office.

> In his room he leaned back in a leather recliner, turned on his flat-screen TV and settled on a series about urban warfare in Brazil. A torture scene came on in which the military police wrapped a bag around a person's neck, prompting him to convulse violently to try to get it off. Nicolás commented knowingly, "Bag." The man on the screen kicked in his chair. "Now take it off so he doesn't die," Nicolás said. Seconds later that is just what happened on the screen, as the interrogators returned to questioning. "That doesn't happen anymore," he said.

Nicolás's claim that torture, or at least the suffocation variety, "doesn't happen anymore" is what interests me. Reliable statistics about torture in Colombia do not exist, though from anecdotes that percolate into the public sphere it is clear that the tactic has not been abandoned.[27] My own inference from a plethora of signs is that the state has substantially reduced its use of torture. This reduction is due in large part to the fact that the state outsourced the more macabre dimensions of the counterinsurgency to the paramilitaries in the 1990s and early 2000s.[28] The paramilitaries' use of torture, which included practices as gruesome as playing soccer with human heads, served to intimidate its enemies and dissuade civilians from collaborating with the guerrilla. As an intelligence-gathering function, however, torture has come under withering critique as ineffective (in addition to common sense outrage regarding its moral reprehensibility).[29] To what extent has the individual demobilization program at the heart of this book displaced torture as a tactic of collecting intelligence? Perhaps those best positioned to answer that question are members of the FARC.

Fast forward to March 2016, when I interviewed one of Nicolás's archenemies. Four years after I concluded the fieldwork for this chapter, I sat in the lower level of the Hotel Palco in Havana, Cuba, across from Rodrigo Granda, a member of the FARC's secretariat, its most powerful body. In 2004 he had been captured by Colombian intelligence officers in Caracas, brought to Colombia, and imprisoned. (Two years later the Colombian government freed him as part of diplomatic wrangling to try to free Franco-Colombian celebrity hostage Íngrid Betancourt.) When I asked him about the individual demobilization program, he said:

> It's buying your consciousness, putting a price on the head of the leaders, weaponry. It's promising the moon and the stars so people desert from the revolutionary organizations, so they betray the goals of the revolution. But in Colombia this has degenerated miserably. Many of the people who abandon the ranks oftentimes do it because the intelligence services have him or his family in their sights. Now when they capture a militant of the FARC or the ELN they don't disappear him, they don't torture him like they did before. They bring him to a five-star hotel and pay for a few nights there. Military intelligence specialists visit him, psychologists come and say, "You should collaborate with us, your mom is over there, your siblings over there, your cousins over there."

The observations of both Nicolás (whose star continues to rise within the army) and Granda coincide. Demobilization policy provided an alternative to torture as a means of collecting actionable human intelligence, and with an added benefit—it generated press favorable to the counterinsurgency as opposed to scathing human rights reports. Recall the motto above the threshold to Nicolás's office: "The army will never be ashamed of me."

Nicolás is part of an elite officer corps that has come of age in a decade of military reforms, which include collecting intelligence through means more subtle than torture.[30] Here it is important to highlight Colombia's role as laboratory for US counterinsurgency and the Obama administration's disavowal of its predecessor's willingness to torture. As investigative journalist Dana Priest reported for the *Washington Post* in 2013: "The CIA also trained Colombian interrogators to more effectively question thousands of FARC deserters, without the use of the 'enhanced interrogation' techniques approved for use on al-Qaeda." By the late 2000s, in the wake of the Abu Ghraib scandal, the fact that torture produces bad press and costs precious legitimacy had again been confirmed. The PAHD, as a testing ground for US policy, managed to collect intelligence that was of paramount interest to the counterinsurgency while also compensating for Colombia's other long-standing deficiency: legitimacy.[31] Through a dialectics of spectacle and secrecy the PAHD has become a vehicle for rebranding the armed forces, and ultimately the state, so that it might project, perform, and—in some ever-deferred future—embody a legitimate sovereign authority capable of monopolizing violence.

Redefining demobilization policy as a form of counterinsurgency may be reprehensible, but what is the moral calculus when the point of comparison is torture? I pose this question not as an apology for the program or as an attempt to relativize its problematic dimensions, but rather as a provocation to grapple with through the rest of this book. Any answer, however partial, must be considered in light of the experiences of former rebels as they transition to civilian life.

Claudia

c: *My dad was a person who always worked with the organization, helping the FARC. Sometimes I saw him leave with pots of food. He would go and we would wonder who those pots of food were for. He never told us anything. One day—you know how when you're a kid and dying of curiosity—we wanted to know. Me and my brother followed him.*

In the countryside many people have thatched canopies [enramadas] where they grind stalks and take out the sugarcane and sugarcane juice, so we saw him arrive at one of those canopies and there was a group of people all dressed in military clothes, but we didn't know who they were or anything. The only thing I remember was saying to my brother, "That's not the army, because my dad is very persecuted by the army. He's not going to meet with the same people who are looking to put him in jail." But I couldn't imagine who they were.

a: How old were you?

c: *I was twelve or thirteen, tiny, and my brother was younger. Later my parents separated. We were four from that marriage, two men and two women. My dad made the decision to divide us like we were a flock of chickens: "You take this one, I'll take that one." So my dad said, "I'll keep my daughters," and my mom kept the boys—that's how it went. . . .*

One day [my cousin and I] were planning to catch a chicken to eat. We were talking trash when we heard the thud of a door crashing. It was my dad who had arrived but couldn't open the door, so kicked it and almost knocked it off. He asked us, "What are you doing here?" We were drinking sugarcane liquor, and we told him we were planning to kill a chicken and make dinner. He said, "No! Get out of here, the paramilitaries are coming, they're following us. Get out of here!"

He took us out. What the kid [her cousin] did was grab me by the hand,

and we took off down through the coffee plants. When we passed through a field we could feel that crazy firestorm. The bullets whistled above us and hit the branches on top of us, and we kept running down through coffee plants. My dad took off in a different direction, and I said to the kid, "We're running but where are we going?"

"Your dad said that we should go down there, that people are waiting for us," he said.

We didn't know who they were, but there were a lot of people: children, women with children, old men already grandfathers. Everyone was huddled together. They introduced themselves as being from the FARC and all that. When I saw them, I thought, "Those people, I saw them that time I followed my dad with the pots. They were dressed the same."

They got us out of there, walking the entire night. They took us and made us go down through some jagged rocks hanging by vines, and from there through some pastures.

Then my dad came. They took all of those people out to Cali, because they knew things were getting complicated. They took my dad out because he was being persecuted, so he couldn't go by bus on a normal road. After walking all night we got to a place that was supposedly their camp, and we stayed there for a week. Since my dad couldn't leave, he told us that we should leave and catch a bus to Cali.

The kid called me over and said, "They are telling me that I should go with them." There was a commander there who had spoken to him and proposed that he join [the guerrilla].

The kid asked me, "What should I do?"

I said, "You're the one who knows, you'll see if you go or not."

Then a commander came to speak with him again. I was right next to him, listening as he explained everything. He talked about how if my cousin went with the guerrillas he couldn't leave, that he would have to follow a set of rules.

I saw how the kid was getting excited, and it started happening to me—as the saying goes, the crazy—and I said to the kid, "If you go, I am going too." [Laughs] I said, "Let's go!"

He said, "Do you really want to come with me?"

I said, "Yeah, let's go, the two of us." But then I started thinking, "How am I going to tell my dad?"

My dad, in the beginning, got angry and said, why was I going to stop going to school? He said, "Just because I am working with these people doesn't mean you have to." He explained, "It's difficult—if you go, you

can't come home, because things will get complicated. After you are in the
hands of those people, you'll have to forget about us."

I said, "It doesn't matter, I am going."

My dad said, "You'll see. Make your decision, but later don't say that
I sent you."

I left with those people. They left me and the kid together for a week,
but then they called everyone together and separated us.

A: Why did you make that decision? What were you thinking in that moment?

C: *[Laughing] I don't know, I don't know, I don't know. It happened quickly.*
I don't know why. Well, I liked it, it seemed cool to be there. I saw that
those people lived well, had a good time.

A: So you are inside and separated from your cousin.

C: *Back then, I remember, it was months of walking. When I began it was re-*
ally, really hard. I cried and said, "My God, why did I have to come here?"
I regretted everything. I thought about my dad and thought, "I don't know
why I am doing this when I was fine before," but you start regretting when
it's too late.

After working as a community organizer within the FARC, she became a messenger, carrying notes to FARC leaders in the extreme highlands. The organization gave her money to buy nice clothes to help her
to pass undetected by the government. When she concluded that she had
been identified, Claudia returned to rank-and-file guerrilla life. She received permission to visit her dad in Cali, which was when she learned
that paramilitaries had killed her cousin. The news demoralized Claudia.

C: *I told some kids that were with me [in the guerrilla], "The truth is, I want to*
leave. I don't want any more of this, I don't know what I am going to do."

The kids told me, "If you want to leave, try to get a formal exit. Don't
escape, because they're not going to forgive you."

I thought about whether I should escape or leave [formally], if I could
talk it through. So I went to a commander and started to talk with him. I
put it to him like this: "What possibilities might there be for a person who
wants to leave, formally leave? Could he do it?"

Then the commander said, "Why are you asking me?"

That's when I said, "The truth is that I am asking for myself. I came to
ask you this because I want to leave. I want to be with my family. I don't
want to continue in this, I don't." I told him, "I give you my word, I'll give
you anything; believe what I am going to say to you: I am not going to in-

*form on anyone, I am not going to turn anyone in, that's not why I would
go. I don't need it, my conscience won't allow that. If I go, I'll work or
maybe continue my studies—wipe the slate clean."*

*He said, "Wait, and I'll think about it. I know you are a truthful person,
I know the family you come from, I know your dad, and I know you're not
going to do that stuff. But I can't give you my word that I'll say yes. You
know what the Secretariat [the FARC's highest body] will think. You know
how others will start coming, saying "Let me go too."*

The commander let Claudia leave, but under the condition that she
stay in one place and keep a low profile to avoid arrest. He warned her
that the authorities or paramilitaries could kill her and blame it on the
FARC, since it would appear as if the FARC had killed her for deserting. Her father was surprised and ecstatic that the group had made an
exception for her. Claudia was worried that the FARC would renege on
its promise to let her leave without any trouble, so her father went to
plead on her behalf. He reiterated her promise that she wouldn't work
with the military or paramilitaries. Eight months after she left, however,
the Secretariat issued an order that the group collect anyone who had
been allowed to leave. A friend from inside the guerrilla tipped her off.

c: *I said to myself, "No, God no, I can't go back there, I can't, I won't, I've
lived a hard life." Imagine walking at night, in the rain, the thunder, getting drenched, diving on the ground, not being able to turn on a light to
see where you're going. It was terrible. Now when [the military] did operations, you would have to go and hide for two or three days without eating
anything. What you ate was water and sugarcane. So I told my friend, "I
know if I go back it's because they've ordered the firing squad for all of us,
or it's so we go back to guerrilla life, but it's not to forgive us just because."
So I left for Silvania, the same place where I had organized people [for the
guerrilla]. When I arrived, I told them I was no longer with [the FARC].*

*They asked, "Then why did you come here? Here you are in more dan-
ger. Here they can find you more easily."*

*I told them, "No, it's that I know that in the city there are many people
with the guerrilla, and they are hidden as civilians—you don't know who is
who. You can be talking with someone and not know that they are a guerrilla. Here at least you know who comes, because they're from the countryside, and the people see who arrives with weapons, dressed in camouflage.
In the city it's more dangerous."*

*I spent my time quietly in houses. I told the people, "Don't tell anyone
I am here. If someone asks who I am, say that I am family, I am the sister
of some cousin."*

She met her husband in a household that gave her cover. Claudia traveled back and forth between Silvania and Medellín for the first year that
she dated the man. Shortly after they moved in together in Silvania,
he was recruited as a *miliciano* for the FARC. After working with the
FARC for two years as a *miliciano*, he told his commander that his wife
used to be with the group. The commander knew her story and proposed
that she rejoin, but as a *miliciana*, not an armed guerrilla.

Claudia began to run errands, "sending money, sending things." Her
husband, however, went on more involved missions. He, like her father,
became "very persecuted." She would help him slip through roadblocks,
driving the car while he held their baby, baseball cap pulled over his
brow. He began to work full time with the guerrilla, far from her, and
visited only occasionally. The military was tracking him closely.

c: *At about two or three in the morning, I heard dogs barking, and said, "My
God, the army is out there," because the dogs were going after people.
That's exactly what it was.*

*At like six in the morning, the chickens got down from the posts, scared.
I got up and opened the door carefully; my kids were sleeping. I didn't see
anyone, nothing, and when I turned my back I felt someone grab my arm.
I turned around carefully, and then I saw the army coming out from under the coffee plants, more and more and more people. I said, "My God,
what's going to happen here?"*

*A commander from the army knew everything about the father of my
kids, everything about me. He said, "You are so-and-so who used this
alias." I was startled. I thought, "This guy knows everything."*

*Hearing the noise, my kids started to get up, crying. The guy took me
out to the road and said to me, "You are detained because you belonged to
an organization, you are from that front."*

"It's over," I thought.

*The guy said, "Tell me about your husband, hand him in, tell me where
he is, who he's with. You are going to tell me. You know where the weapons are buried."*

*I told him, "I don't know anything, I don't even know what you're talk-
ing about. My husband hasn't lived here for many years."*

I said, "You'll take me out dead because I am not taking a step anywhere. If you want to kill me, kill me, do whatever you want. Or you will take me with my kids, because I am not going to leave my kids stranded. Let's see what you do."

I managed to tell my kids, "If, for whatever reason, they take me from here and put me in a car, stick to me, don't let go of me for the world."

A: How old were your kids?

C: *My kids were tiny. My son was eight, my daughter six, the other [son] was four. Imagine, they were still small, and I had another [son] that was only two. I told them not to let them take me.*

Then the guy said, "OK, you don't want to come with me, let's make a deal—keep it positive [por las buenas]."

"What does 'keep it positive' mean?" I said.

He pulled up two chairs, sat down on one, and put another in front of him. He said, "Sit down. We are going to make a deal. I know that you know where weapons and everything else is stashed."

He pulled out a wad of money. I remember it—a ton of money tied up with a rubber band—and he said, "You keep this money, and I'll take what you turn over, and we forget the whole thing."

Then I said, "The truth is I am not going to give you anything, because I don't know anything. Where things are, I don't know that either. That's the truth."

That's when he grabbed my kids. He sat my oldest daughter, who was six, on a stone. The boy, he took him down by the coffee plants. He said, "I know that this kid knows where things are." So he grabbed the child and took him to the coffee plants below. I panicked, thinking, "This guy is going to do something to my son. He could kill him, or who knows what he'll do." That guy looked crazy.

I said to the guy, "If you want to kill me, whatever you want, but not my kids—don't touch them. They are little people who don't even understand why you are treating me this way."

The boy escaped and ran off to where I was. He hugged me and started crying. I asked him what the man had done, and he said, "No, Mom, they didn't do anything to me, but they were saying that I had to turn over things that I knew, and I don't know anything."

I said, "Tell me if they did anything to you or threatened you or anything. Tell me."

He said, "No, mami, no."

I don't know if it was from fear or what, but that moment hurt—a lot.

Shortly after the incident with the army, Claudia had another encounter with the military. When she was returning from the doctor with two of her children, two soldiers started following her and threatened to "leave her sleeping for the rest of her life" if she had any further contact with her husband.

Her husband and the FARC agreed that she should demobilize. While she was in the reintegration program, Claudia's social worker announced a call for job applications for positions cleaning offices and serving coffee to corporate employees and their guests. I asked whether anyone at work knows about her past.

C: *No, no, nobody. I've worked there for five years, and the truth is, I haven't dared to tell anyone, because I'm scared that people will reject me.*

A: Are you still with your husband?

C: *They caught my husband, and now he is in jail. He's been in there for thirteen years. Since then it's been me, by myself, playing the role of mom and dad with my kids.*

I've always told them about my life because I don't like to have secrets with my kids. They know, and they remember many things. They would ask me, "Mom, why did that happen on that day? Why this and that?" So I've had to explain to them, and I've told them the truth so in the future they don't find something out and become upset. I've always told them who I've been—everything.

FIGURE INT.4. Drawing by Lucas Ospina.

CHAPTER FOUR

The Good Life Deferred and Risks of Remobilization

Felipe ducks into a closet lit with heat lamps glowing red. He pulls out a plastic fender for a motorcycle's front wheel, its paint now dried. A friend who has a relationship with a Kawasaki distributor sends Felipe business for his motorcycle repair shop. From the perspective of the Colombian Agency for Reintegration, or ACR, the civilian reintegration program that receives the demobilized from the PAHD, Felipe is a success story. In its language, he is a *micro-empresario*, a micro-entrepreneur, who is carving out a name for himself, growing his customer base, and investing in equipment to expand his small shop.

The sound of a growing crowd outside prompts Felipe to pause his work with the fenders and peer out his third-floor window. Below, a young man is throttling a motorcycle while popping a wheelie, riding with one wheel above his head for the length of the block in a display of motorcycle machismo. Biker jackets, helmets, and reflective vests are packed in kiosks and adorn mannequins that pose outside the storefronts below. The three-block radius of this working-class neighborhood of Raconto is a beehive of buzzing motorcycles, a space of commerce regulated by paramilitary strongmen. Felipe pays $15 a day in extortion charges, $3 to five different groups that each promise "protection." Those groups send men with fanny packs or pleather satchels to collect the informal tax. Felipe's contributions add one more layer to the collectors' fist-sized wads of small bills. The paramilitary-controlled neighborhoods where Felipe lives and works served as a buffer against the FARC, which had sentenced him to death. The paramilitaries run drugs, extort local businesses, and kill young people who dare compete for their customers by selling drugs from street corners (*ollas*). The murders these narcoparamilitaries perpetrate are discussed in a euphemistic discourse of cleanliness as pernicious as it is pervasive in Colombia.[1] Most former guerrillas have settled in such informal urban settlements, and many, like Felipe, strike up relationships of accommodation with local paramilitaries. Whereas the guerrillas often recruited children and adolescents by asking them to carry messages or deliver food supplies, paramilitaries begin to *remobilize* former guerrillas by asking for favors, such as lending a motorcycle or storing some weapons.

The ACR, the civilian component of Colombia's individual demobilization program, strives to keep former combatants from remobilizing with a different group. One pillar of its plan is to transform guerrillas into businesspeople. The ACR gave Felipe $2,200 worth of brand-name equipment to help him get his motorcycle repair business off the ground. To receive a second $2,200 of seed capital, he must stay active in the program. That means checking in with his caseworker once a month, avoiding run-ins with the law, and persevering through ACR's business start-up checklist. "Graduation" from the program, an eight-year process, is only a year away. Felipe spoke to me with enthusiasm about a rumor that President Juan Manuel Santos might preside over his graduation ceremony. As we talked, he daydreamed aloud, imagining his eight-year-old son seeing the president hand him the certificate that would consummate his transition to civilian life.

Seemingly Felipe is playing by the rules of the game. He is motivated by the demobilization program's promise of the good life as an entrepreneur and consumer. He has embraced his civilian identity and appears to be a docile, law-abiding subject of the state. Yet things are not so simple. In one of our many conversations, Felipe said, "I have many enemies," and pulled a handle in the lower level of his workbench to prove it. A handgun lay in the otherwise empty drawer. The more time I spent with Felipe, the more I learned of the varied enemies he has accumulated while fighting on different sides of Colombia's war.

As a peasant from an indigenous community in the east, Felipe lived in extreme poverty. He joined the FARC for the authority it projected in his home province of Guaviare, and for the meals it provided. Between the ages of fifteen and twenty-nine, he rose in the organization's hierarchy, but he left the FARC in 2006 in an acrimonious dispute with his commander. After deserting (but not yet joining the government's demobilization program) he feared that he would be hunted down for having abandoned the guerrilla movement; so he went to work for a paramilitary group in a part of Colombia's western Andes.[2] An altercation about money between the paramilitaries and their military collaborators in an illegal gold-mining racket prompted him to flee to the city of Raconto. When a friend who had demobilized from the guerrilla and was living in Raconto's urban periphery warned Felipe that he was about to be captured (which may have been a self-serving warning to earn a monetary reward from the military), Felipe demobilized too.

As I got to know Felipe better, I learned how his story was even more complex. While maintaining his motorcycle repair business, he was also plotting with a group of former rebels and corrupt military officers to locate a stash of cash that he and two others had buried for the FARC years before. One of his former comrades who helped hide the money had recently demobilized. He told Felipe that the stacks of bills had never been unearthed. Pocketing a cut of the approximately $150,000 (likely guerrilla taxes on cocaine production and trafficking) tantalized Felipe.[3] I visited him while this mission loomed as a possibility. We met at a dive bar, a neighbor's living room decorated with pin-up posters, a jukebox, and plastic tables. Drunk on a mixture of whiskey and beer, Felipe fantasized about buying his own house and raising his son to join the professional class.

Felipe's trajectory prompts a chain of questions. What kind of citizen-subject is he? To what extent has he really disarmed, demobilized, and reintegrated into Colombian society? What does Felipe's chameleonlike ability to navigate between an ever-changing assemblage of armed actors say about Colombia's individual demobilization program?

Campaigns to promote desertion from guerrilla ranks, like the Christmas campaigns described in chapter 2, stoke desires to reunite with family and join the middle class. These sophisticated marketing operations interpellate subjects by promising a comfortable life of family connection and consumer citizenship. However, given the state of the social contract in Colombia, eviscerated by a radical form of neoliberalism, the constructed image of the good life—a nuclear family that has the comforts of housing, utilities, education, quality health care, and occasional indulgences—is easily imagined but nearly impossible to maintain. Principal among the obstacles former guerrillas face as they build their civilian lives is a lack of formal education. Another weight that drags on their prospects of keeping a job or making friends in their neighborhoods is the entrenched stigma of having been a guerrilla. It is a stigma cast and recast through decades of government propaganda and the daily and nightly indoctrination of corporate news broadcasts that represent the FARC as evil incarnate.

For former FARC fighters, the good life is continuously deferred in an often incremental process of disappointment that leaves them adrift in contexts of extreme poverty and rampant criminality. Thwarted aspiration connects former rebels with their working-class neighbors who themselves must figure out how to live an ethical life "at the cusp of soaring aspiration and drowning disappointment."[4] This is how Jocelyn Lim Chua discusses the double-edged nature of the good life in Kerala, India. Amid fraying fantasies of economic success, "adjustment seems like an accomplishment," as Lauren Berlant writes in *Cruel Optimism*.[5] Indeed, a certain cruelty festers in the optimism peddled by the Colombian government's mass publicity campaigns targeting the demobilized. Those campaigns to remake rebel fighters into consumer citizens, dialogically engage a more generalized advertising onslaught in which companies bombard marginal communities where the demobilized settle with advertisements that sow desires for middle-class lifestyles. This is not merely a matter of advertising; it's also a question of urban design and financialization. Between 2003 and 2014 the number of malls more than tripled in Colombia. As anthropologist Arlene Dávila notes, developers build most of these shopping malls in proximity to the poor to help companies seek out "coming-of-age" consumers in poor, densely populated areas of cities.[6] These malls are expressions of efforts to produce middle class-ness. I write "middle class-ness" to highlight the fact that in Latin America, as others have noted, "middle class" is often a catch-all category that includes the racially and ethnically diverse "lower middle classes" or "emerging classes."[7] Malls provide a safe space for young people to stroll, a sharp contrast with gang-ridden neighborhoods where invisible borders dictate who can move where. The rate of proliferation of shopping malls in the urban periphery is rivaled by the growth in credit card opportunities for the poor, which quintupled in the first fifteen years of the millennium.[8] The economic struggles of former FARC rebels resonate with those of internally displaced people and economic migrants who also settle in Colombia's urban peripheries and stitch together a life in the yawning gap between the promised and the possible.

The houses in Felipe's hillside neighborhood may be precariously built with brick and corrugated iron, but they have sweeping views of the Raconto cityscape below. At night the downtown glows in the distance. The lights of the tall buildings signal commerce and possibility. In Felipe's neighborhood, however, the road to the good life is routed through relationships with paramilitary mafias. Informality and illegality closely conjoin in the neighborhoods where ex-combatants settle. The ACR knows that such an environment, often labeled "high risk" by urban planners, poses threats to former combatants' commitment to lead a lawful life and undermines its mission statement: "To promote the return of the demobilized population to legality in a sustainable manner, contributing to Peace, Security and Citizen Coexistence." The bureaucracy's principal objective, "the return of the demobilized population to legality," is then qualified by the catchphrases of sustainability and citizen security—code for what cannot be printed in the agency's glossy pamphlets: *to curtail rearmament and remobilization.*

Quantitative studies about rearmament in Colombia are unreliable because researchers primarily use government statistics and include only criminal activity known to the state. Much slips beneath the state's radar. Government statistics claim that 28 percent of demobilized combatants (paramilitary and guerrilla) break their commitments to legality, while another study by Ideas for Peace, a Bogotá think tank, found a recidivism rate of 24 percent.[9] Both of these figures are likely low, not only because they rely heavily on official data but also because they exclude the thousands of ex-combatants who once officially certified never present themselves to the ACR and enter its rolls; choosing to hide (*perderse*) rather than deal with the hassle and surveillance of reintegration.

The academic literature on disarmament, demobilization, and reintegration processes, which is disproportionately composed of political science scholarship, is focused on the difficulty of economic integration and its relationship to rearmament. Scholars often construct complex matrixes of factors—personal, social, and environmental—that push and pull on ex-combatants.[10] One of the most common findings in this literature is that the impossibility of finding stable work leads many ex-combatants to take up arms once again. Although this is a logical conclusion, designing a policy to address it has proved nearly impossible. Well-educated bureaucrats in the ACR have read the academic literature, surveyed previous reintegration processes in Colombia and in other parts of the world, and concluded that the best approach to economic integration is to transform the demobilized into small business owners.

Business owners are rooted, while alienated employees or people who hustle in the informal economy are prone to remobilize. Owners won't cut, run, and rearm—so the thinking goes.

The government's conception of the demobilized as entrepreneurs is yet another expression of its deep ideological commitment to market fixes, a fixation that parallels the PAHD's reliance on consumer marketers for its propaganda and psychological warfare campaigns. The ACR has placed great emphasis on fomenting small business initiatives (*proyectos productivos*)—nail salons, internet cafés, car mechanic shops—that often end in bankruptcy and acrimony. These projects succumb to a series of structural challenges, not least of which is former guerrillas' preference for work in the countryside. Many do dream of ownership, but of a parcel of land rather than an entrepreneurial venture in the city. Fear of their former comrades, however, has kept them in cities, where a mismatch of skills accumulated in the war and those needed in the city, along with the discrimination that comes with their stigmatized status, grind against their prospects.

The ACR, through the years, has become increasingly aware that former combatants are ill prepared to run businesses.[11] In addition to its efforts to turn guerrillas into entrepreneurs, it also pleads with companies to hire a quota of former combatants. But as one former director of the ACR lamented in an academic conference, the government's appeals almost always fall on deaf ears. Despite the ACR's energetic efforts to convince the private sector to hire former combatants, only a few tokenistic partnerships between the ACR and the private sector provide jobs to the demobilized. The most prominent of these initiatives is that of Coca-Cola Femsa, a Mexico-based Coca-Cola bottling franchise, one of the largest in the world.

The motivations for the corporation's support of the ACR are suspect. In Colombia the company has had to cope with bad press emerging from accusations that it is complicit in paramilitary violence against a labor union. It is a long story, but in brief, SINALTRAINAL, the Spanish acronym for the National Union of Food and Beverage Workers, is the trade union that bore the brunt of the paramilitary aggression allegedly linked to the soft-drink giant.[12] The union counts nine deaths among its members between 1990 and 2012. Via allied unions in the United States, SINALTRAINAL filed a suit in a federal district court in Miami. A judge threw out that suit, arguing that the court did not have jurisdiction. Anthropologist Lesley Gill has compellingly argued that such assassinations of unionists in Colombia eviscerated the labor movement and exemplify a fraternal relationship between the "the evil twins" of neoliberalism and political violence in Colombia.[13]

Although the lawsuit against Coca-Cola failed, the brand battle continues. Activists have sought to tarnish the company's image by creating websites like Killercoke.org.[14] Viewed through the optics of the ongoing public relations war between the company and student activists, Coca-Cola Femsa appears to be attempting to peace-wash its image and curry favor with the Colombian government by acting as one of the few companies to hire former combatants. In a 2015 survey of 1,328 businesses, Bogotá's chamber of commerce found that zero percent employed demobilized guerrilla or paramilitary combatants.[15]

In what follows I offer a glimpse into some of the pitfalls of economic reintegration and begin to illuminate how remobilization works. As shown in chapter 3, the government has transformed demobilized combatants into military informants, which is already a remobilization of sorts.[16] While pomp and publicity accompany demobilizations, the remobilization of combatants with other armed groups takes place quietly— often in furtive acts of last resort, at moments when ex-combatants find themselves broke and broken by the economics of urban life.

Luisa

Of the homes of former FARC members that I have visited, Luisa's feels the most spacious. No doors separate the two bedrooms, small kitchen, and nook with a desktop computer, and their absence gives the place an airy feel. Her second-story apartment felt even more spacious when I returned in early 2012. She had recently pawned most of her appliances. The pawning spree began with the motorcycle of her boyfriend, Simón. He had bought it for $2,200. They sold it for $1,100. When things hit rock bottom, Luisa and Simon hauled their refrigerator to the pawnshop. They were in a financial jam, and her three kids felt the effects. They regularly skipped meals and ate a proper lunch only a few days a week.

Luisa could escape her financial straits quickly, if she wished. The solution was as simple as it was dangerous: accept one of two offers extended by the financial manager of a man called Machete, the local narcoparamilitary boss who ran the hills of Raconto during the late 2000s. The first: launder $55,500, and keep $5,500 for herself once the sum was legalized. The second "opportunity" was to join the ranks of Machete's group and earn a comfortable salary, a job that would involve assassination, or "cleansing" (*limpieza*). How did Luisa find herself in this conundrum? Let's backtrack.

Luisa grew up in an indigenous community in the country's far east. From the age of seventeen to twenty-seven she dedicated her life to the FARC, where she was a rank-and-file member of a front that operated in the southwestern Andes. A guerrilla mole in the attorney general's office passed along information that a warrant for her arrest had been issued. A series of close calls intensified her feeling that either the state or its paramilitary allies would kill or capture her soon. So in 2005 she reluctantly turned herself in, coordinating her demobilization with Edwin, her boyfriend at the time, a *miliciano*. Within three months the interagency committee that certifies the demobilized, the CODA, approved both of them and gave them laminated ID cards.

In civilian life she still considers herself a revolutionary though she has disavowed the armed struggle. Politically she identifies with the FARC's political project and has internalized its antigovernment propaganda. She has channeled her passion for what the FARC calls "organizing the masses" into becoming a local activist who tries to bring together former guerrillas and displaced peasants, populations united by the precarity of urban poverty and violence. With other leaders from the demobilized community, she created an organization called Weaving Society (Tejiendo Sociedad). Five of the groups' members were killed between 2005 and 2015, likely by shadowy right-wing forces. The circumstances of those deaths, like so many other of the "cleansings" that happen in her neighborhood, are hardly ever investigated, much less adjudicated.

In the High Presidential Advisory for Social and Economic Reintegration, the predecessor to the ACR, both Luisa and Edwin dutifully fulfilled the requirements to access the seed capital (the centerpiece of which is a business-planning exercise). They each wrote a plan for an internet café and pooled the capital they were given, more than $8,000 in all. Getting their business going meant working with the vendors approved by the reintegration agency, merchants who not only sold the necessary supplies but also served as brokers for entire small businesses, selling them new or used. Luisa and Edwin bought their business for $9,450 (putting in more than $1,000 of their own money) from an approved vendor whom Luisa would later refer to as "a rat of a guy." (She came to consider the network of vendors used by the reintegration agency "a mafia.")

The couple went to see the business. Reflecting on that visit, she said, "Back then we didn't know anything about computers," a point she made in a tone that split the difference between self-criticism and disdain for the institutional arrangement that put her in that situation. They purchased desktops with Pentium 4 processors, outdated by then. "We barely had gotten them and they started to break down," she said. It was not only the computers that began to break down but also the phone cabins where people make phone calls and are charged by the minute. Until the price of a cell minute fell from ten cents to five, minutes were their shop's most profitable items. A software program controlled the codes to the phone cabins, but between glitches in the program and interruptions in internet service, the calls would drop. When the broker sold her the business, he had showed her registries of sale for similar businesses that made $110–$167 per day. Things did not work out that way for Luisa and Edwin.

Hardware and software were not the only problems. "The employees were the worst," Luisa remembered bitterly.

> They didn't clean the machines; they didn't attend [to the customers]. They spent all of their time on Facebook. I would go every two weeks and found bags of trash piled up; they didn't take them out. Over there the roads aren't paved, so lots of dust comes in; you have to clean a thousand times a day, but you could tell they never touched a rag. . . . I changed the people like a thousand times, but I couldn't manage.

As the business faltered, Luisa fell into a debt cycle through the "drip-drop" system (*gota a gota*) in which loan sharks recover their loans in daily sums that amount to usurious interest rates. She took a $1,670 loan at 20 percent interest and paid it down daily.

It's a common story among former guerrillas uninitiated in the world of finance. In the insurgency, each front has a provisioner (*económo*) who apportions supplies to each member of the unit. The vast majority of guerrillas have little experience with managing resources in any way beyond buying an occasional treat with petty cash distributed by the *económo* on an ad hoc basis. Although the FARC was awash in money from the drug trade, mining, and extortion, only commanders and members in the finance commissions made financial decisions and handled large sums of money.

Luisa and Edwin decided to sell his portion of the business, down-

sizing from eleven computers to six. They used the money from the sale
to paint the shop and service the computers. But the cycle of fixing and
breaking continued, further draining their limited resources. Luisa said,
"Technicians take advantage of you—they know you don't know about
system maintenance." It was a lesson in savage capitalism, a "save yourself if you can" world, in her words. She invoked an aphorism all too relevant to her experience: "The con artist lives off the fool" (*el vivo vive
del bobo*).[17] Con artists abounded. They sold her SIM cards containing a
fraction of the minutes that she had paid for. When she went looking for
the hucksters, they had disappeared.

Nonetheless the internet café was covering its costs, if not making
a profit. In the meanwhile, the "drip-drop" had turned into a waterfall, plunging Luisa deeper into debt. She consistently paid multiple
cell phone bills on time. Her decent credit history enabled the predatory lending practices of the local bank, whose transaction manager (*tra-
mitador*) was a con artist of the corporate stripe. He approved a series
of credit cards and loans that added up to $25,560 of debt. Luisa called
those loans "the stupidest decision of my life." (The transaction manager
collected $2,560 from Luisa for pushing the loans through.)

With her newfound credit she upgraded the equipment in the internet café and bought appliances for her home: a refrigerator, washing
machine, and home computer. But if the appliances indexed her ascen-
sion to the middle class, they were unstable signs that vacillated in time.
Time, after all, was the currency of Luisa's business: a fifteen-minute
internet session, a three-minute phone call. Yet the economics of time
were stacked against her. The interest she owed compounded daily, pro-
pelling her debts much faster than any meager profit she could eke out.

After a four-year battle to keep the internet café running, Luisa conceded defeat. The same vendor who sold them the business for $9,450
bought it back for $2,780. Luisa surmised, "This was all premeditated.
He knew the state of those computers, he knew it wouldn't work. He had
his technicians arrange everything so they only half-worked."

When I visited Luisa three years after her business had folded, it was
still causing headaches, literally. The vendor who bought back the business from Luisa still owed her money. She had traveled by motorcycle-
taxi up the hill to speak with him with the hope of getting paid. The
driver was cut off on a turn along an unpaved road, and the motorcycle tipped over. Luisa's right eye was badly bruised by the impact of

her poorly fitting helmet. The trip yielded a nasty black eye and some scratches, but none of the money she was owed.

Although Luisa lacked business acumen, she had embraced the entrepreneurial spirit. Like many former guerrillas she looked for opportunities wherever she could find them—a constant hedge against the improbabilities that any singular source of income will last. Halfway through her experience with the internet café, Luisa took a position as community liaison with a program to support ex-combatants in Raconto's city government. That position would enable her to learn of other initiatives to support the demobilized, one of which was a collective business venture: a supermarket. Luisa jumped at the opportunity to join the collective. The project gave $38,900 in start-up funds to a group of eleven ex-combatants from different groups: the FARC, ELN, and AUC. Five of the demobilized combatants, Luisa included, administered the half of the store dedicated to selling packaged goods, while the other six managed the produce section. Since Luisa had a job in the municipal government, she didn't involve herself in the day-to-day operations of the supermarket and did not expect any dividends either. "As a partner, the only benefit I got was the opportunity to do my food shopping on credit. At the end of the month, I paid [for what I had taken] and took more food out. We all had that privilege, and it helped us a lot."

The supermarket that doubled as a food bank for its partners began to crumble amid mismanagement and theft. One night, Luisa recalled, "one of the *compañeros*, we don't know who, came in. The building had a security system, alarms, cameras. When the person who woke up at dawn to open the store arrived the next day, he saw that $2,780 had been stolen from the safe." The door had not been forced. The alarm did not go off. The only thing that had been broken was the safe, which had a hole smashed into its side. "In the beginning we worked well together," Luisa said, "but then the biggest con artists who managed the business began to take out [money] to pay debts, furnish their houses, send their families on trips."

Only when one of the partners robbed the store did the former combatants identify a longer trend of embezzlement. As with Luisa's internet café, the solution in a moment of crisis was to take out a loan and downsize. Luisa's two business ventures foundered at the same time. Those experiences as well as her work advising other former combatants led her to the conclusion that "we, the demobilized, don't know how to manage a business. It's been totally proven by the majority of the demobilized. I think 1 percent are good at business."

For many years, it was the modest salary from her job with Raconto city government that kept Luisa and her family afloat (a basic stability that most former guerrillas lack). By 2010 she and Edwin had split up. She began a relationship with Simón, who comes from a family that the FARC had forcibly displaced when he was a child. (Such relationships between the demobilized and the displaced are not uncommon nor illogical, given that the two populations are crammed into the same barrios that ring major cities like Raconto.) Simón contributed to the household by taking odd jobs, low-paid short-term contract work like "the Russian" (*el ruso*). *El ruso* is vernacular for construction work, and it involves waking up at 4 a.m., being exposed to occupational hazards, and coming home at 7 p.m. exhausted. Between Luisa's salary and Simón's sporadic earnings they could pay rent and keep paying down their debts. But they hardly had enough money to buy food for the family, let alone school uniforms for the kids. In the middle of one of our conversations, Luisa recalled how her youngest son would look up at her on occasion and say, "Mom, I am hungry." As she repeated her son's words, her tone and body language combined to express a mix of heartbreak and failure.[18]

Three years earlier Luisa had been equally destitute. That was when a man had walked into the local government office where she worked, the same man who a year later would make Luisa lucrative offers to work with the paramilitaries. The municipal government that employed Luisa to support the ex-combatant community was under no legal obligation to provide services to the demobilized, but it offered them skills training and job placement services. It was late and Luisa was the only social worker there, so the secretary ushered the fellow to her cubicle. The man, a former paramilitary, had demobilized from the AUC in the mid-2000s. He asked if they could speak in a more private setting. "Of course," she said. They stepped into an office and closed the door.

"Don't worry, I am also demobilized," she told him. "I am a social worker, but also demobilized. I'll understand whatever you tell me."

"You see, what happened is that I am demobilized [from the AUC] but I reactivated with Machete," he said.

Machete was the narcoparamilitary boss who controlled the drug trade in Raconto's northern hills in the late 2000s. This man, as he explained, was Machete's financial officer. Luisa immediately recognized the danger and delicateness of the case. Luisa recalled her first impression of the man. "When I met him he had been in the street for two days. He had gotten wet and then dry, he had to sleep on the street, he hadn't eaten, he smelled like shit." She gave him some money to pay for a city bus fare, a night in a hotel, and some food.

The man showed her a series of photos he carried to prove his story: photos of Machete, his kids, his mother-in-law, his bodyguards, even images from the funeral of one of Machete's children, including the body in a casket. He said to Luisa, "I have all of this information and I want to turn it in. I have DVDs here and more information."

Luisa told him, "Look, I am going to tell you, as someone who is demobilized from the FARC—you, as someone who is demobilized from the AUC, you know they have people who are infiltrated everywhere, from the government to where you least expect it. I wouldn't hand in any information, because where are you going to hide? . . . If I were you, I would wash my hands of that information. I don't know why you are carrying around those photos, those videos. They will only bring you more problems. If you want to be in good standing as a demobilized person, dedicate yourself to a job, work for your family, and leave that other stuff alone."

Then he showed Luisa his bank statement. She was taken aback. The account, in his name, held more than $55,500. She didn't understand why he couldn't access the money. The man explained: "What is going on is that the manager of the bank works with us. With one call they can cancel everything." The guy had gone from riches to rags in record time.[19]

The next week he came back to the office transformed into a stylish member of the upper middle class with "a nice outfit, pimped-out watch, a laptop, and cell phones." When Luisa asked what had happened, he responded, "I went back. I am not going to give away that information on Machete. I reported to Machete again, and they activated the account. In fact, I need to go and cash some checks. I am good now; I am paying for a studio apartment in Risaraldo [an upscale part of Raconto]." He thanked Luisa profusely for her solidarity in his time of need.

A few months later the demobilization program fired Luisa in a round of layoffs. Machete's financial henchman called and said, "Luisa, hey, your friends told me that you lost your job, that you're in a tough spot because you're unemployed and have the kids, because your partner isn't working, and your businesses aren't going well. I want to help."

I told him, "No, it's fine. I am OK."

He said, "No, I want to help, because you were one of the people who helped me with clothes and money to buy a room. Not just anybody does that."

I said, "You aren't the first. I always help with what I can."

He said, "No, let me cash these checks and I'll give you some money."

I said, "I am not asking for money. I really can't take money from you."

He said, "In any case, I am going to find a way to help you."

Months later he called and said, "Hey, where are you?"

"In the culture house in Quintales [a popular area of Raconto], in an event with a group of women."

"Perfect, I am heading over. I need to talk to you," he said.

The man arrived in a pickup truck with a chauffeur and took Luisa out to coffee at a nearby bakery. He wasted little time before getting down to business. "I am coming with two proposals that can help you. The first is that we need people to launder some money, and there's a possibility you can help. If you want, I'll recommend you. . . . You know what, that's why I brought the truck. If you want, call Simón and we can go to Cali. If you want, we can get $55,500 today."

He said, "If you want to launder that money for me, I'll leave it with you for a year. You'll be responsible to me, and I'll be responsible to Machete. If you fail me, I fail Machete. He'll charge me, and I'll charge you."

Recounting the conversation, Luisa underlined the threat. "That's what he said!" The risks notwithstanding, Luisa confessed that "the whole situation started to tickle my sense of temptation, and I thought—maybe. But then I said no, we're talking about paras."

She declined the offer, in part on principle, in part out of ignorance. "I don't even know how to launder money. I don't know anything about how to make money look legal."

After Luisa declined the first proposal, the man launched into his next offer—that she work for him in downtown Raconto. "He would give me some men [*unidades*] and I would be responsible for doing some things," Luisa recalled. Among the "things" he mentioned were "cleansings," *limpiezas*, or, in less euphemistic terms, murder. "They would pay me monthly, like any other *paraco*." The second proposal did not appeal to Luisa at all. "That would be getting involved with paramilitaries and narcotrafficking, the worst thing anyone can do." She continued,

"I come from the FARC, and I am not open to changing my ideology and switching groups." Luisa mentioned the exchange to friends who had also demobilized from the FARC. Some responded to the money-laundering scheme by saying, "Oof, let's do it."

Within a year the police killed Machete as he fled a raid in Colombia's Amazonian region. Her friends commented, "You see, you could have kept the money."

"There's always someone who collects the debts," she said.

One of her friends shot back, "No, you're being a fool; some of your colleagues in the program went for the $55,500."

She never learned the identities of her colleagues who became paramilitary money launderers. "I'll tell you the miracle but not the saint" is the religiously loaded flourish Luisa's colleague used to compartmentalize the sensitive information. Although "the saint" who took the narco-paramilitaries up on their offer remains unknown, knowledge about who has declined circulates through the paramilitaries' expansive networks.

When I returned to Luisa's home in 2015, she had managed to get her refrigerator back from the pawn shop. Both she and Simón were working with the municipal government (she was no longer with the demobilization program), but her activities as a community organizer had attracted the attention of a group calling itself Cooperating for Good Living. They slipped a pamphlet written in the style of a press release under her door. Its header was simply a white skull and crossbones over a black box. The first line read: "In defense of the Colombian State." The pamphlet claimed that Raconto had been invaded by sleazy people (de mala muerte), "guerrillas masked as defenders of human rights, the land, the peasants, the victims, the poor." It sentenced Luisa and others to death "wherever they are," but especially in the spaces that they use to organize. It urged the listed individuals "to abandon their [organizing] practices, the neighborhood, the city, or face the consequences with their families." The threat was signed with the exact phrasing of a government memo: "Let it be communicated and fulfilled" ("Comuníquese y cúmplase"). Either Luisa's role as a community organizer or her refusal of the paramilitaries' lucrative offer would have been sufficient to get her name on a death list. The combination could be fatal.

This was not the first time that she had been marked for death since abandoning the FARC. When we were walking in her neighborhood to pick up groceries for lunch, she pointed out the route that she had taken to avoid someone she suspected had been sent to kill her. She recalled how she suddenly cut across a busy avenue to evade her stalker. When it was clear that she had gotten away, Luisa looked back at the man. When their eyes met, the man crossed himself as if he were mourning at a Catholic funeral. The gesture made her heart sink.

The skull and crossbones pamphlet triggered a paranoia that had lingered after the incident. Luisa evaluated her risks and lowered her profile in the barrio. Weaving Society (Tejiendo Sociedad), the organization she was struggling to launch with other former combatants, began to unravel as other leaders left the neighborhood. When I last visited their home in 2015, Luisa and Simón were weighing the pros and cons of moving elsewhere in the city.

Cooperating for Good Living's communiqué is not only a threat but an articulation of the good life in which narcoparamilitaries repress into submission community-based projects that suggest collective organizing. Its response is utterly disproportionate to any real threat to paramilitary hegemony.[20] The community-level activism of former combatants has no budget or any significant projects under way. Luisa's organization and others I have followed are "done by one's fingernails"—a Colombian expression that means scraping together the bare minimum necessary. Enterprising former combatants will often take the initiative to bring people together for small projects with the hope of winning funding from a municipal government office or NGO interested in development or reconciliation.[21] I have witnessed the fitful efforts to launch three different organizations led by former guerrillas. Each has struggled to incorporate as a nonprofit, attract sponsors, and move the organization beyond a series of initial meetings. As members of a population of interest to the expansive international and national NGO sector, charismatic former guerrillas can get an audience in NGO offices. Navigating the paperwork at the chamber of commerce and creating a legal organization, however, is a first, and often insurmountable, hurdle. While former guerrillas like Luisa try to organize, narcoparamilitaries who control the urban periphery violently repress even the most ineffectual of community solidarity initiatives. The vision of the good life that narcoparamilitaries enforce is one in which atomized individuals and nuclear families strive to improve their own lot by laboring under their menacing dominion.

When we overlay the perspectives of narcoparamilitaries and the state toward former guerrillas, their ideological alignment against leftist politics comes into relief. While narcoparamilitaries respond to the specter of leftist politics with violent repression, the state tries to detach former rebels from the political sensibility they forged while in the insurgency. The ACR's dedication to social and economic reintegration brackets out political reintegration, preferring that the demobilized see themselves as apolitical subjects. The ACR worries that political activities might spur ex-combatants to return to the FARC or to a different guerrilla organization. Yet the ACR's model of reintegration, focused on entrepreneurial projects, is far from apolitical. Microcredit schemes throughout Latin America serve as potent tools for integrating marginal populations into existing political economic structures and blunt the possibility that they might embrace revolutionary movements.[22] Peruvian economist Hernando de Soto has argued forcefully for the formalization of the global poor's assets so that capital languishing unrecognized by banks, such as properties without deeds, can be used as collateral for loans. The subtext to this model of development, outlined in his best seller *The Mystery of Capital*, is a political project to buttress liberal capitalism by integrating the abjectly poor—those most prone to rebel—into the economic system partly responsible for their marginality. De Soto makes explicit the politics of his program in an opinion piece he published in the *Wall Street Journal* in October 2014 titled "The Capitalist Cure for Terrorism." There he argues that the fight against the Islamic State should learn from the fight against the Peruvian Maoist group the Shining Path (Sendero Luminoso). He claims that the Peruvian military defeated the Shining Path because of the legal and economic reforms that allowed its peasant base to prosper and ultimately turn on the Shining Path. He points to Peru's relatively fast-paced growth in the 1990s and 2000s, failing to mention the economic polarization, grinding rural poverty in the postconflict moment, and the calamitous environmental consequences of Peru's resource extraction–oriented economy.[23]

Whereas de Soto advocates for integrating the poor into an ownership society, he refuses to look at the ways in which they get locked into an *owership* society. As Luisa's case makes clear, reintegration through entrepreneurialism can easily end in cycles of credit and indebtedness. For most this becomes a downward spiral for which paramilitarism is the only quick solution. Refusal to resolve one's economic problems through remobilization means breaking the unwritten social contract by which paramilitaries solidify their hegemonic position through a combination of gifts and threats.

I don't want to give the impression that *all* small businesses started by former guerrillas end in failure, but over the nine years that I spent

researching this book I did not hear of a single success story. When I returned to Colombia to do follow-up fieldwork in 2016, I got in touch with
a former ACR official. She had spent more than a decade in the organization and oversaw more caseworkers (*reintegradores*) than any other
manager. I asked if she could refer me to a successful small business run
by a former rebel. She sent me the contact information for Ciro.

"What's his business," I wrote in a WhatsApp message.

"He makes briefcases, bags," she replied. "Sewing," she added in the
next bubble.

"Is he the tailor?" I asked.

"Yes"

I should have figured that when I asked for an exemplary business, I
would be referred to the tailor.

Ciro

As it turns out, Ciro was not the person whom the ACR had labeled "the
tailor of the FARC" in 2012. That was Álvaro Pérez. Supposedly Álvaro
specialized in sewing uniforms for the FARC. As a demobilized combatant he created Colfepaz, a sewing business that received the enthusiastic backing of the upper echelons of the reintegration agency.[24] Colfepaz
seized upon the government's scheme to create a brand—Chance—at the
Bogotá Fashion Circle, the nation's premier fashion event. The public relations initiative to launch the Chance brand brought together the ACR,
the Ministry of Defense, and Lowe/SSP3 (from chapter 2). Ciro was one
of Álvaro's close associates in Colfepaz. Leading fashion designer Sandra Cabrales helped Álvaro, Ciro, and other former combatants (from
both the guerrilla and the paramilitaries) design a seasonal fashion line.
When Marcela, who features in chapter 2, invited me to the launch, I
went unprepared for the spectacle that would take place beneath the giant tent pitched in the middle of Bogotá's Ninety-Third Street Park, a
green space surrounded by some of the city's most expensive properties
and restaurants.

Beneath the canopy, models dressed in meticulously tattered T-shirts
and jeans strutted to the music of the Colombian hip-hop group Choc-
quibtown (see figure 4.1). At the end of the runway they would strike
a pose for the photographers and, with a flip of the hip, turn and strut

FIGURE 4.1. Models stride down the runway wearing the Chance fashion line designed by ex-combatants with the help of fashion designer Sandra Cabrales. Photo by author, 2012.

back. The ex-combatant tailors held hands with Cabrales as they walked the catwalk and took a bow to polite applause.

Then came remarks by Juan Carlos Pinzón, Colombia's minister of defense: "During the time I've been minister of defense, and the years before when I was vice minister, I've visited what is known as the naked Colombia. The most isolated places." After listing a series of remote municipalities, he said: "The state, entrepreneurs, civil society, all want the demobilized to dream and to aspire to a better future. Chance by Colombia, Chance *para* Colombia, offers a real opportunity for those who have left the guerrilla to make visible the possibility of a better future, and God willing with a stable income, so that everyone who is there [in the guerrilla] decides to demobilize." He concluded, "Thanks to the Fashion Circle there's hope for the country's future."

After the minister's remarks came an inspirational video extolling the fashionista peace initiative. Up-tempo music accompanied images of former combatants concentrating at sewing machines, a behind-the-scenes look at the production process (figure 4.2). The voiceover proclaimed: "We are going to show that behind every item of clothing, each

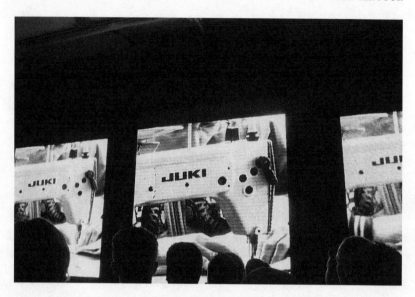

FIGURE 4.2. Image of an ex-combatant sewing in the promotional video for Chance. Photo by author, 2012.

color, each texture, there's much more than fabric and machines, threads and stitches. There's a life story. The brand looks to transform trends into something much more than fashion, transforming it into a motor for social change that generates opportunities for thousands of Colombians. They can show the world that it's always possible to start over, that there's always a chance."

There's always a chance. But for whom? To do what? The word itself has a gambler's edge. Presumably the "chance" (never translated into Spanish) is an opportunity for the demobilized, but that requires some parsing.

To start, let's look at the sartorial clues. The clothes themselves, ripped and pockmarked to suggest bullet holes, bespeak worn combat fatigues and the tatters of urban poverty. The mostly denim garments also evoke the punk culture of the Global North and invite prospective wearers to posture as rebels of the nonthreatening variety.[25] The models, meticulously accessorized, carry shiny red backpacks and red tote bags that resignify the color associated with the Communist Party in an indisputably consumerist register. The demobilized tailors watching on the sidelines dress in business suits and embody rehabilitated subjects, transformed from class-conscious guerrilla fighters or ruthless paramilitaries into successful entrepreneurs ready for the upscale bustle of north Bogotá's workweek. The fiction of their agency in the Chance project and its ostentatious launch is transparent to all. But the Fashion Circle is not about a reality: it's a phantasmagoric world where the demobilized are cast as characters in a morality play in which consumer culture is good and militancy bad. The figure of the rehabilitated demobilized fighter exists only to be consumed by the spectacle itself. The real protagonists of this show are the fashion models. That is who the audience has come to see, the archetypal sirens of consumption. I concur with anthropologist Michael Taussig when he writes that focusing on "the co-existence of glamour and terror in the world" misses the point of "their synergism."[26]

Two blocks beyond the giant white tent in Ninety-Third Street Park stands a five-story brick building that contains the offices of *SoHo*, the Colombian equivalent of *Playboy*. In November 2015, three years after the Chance fashion show, *SoHo* featured a demobilized female FARC rebel, Ana Pacheco, posing erotically with a female police detective, Isabel Londoño (figure 4.3). The gloss of the cover contained the wild sexuality of these dangerous women, immobilized by the photographer's camera. These technologies of capture and display put the uncomfortable matter of this femme fatal pair in its place, the familiar category of objects of male desire. The intentionally provocative cover helps to illuminate the relationship between models and demobilized combatants in the Chance fashion show.

The first point that must be made about this image is a chronological one: it appeared at the end of 2015, when peace negotiations between the Colombian government and the FARC were in an advanced stage. The liberal facet of corporate media had begun to anticipate the collective demobilization and reintegration of the FARC's military structures, while not giving up on the mass media's long-standing project to discredit the FARC by relentlessly drawing attention to its child-recruitment practices and mistreatment of women (valid points often exaggerated for effect). *SoHo*'s editors, in the spirit of peace through dialogue between political opposites, asked right-wing journalist Salud Hernández-Mora to interview Ana Pacheco, the former FARC guerrilla, and left-wing journalist Alfredo Molano to interview former DAS detective Isabel Londoño.

The combination of erotica and stories from the war's protagonists in

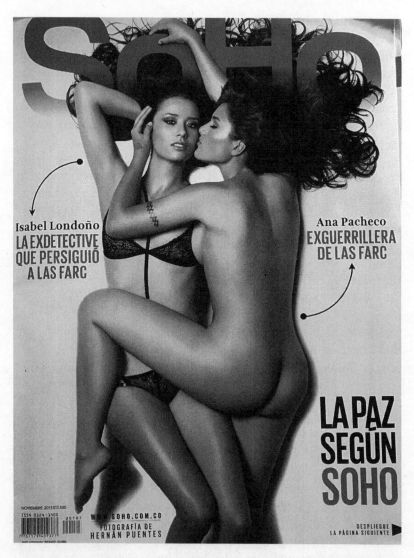

FIGURE 4.3. This November 2015 cover of *SoHo* magazine features a former FARC guerrilla and a former police detective that prosecuted the FARC. In a cheeky reference to its own debasement of the war into airbrushed erotica, the editors title the cover "Peace according to *SoHo*."

SoHo is an iteration of the same recipe behind the Chance fashion show. The amalgam of sex appeal and war drama serves as a two-pronged hook to lure audiences and potential consumers. As in the Chance pageantry, combatants proved a potent weapon for marketing the idea of peace through consumption. That messaging intensified as negotiations between the FARC and the government accelerated during 2016; but the PAHD had been watering the seed of the notion of peace as business since the mid-2000s, when it began its campaigns to sell a new life of consumer citizenship to the demobilized.

With the *SoHo* photo spread and accompanying interviews, the magazine's editors, photographers, and layout artists call on audiences to visually consume the two former adversaries, their curvaceous bodies, and the dramatic twists in their personal narratives. That consumption, in turn, will help the magazine sell advertisements that promote liquor, watches, bicycles, and clothing. A two-page Diesel advertisement that separates the two sets of photos and the interviews features models outfitted in urban camouflage (figure 4.4). The slogan, in English, reads "No military experience required."

FIGURE 4.4. Advertisement between the photos and interviews of two women ex-combatants featured in the *SoHo* cover story, November 2015.

Taken together, the *SoHo* spread—hyphenated by this advertisement—
and the Chance spectacle speak volumes about the urbanization of the
Colombian conflict. In the Diesel ad, the indeterminacy of who is and
who is not a combatant, the cause of so much death and injury, becomes
the basis of a new clothing line. The style could be interpreted as guerrilla chic, offering potential customers the opportunity to express their
inner (depoliticized) rebel, or as inviting them to unwittingly embody a
paramilitary logic whereby civilians serve as extensions of the military.
The otherwise deadly military-civilian ambivalence at the heart of guerrilla warfare is rendered banal beneath the veneer of urban outfitting.
Not to worry, "no military experience required." The larger point is that
the fantastical urbanization of the armed conflict represented in *SoHo*
hides the deadly urban war unfolding on the peripheries of Colombian
cities, like Raconto, where former combatants struggle to remake their
lives in contexts where the war still rages. That urban war, which the demobilized find themselves in the middle of, exceeds classic portrayals of
the Colombian conflict that feature images of armed men and war machines in the countryside. Yet the urbanization of the conflict has existed, persisted, and quietly intensified for decades. While residents of
impoverished swaths of large cities must navigate armed actors that fur-
tively control much of the metropolis, elites in wealthy pockets of those
same cities project very different images of war and urbanism—like this
Diesel advertisement or the photographs that emerged from the event in
Ninety-Third Street Park. Let's return to the scene of the latter.

When the narrator of the inspirational video proclaimed that the
Chance project was about "something much more than fashion," he was
entirely correct. Not because the fashion world is saving the demobilized,
as he insinuates, but rather the contrary. The excess that the disembodied voiceover invokes, I argue, is the surplus value that the fashion industry, often assailed for the exploitation of its workers, stands to reap from
its ostensible commitment to peace in Colombia. The token demobilized
entrepreneurs, their stories, and the feel-good-fable of leaving guns for
sewing machines allow fashion designer Sandra Cabrales, and metonymically her industry, to stake a claim to the category of "ethical fashion."

Ethical fashion has emerged as a current within the world of "ethical capitalism," in which environmental and social values become dis-
tinguishing features of high-end consumption—think sustainable agriculture or fair trade coffee. The inherently contradictory idea of ethical
capitalism relies in large part on the tales that companies tell about their

FIGURE 4.5. The media interview Álvaro, "the tailor" (center), and ACR leader Joshua Mittroti (left). The screen behind Álvaro (not pictured) is filled with the logo of the supermarket chain Éxito. Photo by author, 2012.

supply chains—distributing more profits to impoverished farmers in Honduras, for example.[27] Such stories, always presented in sketch form, not only enable a markup but also allow the fashion industry to refashion itself by posing as a socially concerned. In the process, the industry hides its association with classic capitalist exploitation of the likes highlighted by investigative reports about sweatshop conditions in Bangladesh.

As I watched and reflected on the production that evening, I wondered: who is the real beneficiary of this elaborate show? After the ceremony I watched people pose for photographs with the ex-combatant entrepreneurs in front of backdrops adorned with logos. News media besieged "the tailor" and Joshua Mittroti, then managing director of the ACR (figure 4.5). Scanning the press after the event, I found this quote from Álvaro, "the tailor," appealing to those still in the FARC: "Come out, this is your last chance at life before you are executed over there."[28] Same script, new context, I thought.

As I left the event, I strolled onto the lawn, which was lined with small white tents promoting consumer goods. I walked past a carefully arranged display of creams and soaps beneath pink lighting, a stand for

Dove to promote its brand. I left the launch of Chance overwhelmed by the very subject of my research, the confluence of consumer culture and counterinsurgency. Later that night I reflected: Was this vertigo not the point? Were the over-the-top theatrics not a sensory and cognitive deluge intended to numb one's critical faculties? The spectacle's components— lights, models, garments, music, videos, speeches, commercial kiosks— created a heightened sense of distraction that helped to normalize the questionable conceit of creative entrepreneurship as a strategy for the economic reintegration of ex-combatants. Over the course of the evening, statesmanship (via the minister of defense) and commerce (via the fashion industry) combined to tell a tale of liberal capitalism as the remedy for militant critique run amok.

The scene carried traces of world fairs past. Those fairs did important ideological work. Take the 1939 New York City World's Fair at Flushing Meadow–Corona Park. The organizers transformed the park into a veritable corporate Disneyland that served as the launching pad for magical new technologies, such as television. Edward Bernays, a founding father of public relations, branded the futuristic fair "Democricity." As documentary filmmaker Adam Curtis has noted, the fair equated capitalist-driven technological progress with modernity and liberal democracy.[29] Clearly world fairs, and their heirs, carry a heavy ideological charge. Cultural theorist Walter Benjamin, writing about the exhibitions of those fairs (he was most interested in the Paris World's Fair of 1867), says: "They open a phantasmagoria which a person enters in order to be distracted. The entertainment industry makes this easier by elevating the person to the level of the commodity. He surrenders to its manipulations while enjoying his alienation from himself and others."[30] In the same passage of his unfinished Arcades Project Benjamin connects the exhibitions of the fairs to fashion, which "prescribes the ritual to which the commodity fetish demands to be worshipped." In the technological exhibitions of the world fairs, and in the obsolescence through design of the fashion industry, both of which project into an imminent and fleeting future, Benjamin sees commodity fetishism unhinged—a pleasurable resignation to the deification of commodities. In the Chance show, the thin fiction of demobilized combatants reintegrating into society through a fashion brand was forgotten in an atmosphere thick with desire for the models and the clothing they wore. The event was a call for the demobilized, the attendees, and the consumers of media reports about it to allow themselves the pleasure of entertainment in the presence of defanged ex-combatants, to surrender to the manipulations of the commodity, in Benjamin's terms.

But if the commodity fetish hides the social and political relationships at the heart of a commodity's production, as in Karl Marx's classic formulation, what were those relationships in the Chance project? Clearly the organizers of the Chance spectacle treated the demobilized more like props than people, which only made me more curious about the former combatants' perspective on the event. Who were the tailors? What happened to Chance? The answer to the latter question is simple: nothing. You might say it never had a chance.

In 2016, four years after the fashion show, I posed that question to Ciro, one of the tailors in the Chance project. He was the tailor whom the former reintegration official had put me in touch with (not the one hyped as "the FARC's tailor")—a success story of the ACR's entrepreneurial reintegration model.

A: What was the story with Chance?

C: Chance was from the government. I don't know who invented that thing. But they came out saying that they were helping us, that they were going to give us a shop to sell our products. Nothing came of it. It was all bells ringing but no ice cream. Imagine, we went to register the brand Chance, but then we saw how many brands of chance already existed in the Chamber of Commerce; we couldn't lodge it anywhere.

A: But the idea was to develop a brand?

C: Yes, to develop a brand, but we couldn't. It didn't work.

A: How long did the initiative last?

C: Barely two months—making the products and exhibiting them. That's as far as it got.

A: And with all of that show, with the models and the minister of defense.

C: We were happy because we were naive. When you are just starting you think, "Here comes a big help, we're going to get ahead." What a huge lie. That's as far as it went.

One of the few traces left by the mediated experiment of Chance was Ciro's dedication to building his own personal brand. When we met in 2016, he was standing beneath a white tent assembled over the brick patio at the base of a northern Bogotá office complex known as the World Trade Center. He carefully arrayed his stock of leather purses, wallets, handbags, and satchels on stylized white shelving. Each piece carried the stamp of his brand: his name written in a cursive font that made "ciro" look symmetrical. Shortly after I arrived, a military officer patrolling the patio in pixelated camouflage inquired about a woman's handbag on the top shelf. Twenty minutes later, two suited men approached the stand. One of them was the patrolling soldier who had inquired about the handbag earlier. Ciro explained his personal business initiative to the two men, how it employs vulnerable populations, the demobilized and displaced. (He didn't disclose his own background.) The officer bought the black handbag.

It was Friday afternoon and an elimination soccer match between Colombia's and Peru's national teams compounded the collective relief and excitement that comes at the end of a hard-fought workweek. People had begun leaving work early. One guy in a yellow replica jersey picked up a black wallet with white seams and asked: "How much?"

"$14," Ciro responded.

"Leather?"

"Leather."

Careful not to show too much interest in the wallet, the fellow thought for a moment, then said: "Would you give a little discount?"

"I'll give it to you for $13, my brother," Ciro said.

"Leather?" the guy asked again, pulling out his own wallet to inspect its tattered state.

"Napa leather, good leather—smell it," Ciro replied. "It's a good deal, I won't make almost anything, but it's fine; I am promoting my brand."

"You wouldn't do it for $12?"

Affecting resignation and displeasure, Ciro said, "All set, my brother."

After that sale Ciro began to close his stand. He needed to get home, not to watch the game but to go to a funeral. A few days earlier two assassins had killed his brother-in-law. They had come to his house at the top of the hill on the far outskirts of the city at 3 a.m. Ciro explained the cause of death with a trigger gesture of his right index finger, then added: "He was also demobilized."

"From the same group?" I asked.

"Yeah, also from the FARC," he said.

"It's a bit of a pattern," I said.

Ciro's eyes widened as he nodded in agreement. The deceased had worked in private security and left behind three children, one fifteen years old and the other two "really small." I expressed my condolences.

His brand of leather goods was a still unprofitable side project. Ciro earned his living by running a "satellite workshop" for multinational companies to contract. His sole client is Fapsou, a multinational company that produces backpacks, luggage, clothes, wallets, and shoes for developing markets, especially in Latin America. Ciro turned fabric, padding, and zippers provided by the company into backpacks.

After a manager at Fapsou saw Ciro on the news during the launch of Chance, he called Ciro to fire him, accusing him of having infiltrated the company and suggesting Ciro maintained ties with the guerrilla. Ciro defended himself, insisting he had done nothing wrong. He called the ACR to tell his caseworker the story. The caseworker's advocacy got him reinstated in three days. Pride filled his voice as Ciro finished recounting the episode: "Since then, I have always had work."

The three-story brick building that Ciro has turned into a workshop was lined with backpacks in different stages of assembly. Under his contract with Fapsou, Ciro had one month to deliver three thousand finished black backpacks. The company would pay $2 for each acceptable backpack—one tenth of its retail price. Fapsou provided the plastic padding, precut fabric, and zippers. Ciro provided the machinery, thread, and labor. On the third floor, people bent over sewing machines stitching straps and pockets. Three of the six workers were ex-combatants. Ciro said he paid them between $7 and $14 a day, depending on their productivity— better than a sweatshop but a poor substitute for a stable salary.

We returned to the first floor, and Ciro told me the story of how he joined the FARC only to desert two years later. Until the age of thirty-one, Ciro bought and sold cattle in a rural area five hours from Bogotá. The guerrilla has had a strong presence there but at the time was on the defensive. A FARC *miliciano* stole one of his steers. One morning the two men passed each other. The *miliciano* was herding cattle and Ciro's steer was among them. Ciro said, "I like that steer. Would you sell it to me?" The passive-aggressive exchange soon escalated into a machete duel. "I gave it to him, and he gave it to me," Ciro said, pointing to the scar running diagonally down his left cheek. As the duel wound down, the thief threatened to kill Ciro, so he decided to make a formal complaint to the FARC, which controlled the area. The commander called Ciro and his adversary to a meeting. He told Ciro's enemy, "If anything happens to Ciro, we'll finish you." The commander also told Ciro that if he wanted to stay in the area, he needed to work with the FARC.

Ciro joined but never embraced guerrilla life. He deserted during a paramilitary incursion into the area, shortly after they disappeared his sister. Ciro's sister had been a member of the Communal Action Board, one of the neighborhood councils where most local governance happens in Colombia. On March 30, 2003, she had been driving a truck that the Communal Action Board had contracted to ferry beer and food to an event. The paramilitaries pulled her out of the truck. Ciro told his commander about it, but he refused to do anything. "She's not from our ranks. She has to defend herself," the commander said. Her husband did work for the FARC as a *miliciano*, but that wasn't enough to move Ciro's commander to action. The day after the paramilitaries disappeared his sister (she was never found), the military arrested her husband.

After his commander refused to help confront the paramilitaries over his sister's abduction, Ciro decided to desert, escaping when the commander sent him to fetch supplies. He sought refuge in his cousin's house and started to pick flowers on a large farm that exports roses to the US for Valentine's Day. The company liked his work ethic and began the process of offering him a more stable contract. When it requested his judicial records, the DAS (the Colombian equivalent of the FBI) captured him. I was surprised that the DAS had known of his membership in the FARC and had a warrant. Given that he had entered the insurgency at thirty-one and spent limited time in the guerrilla, I figured he would not yet have been cataloged in the state's files. What I had not accounted for was that the guerrilla reported his defection to the state as a way of punishing him (and a tacit admission that it lacked the resources to track him down). When DAS agents showed up at his cousin's house, he began a conversation that led to his demobilization.

Ciro's demobilization process was smooth. During the reintegration stage he attended vocational courses in private security and tailoring. He presented his small business proposal—to open a tailor shop—to the ACR. I asked about the nuts and bolts.

A: So they gave you $4,400?
c: No, they don't give you money. They pay a vendor who sells you the machine.
A: What's the deal with the vendors?
c: It's a bitch, because everyone sells machines, but they don't pay a fee the SENA [government skills training agency] requires that involves a ton of paperwork. Since they have to pay, they pass it on to you. You can get a [sewing] machine downtown for $389, but there they sell it to you for $670.

Of the $4,400 allotted him, Ciro spent $4,000 on four sewing machines and a riveter, and another $400 on start-up costs. Ciro's other sister was already running a workshop of her own and advised him. I asked how much profit his workshop generated in an average month. He said it varied, and scribbled calculations on a piece of scrap paper in front of him: roughly $1,500 per month (about the salary of a midlevel bureaucrat in the ACR).

His leather business, the Ciro brand, was still losing money, but he remained determined to make it viable. The ACR had alerted him to a series of workshops in which corporate executives taught former combatants how to register brands and export merchandise. Ciro had attended the first training at a Juan Valdéz café (Colombia's gold standard for brands) two days before I visited his workshop. "How many other small business people were there?" I asked.

"Just one other," he said. "A guy with a washing-machine business."

The former reintegration official who directed me to Ciro was right, he was a success story, but one of very few. An extraordinarily rare confluence of factors has enabled him to sustain his manufacturing business. He joined the FARC at the age of thirty-one, which meant he had much more experience in economic exchange as an independent adult than the vast majority of former guerrillas who joined as teenagers. Furthermore, he enjoyed doing business. The fact that his sister already operated a workshop meant he could get reliable advice, and his father gave him loans at key moments. The FARC front he deserted had been all but vanquished, and with only two years in the FARC he did not have access to sensitive information, so his security concerns were relatively low. These contextual factors helped enable Ciro to position himself as a success story via the ACR, which has been consistently desperate for success stories.

Ciro knows he is the exception rather than the rule. The former combatants that he hires lead much more precarious lives and are prone to remobilization. Ciro recalled the story of one employee he had taught to sew. "I told him, 'Have a little, but chew it well,' but no, he couldn't resist the temptation of stuffing himself with money. He went [with the paramilitaries]. The guy was a good worker, but ambitious. He got fucked up looking for easy money."

"What did they promise him?" I asked.

"That he was going to be filthy rich because he was going to go over there and steal that merchandise, pure coca paste," he said.

Not quite understanding, I asked, "Carrying packages between here and there?"

"No, he was supposed to take the merchandise from those who processed it. They robbed from the guerrilla; but the guerrilla, watch out, they're nasty."

Theft and reprisals played out closer to Ciro's workshop as well. His barrio, like the neighborhoods of Raconto where Felipe and Luisa live, is an another overlooked theater of Colombia's urbanized "low-intensity conflict," which feels anything but low intensity to those ensnared in its web. Ciro tells of how, a decade earlier, one former paramilitary living in his neighborhood started a gang of thieves. A subset of the one hundred former guerrillas who had settled in his neighborhood organized and adapted the FARC's heavy-handed style of revolutionary justice to urban vigilantism, killing the thieves. Trouble, however, has persisted in his neighborhood. When I checked in with Ciro in the summer of 2016, he was facing a death threat. A local gang was trying to intimidate him into leaving the area so it could take over the low-income housing block where he kept his workshop. Even for the few success stories, like Ciro, the shadow of violence does not disappear after demobilization.

The Good Life Deferred

What is the good life? The pursuit of self-advancement and the fulfillment of individual desires, or commitment to the collective concerns of ethics, justice, and societal obligations?[31] In Colombia, a country with one of the highest rates of inequality in Latin America, the good life has long been framed as the individual quest for wealth, a historical trend that can be traced back to the Spanish conquest and colonists' search for El Dorado. The country's historical reliance on extractive industries (gold, rubber, oil, emeralds), large-scale agriculture (coffee, bananas, African palm), and illegal drugs (marijuana, heroin, cocaine) has led towns and entire regions to boom and bust. The longue durée of imagining and aspiring to quick riches percolates into the present and molds contemporary conceptions of the good life expressed in the popular Spanish idiom *la buena vida*, which connotes a decadent lifestyle.

The Colombian government's vision of the good life for former guerrillas at once clashes with and reinforces this historical and cultural context in which the good life is routed through often violent shortcuts to wealth. What matters to the government, first and foremost, is that former guerrillas definitively abandon their quixotic misadventure in search of socialist ideals and buy into the existing political economic order. This perspective is intimated by the PAHD's media campaigns but only comes into relief in the ACR's efforts to mold the demobilized into entrepreneurial participants in a neoliberalized economy, and in narco-paramilitaries' quest to co-opt guerrilla knowledge while repressing collective organization. This assemblage of forces serves as shock therapy for the demobilized.[32]

In the first weeks and months after deserting, the demobilized are dazed and disoriented. When they receive their CODA certification they are pushed into an urban landscape in which society is rigidly stratified.[33] The first order of business is to survive. Once the needs of housing, utilities, food, and basic comforts, like a mattress, are secured, ex-combatants look to transcend their abject status by finding a job that might make them an active member of the working class. Ascent through Colombia's rigid class system is measured through patterns of consumption tied to cycles of debt and credit.

What matters to the ACR is that ex-combatants stay on the right side of the law, that recidivism rates are low (and that rearmament is hidden from public view). In this formulation the good life is but the absence of the bad, illegal life. Yet in the everyday worlds of former rebels who live amid latent and less latent forms of paramilitarism, remobilization appears as the most promising road to *la buena vida*. The best chance demobilized guerrilla fighters have to achieve the aspirations that the PAHD stokes in its marketing campaigns and targeted military intelligence operations is either to collaborate with the military or to work with an illegal armed group, most often narcoparamilitaries. These options offer a shortcut to joining the middle class or jumping straight into the nouveau riche's world of conspicuous consumption. But this vision of the good life is extraordinarily dangerous, as the debts incurred in the act of remobilization are often paid with one's life.

Former rebels who pursue the easy money that rearmament and re-mobilization promise risk not only their own lives but their family members' as well. Those who steadfastly refuse that path live in a state of extreme precariousness in which the vision of the good life peddled by the government is continually deferred. Like civilians who live in former combat zones in rural areas where heavy rains wash land mines to imprecise locations downhill, rendering the local geography a shifting terrain of exploding artifacts, former rebels in urban areas traverse a moving minefield of armed actors, economic forces, and moral quandaries.[34] For many ex-combatants, the idiom of struggle for survival viscerally connects life before and after demobilization. "We left one war for another" is a repeated refrain in my interviews. Another common invocation was of "the mountain of concrete" or the "jungle of cement," phrases that connect their time in the guerilla to their experience in an urban economic battlefield.[35]

Faced with this menu of difficult and dangerous options, most former combatants retreat into the private sphere of the family and embrace the popular idiom *sacando adelante a la familia* (pushing the family forward). The phrase expresses a cultural logic of enduring the travails of economic struggle and justifying them with the hope that future generations might join the middle class through a combination of education, hard work, and good luck. The idea of *sacando adelante a la familia*, however, presupposes a stable family life and requires at least minimal employment opportunities. Given the scarcity of both, former rebels hatch short-term schemes known colloquially in Colombia as the *rebusque*, which is perhaps best translated as "scavenging." This scavenging involves juggling piecemeal work in the informal economy, short-term contracts in the official work force, and cycles of indebtedness. In this unforgiving landscape, favors from support networks and the ability to game the meager welfare of the ACR are barely buoyant life rafts. Most see clearly that the prospect of entrepreneurial success is dim, so they don't give the endeavor an earnest shot.

In an email exchange with the former ACR official who introduced me to Ciro and managed a small brigade of caseworkers for more than a decade, she wrote an honest appraisal: "War leaves holes that are significant in civilian life, lack of schooling, distrust in institutions or in others, shortsightedness [*cortoplacismo*], migration to cities and conditions that aren't conducive to a return to the countryside, dysfunctional families and lack of support networks, the lack of a credit or financial history, lack of tolerance and ease of frustration as well as their imaginaries are some of the hurdles." Though her candid analysis identified many structural challenges, she was still somewhat surprised and disappointed that former combatants did not embrace their entrepreneurial projects. "There are demobilized that think paternalistically, who barely fulfill the requirements to get a business plan. Then they fail as a result because their mission from the beginning was not to be creative and self-sufficient but to scam for resources."

With such an array of structural factors pushing against the possibility that a former combatant's small business might succeed, why has the ACR insisted in emphasizing entrepreneurialism as a path toward economic reintegration? The program's senior leadership is aware of the challenges. USAID, one of the ACR's largest foreign patrons, commissioned a group of high-profile US-based researchers to evaluate USAID's support of the ACR. When the final document was completed in 2013, the ACR buried the report, never releasing it publicly. The report recommended creating "a public sector employment program for ex-combatants," as opposed to the inordinate emphasis placed on entrepreneurialism.

As I will argue in the conclusion, the three-step process of disarmament, demobilization, and reintegration of Colombia's individual demobilization program has been designed for ritual failure. What is important to underline here is not failure itself but rather what failure produces: atomized subjects who are locked in a struggle for economic survival that leaves little room for political commitments. Mired in extreme precariousness and condemned by their former comrades, demobilized guerrillas are economically and politically immobilized—unless, that is, they choose to remobilize with their former enemies.

Sergio

s: *I left the house when I was nine to work and pay for school. We were poor, and with so many siblings, we had to leave to pull coca leaves. I grew up away from home. When I was in third grade; a man brought me to a farm — and I turned thirteen there. In those days we would work for eight hours in a small village outside Las Chilupas. That's when a guerrilla called "Restrepo" came to the village. He asked me if I wanted to join. I said, no; taking up arms seemed hard to me, and I was scared.*

A week later I saw him again, I ran into him. I had been drinking. I was drunk and asked to join. The next day I was working and two guys came, Jhon — a black guy — and the other one was José, they called him the Smurf. They came and spoke with the owner. They told her that they had come for me. The owner refused, saying I was a minor and didn't know what I was doing.

They said, "Let's go to the village; we'll talk there and you can decide if you'll go or not." Along the way, four hours later — we were about to get to the river, let's say — they convinced me. They talked about politics, how they were fighting for the people, the peasants, the proletariat. They also said that where I was going, in the guerrilla movement, I would study, and they would support me economically, that I had to do a military course.

Those guys were well dressed, nice uniforms, jewelry, a good pistol, because back then in Caquetá they were getting a lot of money working with coca. I let them convince me. I left with them, walking six hours along a river called Pulobrí. The next day we woke up at 3 a.m. and caught a boat to a village called La Pirga. From there ten hours by foot to a hamlet called Girambo. From Girambo we went seven hours upriver until we got to a camp. There they interviewed me. They told me that from the moment I

passed the guard post I could never return to civilian life because I had
joined a group, a military.

A: At that time what were you thinking, as a young person who was thirteen?
What did you feel?

S: *Well, back then, the truth is I didn't know what I was doing. I walked just to*
walk, to carry a rifle just to carry it, because I wasn't conscious of where I
was going or what I was doing. I became aware of the organization when
I turned sixteen. A girl called Nora came; she was the secretary for Raúl
Reyes [the FARC's no. 2 at the time]. She was very political, and she was
the one who explained what the organization really was, why we had to
fight and be prepared to die. I turned seventeen years old, and they trans-
ferred me to Putumayo.

A: But as a kid, did you miss your family?

S: *Yeah, I missed my mom especially. I thought about my dad too, but he was*
stronger and would lift my mom's spirits by saying I would leave the orga-
nization at any moment. Despite the fact I was in the organization, I was
very sentimental—let's say my heart is soft, weak. For me, what's most im-
portant is the family. It was hard to hear that I had to forget about my fa-
ther and mother, that if they screwed up, if they made some mistake, and I
received the order to kill them, I would have to do it.

Life in the insurgency began to sour for Sergio. Illness made long
treks through the jungle painful. A fight with his commander brewed,
and ultimately his commander emasculated him by stripping him of
his rifle. Sergio began to receive the worst assignments repeatedly: the
front lines, extra guard duty, digging longer trenches. The commander
bragged about sleeping with his ex-lover, and the conflict blew up in a
verbal spat that included death threats.

S: *They tied me up and threw a war trial at me, saying I had infiltrated, that*
I worked with the army, that I was a spy. Jorge, "The Valluno," ordered
me tied up. But there were many people from my family there, we were
about two hundred family members in the guerrilla, almost the majority
of my family have been part of that group. Most of them were killed by
[the FARC]. . . . At the end of the day, [the leadership] punished both of
us [Sergio and the commander he was fighting with]. They sent me back to
my front. He deserted before I did. He made it to Neiva, but that's where
they killed him . . . he had been stealing, something like $19,500.

After the acrimonious war trial, which left Sergio disarmed, he approached the front commander to insist that he be allowed to leave.

s: *I asked that he relocate me with a project because I didn't have anything.*

   I said, "You know I'm a nurse, put me in a business, something where I can work."

   He had someone bring me a pair of shoes, a pair of pants, and a shirt, and said, "Look, here's your ticket so you can go home." It was $14.

   I said, "What do I do with this? If I get off the bus in Puerto Asís the paras will kill me," because back then Puerto Asís was mined with paramilitaries.

   So I made the decision and deserted when they sent me with a commission [a squadron traveling on a mission]. I went to my father's farm. We're from an indigenous community, and they accepted me back. I worked in the house for a year until they came looking to kill me. They tried to kill me seven times in my house.

A: What did you think when you heard they were looking for you?

s: *When they came looking for me at home, the story was that I was working for the paramilitaries. I never had any contact with those people. I asked my dad, "What should I do?" I started to cry because I barely had clothes—financially I was in bad shape. I thought, "If I stay here, they'll kill me." My dad said it was better that I go. He sacrificed and managed to get $56. But I couldn't relax: I had no papers, and someone could always recognize me in a village and ask, "What are you doing here?" I didn't know what to do, I was confused.*

   Then I met a friend who had also been in the guerrilla. He said, "What are you going to do?"

   "Brother, I have no idea. I'm confused. Maybe I shouldn't have left the organization," I said.

   "No, kid, don't even think about going back," he responded. "Look, do you know about the demobilization plan?"

   "No," I said. The truth is I didn't know about it.

   "I am in that program; if you want I'll help you get in the program. You have a ton of information; you know because you [really] were [a member of the FARC]," he said.

   "I've been out for a while," I said.

   "Don't worry, I'll help you," he said.

   But he couldn't help me right then because the lieutenant who received the deserters wasn't there.

I returned to the farm, and that night [the FARC] came back to the house. That's when my dad said, "No, my son, you have to leave here and never come back, because if you come back they'll kill you."

A: They came to the farm looking for you?

S: *Yeah, what saved me was that five minutes earlier we had finished eating lunch—it's way out in the country where we live—and I went to cut some branches for my mom. At that moment, ten guerrillas arrived and rifled through the entire house looking for me. I listened to God; it was like he was telling me to go further in, toward my sister's house. I got to my sister's place, and fifteen minutes later my nephew arrived, he was like ten years old and said, "Uncle, don't leave, Juan is looking to kill you."*

Over there, in the countryside, you live with all sorts of shortages, with no money, nothing—and that's how I left for Puerto Asís. That's where I met Lieutenant Ospina. He said, "All set, brother, I've got it all sorted, join the [demobilization] plan," and he interviewed me and all that. He said, "OK, with these details it seems like you did belong to the group. What front were you in?" I told him I've passed through many. I told them what I had to say, but the program rejected me. They said I hadn't been a part of the guerrilla.

Despite his pleadings, the PAHD expelled him from the halfway house. He went to see a contact he had made in the attorney general's office during one of his interviews.

S: *I said, "Doctor, erase me from the system. If I wasn't [a member of the guerrilla], then why I am going to have a paper trail* [quedar empapelado]*?"*

She said, "No, my son, we have proof you were a guerrilla; you should get the benefits of the program." What saved me is that I appeared in a few videos. She told me that my certification had come through, but when I went to the office they told me I was denied again.

After collecting signatures from other ex-combatants he knew, Sergio picked up the certification that had been approved but was being arbitrarily withheld. Once his reintegration process began, it went fairly smoothly and he received the first half of his seed capital to start a business, $2,200—but then he was imprisoned.

The story Sergio tells is that a friend requested his company on a trip in the eastern province of Meta, only to learn that his "friend" extorted local businesses. The two had planned to meet the day after they collected $900 from a store. His accomplice did not show, but the police did.

Sergio had spent four and a half years behind bars when his contact at the attorney general's office and a member of the demobilization program came to the prison to see if he would help demobilize others. The reward would be $1,670 per person he helped to demobilize. The government managed to contact and demobilize ten members of his former front, six of whom it ultimately certified. Sergio did not receive the promised reward because he had a criminal record (a detail the government officials had omitted when they came to seek his help).

The FARC killed his father while he was in prison. One of his brothers joined the paramilitaries to avenge their father's death. The fact that Sergio's brother joined the paramilitaries further fueled the persecution of members of Sergio's family still in the FARC. As we spoke I grew flabbergasted at the sheer volume of death.

A: How many people in your family have the FARC killed?

S: *I think it's been more than one hundred relatives who've died at the hands of the guerrilla.*

A: *In your generation?*

S: *Yeah, in the generation, and that's on top of those who have been killed by the paramilitaries. Those who [the FARC] killed sympathized with them. They say they're informants, that they've twisted just because they stop working with them—so they shoot them for not helping. They killed seven of my uncle's children.*

I have some hatred. I'd like to avenge it, but it's hard because I can't. When they killed my dad, we all got together and said we would leave it in the hands of God. God will have to pardon the person who killed my father, and who knows who sent them to do it.

And my relatives keep leaving [to join the FARC], minors, twelve, thirteen, fourteen years old, they keep joining—and keep deserting. Right now there's nothing to do, there's no work, the farms are mined, what future does a kid have? . . .

The images in most of my dreams are of being there; sometimes I go there and they tie me up. I've dreamt that they kill me. I've dreamt that they put me in a coffin and I wake up and say, "Oof, I am alive"—always with that psychosis. I've felt, and sometimes I dream, that they come to my house and they're looking for me, wanting to kill me.

My father appears in my dreams every once in a while. My dad was ex-

tremely honest. I'm not saying so just because he's dead; everyone loved him. . . . When he shows up in my dreams he always says, "Be careful." In the dream he's in a coffin, mutilated [deshecho]. *He says, "Take care of your mother and take care of yourself, they're looking for you." When he appears in my dream I get sick. I have that dream every month or two.*

Sometimes I go to church and ask my God to help me. I pray. I cry. I sing. In those moments, I forget everything I've been. But I leave church and come back home and I remember again.

FIGURE INT.5. Drawing by Lucas Ospina.

The Colombian Model

We always thought of post-hostilities as a phase distinct from combat. . . . The future of war is that these things are going to be more of a continuum. . . . We'll get better at it as we do it more often. — Lawrence Di Rita, special assistant to US secretary of defense Donald Rumsfeld, 2003[1]

Colombia is a model for the region. . . . It is an example to the rest of Latin America about what awaits them if we can convince people to make better decisions. — John Kerry, US secretary of state, 2013[2]

Colombia's Program for Humanitarian Attention to the Demobilized, or PAHD, has helped its US patron tailor its military doctrine to the challenges of the early twenty-first century. As the United States muddles through the maintenance of its post–Cold War hegemony, it has grown desperate for ideas to combat increasingly mutable, rhizomatic, and networked enemies. That the US would lean on a close Latin American ally is neither illogical nor historically novel. Historian Greg Grandin argues that Ronald Reagan's anticommunist crusade in El Salvador, Guatemala, and Nicaragua helped the United States reassert its ability to win guerrilla wars and that Latin America more broadly served as a workshop for US empire. Central America in the 1980s, Grandin writes, provided an opportunity for the US to defeat "a much weaker enemy in order to exorcise the ghost of Vietnam."[3] The neoconservatives of the Reagan era returned to power in 2001 in the administration of George W. Bush, bringing with them experience using ruthless paramilitaries, expansive covert operations, scrupulous media management, and rural development schemes. As they refashioned the techniques that they had honed in the 1980s for the post-9/11 world, the ongoing conflict in Colombia offered an ideal testing ground for higher-stakes wars in Afghanistan and Iraq, as well as the proliferating security scenarios spurred by the Global War on Terror.

The multigenerational aspect of Colombia's conflict has made it a laboratory uniquely suited to long-term and iterative experimentation. The alliance between the US and Colombia is rooted in a Cold War history in which Colombia has been an eager collaborator in the anticommunist project. The emblematic act of such solidarity occurred in 1950, when Colombia sent an infantry battalion and three frigates to fight alongside the US in the Korean War. That adventure would help drive the modernization of the Colombian military in the early Cold War years.[4] Feedback between the two militaries has continued uninterrupted since. Whereas modern US counterinsurgency doctrine was forged in Southeast Asia, especially in the Philippines, after World War II, the implementation of Plan Lazo (Snare Plan) in Colombia between 1962 and 1966 provided the Kennedy administration a less distant testing ground for an increasingly codified set of strategies developed by US military intellectuals.[5] Plan Lazo decreased widespread banditry, the criminal residue of political violence in the 1950s.[6] Its success in turn emboldened the US-supported Colombian military to extend its offensives, which included air assaults, attacking communist and liberal dissidents who had formed agrarian collectives known as independent republics. The assault on those independent republics in the mid-1960s transformed a static threat into a mobile guerrilla force, the nascent FARC.[7] Since then Colombia has served as a workshop for the US and Colombian militaries to hone counterinsurgency strategies and practices.

The PAHD layers onto this longer history of Colombian-American military exchange in a global moment when the temporal delineation between war and postwar inherited from interstate conflicts, especially World War II, withered.[8] As many observers have noted, the attacks of September 11, 2001, provided a justification for a war that is not only global in reach but unbounded in time. The idea that warfare is enclosed by a formal declaration of hostilities and a peace treaty has become increasingly anomalous in recent decades. A transnational dialectics of forms of violence that are not quite war, such as the drone strike and the terror attack, further enmesh military conflicts into civilian affairs. At the same time, police forces amass surplus military supplies to the point that they begin to resemble militaries, and militaries often find themselves doing police work.[9] US military strategists have tried to adapt and work more effectively within the indeterminacies of nonwar warfare, formalizing its nonmilitary entanglements as MOOTWs, or Military Operations Other than War.[10] By serving as a theater to develop new strategies tailored to the times, pre-postconflict Colombia has provided the US a testing ground for fighting radical nonstate adversaries in the liminal zone of nonwar-war.[11]

One such strategy is "individual demobilization," a militarized iteration of DDR policy that discards the United Nations' key prerequisite for demobilization: a peace agreement. Through the 1980s and 1990s, Central America demobilizations followed political agreements that formally demarcated a period of war from a period of nonwar. [12] In the 2000s Colombia bent this norm to the point of breaking it. Colombia changed demobilization and reintegration policy from a strictly collective affair, in which all of the people in an armed group's structures laid down their weapons in a singular process, to also include the desertion of individual combatants. This conflation of demobilization and desertion has equated an individual's will and desires with the political determination of a movement's leadership. Colombia's watered-down definition of demobilization is part and parcel of the network approach to twenty-first-century counterinsurgency. By targeting nodal individuals in the guerrilla's structure, the Colombian military has waged a war of attrition against its enemy's network—a strategy akin to drone warfare. Rather than killing its enemies, however, it turns them, like police informants, into sources of pivotal intelligence—tacitly remobilizing them.

The problematic byproducts of this policy that I have flagged over the course of this book—the militarization of social life, the evacuation of meaning from humanitarian discourse, the inability to distinguish between war and peace—have passed uninterrogated in the Colombian public sphere, hidden by the government's publicity machine. With a paucity of critical voices speaking out domestically, the government has marketed its demobilization program internationally and positioned the country as a model for other war-torn nations to follow. Such nation branding, which insists that the country has vanquished terrorists while dazzling tourists, looks to elevate Colombia's international standing to attract foreign investment and vie for regional leadership in Spanish-speaking South America.[13]

Colombia's case for the efficacy of its curious conjunction of war and peace policies grew more compelling on November 30, 2016, when the

Colombian Congress approved a peace agreement with the FARC. The agreement promised a return to the status quo ante, demobilization in a classic United Nations sense. By mid-2017 all sixty FARC fronts formally turned over their weaponry. The accord's historic dimension has eclipsed the public's limited memory of the PAHD, a placeholder in lieu of a peace agreement. Yet the placeholder was not inconsequential. The PAHD had helped to demobilize sixteen thousand FARC fighters between 2003 and 2016, cripple the guerrillas, and rebrand the military as a humanitarian actor, even as it left many former combatants feeling deceived, dejected, and primed to remobilize.

The Colombian military's use of brand warfare is poised to become the policy equivalent of a viral sensation. Foreign policy pundits have since called on the US military to study it as a way of combating ISIS, which has displayed no shortage of brand savvy of its own.[14] The Colombian government has shown great skill and persistence in hawking its expertise abroad and selling the bellicose variety of demobilization as the cutting edge of peace policy, articulating it with the exponential growth of special forces. For instance, consider the hunt for Joseph Kony, warlord of the Lord's Resistance Army (LRA) in central Africa. Patrick Tucker, writing in *Defense One*, a military foreign policy magazine, writes that a US special forces and psychological operations unit deployed a MISO (Military and Information Support Operations) team to disband the Lord's Resistance Army by finding key members of Kony's gang and persuading them to defect."[15] The mediated "come home" campaign, which mostly used radio programming but also leaflets and aerial loudspeakers, offered individual combatants the chance to turn themselves in in exchange for avoiding prosecution.[16] This propaganda campaign, which tapped into NGOs such as the controversial organization Invisible Children, began in 2009, the same year that Colombia ramped up its efforts to infiltrate transnational policy circles dedicated to the minutiae of disarmament, demobilization, and reintegration (DDR) policy.

In 2009 the Colombian government launched a full-scale offensive to spread its vision of DDR policy, hosting the grandiose First International Congress of Disarmament, Demobilization and Reintegration (CIDDR) in Cartagena. The congress brought more than fifteen hundred people from fifty-seven countries to the Caribbean port city renowned for its colonial architecture. Right-wing President Álvaro Uribe presided over the conference, which ended in a formal document that sought to rival the two widely accepted white papers on DDR: the UN's Integrated Standards and the Stockholm Initiative. The final policy document that synthesized the conference's conclusions, the Cartagena Contribution to Disarmament, Demobilization and Reintegration, asserted that "DDR is no longer confined to transitional and postconflict phases, and is increasingly undertaken during 'live conflicts.'" The passive phrasing hides the Colombian government's role in fueling this trend. The next sentence suggests that other countries should follow Colombia's example: "DDR can serve as both a platform for longer-term peace-building processes, as well as an implicit component of counterinsurgency and anti-terror campaigns."[17] With the Cartagena Conference, Colombia boldly asserted a securitized, US-supported vision of demobilization over the United Nations' conception, which privileges political negotiation.

The United States has looked to apply the lessons of its South American client and ally to its imperial ventures in the Middle East. The State Department routed two different ambassadors on the same trajectory from Bogotá to Washington to Kabul in the 2000s and 2010s (William Wood, 2003–9, and Michael McKinley, 2010–16). Afghanistan, US officials reason, is the perfect place to transfer those who have learned from the Colombian experience because of the dual challenges of insurgency and drug trafficking. According to Matt Waldman, a British DDR expert who worked in Afghanistan throughout the 2000s, the Afghan government began its own individual demobilization program targeting Taliban militants in 2006 (three years after the PAHD began).[18] The Afghan program has received support not only from U.S. officials who have rotated between Bogotá and Kabul but also from Colombians working for the PAHD, including Marcela, its communication director.

When I spoke with Marcela about her three-week trip to Kabul and Kandahar in 2010, her voice filled with pride as she assumed the role of international policy adviser. She explained why she thought the Afghan program would not work: "It's not feasible because the limits of forgiveness are not clear." Although Colombia's highly improvisational legal framework for dealing with former rebels is riddled with gray areas, it is a bedrock of jurisprudence compared to Afghanistan's, in Marcela's analysis. Her framing places Colombia on a middle rung of a global hierarchy of security expertise, able to mediate between a superpower and states widely perceived to be on the brink of failure.[19]

The Cultures Are So Different

Whoever heard of a reintegration program having a section for foreign relations? — Samar, a former adviser to the Somalian prime minister

The semantic gymnastics of the Cartagena Conference and the effort to rebrand Colombia as a postconflict country continued on a smaller scale with yearly follow-up tours. The Colombian government, through the Colombian Agency for Reintegration (ACR), invited delegates from other troubled nations to experience its postconflict policy interventions firsthand. In 2012 I accompanied twenty-three people from nineteen countries on a one-week tour.

Colombia's mountains make a strong impression on first-time visitors. The delegates on the tour bus looked out giant windows onto the eastern branch of the Andes Mountains. A wispy patchwork of mist periodically covered and uncovered the views. As the bus climbed higher, the vegetation shrank lower until the only flora to be seen along the rolling panorama were *fraylejones*, hairy-leafed, high-altitude plants that look like stunted palm trees. Through the descent into the piedmont that spills into the eastern plains, the vegetation grew taller and more varied. Two police pickups, three police motorcycles, and two armored 4x4s drove in front, behind, and alongside the bus, escorting it along a route that ten years earlier would have been avoided by even the most intrepid Bogotanos of the professional class. By 2012, however, the military had vanquished the FARC from the highlands and most proximate lowlands surrounding the capital, a point the ACR underlined at every opportunity.

Inside the bus sat delegates from countries either in the midst of an armed conflict or emerging from one (including South Sudan, Afghanistan, Nepal, and Iraq), as well as members of the ACR's highly educated, mostly female staff culled from the Colombian elite. The delegates included a former Taliban ambassador to Pakistan then serving as the second-most senior member of Afghanistan's High Peace Council, a government body charged with negotiating with armed groups; a retired Canadian military officer and transnational DDR guru who advises the Colombian government; a former adviser to the Somali prime minister interested in debilitating Al-Shabaab; an ex-SPLA rebel then leading the demobilization effort in South Sudan ("the world's youngest country," as he liked to remind the group); and an Iraqi working with the US-funded International Organization of Migration in Baghdad to demobilize the Sons of Iraq, a Sunni paramilitary group. Together, the characters embodied a US-backed world order struggling to contain networks of violent actors (some of which had once received US support).

This one-week "South-South Tour"—a framing that brackets out Colombia's northern patron—was the third such follow-up to the extravagant Cartagena Conference of 2009.[20] Like the previous two, it concentrated on a single department. In 2012 the featured department was Meta, which connects the highlands of the eastern Andes with the country's eastern plains and Amazonian south. The weeklong itinerary included a graduation ceremony for ex-combatants who had completed their reintegration process, a demonstration by a military unit charged with demining former battlefields, a visit to one of the halfway houses where former rebels await their official certification as demobilized, a tour of a fish-farming cooperative run by ex-combatants, a one-day wrap-up conference, and an alcohol-infused farewell *fiesta*.

My first impression while on the bus was amazement at this cosmopolitan expert culture. The Canadian delegate insisted that he had "worked pretty much everywhere except Afghanistan." The delegate from South Sudan explained to an ACR hireling how the number of people who suffered amputations in Colombia's war "is nothing" compared to the amputations sustained in the war for succession in South Sudan. After a few stops, the representative from Somalia mused that her country "could never afford this" and that any such demobilization program would have to be funded by the UN or some other multilateral organization. *El Tiempo* interviewed the former Taliban spokesperson-turned-peacemaker about reconciliation. The Filipino man who had worked in a concrete bunker in the Green Zone in Iraq and spent ten years working in Angola joked that wherever in the world he goes, he's always associated with actor Jackie Chan. English was the lingua franca.

As I stared out the window listening to stories from Sierra Leone, Iraq, and Nepal, the lush landscape zipped by at fifty miles per hour. I envisioned the scenes described by each delegate and superimposed them on the Colombian countryside. Such imaginings were part of the purpose of the "South-South" tour—to prod this worldly bunch to rethink their own experiences through the Colombian context. Geographic presence set the stage, but it was the itinerary that drove home the idea that Colombia had become not only a referent in the transnational technocracy of DDR policy but a model.[21]

On the third morning we stopped at an economic reintegration project in which former combatants—paramilitaries and guerrillas—worked together to farm tilapia. The three ex-combatants who spoke emphasized that they had built up their business with the ACR's help. Afterward the group dispersed to walk along the canals and reconvened for lunch a half hour later. At lunch the Ghanaian delegate, who worked at the Kofi Annan International Peacekeeping Training Centre, summed up his feelings about what he had seen: "These people have the political will and the money." He squeezed a lime wedge over his filet of fish and added, "This would never work in Africa." The Filipino and Nepalese members agreed.

The Senegalese attendee added, "What donor will give you the money for six, seven years of reintegration? Nobody, not even for Congo."

Three voices at the table agreed that the presentation that they saw moments earlier would be unfeasible in Africa, where "local governments are weak." That didn't mean DDR should then be entrusted to the UN, because, in the words of the Congolese representative, "you can't give it to the UN—it's always a failure." I observed this discussion quietly and marveled at how well it echoed the tour's unmarked objectives: constructing Colombia as a leader of the war-torn subset of the developing world and displacing the UN's privileged technocratic position in determining demobilization policy in favor of a US-aligned alternative.

The ultimate barometer of success in the three-step DDR process is how well the policy helps former combatants to periodize their lives into a militant past and a civilian present and future. Therefore it was fitting that the delegates' agenda featured a "graduation ceremony" in which one hundred ex-combatants (from guerrilla and paramilitary groups) brought their eight-year reintegration process to a ceremonial end. After a performance of *joropo* music and dance, which is traditional in the eastern plains, and a few pro forma speeches, the master of ceremonies called each of the former combatants to the front of the auditorium to pick up his or her certificate. After the last speech, confetti flew toward the front of the room. The demobilized dispersed to pose for cell-phone photos with the delegates (figure C.1).

After a week of bonding over meals, events, and rides on the bus, the delegates participated in a two-part symbolic sendoff that began with a daylong conference and feedback session. The ACR rolled out Alejandro Eder, its director; General Jorge Enrique Mora Rangel, the country's most decorated veteran and also a lead negotiator for the govern-

FIGURE C.I. A ceremony for former rebels and paramilitaries completing Colombia's DDR program, with Abdul Hakim Mujahid, a member of the Afghan High Peace Council (center), and a Congolese DDR expert (right). Photo by author, 2012.

ment in its then month-old negotiation with the FARC; and Antonio Navarro Wolff, a former militant of the M19 who, eighteen years after disarming, had been elected governor of the department of Nariño. The trio gave gravitas to the closing event while ending on a friendly note. Eder insisted, "We have an open-door policy. . . . Whatever we can contribute to your own peace processes, you are very welcome." General Mora spoke eloquently about his experience with deserters on military bases and offered sweeping assurances that the demobilized are treated respectfully by the military.

In a feedback session between the hosts and the delegation, the visitors clamored for unrestricted access to the demobilized. They had picked up on something that had been grating on me throughout the trip—how the ACR had selected and prepped the former combatants. One former combatant I spoke with privately during the tour claimed that an ACR official had urged them, in a threatening tone, to speak positively about the program. By strictly controlling access to the demobilized, the ACR elided many complaints and horror stories that would have complicated the rosy image it had gone to lengths to compose for the delegates.

The policy recommendations from the delegates were insightful and resonated with the agenda for the peace negotiations that had recently begun in Havana: pay closer attention to the paramilitary threat, focus more on the rural areas, work to create programs that bring together ex-combatants and members of the communities where they resettle, don't pass over the question of justice too quickly (figure C.2). After everyone said their piece, the group disbanded to rest for a few hours before heading out on one final excursion for a lavish dinner at Andrés Carne de Res, a booming tourist trap decorated with purposefully kitschy decor representing Colombia's regional diversity.

After dinner the ACR needed to spend its surplus budget or risk losing it, so the woman charged with paying for dinner ordered two dozen more cocktails. As the Canadian DDR expert danced between two performers dressed as clowns, the former Taliban spokesperson stared into his soup and muttered, "The cultures are so different" before excusing himself by giving the universal sleep gesture, pressed hands to tilted ear. The comment served at once as a statement of the obvious and an understated critique of the idea of "best practices," the buzzword used to stand

FIGURE C.2. International delegates participate in the group discussion that ended the "South-South Tour" organized by the ACR in Meta Department in 2012. Photo by author, 2012.

FIGURE C.3. A celebration at the end of the ACR'S "South-South Tour." At left, deputy director of Afghanistan's High Peace Council and former Taliban militant Abdul Hakim
Mujahid. Photo by author, 2012.

in for the inherently problematic task of grafting the policies of one conflict zone onto another.

Branding the Postconflict State

That branding, an exercise that creates a gaping hole between that which
is projected publicly and that which is guarded secretly, has become the
basis for an emergent mode of governance is fitting for a neoliberal moment in which most state institutions have gradually been gutted.[22] Since
the 1990s Colombia has created a warfare state in lieu of a welfare state.
The government has worked to obscure this unflattering reality through
a marketing offensive that positions Colombia as a postconflict nation.

The relentless bombardment of the public sphere with the PAHD's
marketized propaganda is only one element in a broader framework in
which the Colombian state marshals its bureaucratic, symbolic, and diplomatic resources (as in the ACR's South-South tours) to perform its postconflict future and thereby call it into being. Although the Colombian

government has succeeded in projecting itself internationally as ascendant, creating a narrative of having transcended the plague of political violence that has marred its history, a certain hollowness haunts its efforts. Branding may be a potent way for companies to funnel consumers' affective investments back into a commodity, making shoppers complicit in the production of surplus value, but branding's performative force, that is to say its ability to enact a change in status or identity, is weak. Why weak? By way of comparison, take a classic example of a performative utterance: a judge declaring a couple husband and wife. The power of the pronouncement to change the status of the two individuals before him has legal, ethnic, and religious traditions behind it. In comparison, the freewheeling sign system of branding can muster none of those classic sources of authority. Neither can it call upon a wellspring of moral authority.

Although marketing is capitalism's default system of signification, the relationship it fosters between signs and referents is notoriously loose.[23] Jean Baudrillard, an early critic of consumer culture, decried advertising's role in creating "a giant recombinatorial machine"—a manipulable system of signs in constant flux.[24] While militaries and states have been attracted to the agility of the marketing system, they turn a blind eye to the weakness of its sign system. Can the world of branding, which builds upon the pseudo-scientific claims of marketers, be trusted in such weighty matters as rehabilitating militaries or remaking states?

In Colombia questions smolder. Has the Colombian military really become a humanitarian actor because of its role in demobilizing guerrilla fighters? It is worth pausing to think about demobilization as a ritual. Peace-building technocracy has divided the transition from combatant to civilian into three stages: disarmament, demobilization, and reintegration, or DDR. The overriding purpose of this staged process is to periodize lives into a military before and a civilian after. In this way DDR operates, like graduation, as a ceremonial passage. Following French folklorist Arnold Van Gennep's classic formulation, rites of passage steer individuals from one social status to another: girl to woman, man to husband, profane to sacred—in three steps: separation, liminality, and reincorporation. By the end of a ritual, according to Van Gennep, the subject has delinked definitively from one social category and emerged as a member of another, communing with her new group.[25]

Other than the three-part delineation and the emphasis on transition, however, Colombia's individual demobilization process does not resemble a ritual in any classic formulation. As we have seen, the former guerrillas who pass through the government's staged transition are called upon to inform on their former comrades and undertake military operations. Paramilitaries eager to exploit the knowledge and training of the demobilized make them similar offers. Partly demobilized and partly remobilized, former rebels are left in an interstitial position, civilian but "not entirely free," as one former guerrilla put it. The persistent fear that *someone* is looking for them—their former comrades, the law, the paramilitaries, local gangs—fosters an enduring feeling of being mired "betwixt and between" armed groups and stuck in a liminal stage between military and civilian statuses.[26] Most seek anonymity in the periphery of Colombian cities, where they live as atomized subjects, form nuclear families, and desist from collective organization, denying themselves the communion and community that are the hallmarks of reincorporation in the ritual sense. The result is a dispersed set of individuals living in precarious economic conditions who are politically paralyzed by their own act of betrayal and carry with them an enduring stigma. It is not coincidental that many of my former guerrilla interlocutors use the word *uprooted* (*desarraigado*) to describe their sense of alienation, a feeling exacerbated by their need to adapt to a capitalist system for which they are utterly unprepared. By making demobilization into an individual decision, defection with welfare, the opportunities for former guerrillas to bond with members of their new civilian status are damaged from the start.[27]

From ex-combatants' perspective, Colombia's individual demobilization program is a ritualistic process predisposed to fail.[28] That failure, however, is productive, it does ideological work by demonstrating the state's ability to coerce and co-opt even its most militant detractors and impose on them the attenuated social contract of neoliberal governance. In chapter 2 I presented the individual demobilization program as an adaption of a biblical parable, the return of the prodigal son, and suggested that as former combatants demobilized, they buttressed the patriarchal authority of the state. The care that the forgiving father enacts is a veneer atop a more brutal reality. The reintegration of former rebels reinforces not just any patriarchal state but Colombia's iteration of neoliberalism, which echoes that of its patron and ally, the United States, in which state institutions—other than an expansive security apparatus—are steadily stripped of their capacity. The difference between the two allies is Colombia's more robust allocation of welfare for the conflict's victims and perpetrators.

Government spending on demobilization and reintegration is only part of a broader performance of postconflict statehood. The government has also created expansive programs to return peasants to land they had been displaced from and to compensate victims of the conflict, as well as a government research institute and museum to curate intellectual and cultural production about the conflict. Implementing postconflict policy has entailed a large public expenditure destined for two target populations: perpetrators and victims. Although a staggering eight million victims have registered with the government's Victims Unit, the vast majority of Colombian citizens are beyond the purview of postconflict welfare. Simultaneously, public-private schemes continuously encroach on core state functions, like providing health care and education to all citizens. By using sophisticated public relations techniques the Colombian government shows its commitment to emblematic state functions, such as drawing down the armed conflict, while hiding the structural dysfunction within the state that is creating the conditions for social unrest (and possibly yet another armed movement).

In retrospect, the performance of postconflict statehood that the government had been practicing since 2003 was an elaborate preparation for events that would unfold thirteen years later. The PAHD served as a placeholder between the peace talks of 1999–2002 and those of 2012–16. Between 2010 and 2012, the two sides met clandestinely and established a six-point agenda for the talks.[29] After almost four years of intensive negotiations, the parties reached a historic peace agreement. Although the fieldwork for this book occurred primarily between 2011 and 2013, I returned to Colombia for three months every summer afterward, the fall semester of 2015, and the spring semester of 2018. Those returns allowed me to gauge the shifting political atmosphere over the course of the peace process and its initial implementation, lines of continuity and moments of rupture.

Shortly after the two sides announced a bilateral ceasefire in the summer of 2016, I stopped in at the PAHD's offices. The bustle of staff from one office to another and the incessant ringing of telephones were gone. Desertions from the FARC had diminished to a trickle. People continued to leave the ELN, but at a decreasing rate. The government, and the country as a whole, focused its attention on the incremental progress being made toward a peace agreement in Havana, Cuba, where the negotiations were held. The prospect of an accord signaled a return to the status quo ante, in which a peace agreement creates a temporal divide between a conflict and a postconflict period. *Postconflict* was one of the most frequently uttered phrases on television and radio news and in policy discussion forums and university auditoriums through the negotiating period. The country was discursively preparing for the implementation of rural, political, judicial, and antidrug reforms, not to mention the updated schema for demobilization and reintegration, written into the 310-page agreement. How long would this new postconflict period last? Senior government officials gave ballpark estimates of fifteen years, acknowledging that the dynamics put in motion by the accord would extend into the 2030s. The thirteen-year preparatory "pre-postconflict period," however, is already casting a shadow over the postconflict period.[30] The precedence for remobilization, the lurking threat of paramilitarism, and the enduring logics of espionage and counterinsurgency will not simply fade away. Terms matter. The PAHD emptied demobilization of its prior meaning for thirteen years; that cannot simply be undone with the stroke of a pen.

The PAHD and its belligerent model of individual demobilization is not the only specter that haunts Colombia's postconflict future. Although the demobilization of the FARC's military structures in 2017 appears as a last gasp of armed Marxism in Latin America, class conflict and the spectral presence of Marxist politics loom. When I traveled to Cuba to interview FARC negotiators, one of them, Rodrigo Granda, acknowledged that the result of the negotiation amounted to the implementation of a bourgeoisie reformist agenda, not a radical transformation of the state, which the FARC had declared itself to be fighting to achieve for over five decades.

Rapprochement between Cuba and the US, which took place at the same time as the Colombian negotiations, also signaled a center-left convergence in the hemisphere, even as the region showed signs of swinging back to the right after its left turn in the late 1990s and 2000s. By all outward indications, the militant Marxist left in Colombia had been so far marginalized in the 2010s that it had essentially disappeared from the political stage.

Yet it is precisely now, when the last vestige of the revolutionary ferment catalyzed by the Cuban Revolution of 1959 burns out, that its specter is haunting Latin America. Philosopher Jacques Derrida made a similar point in 1993, amid the implosion of the Soviet Union, arguing that Marxism's political death had lent it a ghostly life. Derrida writes, "Perhaps people are no longer afraid of Marxists, but they are still afraid of certain non-Marxists who have not renounced Marx's inheritance, crypto-Marxists, pseudo- or para-'Marxists' who would be standing by to change the guard, but behind features or quotation marks that the anxious experts of anti-communism are not trained to unmask." The post–peace accord period in Colombia will entail a reckoning with such quasi-Marxist apparitions. This will be a war that is not war and a peace that is not peaceful. In *Specters of Marx* Derrida muses about Hamlet's dialogue with the ghost of his father and picks at Hamlet's observation that "time is out of joint." Teasing apart the logic of spectrality, Derrida notes:

> A spectral moment, a moment that no longer belongs to time, if one understands by this word the linking of modalized presents (past present, actual present: "now," future present). We are questioning in this instant, we are asking ourselves about this instant that is not docile to time, at least to what we call time. Furtive and untimely, the apparition of the specter does not belong to that time, it does not give time, not that one: "Enter the ghost, exit the ghost, re-enter the ghost" (Hamlet).[31]

Colombia's model of individual demobilization may have helped to push the FARC toward the negotiating table, but in the process it unhinged times of war from times of peace, blurring demobilization and remobilization: enter the ghost, exit the ghost, enter the ghost.

The PAHD has cut a widening wake of indeterminacy in which war, peace, policing, culture, marketing, and business flow into and through each other. Though the state has spurred this confluence, it is unclear whether it will be able to navigate its currents. Governance by brand management, after all, is but a compensatory strategy for hollowed-out institutions that are shells of themselves. Students, peasants, women, indigenous peoples, and Afro-Colombians, in their various collectives, have been activated in overlapping social movements, and, like Hamlet, they "know not 'seems.'" As their mobilizations stir, so do dark narco-paramilitary forces intent upon stifling the promise of a more inclusive democracy coded into the peace agreement. As political contestation absorbs the intensity of the armed conflict (an inversion of Prussian general and military theorist Carl Von Clausewitz's dictum that war is but politics by other means), brand warfare has already proved a constant through the transitional period and is projecting into the country's political future. Organizations across the political spectrum, from social media–savvy social movements to the already brand-oriented right-wing opposition, are embracing brand warfare.[32]

A similar pattern emerged through the negotiating period (2012–16). For example, the FARC has sought to rebrand itself as a political movement by creating a YouTube-based news program and trying to build its media operations, a response to its resounding defeat in the propaganda war. (The FARC leaders I have interviewed readily acknowledged that loss but contextualized it by saying that they prioritized military resistance over maintaining the group's media infrastructure.) In the middle of the negotiations, the FARC changed the program's aggressive name, *Insurgent Bulletin*, and slogan, "Breaking the media siege," to the non-militant *New Colombia News* and "Informing for peace." Sergio Marín, head of the FARC's commission for propaganda in its peace delegation, told me in Havana, "We are absolutely clear on the fact that you cannot do politics in the twenty-first century without impacting the media and social networks." He spoke of the group's deliberations about how thoroughly to segment its target audience, prioritizing twenty-six-to-thirty-six-year-olds in the urban middle classes. He noted that FARC *milicianos* have clandestinely solicited feedback on their programing from high-end marketing firms in northern Bogotá (perhaps Lowe/SSP3 or one of its competitors).[33] There is no doubt that the FARC's counterhegemonic project is already deeply inflected by the cultural logic of marketing, a transformation that accelerated through the Havana negotiations.

Brand warfare is poised to proliferate, and not only in post–peace accord Colombia. What the PAHD has modeled for the Colombian government and a US-backed international order is but one case of branding's expansion into the terrain of warfare and governance in the early twenty-first century. The proliferation of the Colombian model of demobilization and brand warfare is disquieting, for it enables a corrosive form of deceit that insists it is not being deceitful, even as it redefines terms and rearranges categories. In the process, the Colombian synthesis of antiguerrilla warfare and consumer marketing that I have traced in this book casts distinctions seminal to the twentieth century—between military and civilian spheres, and the separation of a conflict period from a postconflict period—to the wind. This is more than a little makeup. In the epilogue I take up the issue of making up, or, in the literal translation of the reflexive Spanish verb *maquillarse*, making oneself up.

Diego

D: *I was a very passive guy, even apolitical. I didn't like politics and disliked weapons even more. My life changed when the state, the public force, killed a sister of mine. That's when my thinking changed. I got the worst illness: vengeance. They killed my sister in 1993, and that's when my life began to change.*

I was born into a humble family. My parents were honest workers, peasants. They always instilled in us the value of work. I kept that up until we started to see our family getting killed. So we asked ourselves: where is this situation coming from? At that time there was an absurd, intense war. My classmates would appear dead on the highway and nobody was held accountable. The police did nothing. The military did nothing. They are dead voices, nobody responds.

As time passed, three guys would come to the farm where I worked and would talk about other countries. I remember they spoke about the Russian Revolution, a communist party, they spoke about Carlos Marx, Vladimir Lenin, people who [you never learn about] in your little education. Back then I had only done elementary school and could barely read and write. They started stirring my curiosity. They are people who know what they're doing: they touch on the loss of your family and show how it's the forces of the state, the army and police, who should be defending, but in this case were killing my family.

A: The feeling of vengeance or rage in that moment is why you joined?

D: *It's an ugly feeling, because it's wrapped up with pain and the inability to do anything. Because the enemy is a giant that you can't find, and you don't know how to attack it to defend yourself. When you join an organization like the FARC, a political-military organization, they work on that part of you, so it's not all about vengeance. They talked to us about social change, about how we had to fight the state because this war isn't about a personal objective, that we had to bring it to a different level.*

Suddenly you depend on a weapon. They teach you how to maintain it, how to carry a magazine, about munitions, what caliber of weapon, because there are many weapons of different calibers and models. As they say, "Weapons are made like women: some are big and beautiful, others small, and if you look at their style, very ugly." We learned what a military confrontation is like, but I didn't have a battle for a long time because I was in an area that was very calm.

A: How long did you last in the organization?

D: *Eight years, eight little years . . .*

The conflict began to intensify in 2000 when the military and the supposed self-defense forces, or paramilitaries, began to enter into those areas where the public force had been taking it easy. The paramilitaries knew there were guerrillas [in the area], so then things took on a more ominous dimension, because they didn't only come for the guerrilla but also displacing masses [of people] with a policy of extermination. Then the war fell on the peasant as well as the guerrilla soldier—the peasant also became a military target.

A: In Sucre [a department in northern Colombia]?

D: *Yeah, in a part of southern of Sucre that is very rich in minerals. Many people had illegal crops, which is an illness for Colombia; it exacerbated the violence. It produced easy money, so the war got worse, since everyone wanted to control it: the army, the police, the paramilitaries. And it's no secret that even the guerrilla got corrupted by the easy money.*

A: So why did you decide to leave?

D: *When I decided to withdraw from the organization, well, I had learned a lot there about how to make plans in the long, medium, and short term. I made those plans [for myself]. As I looked around I saw that taking power militarily kept getting postponed. I started thinking, "Am I going to spend my whole life in this? Am I going to keep watching people die?" Many young people had joined with me, and they only lasted a little while, one or two years. Some were captured, others massacred.*

I am going to tell you an anecdote, because the public force and the state didn't believe it. I had made my way through some farms and made friends with some men. Two years later I came back to our camp and found them detained [by the guerrilla]. For security the guys were detained as enemies, since the paramilitaries and military had already entered into the area. But I knew that they were humble peasants, workers. It bothered me because I knew where they came from.

The commander gave the order for me to guard them, which I did for a month. As detainees they could listen to the radio, whatever stations they wanted, until late at night, since they weren't inside [the guerrilla].

I remember that one was an evangelical and the other an agrarian engineer; he had his farm and a house in the city. They talked to me about how the state wasn't only the police and the military, and how I could get in touch with the church to access the [demobilization] program that they talked about on the radio. The church or the mayor, or whoever could do me the favor, if I wanted to turn myself in. They said that when they were released they could help me.

When the day came for them to be released—thank God [the FARC] let them go—they went to their homes. One of them had given me his cell number. When I said good-bye he said, "Call me—I am going to check on a few things in the city." He did. The guy contacted the International Red Cross. At that time the war kept intensifying in southern Sucre. It was 2005 and very ugly, and one day I managed to call him and he transferred me to the Red Cross. That person came to get me, but the military didn't let the Red Cross's truck pass. I lasted three days in hiding until they called again and said they couldn't get through because of a paramilitary checkpoint, but they knew where a military patrol was passing. So I found that municipality and turned myself in.

The military held Diego on a base for three months. Diego feels he would have been marooned there longer and possibly framed, since "the military was cooking up something for the press," had the International Red Cross not arrived at the base asking about him by name.

D: *They finally sent us to Bogotá, and we started another struggle—one that I think is harder than the one we left. It's starting a process from scratch, restarting the daily struggle to survive—to build a life like I've always wanted, a quiet life.*

This mountain of concrete [city] has eaten a ton of people. If you're not smart in this concrete mountain you'll fail quickly.

A: Can you say more?

D: *In the countryside you have your whole life. You don't pay for utilities. I had my farm, and I didn't get a water bill or an electricity bill. There you don't get an internet bill. But here in these mountains of concrete, there's an owner, a state that controls it and even charges for the air you breathe.*

Beyond that, the options to work are minimal. There are compañeros who have had to go back to the mountains. Those who were from the right look to join leftist organizations, and those from the left look to join the [armed] right—and they go back. Or some get together and make a little criminal group because the state can't fulfill Colombia's political constitution and guarantee a decent job, housing, education.

I know people that have gone back. Others say, "No, I won't go back, brother." They are the people who crawl on their elbows in the concrete mountain, scrubbing around for their daily bread, but with honor and dignity. . . .

I suffered from a condition called "postwar." A motorcycle honk would knock me off balance. Sitting and waiting at a traffic light bothered me, would make me stressed and sick. I spent two weeks locked in a room, only reading and drinking water—nothing else.

I started my process in bad shape. But there are people who listen with their heart and help and don't want anything in return. One day I was on the bus and a nurse sat at my side.

She said, "Son, what is going on with you?"

I said, "When I drink water it makes me cold, and if I eat something hot it makes me hot."

"Look, I work in a hospital; come by and I'll take a look."

She talked to other doctors who helped me. In Colombia, if you don't have an EPS or Sisben [insurance] or a certain document, they don't attend to you. The girl from the bus was in odontology but called over the doctor and said, "This guy has all these symptoms." That doctor was from general medicine, but he brought me to a psychologist. I had six sessions with three psychologists, and they said you have this that and the other— they helped me.

The experience with the FARC that most affected Diego psychologically was the death of his girlfriend in combat.

D: *Once they attacked the camp and they killed my woman. I couldn't do anything for her, because when I saw the shots going everywhere I was in my underwear. They train you that your weapon is your woman, and your life is your weapon, and your mother is your weapon—that your life depends on your weapon. It was like 3:30 a.m. in the bunk, and the first thing I did [upon hearing the shots] was drop to the ground, taking down my rifle. But my* compañera *didn't drop to the ground. When I put on the camouflage, my boots, and started to look for where the lead was coming from, I moved her, but she was already bathed in blood. I tried to get her out but I couldn't. They had killed her.*

You get another woman, another compañera. *Now I have a* compañera, *but I don't know—love kind of goes with that person. You don't fall in love again.*

They say that in war you don't have any friends, but that's not true. I had friends who left for a different operation. I went one way and they went another. We would see each other again after two or three months and it's such a tremendous happiness, it's like a blood relative. You don't forget about some people. I have demobilized friends who I see on the internet [social networks]. I haven't had the chance to meet them in person, but it would be nice. I've said this to the psychologists who supposedly give us psychosocial workshops [in the ACR], but they say it's bad, they say we'll reorganize and become delinquents. But no, everyone decides for himself.

A: What has your experience been like in the [demobilization] program?

D: *What I have deduced is that the only interest the state has is that the demobilized turns himself in, and turns in his weapon, and to be able to say, "We have one combatant less." But do they solve your problems and follow up on what they promise?*

For example, they tell you that you have the right to higher education; you can go to the office and get credits in ICETEX [government agency that distributes loans for higher education] to study. I've done it. What did they ask of me? Real estate, a cosigner, a salary three times the minimum. Where the hell am I going to get that? Who is going to be my cosigner?

A: When you were on the battalion, did they ask you to be a guide or to . . .

D: *They invited me to join in operations. I came conscious of what I was doing. If I leave one struggle that I saw as justified, I can't come and keep on fighting for some money. What does the army offer? "Come, turn yourself in, and come and kill your* compañeros—*and make some money." That's money I've never wanted to earn.*

A: But did they take you anyway?

D: *No, no. They don't force you, but they do offer. Some people let themselves be wooed by the money, or want to go. I know cases of people who testified against people for $170. They would go in and point at peasants and fill up trucks with them, calling them guerrilla collaborators to earn $170 for every person they convict.*

As someone who has demobilized, I don't agree with this. I don't agree that they take the demobilized on operations. Because if it's a demobilization program, and if we look at the international side, a demobilized [person] can't use weapons. But our state sends them with the army, with the police. What they are doing is taking off one set of camouflage and putting on another.

I've seen people get $110,000 and have a party for two weeks, ten days, four days, drinking and saying, "As soon as the money runs out I'll go on another operation."

Here, when you arrive, you leave behind your previous life. Today I have friends from the AUC whom I've exchanged fire with on more than one occasion. We say, "Brother, the war is over for us, but in this concrete jungle we need to apply the law of survival."

A: How did you know that it was the same people you had exchanged lead with?

D: *I have a story with a friend, a* paisa *[person from Antioquia]. We were doing our high school [equivalency] courses together. One day during the break we were drinking soda, and he overheard me talk about the area where I used to patrol. It got his attention and we started talking. He even knew my alias. He used to stalk me. He said, "Look, now I can look at my enemy who I went hunting for, who I exchanged fire with, and here we are having a soda."*

A: What was that conversation like?

D: *As soon as we left the school we drank soda and talked for like two hours. We are still friends. He's an amazing person. We call each other, we talk, we help each other. He defended Puerto Pérez in northwest Antioquia, and I was in the same area. In civilian life you get into heated discussions and say ugly words, but not over there. There you only see the camouflage, take the safety off your rifle, and go. There are no words, nothing. Today we'll discuss a subject for the whole day, if he's right or if I am right.*

FIGURE INT.6. Drawing by Lucas Ospina.

Target Intimacy

September 2016

D own in the camp where guerrillas and journalists bunked and bathed together, men were shaving and women putting on makeup (figures E.1, E.2). Spirits ran high as FARC rebels broke out their civilian clothes and prepared for a party. This was the last night of the Décima, the FARC's tenth guerrilla conference, in the Plains of Yarí, deep in the insurgency's southern territory. Journalists had flocked to document the last of a type, the Latin American jungle revolutionary.

The FARC had made extensive preparations to do some guerrilla marketing of its own. Two hundred delegates representing all the FARC's fighters had lent their approval to the peace accord just hours earlier. A closing ceremony and one more nighttime concert on a stage fit for the Rolling Stones were all that remained of the six-day extravaganza (figure E.3). Throughout the festivities journalists would snark about "FARC in the park" or "FARC Woodstock," while also indulging in the eco-conflict tourism / experiential marketing adventure that the FARC had orchestrated.

The sky had been ominous all day. By the time everyone gathered in front of the giant stage for the closing event, the wind was gusting across the open field, swinging the giant LED screens from the chains that suspended them on either side of the stage. As I walked through the crowd, two guerrillas, a couple, recognized me and waved me over. Seated under a square canopy that advertised Aguila Light beer, they convinced me to claim a plastic chair by their side. The position offered a sweeping panorama of the grounds.

Timochenko, the FARC's commander, launched into a speech. In

FIGURE E.I. A FARC fighter shaving before the closing event of the Décima conference. Photo by author, 2016.

FIGURE E.2. A FARC fighter putting on makeup before the closing event of the conference. Photo by author, 2016.

FIGURE E.3. Esteban, a young rapper and member of the FARC, performs onstage with the Bogotá-based reggae band Alerta Kamarada. Photo by author, 2016.

a voice more impassioned than usual, he declared: "We dream that it will never again be necessary for Colombians to rise up in arms so their voices can be heard and their demands felt, like we've had to do in a fratricidal war that we never wanted." Rolling thunder filled the pause between that sentence and the next: "Our horizon has always been a political solution, which is why peace is the most beautiful victory." The guerrilla leader's reflections on peace wrestling to overtake war resounded in the late afternoon sky. Orange sunset light glowed unevenly across the horizon, as if a giant egg yolk were oozing east, only to gradually fuse with the darkening charcoal clouds of a gathering storm (figure E.4).[1] A faint rainbow appeared as a witness to the proceedings. It was more of an eerie apparition of a rainbow, really, soon snuffed out by the thickness of the air. Though the atmospherics were coincidental, it is hard to resist the temptation to read the rainbow's fleeting presence as a metaphor for the precariousness of the peace being celebrated.

Timochenko concluded his address, and then, fifteen minutes later, rain poured down. Most everyone had managed to retreat to their dinner stations in time to avoid getting drenched. While having drinks with

FIGURE E.4. Closing ceremony of the Décima conference. Photo by Andrés Cardona, 2016.

a group of photographers after dinner, I saw James and Javier seated across the tent. I had seen them in nearly the same place two days earlier. On that occasion a wave of disorientation had rippled from my head to my knees as I recognized James. I was not expecting to find government agents at the Décima. I had spied James doing his best to look the part of a communist, with an Arab shawl slung over his shoulders and a duck-bill cap pulled down on his forehead. We had met for the first time in the summer of 2007, in the office of Nicolás, the commander of the military intelligence unit discussed in chapter 3. Back then Nicolás was direct-ing the PAHD's strategic area team and James was his right-hand man. James, perhaps more than anyone else I met during my research, sus-pected that I was a spy. He would "jokingly" suggest that I was inform-ing for the CIA, the Mossad, or the FARC. By way of cross-examination and intimidation, he would ask what class I taught at the university and what brand of cell phone I carried. I recognized these questions for what they were: efforts to sow paranoia. His cautiousness helped James earn the trust of Sergio Jaramillo, the high commissioner for peace in the Santos administration (2010–18), who is commonly considered the mas-termind of the peace process. From 2010 to 2016 James served as the human link between the PAHD and the presidency, enabling a seamless flow of strategic intelligence emanating from interviews with former guerrillas to key decision makers in the Colombian government.

When I first recognized James from across the catering tent at the Décima, a series of loosely connected thoughts ran through my head: *What secret mission is he on? He's probably here with a special gadget to capture all the electronic communication in the area. Should I say hi to him? I do not want to be presumed to be in cahoots with the government.* When our eyes locked, he tilted his head, suggesting that I come over. My legs responded for me. With a wide grin, he said, "Alex Fattal," emphasizing my last name's consonance with "fatal." "Sit down," he said, grinning with pleasure at my bewilderment.

As I sat, I recognized the man next to him, Javier. We had met only once, six months earlier, at the Yellow Submarine, a venue in Havana that features Western rock and roll. I had gone to the club to meet with Jaramillo. Conversing in a loud music venue was not ideal, but, pressed with negotiations, that had been the only time Jaramillo could talk.

James and Javier handled the most sensitive tasks for Jaramillo in his wide-ranging portfolio as the high commissioner for peace. James admitted that he was on a top-secret mission, and pulled out his cell phone to prove it. He swiped through photographs and stopped at an image of himself standing next to Iván Márquez, the FARC's lead negotiator. *Phew, the FARC knew he was there.* Javier and James had traveled to the Plains of Yarí to tie up loose ends in the negotiation. Although the peace accord would be signed in a stately ceremony in Cartagena attended by UN Secretary General Ban Ki-moon and fifteen heads of state only three days after the conference ended, many details still needed to be resolved. The negotiators had rushed to the finish line in the summer of 2016. Perhaps they accelerated to sign an agreement before the Nobel Peace Prize committee selected a winner in the fall. (President Santos would go on to receive the Peace Prize that year.) Maybe they sensed the Colombian public growing weary of the negotiations as they neared the four-year mark. Whatever the reason, the accord still needed massaging.

When I saw James and Javier the night of the closing ceremony, I overcame my paranoia about being mistaken for an intelligence agent, and I joined them for a drink. A group of five guerrillas milled around them, keeping a watchful eye. James explained that the young men were their security detail. I marveled at how the FARC was protecting, rather than holding hostage, senior members of the government. The expression *el mundo da muchas vueltas* (the world takes many turns), used to the point of cliché in Colombia, came to mind. I asked James about what I was most interested in, the model of demobilization and reintegration for FARC fighters that the two sides had agreed upon in the third point of the accord, which was ambitiously titled "End of the Conflict." As one of the thorniest issues of the negotiation, it had been left for last. Two weeks before the agreement was announced, the sides had still been far from each other on the question of what model of reintegration to adopt. How had the parties managed to close the gap so quickly? James suggested that they hadn't entirely, that the issue had been resolved hastily as politicians rushed toward the extravagant signing ceremony (*el plumazo*).

The root of the disagreement was the degree to which the reintegration process should be collective versus individual. The FARC wanted to pool the resources that would be disbursed to its former combatants to help preserve the group's cohesion as a political movement. The government, in an adaptation of its existing strategy of using demobilization as a counterinsurgency weapon, wanted to maintain its emphasis on the individual in order to dilute the FARC and fragment its political movement. The two sides resolved a hybrid scheme. Reintegration would be primarily administered via what the agreement calls ECOMUN, which stands for Communal Social Economies, a newly established network of collectives. *But* it would also have an individual option for those who preferred to strike out on their own and receive a personal welfare package. Under the agreement, each individual combatant would decide which of the routes to take.

"These guys," James said, pointing to his security detail behind us, "in four years, what are they going to be worried about?" I turned to look at the young men horsing around with each other. I pondered his question, a variation on the same question journalists had been posing and re-posing to guerrillas throughout the conference. "What happens when they need to earn a living? How will they get everything they want when they leave this world?" James continued, gesturing to indicate the conference grounds. James saw that I was following his logic: once guerrillas were no longer obligated, under threat of violence, to remain in the organization and deferential to their leaders, and when they faced the harsh reality of earning a living, the FARC's collective project would stumble. He was counting on late liberal capitalism's proven ability to engulf the individual and co-opt its ideological challengers.

I expressed surprise that the government had agreed to the FARC's proposal of the ECOMUN. Paraphrasing the government's thinking, James replied in a sardonic tone, "ECOMUN, what's that? Whatever, let's do it, it doesn't matter." The government had managed to maintain the individual reintegration option, which it believed would siphon off a significant percentage of the FARC's combatants–cum–political operatives.

Both the FARC and the government realized that the next battle would center on the implementation of the accords and the FARC's ability to provide a viable economic alternative for its ex-combatants in the regions where its political movement would concentrate. The economic question was interlaced with an affective one. How would the practical economic challenges square with guerrillas' reconnection with their families after years, if not decades, apart? This was not some hypothetical concern for the postdisarmament future. The magnetic drive of familial reconnection pulsed along the edges of the culture industry–like spectacle of the Décima.

One evening in the middle of the conference, Aries Vigoth, a regional star of folkloric music from the eastern plains, read scribbled notes passed to him from audience members in the pit below. Most of these were song requests and dedications. One of the notes, however, read, "Carrillo, from the Yarí Front, your family hasn't seen you for twenty years and it needs you urgently. If you are here, please come toward the stage and let yourself be seen. Your family is here, waiting, hoping to see you." The crowd let out a collective gasp. After a moment of silent staring toward the stage, applause erupted, and journalists swarmed the guerrilla and his mother to record their reunion in the pit below the stage. Mothers and other family members had flocked to the Plains of Yarí. They approached the FARC's media team, the conference's most visible representatives, prompting its staff to create a special sign-up sheet for people who had come looking for their loved ones. As I observed family members in their felicitous and frustrated family reunions, I recalled the slogan of Lowe/SSP3's 2013 Christmas campaign: "Before being a guerrilla, you are my child." Beneath the surface of the Décima ran a more personal current that included not only family members' trips to Yarí but also phone calls, email messages, and Facebook searches.

The internet, however, was the one piece of infrastructure that the FARC arranged for the conference that had faltered. The company it had contracted, Amazon Connection, failed to provide the wifi it promised leaving only a single antenna outpost where people could connect.

One evening, while waiting in line for a half hour of connectivity for my cell phone, I struck up a conversation with David, a FARC rebel living among the journalists. He had opened a Facebook account a week earlier in hopes of finding his family. Like the majority of rebels, he carried no family photographs with him. If the military captured him or raided his camp and got hold of such photos, his relatives could be endangered. Facebook had been a revelation. He downloaded as many photos from his siblings' accounts as his phone could store and his connection time allowed. He showed me one image of himself seated before a cake, surrounded by siblings and cousins. The picture from his thirteenth birthday was remarkable in its universality. It could have been any band of siblings and cousins giddily leaning their heads toward the birthday boy who was seated in the center and smiling widely for the camera. That was David's last birthday at home. He joined the FARC nine months later. The kids in that photograph, he explained, had become the adults in the images he then showed me, young men and women in their thirties posing with children of their own.

David slept in the camp below, among the journalists. His left leg had been amputated above the knee, and the visual aspect of his injury attracted journalists looking to tell the story of the FARC's transition through an individual guerrilla. I didn't want to burden him by asking him to retell his story, so I asked only about his plans to see his family. As soon as the FARC put down its guns, he said, he would travel to see them. Would he continue to participate in the political movement? "Yes," he said, unenthusiastically, "but in an area near [my family]." For David and his cohort of approximately eight thousand other FARC fighters who disarmed in 2017, family—in whatever form it may take— matters.[2] Inevitably they will need to juggle the competing priorities of their political commitments, friendships forged in the war, and reconnection with kin.

What connects that story to the rest of this book is the transformation of intimacy into a battleground. As we have seen, the military and its partners in the consumer marketing industry have worked together to game a matrix of allegiance, paranoia, emotional bonds, and seduction to precipitate the desired betrayal: a guerrilla's abandonment of the armed struggle. Intimacy is the common denominator in this matrix, and its appropriation by counterinsurgency doctrine correlates with a structural transformation in advanced capitalism, in which the creation of surplus value is tied to the production and exploitation of consumers' affective investments in commodities.[3] Love, as we have seen throughout this book, is the war's ultimate target.

Kevin Roberts, the CEO of the advertising firm Saatchi & Saatchi, writes, "Lovemarks . . . represent the next step in the evolution of brands. Lovemarks are brands that are not simply respected and trusted, but loved."[4] Anthropologist Robert Foster notes that lovemarks "signal an emotional connection and attachment to a brand that goes beyond reason—and for which a premium price can be charged."[5] Like emergent marketing tactics that build value and create new markets by insinuating themselves into increasingly intimate spheres, wars waged principally through human intelligence operate on ever more personal levels. The government has been honing this intimate mode of brand warfare for thirteen years through the PAHD. To contain the effects of this affective onslaught, the FARC took disciplinary measures such as increasing the threat of violence against deserters and their families and redoubling its ideological work with the rank and file. But the FARC's leadership was rightfully worried about what would happen after its troops turned over their weapons, dispersed, and found their families.

Boris is the FARC's lead videographer and a central member of its communications division. He speaks in ultra-quotable phrases such as "We are going to put down our rifles and pick up our cameras," a comment he made to the PBS program *NewsHour*. I spoke with him and his girlfriend, Tanja, the FARC's Dutch foreign-fighter celebrity, at the Décima. They drew a parallel between the then-imminent demobilization and the situation of FARC guerrillas who had left prison after serving jail sentences. The FARC had appealed to the former prisoners to return to the movement, but they had chosen to go home to their families instead. After a while, however, many returned to the FARC. Boris said, "They got home and it was worse than before. Their mothers were in a difficult fix—no money. The first two days they cooked them chicken, but after two or three days they'd say, 'My child, what are you going to do?'" Boris claimed that the people freed from prison had started returning to the FARC "to get a better future," suggesting that the structural conditions of entrenched poverty would make the FARC's collective initiatives appealing.

When my discussion with Boris and Tanja turned to the economic reintegration on the horizon, Tanja said, "We have to offer them something. If they want to leave, that's fine, but it shouldn't be because we didn't have anything to offer."

"Something that works in the long term, that's worthwhile," Boris said. "Money, work—that's what we need to provide the guerrilla once he leaves."

"I think that the world really doesn't know the guerrilla, its work ethic," Tanja said. "The guerrilla builds a village in a week."

"They built [the conference grounds] in three weeks. They're ants," Boris said.

Should the vast majority of guerrilla fighters choose the ECOMUN, as opposed to individual reintegration, this army of "ants" could create ecotourism initiatives marketed to travelers curious about the conflict, start agriculture collectives, export fair-trade coffee, build regional transportation companies. Such a collectivist economy would fold into the FARC's political project. That's the FARC's utopian vision.[6] Will that vision materialize? Will the group and its allies on the left be able to instantiate their socialist ideals at the local level and link their various regional initiatives in a national movement? Key among the challenges before them are a historical penchant of the extreme right to assassinate the unarmed left; macroeconomic development schemes planned for territories long held by the guerrilla; the persistence of illegal economies that stir temptation toward self-enrichment; and an uncertain national political picture that could roll back or scrap large parts of the peace agreement. Though the future is uncertain, what is clear is that the dream of a postconflict future will continue to be deferred.[7]

The peace agreement of 2016 sketched an ambitious plan for the postconflict state's regeneration. To what extent the changes were real or merely cosmetic is hard to say. For example, the Colombian Agency for Reintegration (ACR) became the Agency for Reincorporation and Normalization (ARN), while retaining key personnel and much of the previous organizational structure. I asked James about the bureaucratic renaming and reshuffling, observing that agencies that have honed their services over thirteen years seemed to be out of the picture in the final accord. He brushed aside my observation, saying, "We'll put makeup on that later" ("Esto lo maquillamos después"). Supposedly this metaphorical makeup would hide the fact that the new policy bears close parallels to the old. Makeup might hide the wrinkles of the postconflict state and give it a fresh mask; but how many layers of makeup can be applied to how many surfaces for how long before it all starts to crack up?

Ten days after the Décima ended, workers from the Civil Registry tallied votes from the plebiscite to approve or reject the accord. The

No vote won by a margin of 0.4 percent, sending negotiators back to tweak the agreement. Nearly two months later, on November 30, 2016, Congress passed a slightly modified accord (a form of ratification that avoided a potentially embarrassing second defeat at the polls). The Yes campaign's universal message of peace fell flat against an opposition that targeted different audiences with specious, often distorted messages. To the poor, the No campaign argued that imprisoned guerrillas would get out of jail free and receive handsome reintegration welfare that exceeded the assistance available to the working poor and the unemployed. To Christian-conservative audiences, the campaign preached of a hidden "gender ideology" in the agreement, a cryptic but effective way of channeling the backlash against advances in LGBTQ rights. Regionally, in the north and east, the No campaign—financed by the largest economic conglomerates in the country[8]—played up fears of the agreement paving the way for a leftist political takeover and a descent into the economic chaos then playing out in Venezuela.[9]

The Yes campaign comprised a multiplicity of political parties and civil-society coalitions, each conducting its own mini-campaign that operated on the edges of the government's official campaign. When I saw the central advertisement for the government campaign, I immediately recognized it as the work of Lowe/SSP3 (which by then had become MullenLowe SSP3 on account of a transnational merger). The narrator's voice, the rhythm of the editing, the gradual build of uplifting music— the style was unmistakable.

The two-minute spot starts with a time-elapsed breaking of dawn over Bogotá and then cuts to a morning scene of silhouetted fisherman on a river. The narrator says, "Today is October 3, 2016—yesterday Colombians voted Yes." Cut to an image of a baby in the hospital in her first moments of life. "This is Juliana. The war with the FARC just ended, and she just arrived in the world." The video shows a few seconds of archival footage, seemingly of guerrillas from the 1960s, before cutting back to the baby. "After fifty years, she's the first Colombian to be born in this country without the armed conflict." The video goes on to create a touching montage of people sharing the story of newborn Juliana online, and the country abuzz with the news that the war is over. Forty-three seconds in, the narrator says, "Headlines around the world are talking about the same thing," which cues a montage of newspapers and television broadcasts reporting on the news. One scene includes a newscaster at a desk with the digital overlay, in English, announcing, "Breaking News: Colombia Is a New Country." The theme of viral diffusion continues as the montage and narrator then show and describe people holding handwritten messages of peace in their native languages. The story returns to Colombian soil as the narrator concludes, over a montage of images of celebration and an inspiriting soundtrack:

> Today we woke up in a different country. Peasants and guerrillas went back to their villages, their homes. Soldiers celebrate their triumph and receive the gratitude of all Colombians. People left their jobs and went out to shout about how the history of the country has started to change, to celebrate that at last in Colombia there's the chance to live in peace, to celebrate that from today onward we can build a new country and give it to our children and grandchildren—the Julianas yet to come. A country where war no longer exists and peace can last forever. The country's history *can change*—it depends on everyone. On October 2nd, vote Yes—everyone for peace.[10]

I rewatched the commercial on October 3. The juxtaposition of the fictive future conjured by the commercial and the reality playing out in the news coverage of the No victory could not have been more jarring.[11]

The generic message of peace spouted by the Yes campaign foundered on the shoals of a jaded public that saw through the marketers' attempts to periodize history into a conflictive past and a peaceful future. The result of the plebiscite astonished many commentators who thought, like President Santos, that in a decisive moment Colombians would not reject peace after more than fifty years of uninterrupted war. But those categories, "peace" and "war," had ceased to be meaningful. Agreement or no agreement, the cold calculation of interests would persist, as would violence of different stripes. The government does not bear the responsibility for such radical skepticism alone, but it bears much of it. For thirteen years the Uribe and Santos administrations resignified demobilization in a Machiavellian bid to gain military and political advantages. The charade of the paramilitary demobilizations and the individual demobilizations of guerrilla fighters had rendered the term a floating signifier used for manipulations of all sorts. Remember the assessment of Juan Carlos, the young anthropologist charged with evaluating the launch event for the 2011 Christmas campaign, Operation Rivers of Light, in Tibú. "The people don't believe in demobilization. What they say is 'Demobilization is a farce.' . . . [They] perceive [demobilization] as a political strategy, the government of the moment trying to show success, not a form of reparation or justice."

This brings me back to makeup. Even before James's comment—"we'll put makeup on that later"—I had makeup on my mind. Over the course of doing research I found one image that illustrated my argument about the radical convergence of counterinsurgency and marketing particularly poignantly. I do not have permission to reproduce the image because the model Lowe/SSP3 contracted no longer wanted to be asso-

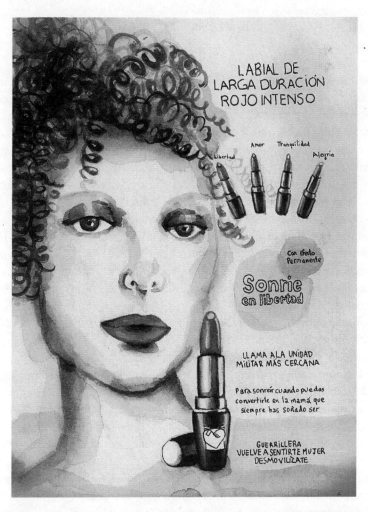

FIGURE E.5. A lipstick "advertisement" as part of the "Guerrilla Feel like a Woman Again" campaign. Image courtesy of Ivon Salazar.

ciated with the subject of demobilization, so I have asked a Colombian artist to interpret it (figure E.5).

The image is a cryptogram of sorts. From top to bottom the text reads:

Long lasting lipstick, intense red.
Freedom, love, tranquillity, happiness
Smile with freedom, a permanent effect
Call the closest military unit
So you can smile and be the mother you've always dreamed of
Guerrilla, feel like a woman again
Demobilize

The last line, "Guerrilla, feel like a woman again. Demobilize," was the campaign's slogan. The PAHD launched the campaign in the southern town of Cartagena de Chaira, in the midst of FARC territory, calling on female guerrillas to resume their place in a deeply gendered and market-oriented society. The familiar female gaze that has long signaled the confluence of seduction and consumption mimicked a Revlon advertisement, while the red-tipped cartridges of lipstick evoked bloodied bullets. The poster, like the videos for the campaign (which also mobilized the commodity image of moisturizing cream), implies a transformation: from being a captive of the harsh conditions of guerrilla life where women abdicate their femininity, to being a free, feminine individual. You need not be an anthropologist of gender to recognize the most salient problems with such a construction. Clearly it relies upon and reinforces dominant notions of gender roles, women being valued for their appearance or as potential child bearers. It also presumes that women in the guerrilla do not feel feminine and are beyond the reach of the market.

I wanted to learn more about how women who had been in the guerrilla responded to the "Feel Like a Woman Again" campaign, so I convened two focus groups with women who had deserted from the FARC to discuss it. What did they see in the posters and the thirty-second television spots?

"It's a life change," Carolina said. She had spent twelve years in the FARC and had left two years prior. "Over there [in the guerrilla] you don't have anything, there's jungle, trees, but in the city it's different because here there's a shift, a life change, here you can indulge your desires [*darse sus gustos*]. You can work and buy your things."

Mariela added: "Honestly, over there they don't think about this stuff . . . the women from the countryside, those who were born and raised in the countryside, and are still there, don't care about this."

There was little consensus in the discussion, but what became clear through the two ninety-minute sessions was that the Feel Like a Woman Again campaign was not about communicating to guerrilla fighters on their own terms, but rather telling a story of female guerrillas oppressed by the rigors of the insurgency and by their exclusion from the market. In telling this tendentious tale, the marketers militarized the representations of gender to establish a difference and stoke a desire.

When conceiving the campaign, Lowe/SSP3 organized a pair of focus groups to brainstorm ideas. In male and female sessions, ex-combatants highlighted the egalitarian gender roles in the FARC—how at the level of the rank and file everyone, regardless of gender, hauls equal weight in their packs, digs the same length of trenches, cooks, and spends the same amount of time on lookout.[12] It was this relative equality at the level of the rank and file that the young men in Lowe/SSP3 conceived as unfeminine. Francisco, a creative talent who had recently arrived in Bogotá from the company's Madrid branch, lamented the sessions' failure to yield any piercing "insights." But one female ex-guerrilla, when asked what she had enjoyed since demobilizing, said, "Putting on makeup." She blushed as she said it. The marketers saw an opportunity to reinforce the message at the core of their brand: "There's another life, demobilization is the way out." Like the propagandistic dimension of US-led wars in the Middle East, the appearances, representations, and rights of women had become an intricate and often intimate battleground, each side accusing the other of abusing and controlling women and also distorting the realities of "their" women.[13]

I wanted to get the FARC's side of the story. While researching at the Décima I spoke with a dozen female guerrillas about the subject. I asked Natalia, a woman in her late twenties who had spent twelve years in the FARC and had red highlights in her hair (a trend among guerrilla women at the Décima), about the Feel Like a Woman Again" campaign. She had not heard of it. After I described it, she objected.

N: It's a lie. When I entered I brought my eye shadow and everything. They never said, "You can't use that."

A: So you carried lipstick in your pack?

N: Not just me. Lots of women like to paint their nails. I don't really [laugh-

ing], but yeah, a lot of girls paint their nails, shave, put on lipstick, use
shadow, all that stuff, of course—lotion, everything, it's normal.

A: All of that? Isn't it additional weight?

N: Yeah, but if you want it, you carry it.

A: Why do you think the government made a spot like that?

N: Well, I am not sure. I guess to make us seem like women who are very
macho, like monsters, I think—that we don't like to put on makeup and
look beautiful. It's a lie that paints another face on the FARC, shows us
as ogres.

A: But how do you get all that stuff? Through *milicianos*?

N: People who are in charge of it, they'll come to an area on muleback, or
guerrillas who come into the camp—the same way food gets to the camp,
the normal way.

Though I have my doubts about the ubiquity of makeup during times
of siege, Natalia and the other female guerrillas I spoke to rejected
the idea that female guerrillas have lived an ascetic, unfeminine life—
though they didn't challenge the equation of cosmetics with femininity
on which the propaganda piece was predicated. The lipstick "advertisement" produced by Lowe/SSP3 for the Ministry of Defense set out to divide the country into those who agree with the idea of selling lipstick,
and with dominant ideas about feminine beauty wrapped up in that sales
pitch, and an outlaw band of communists supposedly operating outside
of the market and its cultural constructions.

This specious segmentation began to fall apart through the negotiating period. Once the FARC had access to microphones, cameras, and a
basic studio in Havana, it went to lengths to undo this division by prominently featuring its women fighters as anchors and correspondents. They
often presented themselves in the style of the glamorous women who
anchor television news in Colombia.[14] Fronts in Colombia invited journalists to photograph their combatants, resulting in photo essays that
showed guerrillas bathing in their underwear, embracing their partners,
wearing pink clothes and accessories, and applying cosmetics. In 2015
the FARC suspended its mandatory birth-control policy, and in 2016 reports began to circulate of a "baby boom" in guerrilla camps. Photographers rushed to depict expectant guerrilla couples, creating images that
signified the renewal promised by peace and the return to a rhythm of
biological and social reproduction no longer constrained by the war. The
government would no longer be able to portray the FARC as a monster

in the jungles and mountains that imposed birth control and abortion on its women; it could no longer depict guerrilla women and men as beyond the pale of the marketing nation.

The genius of the PAHD's brand warfare was its ability to operate across military, cultural, affective, and ideological registers. This total mobilization drew strength from the relative sovereignty of the market vis-à-vis the Colombian state. Although the Colombian state does not function in all of the communities in its expansive territory, the market does. The ubiquity of commodities and their images, and the professional practice of channeling consumers' affective investments into them, proved an alternate mode of governance. In the early 2000s, as documented here, the state turned to marketing experts to harness the authority of the market and use it to set the terms of war and peace.

What does the cryptogram that is this lipstick "advertisement" reveal? Quite simply that lipstick is not a means to demobilization, but rather that individual demobilization is a form of lipstick—one piece in a bag of cosmetics that the state uses to co-opt its ideological challengers and give itself and its enemies a new face. As the FARC embraces the arsenal of brand warfare, the post–peace accord period is bound to be a masquerade in which the country is mired somewhere between its peaceful postconflict aspirations and the specter of a war yet to come.[15] In that liminal space that is not quite war nor peace, it will be worth paying critical attention to the shifting means of mass persuasion, for they illuminate how economics, governance, and culture coalesce in an affective regime ever more tightly connected by the tissue of marketing.

Acknowledgments

The research and writing of this book has been a long process, and it would not have been possible without the generosity and guidance of many individuals and institutions. Given the sensitivity of the subject matter in Colombia, many of the people who contributed most to this endeavor remain nameless. Among these anonymous collaborators, I am particularly grateful to former rebels who confided in a curious gringo with a suspicious last name. Some appear under pseudonyms in the text. I was unable to include the stories of many others, though their experiences and insights are seminal to this book. Government officials constitute the second category of nameless interlocutors without whom this project would not be possible. Although my relationships in the Ministry of Defense and the Colombian Agency for Reintegration at times suffered from the unavoidable tension generated by conducting academic research in the middle of the national security state, the hospitality and kindness of many officials proved crucial. The marketing professionals at Lowe/SSP3 gave generously of their time and knowledge. The individual demobilization program in Colombia is labyrinthine, and every time I hit a cul-de-sac, someone else appeared to show me an entirely new path.

I am indebted to the professors with whom I worked most closely at Harvard, especially Kimberly Theidon, Jean Comaroff, Michael Herzfeld, and Arthur Kleinman, who all provided insightful suggestions and encouragement. Other faculty in Cambridge who enriched my thinking include the late Mary Steedly, John Comaroff, Michael M. J. Fischer (MIT), Steven Caton, Ajantha Subramanian, Byron Good, María Clemencia Ramírez, Andy Klatt, Jean Jackson (MIT), Catalina Laserna, Kerry Chance, George Paul Mieu, and Laurence Ralph. I would also like to thank Michael Hardt, a mentor from my undergraduate studies at Duke University, for his willingness to talk through this project on multiple occasions. Orin Starn is responsible for having piqued my interest in anthropology when I was an impressionable eighteen-year-old, and despite existential doubts along the way, I am very grateful he did.

Friends at Harvard and elsewhere have been key sources of intellectual and personal sustenance. My first thanks go to Abbey Steele, my dear friend, who provided a crucial introduction that enabled this project to happen. Special thanks are due to Federico Pérez, with whom I have shared the travails of the field and dissertating. His companionship and the boundless optimism of Ivette Salom, his wife, infused the process with a sense of camaraderie. This project bears traces of Claudio Sopranzetti's passionate belief that intellectual concerns are inseparable from everyday life. Conversations with fellow graduate students Hassan Al-Damluji, Julie Kleinman, Bridget Hanna, Jennifer Mack, and Anand Vaidya helped to frame the project's earliest iteration. I learned a great deal about the Colombian conflict from late-afternoon discussions with Juana Dávila in Bogotá and in Cambridge. In a postfieldwork moment, after nearly five years away from Cambridge, I was lucky to connect with a superb group of young scholars who helped stave off the alienation of writing: Nancy Khalil, Maude Baldwin, Catherine Kelly, Natalia Ramirez-Bustamante, Juan Rafael Martinez Galarza, Lara Versari, Namita Dharia, Nicolas Sternsdorff-Cisterna, Claudia Gastrow, Liz Korner, Liz Maynes-Aminzade, Stephanie Dick, Aryo Danusiri, Kimberly Wortmann, Meghan Morris, Joshua Walker, and Alejandra Azuero Quijano.

A Mellon fellowship at Harvard University's Mahindra Humanities Center provided a sumptuous interdisciplinary forum for discussing the fuzzy frontiers between war and nonwar. Thanks are due to Homi Bhabha, Steven Biel, Mary Halpenny-Killip, and the staff at the center, and especially to fellows Hiba Bou Akar, Ram Natarajan, Joseph Fronczak, Samuel M. Anderson, and Thiemo Breyer for creating such a vibrant climate of intellectual exchange.

At Penn State I have been fortunate to work in an interdisciplinary environment with extraordinary colleagues. I am grateful to the faculty at the Bellisario College of Communications for creating a collegial and thought-provoking setting for finishing this book, especially Anthony Olorunnisola, Shyam Sundar, Matthew McCallister, Matthew Jordan, Mary Beth Oliver, Jo Dumas, Pearl Gluck, Richie Sherman, Anita Gabrosek, Boaz Dvir, Michelle Rodino-Colocino, Russell Frank, Kevin Hagopian, Colleen Connolly-Ahern, Lee Ahern, Yael Warshel, Sascha Meinrath, Matthew Jackson, Marie Hardin, and Ford Risley. Outside of the college Sophia McClennen, Courtney Morris, Martín Perna, Juan Carlos Garzón, Matt Tierney, Anita Starosta, Heidi Pernett, Salua Kamerow, Harry Kamerow, Hoda El Shakry, Ebony Coletu, Clio Andris, Sarah Townsend, Matthew Restall, Eric Hayot, Jonathan Marks, John Christman, Douglas Bird, José Capriles, Erica Smithwick, Idan Shalev, Jonathan Eburne, Greg Eghigian, and Natascha Hoffmeyer, among others, have created a fun and stimulating environment to complete the manuscript. Special thanks are due to Denise Bortree and the Arthur W. Page Center for its support to index *Guerrilla Marketing*.

In Colombia I have benefited from a two-decade dialogue with a vibrant, cosmopolitan community of scholars, journalists, activists, and artists who nurtured my intellectual engagement with Colombian politics and inspired me with their commitment to building a more peaceful, just, and equitable country. My deepest thanks and admiration are due to Darío Villamizar, Camilo Ruiz Anzola, Consuelo Cifuentes de Ruiz, Jose Antequera Guzmán, Lorena María Aristazábal, Vladimir Rodríguez Valencia, Juan Felipe Hoyos García, Stephen Ferry, Roméo Langlois, Pascale Mariani, Juan Orozco, Claire Launay-Gama, Luis Eduardo Gama, Monstruo Prometedor (John de los Rios), Joe Broderick, Julien Petit, Juliana Díaz Franco, Jim Wyss, Ana Soler, Nadja Drost, Bruno Federico, Claudia Rodríguez Valencia, Carlos Villalón, Juan Forero, John Otis, Steven Dudley, Nicole Jullian, Adelaida Pardo, Alejandra Gaviria, Sibylla Brodzinsky, Simone Bruno, Oriana Alonso, David Rojas, Jesús Abad Colorado, Edwin Cubillos, Cristina Lleras, Nicolás Van Hemelryck, Clare Weiskopf, Felipe Gómez Ossa, Julían Mejía Villa, Jairo Valenzuela, Fabio Cuttica, Ángela Gómez, Lorraine Leete, Paula Rodríguez, Celia Dávila, Helkin René Díaz, Gerald Bermudez, Thomas Wagner, Max Schoening, and Fábrica Visual Ojo Rojo. *La vida macarense* provided a base and fountain of energy and ideas.

Colombian universities have hosted me and helped me along the way. At Universidad de los Andes I am grateful to Lucas Ospina, who stirringly illustrated the testimonials, as well as Pablo Jaramillo, Mónica Espinosa, Carlos Alberto Uribe, María Claudia Steiner, Juan Ricardo Aparicio, Ómar Rincón, Friederike Fleischer, Margarita Serje, Enzo Nussio, and Arlene Tickner. A fellowship at the Pontificia Universidad Javeriana provided summer support in the last phase of writing and editing. Jefferson Jaramillo and Germán Mejía Pavoni welcomed me graciously. Academic units at the Universidad Nacional (Bogotá), Universidad de Antioquia (Medellín), Universidad ICESI (Cali), Universidad del Norte (Barranquilla), and the Instituto Colombiano de Antropología e Historia (or ICANH, Bogotá) also provided forums in which to share work at key moments of the research and writing process. At these institutions I am particularly thankful to Jonathan Echeverri Zuluaga, Elsa Blair Trujillo, Margarita Chaves, Marta Zambrano Escovar, Andrés Salcedo Fidalgo, Inge Helena Lilia Valenica Peña, Diana Rico, and Luis Fernando Trejos. Special thanks are due to my research assistant, Lorena Parra, for her thorough work tracking down sources and transcribing interviews, and to Juan Felipe Forero Duarte, Ana María Caballero, and Johanna Espinel Romero for follow-up work. Brad Tyer and Ruth Goring have copyedited the manuscript with professional skill.

A Fulbright scholarship in 2001–2 initially took me to Colombia, five years before this project began, and then again as the book entered production in the spring semester of 2018. During my first year in Colombia the war was at full boil, a fact I did not fully appreciate at the time. The immersive experience of that year, 2001–2, set in motion the gears that led to *Guerrilla Marketing*. Various institutions have financially supported this research. Principal among them are the Fulbright IIE, the National Science Foundation, the Social Science Research Council, the Wenner-Gren Foundation, the Swedish Institute, and the US Institute for Peace. At Harvard, the Sheldon traveling fellowship, the Weatherhead Center for International Affairs, and the David Rockefeller Center for Latin American Studies all pitched in. Faculty research support at Penn State, especially through the Bellisario College of Communications and the Center for Global Studies, has helped me complete the manuscript. I would like to acknowledge three administrators who gave these institutions a wonderful human touch: Daniella Sarnoff (SSRC), Margot Gill (Harvard), and Steven Bloomfield (Harvard).

A pair of workshops in Villa de Leyva, Colombia, and Aguascalientes, Mexico, each part of the Social Science Research Council's Drugs, Security, and Democracy in Latin America program, were uniquely stimulating. On both occasions the cohorts clicked, creating lasting friendships and a scholarly community spread throughout the Americas. There are too many fellow fellows to name, but very special thanks are due to Kevin L. O'Neill and Winifred Tate. To say that their mentorship has been generous would be a terrible understatement. Both Kevin and Winifred gave detailed comments on the manuscript and wonderful advice along the way. Teo Ballvé and Anthony Fontes provided excellent feedback on chapters. I extend a warm shout-out to a few other DSDers for their support: Robert Samet, Yanilda González, Graham Denyer Willis, Lina Britto, Annette Idler, Diana Bocarejo Suescún, Ana Arjona, Jaime Alves, and Adam Baird. Other colleagues I would like to acknowledge are Richard Grinker, Catherine Lutz, Daniel Goldstein, James Robinson, María Angélica Bautista, Ieva Jusionyte, Hugh Gusterson, Catherine L. Besteman, Karen Strassler, Robert Karl, Joanne Rappaport, Kedron Thomas, Pablo J. Boczkowski, Matthew Durington, João Biehl, Rebecca Stein, John L. Jackson Jr., Deborah Thomas, Alma Blount, Marwan M. Kraidy, Alireza Doostdar, Paula Moreno, Amit Schejter, Michael Elavsky, Bernardus Van Hoof, Juno Salazar Parreñas, Narges Bajoghli, Noah Tamarkin, Jeffrey S. Kahn, Adia Benton, Jaime Arocha, Carlo Tognato, Paolo Vignolo, Doris Sommer, José Luis Falconi, Michael Taussig, César Abadía-Barrero, Diana Pardo Pedraza, Juan Pablo Vera, Danny Hoffman, Carlos Duarte, Parker VanValkenburgh, Maple Razsa, Diana Allan, Noelle Stout, Austin Zeiderman, Maria L. Vidart-Delgado, Kristina Lyons, Sara Lipka, Peter Andreas, Gavin Sullivan, Elizabeth Ferry, the late Marc Chernick, and the late Virginia M. Bouvier.

This book has also benefited greatly from a morning of intensive discussion with the editors of the Chicago Series in Practices of Meaning and Joseph Masco. I am especially thankful to William Mazzarella for seeing the promise of this project and providing a sounding board along the way. At the University of Chicago Press, I am grateful to David Brent for taking an interest in *Guerrilla Marketing*, to Priya Nelson for her keen editorial eye and astute suggestions, and to Dylan Joseph Montanari for shepherding the manuscript through a smooth publication process. Two anonymous peer reviewers have enriched the manuscript with thoughtful critiques and superb recommendations.

Patricia Alvarez Astacio provided insightful commentary on this manuscript, while also giving so much more. She endured my commitment to this book graciously while challenging me to be a better scholar and person.

My most foundational thanks are to my family. I paused research for two years to advocate for the release of my dear brother Josh. For twenty-five months the Islamic Republic of Iran detained him arbitrarily after he strayed too close to the Iranian border on a hiking trip in Iraqi Kurdistan with two friends. Many people supported the Free the Hikers campaign that I coordinated in those two years (2009–11), but that is an even longer list of acknowledgments. Here I will restrain myself to naming only Paul Holmes, Jake Sullivan, Cindy Hickey, Farah Mawani, Samantha Topping, Yolanda Ali, Fred Felleman, and Brian Gralnick. The experience of running an international media campaign in the midst of a propaganda war between the United States and the Islamic Republic of Iran inevitably informed this book, even if I am not entirely conscious of how. Josh is now a budding young scholar. He sent me germane historical references and served as my final and most careful reader. I never fail to appreciate each evening we spend discussing everything from our projects to our parents. Josh, his partner Jenny Bohrman, and the latest addition to the family, Isaiah Azad, have provided much-needed perspective as I've hunkered down to bring this project to completion.

Only six months after Iran freed my brother, the FARC shot and captured my friend and roommate Roméo Langlois in an ambush on a Colombian antinarcotics mission with which he was embedded. Even then my parents, Laura and Jacob Fattal, never suggested that maybe I should not be wading into the thick of guerrilla politics in Colombia. While they may have been flummoxed by my life choices at times, they never failed to support me with their unconditional love.

My grandfather Carroll Felleman did not live to see this book's completion, which is a shame, as I would have taken great pleasure in discussing it with him. This book might never have been written had it not been for his experience demobilizing after World War II with the help of the GI Bill. My maternal grandmother, Muriel Felleman, and all of my extended family on both sides of the Atlantic are a force that quietly gives me strength.

To all those named here, and to those left unnamed, thank you! Any faults in the text are my own.

Notes

Preface

1. In 2015, toward the end of the negotiating period, the FARC requested that the government not produce any more advertising campaigns for its individual demobilization program. The government complied with the FARC's request.

2. Due to a 2015 merger of two global consumer marketing firms, Mullen Group and Lowe and Partners, Lowe/SSP3 became MullenLowe SSP3. (Such mergers are exceedingly common in an industry that seeks as to achieve high levels of vertical and horizontal integration.) I refer to the company as Lowe/SSP3 because that is how it was known during the majority of my fieldwork.

3. Brit McCandless, "Advertising to Sell Peace Not Products," *60 Minutes*, December 11, 2016, http://www.cbsnews.com/news/60-minutes-colombia-advertising-to-sell-peace-not-products/.

4. In May 2017, Fernando Londoño, an ex-minister in the Uribe administration, rallied the faithful of the right-wing Centro Democrático party by saying, "The first challenge for the Centro Democrático will be to shred that damned paper known as the Final Agreement with the FARC." On June 17, 2018, the Colombian people elected the Centro Democrático's candidate, Iván Duque, to be president.

Introduction

1. During my fieldwork the PAHD officially changed its acronym to GAHD, substituting Group for Program as the first word of its name. For consistency I have chosen to use PAHD.

2. Ricardo Castaño Z., "Colombia y el modelo neoliberal," *Agora Trujillo* 5, no. 10 (2002): 59–77. César Abadía-Barrero, "Neoliberal Justice and the Transformation of the Moral: The Privatization of the Right to Healthcare in Colombia," *Medical Antropological Quarterly* 30, no. 1 (2015): 62–79.

3. Kimberly Theidon, "Transitional Subjects: The Disarmament, Demobilization, and Reintegration of Former Combatants in Colombia," *Human Rights Quarterly* 31(2007): 66. For a sociological analysis of the National Center for Reparation and Reconciliation, the bureaucratic structure created by President Uribe to compensate victims and write reports about the conflict, the precursor to the Center for National Memory, see Paula Castaño, "In the Time of the Victims: Understandings of Violence and Institutional Practices in the National Commission of Reparation and Reconciliation in Colombia," (PhD diss., University of Chicago, 2013).

4. Centro Nacional de Memoria Histórica, *¡Basta ya! Colombia memorias de guerra y dignidad* (Bogotá: Centro Nacional de Memoria Histórica, 2013), 20.

5. For a detailed historical analysis of the early years of the Frente Nacional and the founding of the FARC, see Robert A. Karl, *A Forgotten Peace: Reform, Violence, and the Making of Contemporary Colombia* (Berkeley: University of California Press, 2017).

6. Darío Villamizar Herrera, *Las guerrillas en Colombia: Una historia desde las orígenes hasta los confines* (Bogotá: Random House, 2017).

7. In Colombia departments are the equivalent of states or provinces.

8. "Colombia, el país más desigual de A. Latina en el reparto de la tierra," *El Tiempo*, November 29, 2016, http://www.eltiempo.com/vida/ciencia/concentra cion-de-la-tierra-en-america-latina-oxfam-52376.

9. For a detailed historical account of the marijuana boom in the 1970s that created the infrastructure for cocaine traffic to flourish in the 1980s, see Lina Britto, "Hurricane Winds: *Vallenato* Music and Marijuana Traffic in Colombia's First Illegal Drugs Boom," *Hispanic American Historical Review* 91, no. 1 (2015): 71–102. The wealth created gradually seeped into the groundwater of Colombian society, becoming interwoven with the legal economy and driving a spatial reorganization of then-burgeoning cities. For a thoughtful unpacking of the geographic implications of narco-development, see Kevin Lewis O'Neill, "*Narcotecture*," *Society and Space* 34, no. 4 (2016): 672–88.

10. Bruce Bagley, "Drug Policy, Political Violence and U.S. Policy in Colombia in the 1990s," working paper (2001), electronic document, http://clasarchive .berkeley.edu/Events/conferences/Colombia/workingpapers/working_paper _bagley.html, (accessed March 28, 2016). For an ethnography of the political economy of the drug trade in the Putumayo, see Oscar Jansson, "The Cursed Leaf: An Anthropology of the Political Economy of Cocaine Production in Southern Colombia" (PhD diss., University of Uppsala, Department of Anthropology 2008).

11. For a regional accounting of the FARC's expansion, see Carlos Medina Gallego, ed., *FARC-EP flujos y reflujos: La guerra en las regiones* (Bogotá: Universidad Nacional de Colombia, 2011).

12. See Ana M. Arjona and Stathis Kalyvas, "Recruitment into Armed Groups in Colombia: A Survey of Demobilized Fighters," in *Understanding Col-*

lective Political Violence (London: Palgrave-Macmillan, 2011), for a quantitative study of recruitment by armed groups in Colombia.

13. Central Intelligence Agency, Directorate of Intelligence, Office of African and Latin American Analysis, "Colombian Counterinsurgency, Steps in the Right Direction," intelligence memorandum, MORI doc 951603 (approved for release October 2001), http://www2.gwu.edu/~nsarchiv/colombia/19940126.pdf.

14. Michael Taussig, *Law in a Lawless Land: Diary of a Limpieza in Colombia* (Chicago: University of Chicago Press, 2003), xi.

15. For a detailed analysis of paramilitaries as a proxy force, see chapter 3 of Winifred Tate, *Drugs, Thugs, and Diplomats: U.S. Policymaking in Colombia* (Stanford, CA: Stanford University Press, 2015). For historical accounts detailing the emergence and expansion of the paramilitaries, see Mauricio Romero, ed., *Parapolítica: La ruta de la expansión paramilitar y los acuerdos políticos* (Bogotá: Corporación Nuevo Arco Iris, 2007); María Teresa Ronderos, *Guerras recicladas: Una historia periodística del paramilitarismo en Colombia* (Bogotá: Aguilar, 2015).

16. Francisco Gutiérrez Sanín, "Colombia: The Re-structuring of Violence," in *Economic Liberalization and Political Violence: Utopia or Dystopia?*, ed. Francisco Gutiérrez Sanín and Gerd Schönwälder (London: Pluto, 2010), 228.

17. Winifred Tate, *Counting the Dead: The Culture and Politics of Human Rights Activism in Colombia* (Berkeley: University of California Press, 2007).

18. The most comprehensive documentation of the fragmentation and remobilization of the paramilitaries after the government "demobilized" the AUC in the mid-2000s can be found in Centro Nacional de Memoria Histórica, *Desmovilización y reintegración paramilitar: Panorama posacuerdos con las AUC* (Bogotá: Centro Nacional de Memoria Histórica, 2015).

19. Human Rights Watch, *Smoke and Mirrors: Colombia's Demobilization of Paramilitary Groups* (New York: Human Rights Watch, 2005).

20. Colombian historian Gonzalo Sánchez has argued that amnesties have bequeathed this history its de facto periodization. Gonzalo Sánchez, "Raices históricas de la amnistía o las etapas de la guerra en Colombia," in *Ensayos de historia social y política del siglo XX* (Bogotá: El Áncora Editores, 1984).

21. Charles Tilly, *The Formation of National States in Western Europe* (Princeton, NJ: Princeton University Press, 1975), 42.

22. Stories of the military arming demobilized combatants concentrated in the PAHD's early years. One officer I spoke with said that the reason the military armed them and gave them uniforms was because the lack of those elements had enabled guerrilla sharpshooters to target former guerrillas who accompanied the military on operations. A series of findings from the Inspector General's Office (la Procuraduría) have compelled the military to build nominal safeguards into this practice. According to a 2006 report from the public ministry, "The death of ex-combatants in operations to support the Public Force show a lack of the state's responsibility in protecting this population that has chosen to voluntarily put down

their arms." "Seguimiento a políticas públicas en materia de desmovilización y reinserción: Tomo 2," (Bogotá: Procuraduría General de la Nación, 2006), 61.

23. The United Nations, eager to assert its political relevance with the sub-
sidence of superpower rivalry in the early 1990s, oversaw the implementation of
peace agreements. As the UN accumulated experience, it transformed demobilization into a technocratic exercise and a three-step ritualistic process: disarmament, demobilization, and reintegration, or DDR. United Nations, "Integrated
Disarmament, Demobilization and Reintegration Standards," http://unddr.org/
iddrs-framework.aspx, (UNDDR, 2006), 2.1:1.

24. Demobilization, as a term that signified the inverse of mobilization,
emerged from the post–World War I moment, when Germany and the United
Kingdom struggled to reintegrate their soldiers, many of whom had been
maimed in combat. Adam R. Seipp, *The Ordeal of Peace: Demobilization and
the Urban Experience in Britain and Germany, 1917–1921* (Farnham, UK: Ashgate, 2009). The GI Bill in the US is paradigmatic of policymakers' more systematic attention to the question of demobilization after World War II. Yet it was
only with the formal end of the Cold War in the early 1990s that the meaning of
demobilization grew to encompass attempts to end civil wars rather than only to
manage the aftermath of interstate conflicts. This shift has meant that nonstate
armed actors, such as the Farabundo Martí National Liberation Front (FMLN)
in El Salvador and the Mozambique Resistance Movement (RENAMO), could
also demobilize formally (which both did in 1992).

25. A group of political scientists have tried to disaggregate the gradations of
commitment to the insurgency in Colombia and to understand the motivations
of those who desert and those who inform against their former comrades. See
Benn Oppenheim et al., "True Believers, Deserters, and Traitors: Who Leaves Insurgent Groups and Why," *Journal of Conflict Resolution* 59, no. 5 (2015): 794–823.

26. In an exercise of legal archaeology, I have traced the practice of individual
demobilization back to a temporary measure to deal with cadre of paid assassins orphaned by Pablo Escobar's death. The government reinterpreted a transitional article of the 1991 Constitution (Decree 1385 of 1994, transitional article 13) that enabled the demobilization of the M19 and other guerrilla groups to
"demobilize" the hitmen of the Medellín Cartel who wreaked havoc on the city's
streets after the police killed the drug boss. Decreto 1385, June 30, 1994, *Diario
oficial 45420 de julio 5de 1994*, http://www.alcaldiabogota.gov.co/sisjur/normas/
Norma1.jsp?i=9138, accessed April 21, 2017. What this legal history reveals is a
gradually blurring of the categories of counterinsurgency and policing, and collective and individual demobilization.

27. Neither side placed much faith in the negotiations, which were as ambitious as they were impractical. Agenda items included topics as vast and irreconcilable as "the economic model."

28. In Spanish the word *propaganda* signifies both advertising and the ma-

nipulation of information in war or in politics, a double meaning that anticipates this blurring of vocations.

29. Claudia Gordillo and Bruno Federico, "*Apuntando al corazón* / Pointing at the Heart" (La Danza Inmovil, 2013), YouTube video, 53:11, posted by "La Danza Inmovil," April 4, 2014, https://www.youtube.com/watch?v=Lbu XjhEDUYY.

30. John Rendon describes himself as "an information warrior." He began advising the Colombian military as part of a contract with the US Department of Defense's unit on Special Operation / Low Intensity Conflict in 1999. He operates in a shadowy world of unscrupulous tactics, commonly known as "black propaganda." Of course black propaganda is metonymically related to commonplace forms of "dirty" politics. For a fascinating take on the electoral apparatus in Colombia, see María L. Vidart-Delgado, "Cyborg Political Machines: Political Brokering and Modern Political Campaigning in Colombia," *HAU: Journal of Ethnographic Theory* 7, no. 2 (2017): 255–77.

31. For a detailed analysis of President Uribe's populist discourse and his manipulation of the media, see Fabio López de la Roche's *Las ficciones del poder: Patriotismo, medios de comunicación y reorientación afectiva de los colombianos bajo Uribe Vélez* (Bogotá: Universidad Nacional, IEPRI, 2014).

32. "Política de defensa y seguridad democrática" (Bogotá: Presidencia de la Republica y Ministerio de Defensa Nacional, 2003), 14.

33. "Política de consolidación de la seguridad democrática" (Bogotá: Ministerio de Defensa Nacional, 2007), 18.

34. Quoted in Gutiérrez Sanín, "Colombia: The Re-structuring of Violence," 231.

35. Ernst Jünger, *Der Kampf als inneres Erlebnis* (Berlin: E. S. Mittler & Sohn, 1922), 57. Walter Benjamin considered Jünger's theory of war "nothing other than the unrestrained transposition of the theses of l'art pour l'art to war." Benjamin decried Jünger's valorization and aestheticization of war and foresaw its fascistic forebodings. Richard Wolin, "Introduction: Ernst Jünger," in *The Heidegger Controversy: A Critical Reader*, ed. Richard Wolin (Cambridge, MA: MIT Press), 121–22. Yet Wolin also points out that despite Benjamin's critique of Jünger, the two Weimar intellectuals of opposing political dispositions shared a similar set of philosophical influences and penchant for "anthropological materialism." Richard Wolin, *Walter Benjamin: An Aesthetic of Redemption* (Berkeley: University of California Press, 1994), xxxiii–xxxvi.

36. Ernst Jünger, "Total Mobilization," in *The Heidegger Controversy: A Critical Reader*, ed. Richard Wolin (Cambridge, MA: MIT Press), 126.

37. Ibid.

38. Inger L. Stole, *Advertising at War: Business, Consumers, and Government in the 1940s* (Urbana: University of Illinois Press, 2012), 129.

39. During the 1970s, budgets for public relations within the Pentagon became bloated. Senator William Fulbright led the effort to clarify why the military was spending so much money on propaganda, and focused his criticism on image management during the Vietnam War. William J. Fulbright, *The Pentagon Propaganda Machine* (New York: Liveright, 1970).

40. Maureen Dowd, "After the War: White House Memo; War Introduces a Tougher Bush to Nation," *New York Times*, March 2, 1991, http://www.nytimes.com/1991/03/02/world/after-the-war-white-house-memo-war-introduces-a-tougher-bush-to-nation.html?pagewanted=all.

41. Roger Stahl, *Militainment, Inc.: War, Media, and Popular Culture* (New York: Routledge, 2008).

42. Paul Virilio, *Desert Screen: War at the Speed of Light* (London: Continuum, 2005), 34.

43. Michael Serazio, *Your Ad Here: The Cool Sell of Guerrilla Marketing* (New York: NYU Press, 2013), loc 821.

44. For more on such virtual training, see Nomi Stone, "Living the Laughscream: Human Technology and Affective Maneuvers in the Iraq War," *Cultural Anthropology* 32, no. 1 (2017): 149–74.

45. James Der Derian, *Virtuous Wars: Mapping the Military-Industrial-Media-Entertainment Network* (Boulder, CO: Westview, 2001).

46. I do not mean to suggest that McLuhan's insights into the consequences of technological form have become irrelevant. Hito Steyerl, for example, brilliantly demonstrates how the computational photography of cell phone cameras is an inherently political form in the way it selectively determines which digital information is signal and which is noise. See Hito Steyerl, "Proxy Politics: Signal and Noise," *e-flux journal* 60 (2014): 12.

47. For a theoretical rumination on advertising and mass publicity as modern magic, see William Mazzarella, *The Mana of Mass Society* (Chicago: University of Chicago Press, 2017), 31–37.

48. Gayatri Chakravorty Spivak, "Cultural Talks in the Hot Peace: Revisiting the 'Global Village,'" in *Cosmopolitics: Thinking and Feeling Beyond the Nation*, ed. Pheng Cheah and Bruce Robbins (Minneapolis: University of Minnesota Press, 1998), 329.

49. On the concentration of drone warfare in Waziristan, see Hugh Gusterson, *Drone: Remote Control Warfare* (Cambridge, MA: MIT Press, 2016).

50. On marketing's mutation into a system of global provisioning, see Kalman Applbaum, *The Marketing Era: From Professional Practice to Global Provisioning* (New York: Routledge, 2003).

51. Joseph Masco, *The Theater of Operations: National Security Affect from the Cold War to the War on Terror* (Durham, NC: Duke University Press, 2014), 201–2.

52. Herbert Marcuse, *One-Dimensional Man* (Boston: Beacon, 1991), 89–90.

53. Stuart Ewen, *PR! A Social History of Spin* (New York: Basic Books, 1996).

54. Naomi Klein heralded this process in her best seller *No Logo* (New York: Picador, 2000).

55. On market segmentation and the production of the category of "Latino," see Arlene Dávila, *Latinos, Inc.: The Marketing and Making of a People* (Berkeley: University of California Press, 2001).

56. For books about the tactics of data capitalism in the early twenty-first century, see Joseph Turow, *The Daily You: How the New Advertising Industry Is Defining Your Identity and Your Worth* (New Haven, CT: Yale University Press, 2011); Mara Einstein, *Black Ops Advertising: Native Ads, Content Marketing, and the Covert World of the Digital Sell* (Berkeley, CA: OR Books, 2016). For a legalistic argument against the invasiveness of marketing, see Mark Bartholomew, *Adcreep: The Case against Modern Marketing* (Stanford, CA: Stanford University Press, 2017).

57. Grégoire Chamayou, *A Theory of the Drone* (New York: New Press, 2013), 56.

58. The tendency to invisibilize advertising is often subdivided into "native advertising" and "content marketing," which seek to blend advertisements into cultural and media content respectively.

59. Tom Himpe, *Advertising Is Dead: Long Live Advertising!* (New York: Thames & Hudson, 2006), 14.

60. Gabriel Stricker, *Mao in the Boardroom: Marketing Genius from the Mind of the Master Guerrilla* (New York: St. Martin's Griffin, 2003).

61. Todd C. Helmus, Christopher Paul, and Russell W. Glenn, *Enlisting Madison Avenue: The Marketing Approach to Earning Popular Support in Theaters of Operation* (Washington, DC: Rand Corporation, 2007), xvii. The Rand Corporation wrote *Enlisting Madison Avenue* in the mid-2000s when US forces found themselves mired in quagmires in Iraq and Afghanistan and looking to change the momentum of those conflicts.

62. Increasingly, marketing has sought not only to insinuate its messages into cultures and their subcultures, but to produce culture itself. John Comaroff and Jean Comaroff analyze a corollary of this convergence of marketing strategy and cultural representation, parsing the ways in which ethnic groups deploy marketing as a means of self-commodification and ethno-entrepreneurialism: *Ethnicity, Inc.* (Chicago: University of Chicago Press, 2009).

63. Interbrand, "2016 Ranking, Coca-Cola," accessed May 6, 2017, http://interbrand.com/best-brands/best-global-brands/2016/ranking/cocacola/.

64. Cited in, Applbaum, *Marketing Era*, 54.

65. Stahl, *Militainment Inc.*, 6.

66. ANNCOL, from what I could tell, lacked any geographic headquarters, pulling together a loose global network of contributors. Luis Trejos has written about the FARC's presence in Europe and its use of the internet; see Luis Trejos, "Las FARC-EP en Europa y Centroamérica: Una mirada desde la categoría de actor no estatal," *Opera* 13 (2013): 109–21. Luis Trejos, "Uso de la internet por parte de las FARC-EP: Nuevo escenario de confrontación o último espacio de difusión política," *Revista Encrucijada Americana* 5, no. 1 (2012): 25–50.

67. For a comparative analysis of why certain resistance movements are celebrated internationally and others left to fight in obscurity, see Clifford Bob, *The Marketing of Rebellion: Insurgents, Media, and International Activism* (Oxford: Oxford University Press, 2005). It is interesting to read Clifford's book alongside histories of how public relations and branding strategies have been used by state bureaucracies, such as Mathew Cecil, *Branding Hoover's FBI: How the Boss's PR Men Sold the Bureau to America* (Lawrence: Kansas University Press, 2016).

68. I have produced a book of the students' images; see Alexander L. Fattal, *Shooting Cameras for Peace: Youth, Photography, and the Colombian Armed Conflict* (Cambridge, MA: Harvard University Press, forthcoming).

69. The ACR has its own public relations section that works to manage public perceptions of the demobilization process. I have not researched that office for this book; however, many former combatants have spoken about feeling intimidated into speaking positively of the government's program when talking with the press.

70. See the excellent collected volume of articles on DDR: Enzo Nussio, ed., "Desarme, desmovilización y reintegración de excombatientes y actors del postconflicto," *Colombia Internacional* 77 (2013), as well as a series of monographs and chronicles by Colombian scholars and journalists: José Armando Cárdenas Sarrias, *Los parias de la guerra: Análisis del proceso de desmovilización individual* (Bogotá: Ediciones Aurora, 2005); Juan Felipe Hoyos Garcia, "Capitales para la guerra y el testimonio en un contexto transicional: Etnografía de la producción narrativa de desmovilizados" (master's thesis, Universidad Nacional de Colombia, Departamento de Antropología Social, 2011); Camila Medina Arbeláez, *No porque seas paraco o seas guerrillero tienes que ser un animal* (Bogotá: Ediciones Uniandes, 2009); Andrés Peralta G., ed., *La vida no da tregua: Memorias de desmovilizados* (Bogotá: Alcaldia de Bogotá, 2010); Alfredo Molano, *Ahí les dejo esos fierros* (Buenos Aires: Aguilar, 2009); Enzo Nussio, *La vida después de la desmovilización: Percepciones, emociones y estrategias de exparamilitares en Colombia* (Bogotá: Ediciones Uniandes, 2012); Juan Diego Prieto Sanabria, *Guerras, paces, y vidas entrelazadas: Coexistencia y relaciones locales entre víctimas, excombatientes y comunidades en Colombia* (Bogotá: Uniandes, 2012).

71. On the messiness of the categories of victim and perpetrator in Colombia,

see Ivan Orozco, "La postguerra colombiana: Divagaciones sobre la venganza, la justicia y la reconciliación," Working Paper 306, Helen Kellogg Institute for International Studies, May 2003.

72. In *Democracy and Displacement in Colombia's Civil War* (Ithaca, NY: Cornell University Press, 2017), Abbey Steele sheds light on the political motivations of forced displacement in Colombia.

73. On January 1, 2012, the new general who arrived to command the PAHD ordered all active military to wear their uniforms. That policy changed the feel in the office, drew complaints from the military personnel in the PAHD that it was putting them at risk, and made visible the military orientation of the program.

74. See the award-winning documentary *Caught in the Crossfire* that Langlois produced about the ordeal. Roméo Langlois (for France 24), 2012, http://www.france24.com/en/romeo-langlois-colombia-farc-caught-crossfire.

75. The subject touched a nerve for me. Seven months earlier the Iranian government had released my brother, whom it had detained arbitrarily for more than two years. During that time I took a leave from my graduate studies to coordinate the "Free the Hikers" campaign for his release and that of his two friends.

76. Even when people have authorized me to use their names, I have chosen to use only their first names to be consistent in my pattern of naming my interlocutors.

77. Here I draw on an insight from one of Steven Dudley's subjects in his book about the systematic assassination of members of the Patriotic Union, a FARC-affiliated party in the 1980s. Steven Dudley, *Walking Ghosts: Murder and Guerrilla Politics in Colombia* (New York: Routledge, 2006), 214.

78. *Dreams from the Mountain* (*Sueños del monte*) uses the payload of a truck that I transformed into a giant camera obscura as a mobile cinema space. In this "truck camera" I interviewed former combatants about their lives and dreams. The project is an experimental engagement with form and refracts questions raised in this book through a style of representation that I call ethnographic surrealism. For more information, see www.alexfattal.net.

Chapter One

1. Peter Kenez, *Birth of the Propaganda State: Soviet Methods of Mass Mobilization* (Cambridge: Cambridge University Press, 1985), 7–8.

2. Lynn Mally, "Shock Workers on the Cultural Front: Agitprop Brigades in the First Five-Year Plan," *Russian History / Histoire Russe* 23 (1996): 263–75.

3. Carlos Marighella, a Brazilian who wrote the highly influential call to urban warfare *Minimanual*, was the most prominent intellectual of this urban wave. However, because texts circulated more fluidly within Spanish-speaking Latin America, M19 militants' had greater access to knowledge about the Tupa-

maros, and many carried the book *Actas Tupamaras,* a compilation of the Uruguayan group's actions, in their packs.

4. The name Movimiento 19 de Abril, or M19 for short, alluded to April 19, 1970, the date of a presidential election purported to have been stolen by conservative candidate Misael Pastrana. Arjaid, a founding member of the M19, also noted that the M19 name was "a cheap copy" of Fidel Castro's M26 (Movimiento 26 de Julio). The M19 went on to develop close ties to Cuba. For an encyclopedic take on armed insurrection in Colombia, see Villamizar Herrera, *Guerrillas en Colombia.*

5. For a richly detailed and meticulously researched biography of Jaime Bateman, see Darío Villamizar Herrera, *Jaime Bateman: Biografía de un revolucionario* (Bogotá: Planeta, 2002). A compilation of interviews with the guerrilla leader is also illuminating: Darío Villamizar Herrera, ed., *Jaime Bateman: Profeta de la paz* (Bogotá: Corporación Compañía Nacional para la Paz, 1995).

6. Quoted in Olga Behar, *Las guerras de la paz* (Bogotá: Planeta, 1985), 137.

7. Ibid.

8. Villamizar Herrera, *Jaime Bateman,* 245.

9. Ibid., 252.

10. Carlos's father, Luis Vidales, was a poet who cofounded the Colombian Communist Party in the 1920s and had lived in the literary milieu of Latin American writers in Paris in the 1930s. He fled Colombia's political violence to Chile with his family in 1953. Seventeen years later, after spending a brief period in Argentine prison for attempting to join Che Guevara in Bolivia in 1966, and having narrowly escaped Pinochet's military takeover of the Casa de la Moneda on what Chilean playwright Ariel Dorfman calls "the other September 11" in 1973, Carlos returned to Colombia just as the M19 was forming. Carlos died in exile in Stockholm in 2015.

11. Behar, *Guerras de la paz,* 140.

12. The solidarity of intellectuals, especially the literary community, proved crucial in keeping the sword from falling into the military's hands, even when many members of the M19 were not so fortunate themselves.

13. The sword probably never belonged to Bolívar. The museum has no record of how it entered the collection other than that it was purchased from a citizen in the 1920s. An investigation by the museum staff, in consultation with the Musée de l'Armée in Paris, determined that the sword the M19 stole entered into circulation only in the 1830s, after Bolívar's death. Alexander L. Fattal, "Narco-novelas as Faux Historical Memory: Resignifying the M19's Acts of 'Armed Propaganda' and the Foreclosure of Left Politics in Colombia," unpublished manuscript.

14. Villamizar Herrera, *Jaime Bateman: Profeta de Paz,* 179.

15. Darío Villamizar Herrera, *Aquel 19 será* (Bogotá: Planeta, 1995), 81–89.

16. Those few civilians, however, tended to be from the intelligentsia and

included poets Leon De Greiff and Luis Vidales. "La ruta de la espada," *Semana*, December 29, 1997, http://www.semana.com/imprimir/34708.

17. Villamizar Herrera, *Jaime Bateman*, 123–41.

18. On the systematic assassination of members of the Patriotic Union, see Roberto Romero Ospina, *Unión Patriótica: Expedientes contra el olvido* (Bogotá: Alcaldía Mayor de Bogotá D.C., 2012); Dudley, *Walking Ghosts*.

19. Ospina, *Unión Patriótica*, 23–138.

20. Antonio Nariño was an independence hero who had translated Thomas Paine's *Rights of Man* into Spanish. The invocation of that text dovetailed with the M19's initial intent to seize the Palace of Justice during a state visit by French president François Mitterrand. That effort had been thwarted when the military raided an urban cell just before the visit. Conspiracy theories abound that posit the military had learned about the M19's plans for the Palace of Justice invasion and allowed it to happen so that it could entrap the group's leadership.

21. Ana Carrigan, *The Palace of Justice: A Colombian Tragedy* (New York: Four Walls Eight Windows, 1993), 142.

22. Carrigan, *Palace of Justice*.

23. The military unit charged with retaking the Palace of Justice, the Thirteenth Brigade, had suffered a terrible embarrassment six years earlier when the M19 tunneled into its arms depot and stole approximately five thousand weapons. Ramon Jimeno, *Noche de lobos* (Bogotá: Editorial Presencia, 1989), 79.

24. Carrigan, *Palace of Justice*, 128.

25. Ibid., 143.

26. Gustavo Petro, a former militant of the M19, and mayor of Bogotá in 2014–15, wrote, "You can't have a national dialogue, which is what Bateman proposed and what we kept trying to achieve unsuccessfully for years, over the dead body of a magistrate." Maureén Maya and Gustavo Petro, *Prohibido olvidar: Dos miradas sobre la toma del Palacio de Justicia* (Bogotá: Editorial Pisando Callos, 2006).

27. In 2014 the Inter-American Court for Human Rights found the Colombian state guilty of disappearing ten survivors of the Palace of Justice tragedy, treating some survivors, including those who had worked in the cafeteria, as collaborators with the guerrilla group. José Meléndez, "Corte IDH condena a Colombia por el caso del Palacio de Justicia," December 10, 2014, http://www.eltiempo.com/archivo/documento/CMS-14955458.

28. Media representations, such as Caracol's TV series *Escobar: The Father of Evil*, have fueled rumors that drug cartels financed the M19's takeover of the Palace of Justice to destroy the records on which mafia bosses were arraigned. No evidence, however, has ever been provided to support that theory. See Yamid Amat, "Secretos de la Toma del Palacio de Justicia," *El Tiempo*, November 7, 2004, http://www.eltiempo.com/archivo/documento/MAM-1516427.

29. Nicolas Entel, dir., *Sins of My Father* (Red Creek Productions, 2009).

30. Gabriel García Márquez, *News of a Kidnapping*, trans. Edith Grossman (New York: Penguin, 1998), 181.

31. John Jairo Velásquez, better known by his alias, Popeye, was one of Escobar's closest lieutenants and a member of the Extraditables. He has confessed to killing more than three hundred people, and he authorized the assassination of ten times that many. In 2014 he walked out of jail a free man after serving twenty-two years. He quickly became a social media celebrity, declaring himself the historical memory of the Medellín cartel. Jim Wyss of the *Miami Herald* writes, "His YouTube Channel 'Popeye Arrepentido,' or 'Remorseful Popeye,' has racked up more than 15 million views, a following that has helped him sell books and pitch projects to Hollywood." Jim Wyss, "He Murdered 300. Now Popeye the Assassin Is a Colombian Media Star," *Miami Herald*, November 11, 2016, http://www.miamiherald.com/news/nation-world/world/americas/colombia/article114199558.html. Popeye has quickly adapted to the self-branding logics at the heart of social media. Alice Marwick, *Status Update: Celebrity, Publicity and Branding in the Social Media Age* (New Haven, CT: Yale University Press, 2013), 163–204. Ilana Gershon, "'I Am Not a Businessman, I'm a Business, Man': Typing the Neoliberal Self into a Branded Existence," *HAU: Journal of Ethnographic Theory* 6, no. 3 (2016): 223–46.

32. García Márquez, *Noticias de un secuestro*, 14.

33. It is noteworthy that marketing was expanding into electoral politics at the time. For a thorough analysis of political marketing in Colombia, see María Lucia Vidart-Delgado, "The Pragmatics of Hope: Class, Elections, and Political Management in Contemporary Colombia" (PhD diss., MIT, 2013), http://search.proquest.com/openview/4c9c375ac14cc12abb1bcc73adb2442f/1?pq-origsite=gscholar&cbl=18750&diss=y.

34. On *détournement*, see Tom McDonough, *"The Beautiful Language of My Century": Reinventing the Language of Contestation in Postwar France, 1945–1968* (Cambridge, MA: MIT Press, 2007), 190–94.

35. On the semiotics of violence, see María Victoria Uribe, "Dismembering and Expelling: Semantics of Political Terror in Colombia," *Public Culture* 16, no. 1 (2004): 79–95. Uribe demonstrates how paramilitaries refashioned peasants' skill at butchering and manipulating the bodies of cattle, poultry, and fish to relegate their victims to less-than-human status.

36. Entel, *Sins of My Father*.

37. Rodrigo Lara Bonilla campaigned with Luis Carlos Gálan as part of the New Liberalism movement, which had forcefully denounced Escobar. Gálan continued to rail against Escobar and the drug mafias even after Escobar had Lara Bonilla assassinated. Escobar's assassins killed Gálan at a campaign rally in 1990, when he was at the height of his popularity. Of all the deaths Escobar is responsible for, Gálan's is perhaps the most infamous.

38. The Medellín cartel's practice of kidnapping also had a more direct

dialogue with the M19. In 1981 the M19 infuriated the clique at the center of the Medellín cartel when it kidnapped Martha Nieves Ochoa, the sister of Escobar's close associates the Ochoa brothers: Jorge Luis, Juan David, and Fabio. In response, a group of regional power brokers in the Department of Antioquia created Death to Kidnappers, or MAS, its Spanish acronym. Rather than negotiate for Nieves Ochoa's release, MAS created a private army that assaulted the M19. In a show of overwhelming force, MAS kidnapped more than a dozen people close to Bernal (including his wife). The M19 released Nieves Ochoa without receiving a single peso of the $12 million it had demanded for her freedom. The creation of MAS is often considered a foundational moment in the wave of paramilitarism that gripped Colombia in the late twentieth century. See Verdad Abierta, "Muerte a Secuestradores MAS: Los orígenes del paramilitarismo," September 20, 2011, http://www.verdadabierta.com/component/content/article/11-periodo-1/3556-muerte-a-secuestradores-mas-los-origenes-del-paramilitarismo-.

39. María Teresa Herran, *La industria de los medios masivos de comunicación en Colombia* (Bogotá: FESCOL, 1991), 136.

40. Bolívar called the printing press "the infantry of the Army of Liberation!" Marie Arana, *Bolívar: American Liberator* (New York: Simon and Schuster, 2013), 215.

41. W. J. T. Mitchell, *Cloning Terror: The War of Images, 9/11 to the Present* (Chicago: University of Chicago Press, 2011), loc. 1213.

42. Gabriel García Márquez, *News of a Kidnapping*, trans. Edity Grossman (New York: Alfred A. Knopf, 1997), 86–87.

43. In 2016 *El Espectador* cast doubt on the accepted narrative that Escobar had downed the plane in an attempt to kill then-presidential candidate Gaviria, insinuating that the plane crashed because of a technical failure. "Avianca 203, la historia que nunca nos contaron," *El Espectador*, November 27, 2016, http://www.elespectador.com/noticias/nacional/avianca-203-historia-nunca-nos-contaron-articulo-667717.

44. "Ordenan liberar a Francisco Santos," *El Tiempo*, May 20, 1991, http://www.eltiempo.com/archivo/documento/MAM-86595.

45. García Márquez, *Noticias de un secuestro*, 126.

46. Ibid.

47. Jeff Zimbalist and Michael Zimbalist, dirs., *The Two Escobars* (All Rise Films, 2010).

48. For an ethnography of the social dimension of coca cultivation, see María Clemencia Ramírez, *Between the Guerrillas and the State: The Cocalero Movement, Citizenship, and Identity in the Colombian Amazon* (Durham, NC: Duke University Press, 2011).

49. *FARC: Guerrilla, infamia y dolor* (Bogotá: Ejército Nacional de Colombia, Dirección de Inteligencia, 2012).

50. Correspondence with a senior official at Google did not illuminate the mechanics of removing a video. Rather, I was directed to the "Dangerous Acts" clause of YouTube's community guidelines (2013) that would authorize the removal of videos that incite violence or train terrorists. I suspect the military takes a multipronged approach, flooding YouTube with requests to block a user or flag FARC content, having lawyers send take-down requests, and hacking troublesome accounts. Given restrictions on access, I was only able to approximate the edges of the cyber dimensions of Colombia's war.

51. Alex Fattal, "Hostile Remixes on YouTube," *American Ethnologist* 41, no. 2 (2014): 320–35. For an exploration of the confluence of social media platforms and militarism at the beginning of the twenty-first century, see Adi Kuntsman and Rebecca L. Stein, *Digital Militarism: Israel's Occupation in the Social Media Age* (Stanford, CA: Stanford University Press, 2015).

52. ANNCOL, "Muerte de 11 diputados en Colombia: Comunicado de las FARC," June 28, 2007, http://www.elmundo.es/elmundo/2007/06/28/inter nacional/1183026099.html.

53. Sigifredo López, *Sigifredo: El triunfo de la esperanza* (Bogotá: Planeta, 2011), 178–83.

54. Alex Fattal, "Facebook: Corporate Hackers, A Billion Users, and the Geo-politics of the 'Social Graph,'" *Anthropological Quarterly* 85, no 3 (2012): 927–56.

55. I have interviewed former members of the FARC's First Front who echo the FARC's official position about Operation Check, that it was an inside job rather than a brilliant military intelligence operation. They claim that a deal was cut between the military and the front's leadership, César and Gafas. According to this theory, César and Gafas expected to receive a sizable sum of money in exchange for turning in the hostages, until the military betrayed them upon boarding the helicopter. The conspiracy theory, which spins on the figure of Doris, César's partner who had demobilized shortly before the operation and was working with the military, is not implausible.

56. Conspicuously absent from my account are the ways in which paramilitaries used public relations strategies to pivot toward a more political platform. See Winifred Tate, "From Greed to Grievance: The Shifting Political Profile of the Colombian Paramilitaries," in *Building Peace in a Time of War*, ed. Virginia Bouvier (Washington, DC: United States Institute of Peace Press, 2009), 111–31.

Chapter Two

1. Raymond Williams describes "structures of feeling" as that composite of materiality, social structure, and ideology whose interconnectedness can be fully sensed only by those living through a given period. While the structure of feel-

ing of one period is elusive to later generations, art, Williams claims, provides the best recourse for conveying it. Raymond Williams, "Film in the Dramatic Tradition," in *The Raymond Williams Reader* (Oxford: Blackwell, 2001), 32–34.

2. To view the Mazda ad by Lowe/SSP3, posted by mercadeoypublicidad, see https://www.youtube.com/watch?v=kiT-wzngrNE (accessed May 22, 2017).

3. The theory is articulated in A. H. Maslow, "A Theory of Human Motivation," *Psychological Review* 50 (1943): 370–96. For a critique of how Maslow's theory takes on evolutionary overtones as it is applied across geographic contexts, see Kalman Applbaum, "Crossing Borders: Globalization as Myth and Charter in American Transnational Consumer Marketing," *American Ethnologist* 27, no. 2 (2000): 268–73.

4. The corporatization of Christmas had already redefined the holiday as an extraordinary period to give in to impulsive desires, even if that means miring oneself in debt. Rebecca Bartel parses the financialization of Christmas. She notes that "the credit-fueled gift is the proverbial gift that keeps on taking." Rebecca Bartel, "Giving is Believing: Credit and Christmas in Colombia" *Journal of the American Academy of Religion*, May 10, 2016, 1–23, 11. On Christmas's turn toward consumerism more broadly, see chapter 5 of Bruce David Forbes, *Christmas: A Candid History* (Berkeley: University of California Press, 2007).

5. I am indebted to Jean Comaroff for this keen interpretation.

6. FARC commanders frequently have their troops watch the 7 p.m. news and then lead their units in counterhegemonic readings of the broadcast. Market research by the PAHD and Lowe/SSP3 revealed that guerrillas often managed to watch major soccer matches, especially those of the national team.

7. Marcela's commitment to nationalist symbols parallels William Mazzarella's findings while studying an Indian advertising agency. Mazzarella notes that the everyday practice of marketing looks "more like charismatic prophecy than scientific idiom." William Mazzarella, *Shoveling Smoke: Advertising and Globalization in Contemporary India* (Durham, NC: Duke University Press, 2003), 186.

8. There has been a series of important ethnographic and historical works done about indigenous struggles and questions of representation in Cauca: David Gow and Joanne Rappaport, "The Indigenous Public Voice: The Multiple Idioms of Modernity in Native Cauca," in *Self-Representation and the State in Latin America*, ed. Kay B. Warren and Jean E. Jackson (Austin: University of Texas Press, 2003); Brett Troyan, *Cauca's Indigenous Movement in Southwestern Colombia: Land, Violence, and Ethnic Identity* (Lanham, MD: Lexington Books, 2015); Joanne Rappaport, *Intercultural Utopias: Public Intellectuals, Cultural Experimentation, and Ethnic Pluralism in Colombia* (Durham, NC: Duke University Press, 2005).

9. President Santos's image managers deemed a cameo in the Christmas commercial too conciliatory. After Cano's death, Santos chose to posture as

the hard-handed statesman in large part because of withering attacks from his predecessor Álvaro Uribe, who accused Santos of going soft on the counterinsurgency. At the same time, President Santos needed to be mindful of his enemy, since he had already initiated clandestine peace talks with the FARC under the leadership of Alfonso Cano, who presciently told his comrades "The government wants to drag my body over the negotiating table before starting the talks." Gabriel Angel, "Alfonso Cano anticipó su muerte: 'Lo sé. Quieren arrojar mi cadáver sobre la mesa antes de empezar los diálogos,'" *Las2Orillas*, November 4, 2016, http://www.las2orillas.co/alfonso-cano-anticipo-su-muerte-lo-se -quieren-arrojar-mi-cadaver-sobre-la-mesa-antes-de-empezar-los-dialogos/.

10. Hoyos García, "Capitales para la guerra," 82.

11. On the analysis of the demobilized as prodigal sons, also see Cárdenas Sarrias, *Parias de la guerra*.

12. For an accounting of the FARC's mechanisms of maintaining social control through often bureaucratic means, see Ana Arjona, *Rebelocracy: Social Order in the Colombian Civil War* (Cambridge: Cambridge University Press, 2016).

13. Ieva Jusionyte shows how borders in Latin America serve as intensely mediated zones where journalists emerge as key mediators amid murky combinations of legal and illegal activities, *Savage Frontier: Making News and Security on the Argentine Border* (Berkeley: University of California Press, 2015).

14. For a detailed investigation into the Colombo-Venezuelan border in the 2000s, see Ariel Fernando Ávila and Carmen Rosa Guerra Ariza, eds., *La frontera caliente entre Colombia y Venezuela* (Bogotá: Corporación Nuevo Arco Iris, 2012).

15. Human Rights Watch, "The Ties That Bind: Colombia and Military-Paramilitary Links," *Reports* 12. no. 1 (2000), http://www.hrw.org/reports/2000/ colombia/.

16. For a more thorough contextualization of the La Gabarra massacre, see Tate, *Counting the Dead*, 238–41.

17. Compelling photographs of the demobilization of the AUC's Catatumbo Bloc can be found in Stephen Ferry, *Violentology: A Manual of the Colombian Conflict* (Bogotá: Icono, 2012), 98–102.

18. For a detailed analysis of gifts and humanitarianism see Erica Bornstein, *Disquieting Gifts: Humanitarianism in New Delhi* (Stanford, CA: Stanford University Press, 2012). Marcel Mauss, *The Gift: Forms and Functions of Exchange in Archaic Societies* (New York: W. W. Norton, 1967).

19. Mariella Pandolfi, "Humanitarianism and Its Discontents," in *Forces of Compassion: Humanitarianism between Ethics and Politics* (Santa Fe, NM: School for Advanced Research Press, 2010), 228.

20. Juan Carlos's work for Vanera exemplifies the fluid borders connecting military intelligence, market research, and anthropological knowledge. This fluidity resonates with but differs from the controversies surrounding the Human

Terrain System (HTS) in the US, where the Department of Defense employed social scientists and often embedded them in US military units. Montgomery McFate, "The Military Utility of Understanding Adversary Culture," *Joint Forces Quarterly* 38 (2005): 42–48. Exemplary in the surge of critical scholarship about the military's cultural (re)turn is David Price, *Weaponizing Anthropology: Social Science in the Service of the Militarized State* (Petrolia, CA: Counterpunch, 2011). In Colombia, marketers and market researchers have increasingly served as the experts whom the military has mobilized to instrumentalize knowledge about "adversary culture," which raises interesting questions about the ways in which marketers position themselves as public intellectuals.

21. That statistic is pulled from Agencia Colombiana para la Reintegración, *Reporte anual: Reintegración en Colombia—Hechos y Datos* (Bogotá: Presidencia, 2011). It is important to note that although official statistics collated by the ACR and the PAHD correspond generally; they do not match. Furthermore, government statistics on demobilization are never independently verified, so they must be read with healthy skepticism.

22. The acronym for the Colombian air force is FAC. A certain poetic irony haunts the fact that the FAC has spent much of its time hunting the FARC. The one-letter difference in the two acronyms signals an unbridgeable divide, the idea of revolution, at the same time that its sonority alludes to the fratricidal dimension of the Colombian conflict.

23. Since the early 2000s the US has paid the salaries of five Colombian professionals who work in the Presidency and the PAHD. These are a mixture of lawyers, image managers, and intelligence analysts. Although these five salaries, paid on a US diplomatic pay scale, are a pittance of overall US support to Colombia, they provide the US government with visibility into some of the most sensitive decisions of the Colombian government. The practice is an index of how closely allied the two governments have become and raises questions about Colombian sovereignty.

24. Virginia Hewitt, *Beauty and the Banknote: Images of Women on Paper Money* (London: British Museum Press, 1994), 11.

25. In our conversation Federico said that they used special effects "like crazy" to multiply the lights in the river for the commercial.

26. Andrew Graan defines nation branding as "strategic efforts to formulate national identity as a branded commodity" and goes on to argue that "nation-branding practices represent a new modality of neoliberal governance in which the state is imagined as an entrepreneurial subject" and "charges itself with the task of attracting outside capital as a means of wealth creation." Andrew Graan, "Counterfeiting the Nation? Skopje 2014 and the Politics of Nation Branding in Macedonia," *Cultural Anthropology* 28, no. 1 (2013): 164–165. On nation branding see Melissa Aronczk, *Branding the Nation: The Global Business of National Identity* (Oxford: Oxford University Press, 2013); James B. Twitchell, *Branded*

Nation: The Marketing of Megachurch, College Inc. and Museumworld (New York: Simon and Schuster, 2005); Nadia Kaneva, *Branding Post-communist Nations: Marketized National Identities in the "New" Europe* (New York: Routledge, 2012); William Mazzarella, "Branding the Mahatma: The Untimely Provocation of Gandhian Publicity," *Cultural Anthropology* 25, no. 1 (2010): 1–39.

27. The invocation of Colombia as a "land of magical realism" is a crass effort to capitalize on the literary style and fame of Nobel Laureate Gabriel García Márquez, whose political sympathies have tended toward the left, often the militant left, and especially the M19. Villamizar Herrera, *Jaime Bateman: Biografía de un revolucionario.*

28. Colombia Travel, "Colombia el riesgo es que te quieres quedar: ¿De dónde nace la campaña?" February 24, 2010, http://www.colombia.travel/po/descargas/colombia_campanadeturismo.pdf. Robert Fletcher analyzes Colombian tourism campaigns and coined the term "fortress tourism" to describe the Colombian variety: "'The Only Risk Is Wanting to Stay': Mediating Risk in Colombian Tourism Development," *RASAALA: Recreation and Society in Africa, Asia, and Latin America* 1, no. 2 (2011).

29. Anthropologists of branding rightly point out that the surplus value created through branding is always at risk of being siphoned off by knock-offs, pirates, pranksters, and political opponents. See Constantine V. Nakassis, "Brands and Their Surfeits," *Cultural Anthropology* 28, no. 1 (2013): 111–26; Kedron Thomas, *Regulating Style: Intellectual Property Law and the Business of Fashion in Guatemala* (Berkeley: University of California Press, 2016).

Chapter Three

1. Jodi Dean, *Publicity's Secret: How Technoculture Capitalizes on Democracy* (Ithaca, NY: Cornell University Press, 2002), 47.

2. Dean, *Publicity's Secret.* Jill Lepore historicizes the relationship between secrecy and publicity in her insightful essay "Privacy in an Age of Publicity," *New Yorker*, June 24, 2013.

3. For a fascinating rumination on the interplay between secrecy and media, see Melley's accounting of a US-funded melodrama series in Afghanistan. Timothy Melley, *The Covert Sphere: Secrecy Fiction and the National Security State* (Ithaca, NY: Cornell University Press, 2012). Also on secrecy see Lilith Mahmud, *The Brotherhood of Freemasonry Sisters: Gender, Secrecy, and Fraternity in Italian Masonic Lodges* (Chicago: University of Chicago Press, 2014), 6–17.

4. I am all too aware that such indistinctions are not new. Each has a history that can be traced across contexts. The point here is a general one: the contem-

porary moment is decreasingly invested in maintaining modernist distinctions and the fiction of fixed categories.

5. For a thoughtful reflection on trends in anthropologists embedding themselves in institutions, see Tate, *Drugs, Thugs, and Diplomats*, 14–18.

6. Other décor in Nicholas's office included plaques and medals from his time in a Special Forces unit, and his training at Fort Bragg in North Carolina and Fort Benning in Georgia. Fort Benning hosted the infamous School of the Americas, now renamed the Western Hemisphere Institute for Security Cooperation. For an ethnography of that troubled institution (in which nearly half of all participants were Colombian), see Lesley Gill, *The School of the Americas: Military Training and Political Violence in the Americas* (Durham, NC: Duke University Press, 2004).

7. Mark Duffield, *Global Government and the New Wars: The Merging of Development and Security* (London: Zed Books, 2014); Mary Kaldor, *New and Old Wars: Organized Violence in a Global Era*, 3rd ed. (Stanford, CA: Stanford University Press, 2012).

8. Tate unpacks how the Colombian military has appropriated human rights discourse and folded it back into the counterinsurgency. Tate, *Counting the Dead*, 275–84. The Reagan White House used a similar strategy of creating elite units within the Salvadoran army to parry accusations of funding extreme right-wing elements of the military. Grandin, *Empire's Workshop*, 100–120.

9. For an extended treatment of military culture in Colombia, see Elsa Blair Trujillo, *Conflicto armado y militares en Colombia: Cultos, símbolos e imaginarios* (Medellín: Editorial Universidad de Antioquia, 1999.

10. Although the military continued to refer to the bloc as the Caribbean Bloc, the FARC changed its name to Martín Caballero Bloc in 2007 to honor its militarily assertive commander after his death. (Caballero allegedly tried to plant explosives along the route of President Clinton's motorcade in Cartagena in 2000.) Investigative reporter Dana Priest revealed that the military operation that slayed Caballero used smart-bomb technology courtesy of the CIA. Dana Priest, "Covert Action in Colombia: U.S. Intelligence, GPS Bomb Kits Help Latin American Nation Cripple Rebel Forces," *Washington Post*, December 21, 2013.

11. For a regional history that documents and analyzes the social, ethnic, and political context of the armed conflict in the Sierra Nevada de Santa Marta, a mountain range that is sacred to numerous indigenous groups, see *Cuando la Madre Tierra llora: Crisis en derechos humanos y humanitaria en la Sierra Nevada de Gonawindúa* (Bogotá: FUCUDE, 2009).

12. While looking at one image of rebels bathing in a river, José commented, "They're doing perfectly fine over there," a dig at Venezuela for providing the FARC safe haven. See Annete Idler, "Espacios invisibilizados: Actores violentos–no estatales en las zonas fronterizas de Colombia," in *Las agendas de*

lo indígena en la larga era de globalización, ed. Römy Kohler and Anna Ebert (Berlin: Gebr. Mann Verlag, 2015).

13. For an example of an intrepid denunciation of the practice of cajoling deserters to collaborate by offering them rewards, see Santiago Villa, "El peligro de cobrar recompensas," *El Espectador*, February 11, 2011, http://www .elespectador.com/opinion/columna-404247-el-peligro-de-cobrar-recompensas.

14. In 2006 Luis Carlos Restrepo, acting as high commissioner for peace, oversaw an entirely staged demobilization ceremony in which unemployed men and women, some of whom were living on the street, were cast as disarming guerrillas for $200 each.

15. The military kept Directive 29 of 2005 secret until the W radio station sued to gain access, a sharp contrast to the highly publicized Directive of 300-28 of 2007 declaring that the military would value demobilizations more than kills or captures in the institution's incentive structure.

16. *Bajas* also refers to dismissal or demotion within the armed forces, the equivalent of institutional death.

17. Human Rights Watch, "Colombia: Top Brass Linked to Extrajudicial Executions: Generals, Colonels Implicated in 'False Positive' Killing," June 24, 2015, https://www.hrw.org/news/2015/06/24/colombia-top-brass-linked-extrajudicial -executions. Also see a documentary film by Simone Bruno and Dado Carillo, *Falsos positivos* (2009).

18. See "Statement by Professor Philip Alston, UN Special Rapporteur on Extrajudicial Killings—Mission to Colombia," UN Human Rights Council, August 8–18, June 2009, http://www.unhchr.ch/huricane/huricane.nsf/0/C6390E2 F247BF1A7C12575D9007732FD?opendocument (accessed December 29, 2013). The same unintended consequences of military incentives affected demobilizations. During my time on the military base, Nicolás expressed concern about "kids who want to demobilize people who aren't [members of guerrilla groups]." He continued, "That's called a demobilization false positive."

19. Agustin Iguarán, "En el Caribe, 40 guerrilleros de FARC y ELN se entregaron." *El Heraldo*, July 10, 2012. http://www.elheraldo.co/region/en-el-caribe -40-guerrilleros-de-farc-y-eln-se-entregaron-74226.

20. In June 2008 Chávez gave a landmark speech in which he said that guerrilla warfare "has passed to history" and called on the FARC to abandon the armed struggle and focus on effecting change politically. "Chávez: La guerrilla pasó a la historia," *BBC Mundo,* June 9, 2008, http://news.bbc.co.uk/hi/spanish/ latin_america/newsid_7443000/7443091.stm.

21. For an analysis of the slippage between the legal and the permissible, see Janet Roitman, "The Ethics of Illegality in the Chad Basin," in *Law and Disorder in the Postcolony*, eds. Jean Comaroff and John L. Comaroff (Chicago: University of Chicago Press, 2006).

22. Bonaventura de Sousa Santos and Mauricio García Villegas, eds., *El ca-*

leidoscopio de las justicias en Colombia: Análisis socio-jurídico, 2 vols. (Bogotá: Siglo de Hombre Editores, 2001).

23. The tactics raise urgent questions about the relationship between affect and ethics; see William Mazzarella, "Sense Out of Sense: Notes on the Affect/ Ethics Impasse," *Cultural Anthropology* 32, no. 2 (2017): 199–208.

24. In a letter Che Guevara wrote from Africa to the editor of the Uruguayan weekly *Marcha*, he said, "The true revolutionary is guided by a great feeling of love. It is impossible to think of a genuine revolutionary lacking this quality." In *Socialism and Man in Cuba* (Atlanta: Pathfinder, 1989).

25. For a provocative parsing of why the US military put a premium on intimate knowledge and cultural awareness when it stumbled in its occupation of Iraq in the mid-2000s, see Derek Gregory, "'The Rush to the Intimate': Counterinsurgency and the Cultural Turn," *Radical Philosophy* 150 (2008): 8–23.

26. Joseph Masco, "Counterinsurgency, *The Spook*, and Blowback," in *Anthropology and Global Counterinsurgency*, eds. John D. Kelly et al. (Chicago: University of Chicago Press, 2010), 202–3.

27. See World Organisation Against Torture, "State Violence in Colombia: An Alternative Report to the United Nations Committee Against Torture" (Geneva: World Organisation Against Torture, 2004), http://www.omct.org/files/2004/06/2421/stateviolence_colombia_04_eng.pdf.

28. Tate, *Drugs, Thugs, and Diplomats*, chap. 3.

29. Christopher M. Sullivan, "The (In)effectiveness of Torture for Combating Insurgency," *Journal of Peace Research* 51 (2014): 388–404.

30. For more on the intelligence reforms in the Colombian military at the turn of the millennium, see Porch and Delgado, "'Masters of Today': Military Intelligence and Counterinsurgency in Colombia, 1990–2009," *Small Wars and Insurgencies* 21, no. 2 (2010): 277–302. Also see John A. Gentry and David B. Spencer, "Colombia's FARC: A Portrait of Insurgent Intelligence," *Intelligence and National Security* 25, no. 4 (2010): 453–78, which appraises the FARC's intelligence capabilities and weaknesses and was written by affiliates of the US Department of Defense's Southern Commando, SOUTHCOM, who had "unfettered" access to captured FARC documents and deserters.

31. As Samuel Huntington and others have noted, legitimacy is a "mushy" concept. By invoking the term here I mean an admixture of popularity and moral authority. Samuel P. Huntington, *The Third Wave: Democratization in the late Twentieth Century* (Norman: University of Oklahoma Press, 1991), 46. I am indebted to Lisa Wedeen for urging me to think more about the forms of legitimacy at play in the PAHD's symbolic production. For a further disaggregation of the term's commonly muddled meanings, see Lisa Wedeen, *Ambiguities of Domination: Politics, Rhetoric, and Symbols in Contemporary Syria* (Chicago: University of Chicago Press, 1999), loc. 228–97.

Chapter Four

1. Michael Taussig, *Law in a Lawless Land: Diary of a Limpieza in Colombia* (Chicago: University of Chicago Press, 2003).

2. For an anthropological and photographic exploration of artisanal gold mining in Colombia, see Elizabeth Ferry and Stephen Ferry, *La Batea: Impresiones del oro en Colombia / La Batea: Impressions of Gold in Colombia* (Bogotá, ICONO, 2017).

3. I was careful never to learn too much about this story. For some reason, the mission fell apart.

4. Jocelyn Lim Chua, *In Pursuit of the Good Life: Aspiration and Suicide in Globalizing South India* (Berkeley: University of California Press, 2014), 2.

5. Lauren Berlant, *Cruel Optimism* (Durham, NC: Duke University Press, 2011), 11.

6. Arlene Dávila, *El Mall: The Spatial and Class Politics of Shopping Malls in Latin America* (Berkeley: University of California Press, 2016), 2, 9, 12.

7. Dávila, *El Mall*, 3.

8. Superintendencia Financiera Colombiana, "Informe sobre sector financiero: Tarjetas de crédito en Colombia" (Bogotá, DC: Gobernación de Colombia, 2015).

9. Oliver Kaplan and Enzo Nussio, "Explaining Recidivism of Ex-combatants in Colombia," *Journal of Conflict Resolution*. Ma, 2016, 1–30; Fundación Ideas para la Paz, "Retorno a la legalidad o reincidencia de ex-combatientes en Colombia: Dimensión del fenómeno y factores de riesgo," *Informes FIP* 22 (2014): 29; Alejandro Éder, "Política de reintegración es un caso de éxito en desarrollo social," interview by Milena Sarralde D., *El Tiempo*, November 14, 2014, http://www.eltiempo.com/multimedia/especiales/debates-de-paz-entrevista-con -alejandro-der/14834955.

10. Here I am speaking in broad strokes about the political science and policy literature, which has many subliteratures and methodological nuances. A few references that speak to the breadth and richness of this work are Macartan Humphreys and Jeremy M. Weinstein, "Demobilization and Reintegration," *Journal of Conflict Resolution* 51, no. 4 (2007): 531–67; Oliver Kaplan and Enzo Nussio, "Community Counts: The Social Reintegration of Ex-combatants in Colombia," *Conflict Management and Peace Science*, 2015: DOI 10.1177/ 0738894215614506; Robert Muggah, ed., *Security and Post-conflict Reconstruction: Dealing with Fighters in the Aftermath of War* (Abingdon, UK: Routledge, 2009); Christopher Blattman and Jeannie Annan, "Reintegrating and Employing High Risk Youth in Liberia: Lessons from a Randomized Evaluation of Landmine Action, an Agricultural Training Program for Ex-Combatants," report, Innovation for Poverty Action, Yale University, 2011, https://www.poverty-action.org/sites/default/ files/publications/blattman_annan_ex-com_reintegration_ipa_liberia_1.pdf.

11. The ACR's belated realization that former combatants make poor business owners is thanks in part to academic critique in Colombia. See, for example, Stefan Thorsell, "¿Hacia una reintegración económica centrada en las personas? Análisis de la estrategia de reintegración económica de combatientes desmovilizados en Colombia," *Colombia Internacional* 77 (2013): 177–215.

12. Robert Foster, *Coca-Globalization: Following Soft Drinks from New York to New Guinea* (London: Palgrave MacMillan, 2008).

13. Lesley Gill, *A Century of Violence in a Red City* (Durham, NC: Duke University Press, 2016), Kindle ed., loc. 2532, 2035.

14. For a harrowing story about how the soft-drink industry in Colombia intimidates its adversaries, see Andrew Jacobs and Matt Richtel, "She Took on Colombia's Soda Industry. Then She Was Silenced." *New York Times*, November 13, 2017.

15. Cámara de Comercio de Bogotá, "Encuesta de percepción de seguridad empresarial 2015," report, http://www.ccb.org.co/Sala-de-prensa/Noticias-CCB/2015/Marzo/Encuesta-de-Percepcion-de-Seguridad-y-Victimizacion-en-Bogota, accessed October 15, 2016. A notable exception to this trend is the private security industry, which values former combatants' skills.

16. I have heard stories from villagers of the military passing demobilized rebels to paramilitaries, who mask the former rebels and bring them to towns to identify guerrilla collaborators, many of whom end up on blacklists and are killed. Stories of this phenomenon concentrate in the early years of the PAHD, 2003–6, before my own fieldwork began. I visited one community where villagers said that if that former rebel returned (they claim to know his identity despite his having been masked), they would kill him.

17. For an analysis of the term *vivo*, which as an adjective means lively and vigorous but as a noun is used to refer to someone who is conniving and self-interested, see Austin Zeiderman, *Endangered City: The Politics of Security and Risk in Bogotá* (Durham, NC: Duke University Press, 2016), 115.

18. Luisa's experience is illustrative of what Clara Han, in the Chilean context, calls "the indebted subject" who is pulled between ethical and monetary demands. Clara Han, "The Work of Indebtedness: The Traumatic Present of Late Capitalist Chile," *Culture, Medicine and Psychiatry* 28, no. 2 (2004): 169–87.

19. Later in the conversation he added, "You can't imagine the people who work with us," and listed high-level officials of major cities.

20. This repression of community organizing should be read in light of Teo Ballvé's work on paramilitary grassroots organizing in the Urabá region. Ballvé documents how paramilitaries who wrest territorial control from the guerrillas then adapt and apply similar community-relations tactics to consolidate their dominion and make legal claims on seized land. "Grassroots Masquerades: Development, Paramilitaries, and Land Laundering in Colombia," *Geoforum* 50 (2013): 62–75.

21. Many of these community-based initiatives seek to capitalize on the cultural currency of their indigenous heritage, a process that echoes the self-commodification of ethnic groups analyzed by Jean and John Comaroff in *Ethnicity Inc.*

22. The case of postdictatorship Chile is illustrative of the political logic operating in the drive to economically include classes perceived as dangerous (Han, *Life in Debt*). Also see Caroline E. Schuster, *Social Collateral: Women and Microfinance in Paraguay's Smuggling Economy* (Berkeley: University of California Press, 2015).

23. For a superb ethnography on postconflict Peru and the legacies of the war, see Kimberly Theidon, *Intimate Enemies: Violence and Reconciliation in Peru* (Philadelphia: University of Pennsylvania Press, 2012).

24. The leadership of the ACR has always hailed from the upper rungs of Colombian society. Frank Pearl, who ran the reintegration agency from 2006 to 2010, is a businessman who worked for McKinsey Consulting and served as president of the corporate conglomerate Valores Bavaria. Alejandro Éder, Pearl's successor, is an heir to a fortune from one of the largest sugar manufacturers in Colombia.

25. I am heavily indebted to Patricia Alvarez Astacio for her insights into this scene, particularly her observations about the clothing and the ethical fashion industry.

26. Michael Taussig, *Beauty and the Beast* (Chicago: University of Chicago Press, 2012), e-book, loc. 51.

27. On ethical fashion see, Patricia Alvarez Astacio, "Moral Fibers: Making Fashion Ethical in Post-Authoritarian Peru," (PhD diss., University of California, Santa Cruz, 2015). On ethical capitalism, see Sarah Besky, *The Darjeeling Distinction: Labor and Justice on Fair-Trade Tea Plantations in India* (Berkeley: University of California Press, 2013); Daniel R. Reichman, *The Broken Village: Coffee, Migration, and Globalization in Honduras* (Ithaca, NY: ILR Press, 2011).

28. KienKe, "El Sastre de las FARC entra a las pasarelas," *Kienyke*, May 20, 2012, http://www.kienyke.com/historias/el-sastre-de-las-farc-entra-a-las-pasarelas/.

29. Adam Curtis, *The Century of the Self*, BBC documentary (2002).

30. Walter Benjamin, *The Arcades Project*, trans. Howard Eiland and Kevin McLaughlin (Cambridge, MA: Harvard University Press, 1999), 7.

31. For an anthology of excerpts on philosophers' ruminations on what constitutes the good life, see Charles Guignon, ed., *The Good Life: Readings in Philosophy* (Indianapolis: Hackett, 1999).

32. Such "shock therapy" aligns with the idea of the "shock doctrine" developed in Naomi Klein, *The Shock Doctrine: The Rise of Disaster Capitalism* (New York: Metropolitan Books, 2007).

33. The stratification of classes is codified in numeric ratings, 1–6, of each zone's economic status. This was originally a progressive policy to subsidize the utilities of lower-income communities. For more information on the history and consequences of this policy see Federico Pérez, *Urbanism as Warfare: Planning, Property, and Displacement in Bogotá* (PhD diss., Harvard University, Department of Anthropology, 2014).

34. I thank Diana Pardo Pedraza for sharing this poignant detail about the shifting geographical terrain of minefields with me. For a cultural analysis of demining efforts, see Diana Pardo Pedraza, "When Landmines Do Not Explode: Peasant Life in the Colombian War and Post-conflict" (PhD diss., University of California, Davis, in process).

35. For an account of how demobilization in Sierra Leone transcends linear progressions in time or space, with particular attention to the breakdown in the rural-urban divide, see Danny Hoffman, "Violent Events as Narrative Blocs: The Disarmament at Bo, Sierra Leone," *Anthropological Quarterly* 78, no. 2 (2005): 328–53.

Conclusion

1. Mark Fineman, Robin Wright, and Doyle McManus, "Preparing for War, Stumbling to Peace," *Los Angeles Times*, July 18, 2003, http://articles.latimes .com/2003/jul/18/nation/na-postwar18/6.

2. John Kerry made this statement in 2013 at his Senate confirmation hearing, quoted in Tate, *Drugs, Thugs, and Diplomats*, 219.

3. Greg Grandin, *Empire's Workshop: Latin America, the United States, and the Rise of the New Imperialism* (New York: Metropolitan Books, 2006), 5.

4. Alberto Ruiz Novoa: *Enseñanzas de la Campaña de Corea* (Bogotá: ANTARES, 1956), Álvaro Valencia Tovar and Jairo Sandoval Franky, *Colombia en la Guerra de Corea: La historia secreta* (Bogotá: Planeta, 2001).

5. Edward Lansdale, who stayed on in the Philippines after World War II, began to codify modern counterinsurgency doctrine based on his experience fighting the Communist Hukbalahap rebellion. For a biography of Lansdale, see Cecil B. Currey, *Edward Lansdale: The Unquiet American* (Boston: Houghton Mifflin, 1988). Though Colombian military intellectuals do not cite Lansdale directly, their writings carry heavy traces of his theories about managing civil-military relations and the importance of psychological warfare. See, for example, Ruiz Novoa, *Enseñanzas de la Campaña de Corea*, 243–45, 336–41. I was fascinated to learn that Landsdale was an advertising executive before becoming a CIA operative, Daniel Immerwahr, *Thinking Small: The United States and the Lure of Community Development* (Cambridge, MA: Harvard University Press, 2015), 106.

6. See chapter 9 of Robert Alexander Karl, "State Formation, Violence, and Cold War in Colombia, 1957–1966," (PhD diss., Harvard University, 2009).

7. This foundational moment for the FARC has been written about extensively. Exemplary among this literature are Eduard Pizarro Leongómez, *Las FARC, 1949–2011: De guerrilla campesina a máquina de guerra* (Bogotá: Norma, 2011), and Robert Alexander Karl, *The Forgotten Peace: Reform, Violence, and the Making of Modern Colombia* (Berkeley: University of California Press, 2017).

8. For a thorough accounting of the tectonic shifts that Europe experienced during the postwar period, see Tony Judt, *Postwar: A History of Europe since 1945* (New York: Penguin Books, 2005).

9. Rosa Brooks, *How Everything Became War and the Military Became Everything* (New York: Simon and Schuster, 2016).

10. Another telling euphemism is "overseas contingency operations"; see Masco, *Theater of Operation*, 194. For a more thorough discussion of the porosity of the distinctions between the green of military affairs and the blue of policing, see Beatrice Jauregui, "Bluing Green in the Maldives: Countering Citizen Insurgency by 'Civil'-izing National Security," in *Anthropology and Global Counterinsurgency* (Chicago: University of Chicago Press, 2010).

11. Tate, *Drugs, Thugs, and Diplomats*.

12. Denise Spencer, "Demobilization and Reintegration in Central America," Paper 08 (Bonn, Germany: BICC, 1997). Electronic document: http://reliefweb.int/sites/reliefweb.int/files/resources/D4EA83D23A60E77EC12574410047F9AF-bicc_sep1997.pdf, accessed February 2, 2017. The post-accord trajectory of these Central American nations has not been all that peaceful, with the expansion of deadly gangs involved in the drug trade. In arguing against the Colombian model of reintegrating ex-combatants, I am not proposing the uncritical embrace of the status quo ante.

13. After leading the Colombian police force, Óscar Naranjo, a decorated general, traveled to Mexico to advise President Peña Nieto on how to reform Mexico's security policies. This two-year consultancy has been controversial, especially in Mexico, where many experts questioned Naranjo's credentials. Security conditions in Mexico since Naranjo's advising stint have deteriorated further.

14. Thomas E. Ricks, "The Lesson of Colombia's Demobilization of FARC Can Help Us Work against ISIS," *Foreign Policy*, January 28, 2016, http://foreignpolicy.com/2016/01/28/the-lesson-of-colombias-demobilization-of-farc-can-help-us-work-against-isis/.

15. Patrick Tucker, "How Special Forces Helped Take Down Joseph Kony's Army with Tailored Messages," *Defense One*, October 17, 2017, http://www.defenseone.com/technology/2017/10/how-4-green-berets-took-down-joseph-konys-army-tailored-messages/141851/.

16. For a contextual analysis of the "come home" radio campaigns in the Great Lakes region, see Scott Ross, "Encouraging Rebel Demobilization by Radio in Uganda and the D.R. Congo: The Case of 'Come Home' Messaging," *African Studies Review* 59, no. 1 (2016): 33–55.

17. "The Cartagena Contribution to Disarmament, Demobilization and Reintegration," final report of the International, Disarmament, Demobilization and Reintegration Conference, May 4–6, 2009, 72. Electronic document: https://www.academia.edu/3586330/The_Cartagena_Contribution_to_Disarmament_Demobilization_and_Reintegration_DDR_, accessed February 16, 2017.

18. Personal interview with Matthew Waldman, Cambridge, MA, September 19, 2013. Also see Steven A. Zyck, "Former Combatant Reintegration and Fragmentation in Contemporary Afghanistan," *Conflict, Security and Development* 9 (2009): 111–31.

19. Colombia's intermediary role in this global hierarchy of security knowledge can be seen vis-à-vis Somalia, which adopted a militarized DDR policy in the early 2010s. As Muggah and O'Donnell make clear, the UN mission in Somalia, UNSOM, has coordinated with NISA, Somalia's intelligence service, as it works to wring former Al Shabaab fighters of intelligence. The Somali program follows in the footsteps of the individual demobilization initiatives in Colombia and Afghanistan. Robert Muggah and Chris O'Donnell, "Next Generation Disarmament, Demobilization, and Reintegration," *Stability: International Journal of Security and Development* 4 (2015): 2–5.

20. The Colombian government's "south-south" framing appropriates activist conceptions of "the Global South." See Paul Amar, *The Security Archipelago: Human Security States, Sexuality Politics, and the End of Neoliberalism* (Durham, NC: Duke University Press, 2013).

21. It is interesting to juxtapose the ACR's tour for the international delegates to Winifred Tate's account of US congressional delegations visiting southern Colombia to meet with the Colombian police and army so that they can forge a connection with those fighting on the front lines. Those war tours, a form of experiential marketing that public relations experts cum lobbyists have used since the 1950s (in the campaign to overthrow Jacobo Árbenz in Guatemala, for example), proved pivotal in motivating the US Congress to approved billions of dollars of military aid to the Colombian government. Tate, *Drugs, Thugs, and Diplomats*, 183–90.

22. On branding as neoliberal statecraft, see Graan, "Counterfeiting the Nation?"

23. On marketing as the meaning system of capitalism, see Applbaum, *Marketing Era*, 6–11.

24. Though the hangover after postmodernism has not treated Jean Baudrillard kindly, his early work that drew attention to what he called "sign value" remains an important intervention in thinking about how symbolic value and eco-

nomic value are interpenetrated. Kim Sawchuck, "Semiotics, Cybernetics, and the Ecstasy of Marketing," in *Baudrillard: A Critical Reader*, ed. Douglas Kellner (Oxford: Blackwell, 1994), 95. Gary Genosko, *Baudrillard and Signs: Signification Ablaze* (London: Routledge, 1994).

25. Arnold Van Gennep, *The Rites of Passage* (Chicago: University of Chicago Press, 1960).

26. Victor Turner, "Betwixt and Between: The Liminal Period in *Rites of Passage*." in *Reader in Comparative Religion: An Anthropological Approach*, 4th ed., ed. William A. Lessa and Evon Z. Vogt (New York: Harper and Row, 1979).

27. I do not mean to create the impression that United Nations–administered DDR programs implemented after a peace accord are not also flawed and deserving of criticism. Many classic DDR programs have led to rolling interventions that accommodate a mutating set of armed actors and have made no substantive impact on their heady goals. For a review of some of the critiques of the insufficiency for the UN's model of DDR as codified in its international standards (last updated in 2006), see Muggah and O'Donnell, "Next Generation Disarmament, Demobilization, and Reintegration," 1–12. The article makes palpable my argument about Colombia's role in promulgating a US-backed realpolitik vision of DDR at the expense of the UN's ostensibly neutral technocratic vision. (See note 18 about the Somali case.) Muggah and O'Donnell acknowledge that the very idea of international standards has essentially been abandoned (a finding made all the more poignant by the fact that O'Donnell works in the Department of Peacekeeping at the UN).

28. Pace Max Gluckman, who criticized Van Gennep for isolating ritual from social structure, that failure is due in large part to the ideological denials of the very idea of social structure. Max Gluckman, "Les Rites de Passage," in *Essays on the Ritual of Social Relations* (Manchester: Manchester University Press, 1962). A counterpoint to the government's policy toward former combatants would be the position of indigenous communities in Colombia that have developed their own ritualistic processes for administering a form of punishment and reintegrating former combatants. I have interviewed indigenous former guerrillas who have intensive reckonings with their past through yagé (ayahuasca) rituals. One former guerrilla commander recalled seeing "an entire hardware store" of war material in his vomit, a purge brought on by the yagé. See *Sueños del monte* (dir. Fattal, n.d.), a documentary film that explores a guerrilla fighter's use of psychotropic medicine to reckon with his past.

29. Henry Acosta offers a detailed first-person account of the initial contacts that brought the two sides together. Henry Acosta, *El hombre clave: El secreto mejor guardado del proceso de paz de Colombia* (Bogotá: Aguilar, 2016).

30. Theidon, "Transitional Subjects," 66.

31. Jacques Derrida, *Specters of Marx: The State of the Debt, the Work of Mourning and the New International* (New York: Routledge, 1994), xix.

32. The situation bears strong resonances with Chile's emergence from authoritarian rule. Anthropologist Julia Paley has argued that the advertising strategies and market research tactics used by the No campaign in the 1988 plebiscite to remove Augusto Pinochet from power in Chile have cast a long shadow over that country's political culture. She shows how such marketized tactics filtered down to the level of community organizing, becoming the very ground of politics at the local and national levels. Julia Paley, *Marketing Democracy: Power and Social Movements in Post-dictatorship Chile* (Berkeley: University of California Press, 2001).

33. See a full transcript, Fattal "Interview with alias Sergio Marín, Leader of the Commission for Propaganda and Communication in the FARC's Peace Delegation and Commander of the Antonio Nariño Front," at the Palco Hotel, Havana, Cuba, March 11, 2016, https://www.academia.edu/31226866/Interview_with_alias_Sergio_Mar%C3%ADn_leader_of_the_commission_for_propaganda_and_communication_in_the_FARCs_Peace_Delegation_and_commander_of_the_Antonio_Nari%C3%B1o_Front.

Epilogue

1. I borrow the egg yolk metaphor from the chronicle of the Décima in *La Silla Vacía*: Catalina Lobo-Guerrero, "Bailando cumbia con las FARC," *La Silla Vacía*, September 25, 2016, http://lasillavacia.com/historia/bailando-cumbia-con-las-farc-58080.

2. According to official statistics emerging from a census taken by the Universidad Nacional (in conjunction with the United Nations) of disarmed guerrillas in 2017, 10,015 guerrillas were officially registered as disarmed. Of these, 5,508 were guerrilla fighters, 2,904 were *milicianos*, and 1,603 were prisoners that the government freed. In rounding to 8,000 above I am approximating the combined number of guerrilla fighters and *milicianos*. The census is a fascinating snapshot of the FARC disarmament. See Universidad Nacional de Colombia, "Caracterización comunidad FARC-EP: Resultados generales," Censo Socioeconómico UN-CNR 2017, July 6, 2017. The PDF is available here: http://www.reintegracion.gov.co/es/sala-de-prensa/SiteAssets/Presentaci%C3%B3n%20rueda%20de%20prensa%20Julio%206%202017.pdf.

3. For a thoughtful unpacking of brand valuation, see Robert Foster, "The Work of the New Economy: Consumers, Brands, and Value Creation," *Cultural Anthropology* 22, no. 4 (2007): 707–31.

4. Kevin Roberts, *Lovemarks: The Future beyond Brands* (New York: Powerhouse Books, 2004), 74.

5. Robert Foster, "Things to Do with Brands," *HAU: Journal of Ethnographic Theory* 3 (2013): 708.

6. In fleshing out this vision of a collectivist economy run via cooperatives, the FARC has relied upon Henry Acosta, a key facilitator of the peace process who made his career as a leader of the cooperative sector of the Colombian economy. The effectiveness and sustainability of such initiatives will be a crucial component of a relatively stable post–peace accord period. For other reflections on the prospects of post–peace accord reintegration, see Alex Fattal and Juan Camilo Hoyos, "Hacia una reforma del DDR para la paz: Propuestas desde la academia y las experiencias actuales de desmovilización," November 19, 2013, https://www.academia.edu/7090339/Hacia_una_reforma _del_DDR_para_la_paz_Propuestas_desde_la_academia_y_las_experiencias _actuales_de_desmovilizaci%C3%B3n.

7. By early 2018, many of the transitional camps where the FARC collected to administer their collective projects are shells of what they were before the disarmament in 2017. Though it is hard to determine where most guerrillas have gone, early reports indicate that many sought out family, others integrated into ranks of the ELN, while yet others have created dissident fronts that took up arms again. The phenomenon of the dissident fronts is particularly troubling and echoes the rearmament of paramilitaries in the late 2000s. At the time of writing, March 2018, the implementation of the peace agreement has been marred by lack of follow-through, especially from the state's side. Dissident fronts may in fact be a contingency plan by the guerrilla, a hedge against the prospect of the peace agreement disintegrating further.

8. Juliana Ramírez, "El No ha sido la campaña más barata y más efectiva de la historia," *La República*, October 5, 2016, http://www.larepublica.co/el-no-ha -sido-la-campa%C3%B1a-m%C3%A1s-barata-y-m%C3%A1s-efectiva-de-la -historia_427891.

9. "La cuestionable estrategia de campaña del NO," *El Espectador*, October 6, 2016, http://www.elespectador.com/noticias/politica/cuestionable-estrategia-de -campana-del-no-articulo-658862.

10. This video, central to the "Todos por el Sí" campaign, which was published on YouTube on September 10, 2016, was removed and scrubbed from the internet in mid-2017.

11. In a prescient article, Alfonso Acosta Caparrós, himself a marketer, urges Sokoloff, the most public partner of MullenLowe/SSP3, to radically rethink his strategy for the Yes campaign. Acosta argues that a generic, warm and fuzzy conceit would insult people's intelligence and not be believable. Alfonso Acosta Caparrós, "Respuesta al artículo de Sokoloff y su campaña por el Sí en el plebiscito," *Las 2 Orillas*, February 26, 2016, http://www.las2orillas.co/respuesta-al -articulo-sokoloff-campana-plebiscito/.

12. The discussion of gender in the focus groups highlighted contradictions, such as the difficulty for female guerrillas to rise in the ranks. In feminist circles in the Colombian left, the term Machista-Leninista (a riff on Marxista-

Leninista) is used to describe the machismo rife within the militant left. For an extended discussion of gender and demobilization in Colombia, see Kimberly Theidon, "Reconstructing Masculinities: The Disarmament, Demobilization, and Reintegration of Former Combatants in Colombia," *Human Rights Quarterly* 31(2009): 1–34. For a discussion of the role of women in the FARC, see Gloria Yaneth Castrillón Pulido, "Víctimas o victimarias? El rol de las mujeres en las FARC: Una aproximación desde la teoría de género," *Ópera* 16 (2015): 77–95.

13. In Colombia, the government has selectively focused on the question of women's rights by highlighting the FARC's policy of mandatory birth control and forced abortions.

14. Fattal, "Uploading the News after Coming Down from the Mountain: The FARC's Uncanny Experiment with Online Television, in Cuba, 2012–2016," *International Journal of Communication* 11 (2017): 3832–56.

15. On the concept of the "war yet to come," see Hiba Bou Akar, *For the War Yet to Come: Planning Beirut's Frontiers* (Stanford, CA: Stanford University Press, 2017).

Bibliography

Abadía-Barrero, César. "Neoliberal Justice and the Transformation of the Moral: The Privatization of the Right to Heathcare in Colombia." *Medical Anthropology Quarterly* 30, no. 1 (2015): 62–79

Acosta, Henry. *El hombre clave: El secreto mejor guardado del proceso de paz de Colombia.* Bogotá: Aguilar, 2016.

Acosta Caparrós, Alfonso. "Respuesta al artículo de Sokoloff y su campaña por el Sí en el plebiscito." *Las 2 Orillas* (Bogotá), February 26, 2016. http://www.las2orillas.co/respuesta-al-articulo-sokoloff-campana-plebiscito/.

Agencia Colombiana para la Reintegración (ACR). *Reporte anual: Reintegración en Colombia—Hechos y Datos.* Bogotá: Presidencia de la República de Colombia, 2011.

Akar, Hiba Bou. *For the War Yet to Come: Planning Beirut's Frontiers.* Stanford, CA: Stanford University Press, 2017.

Alvarez Astacio, Patricia. "Moral Fibers: Making Fashion Ethical in Post-authoritarian Peru." PhD diss., University of California, Santa Cruz, 2015.

Amar, Paul. *The Security Archipelago: Human Security States, Sexuality Politics, and the End of Neoliberalism.* Durham, NC: Duke University Press, 2013.

Amat, Yamid. "Secretos de la Toma del Palacio de Justicia." *El Tiempo*, November 7, 2004. http://www.eltiempo.com/archivo/documento/MAM-1516427.

Angel, Gabriel. "Alfonso Cano anticipó su muerte: 'Lo sé. Quieren arrojar mi cadáver sobre la mesa antes de empezar los diálogos.'" *Las2Orillas* (Bogotá), November 4, 2016. http://www.las2orillas.co/alfonso-cano-anticipo-su-muerte-lo-se-quieren-arrojar-mi-cadaver-sobre-la-mesa-antes-de-empezar-los-dialogos/.

ANNCOL. "Muerte de 11 diputados en Colombia: Comunicado de las FARC." *El Mundo.es*, June 28, 2007. http://www.elmundo.es/elmundo/2007/06/28/internacional/1183026099.html.

Applbaum, Kalman. "Crossing Borders: Globalization as Myth and Charter in American Transnational Consumer Marketing." *American Ethnologist* 27, no. 2 (2000): 257–282.

Applbaum, Kalman. *The Marketing Era: From Professional Practice to Global Provisioning.* New York: Routledge, 2004.

Arana, Marie. *Bolívar: American Liberator.* New York: Simon and Schuster, 2013.

Arjona, Ana M. *Rebelocracy: Social Order in the Colombian Civil War.* Cambridge: Cambridge University Press, 2016.

Arjona, Ana M., and Stathis Kalyvas. "Recruitment into Armed Groups in Colombia: A Survey of Demobilized Fighters." In *Understanding Collective Political Violence.* London: Palgrave-Macmillan, 2011.

Aronczyk, Melissa. *Branding the Nation: The Global Business of National Identity.* Oxford: Oxford University Press, 2013.

Ávila, Ariel Fernando, and Carmen Rosa Guerra. *La frontera caliente entre Colombia y Venezuela.* Bogotá: Corporación Nuevo Arco Iris, 2012.

Bagley, Bruce. "Drug Policy, Political Violence and U.S. Policy in Colombia in the 1990s." Working paper, 2001. http://clasarchive.berkeley.edu/Events/conferences/Colombia/workingpapers/working_paper_bagley.html.

Ballvé, Teo. "Grassroots Masquerades: Development, Paramilitaries, and Land Laundering in Colombia." *Geoforum* 50 (2013): 62–75.

Bartel, Rebecca C. "Giving Is Believing: Credit and Christmas in Colombia." *Journal of the American Academy of Religion* 84, no. 4 (May 2016)) 1006–28.

Bartholomew, Mark. *Adcreep: The Case against Modern Marketing.* Stanford, CA: Stanford University Press, 2017.

BBC Mundo. "Chávez: 'La guerrilla pasó a la historia.'" *BBC Mundo*, June 9, 2008. http://news.bbc.co.uk/hi/spanish/latin_america/newsid_7443000/7443091.stm.

Behar, Olga. *Las guerras de la paz.* Bogotá: Planeta, 1985.

Benjamin, Walter. *The Arcades Project.* Cambridge, MA: Harvard University Press, 1999.

Berlant, Lauren. *Cruel Optimism.* Durham, NC: Duke University Press, 2011.

Besky, Sarah. *The Darjeeling Distinction: Labor and Justice on Fair-Trade Tea Plantations in India.* Berkeley: University of California Press, 2013.

Blair Trujillo, Elsa. *Conflicto armado y militares en Colombia: Cultos, símbolos e imaginarios.* Medellín: Editorial Universidad de Antioquia, 1999.

Blattman, Christopher, and Jeannie Annan. "Reintegrating and Employing High Risk Youth in Liberia: Lessons from a Randomized Evaluation of Landmine Action an Agricultural Training Program for Ex-combatants." *Innovation for Poverty Action,* 2011, https://www.poverty-action.org/sites/default/files/publications/blattman_annan_ex-com_reintegration_ipa_liberia_1.pdf.

Bob, Clifford. *The Marketing of Rebellion: Insurgents, Media, and International Activism.* Cambridge: Cambridge University Press, 2005.

Bornstein, Erica. *Disquieting Gifts: Humanitarianism in New Delhi.* Stanford, CA: Stanford University Press, 2012.

Britto, Lina. "Hurricane Winds: Vallenato Music and Marijuana Traffic in Colombia's First Illegal Drugs Boom." *Hispanic American Historical Review* 95, no. 1 (2015): 71–102.

Brooks, Rosa. *How Everything Became War and the Military Became Everything: Tales from the Pentagon.* New York: Simon and Schuster, 2016.

Bruno, Simone, and Dado Carillo. *Falsos positivos.* Film, 55 minutes. Bogotá: Mediakite, 2009. Posted by La Silla Vacía, https://www.youtube.com/watch?v =Srxt7bGBsr4, March 6, 2012.

Cámara de Comercio de Bogotá. *Encuesta de percepción de seguridad empresarial 2015.* N.d. Accessed October 15, 2016. http://www.ccb.org.co/Sala-de -prensa/Noticias-CCB/2015/Marzo/Encuesta-de-Percepcion-de-Seguridad-y -Victimizacion-en-Bogota.

Cárdenas Sarrias, José Armando. *Los parias de la guerra: Análisis del proceso de desmovilización individual.* Bogotá: Ediciones Aurora, 2005.

Carrigan, Ana. *The Palace of Justice: A Colombian Tragedy.* New York: Four Walls Eight Windows, 1993.

"The Cartagena Contribution to Disarmament, Demobilization and Reintegration (DDR)." Final report of the International, Disarmament, Demobilization and Reintegration Conference, 2009. https://www.academia.edu/3586 330/The_Cartagena_Contribution_to_Disarmament_Demobilization_and _Reintegration_DDR_.

Castaño, Paula. "In the Time of the Victims: Understandings of Violence and Institutional Practices in the National Commission of Reparation and Reconciliation in Colombia." PhD diss., University of Chicago, 2013.

Castaño, Ricardo Z. "Colombia y el modelo neoliberal." *Agora* 5, no. 10 (2004), 59–78.

Castrillón Pulido, Gloria Yaneth. "¿Víctimas o victimarias? El rol de las mujeres en las FARC: Una aproximación desde la teoría de género." *Ópera* 16 (2015): 77–95.

Cecil, Mathew. *Branding Hoover's FBI: How the Boss's PR Men Sold the Bureau to America.* Lawrence: Kansas University Press, 2016.

Central Intelligence Agency. "Intelligence Memorandum: Colombian Counterinsurgency, Steps in the Right Direction." Approved for release October 2001. http://www2.gwu.edu/~nsarchiv/colombia/19940126.

Centro Nacional de Memoria Histórica. *¡Basta ya! Colombia memorias de guerra y dignidad.* Bogotá: Centro Nacional de Memoria Histórica, 2013.

Centro Nacional de Memoria Histórica. *Desmovilización y reintegración paramilitar: Panorama posacuerdos con las AUC.* Bogotá: Centro Nacional de Memoria Histórica, 2015.

Chamayou, Grégoire. *A Theory of the Drone.* New York: New Press, 2015.

Chua, Jocelyn Lim. *In Pursuit of the Good Life: Aspiration and Suicide in Globalizing South India.* Berkeley: University of California Press, 2014.

Colombia Travel. "Colombia, el Riesgo es que te quieres quedar: ¿De dónde

nace la campaña?" Last modified February 24, 2010. http://www.colombia
.travel/po/descargas/colombia_campanadeturismo.pdf.

Comaroff, John L., and Jean Comaroff. *Ethnicity, Inc.* Chicago: University of
Chicago Press, 2009.

*Cuando la Madre Tierra llora: Crisis en derechos humanos y humanitaria en la
Sierra Nevada de Gonawindúa.* Bogotá: FUCUDE, 2009.

Currey, Cecil B. *Edward Lansdale: The Unquiet American.* Boston: Houghton
Mifflin, 1988.

Curtis, Adam. *The Century of the Self.* Film, three parts, 180 minutes. London:
BBC, 2005.

Dávila, Arlene. *El Mall: The Spatial and Class Politics of Shopping Malls in
Latin America.* Berkeley: University of California Press, 2016.

Dávila, Arlene. *Latinos, Inc.: The Marketing and Making of a People.* Berkeley:
University of California Press, 2001.

Dean, Jodi. *Publicity's Secret: How Technoculture Capitalizes on Democracy.*
Ithaca, NY: Cornell University Press, 2002.

Decreto 1385 de 1994. *Diario Oficial 45420 de 5 de julio, 1994.* Bogotá: Ministerio de Gobierno, 1994. http://www.alcaldiabogota.gov.co/sisjur/normas/
Norma1.jsp?i=9138.

Der Derian, James. *Virtuous War: Mapping the Military-Industrial-Media-
Entertainment Network.* Boulder, CO: Westview, 2001.

Derrida, Jacques. *Specters of Marx: The State of the Debt, the Work of Mourning
and the New International.* New York: Routledge, 1994.

De Soto, Hernando. "The Capitalist Cure for Terrorism." *Wall Street Journal,*
October 14, 2014.

De Soto, Hernando. *The Mystery of Capital: Why Capitalism Triumphs in the
West and Fails Elsewhere.* New York: Basic Books, 2003.

Dowd, Maureen. "AFTER THE WAR: White House Memo; War Introduces a
Tougher Bush to Nation." *New York Times,* March 2, 1991.

Dudley, Steven S. *Walking Ghosts: Murder and Guerrilla Politics in Colombia.*
New York: Routledge, 2004.

Duffield, Mark. *Global Government and the New Wars: The Merging of Development and Security.* London: Zed Books, 2014.

Éder, Alejandro. "Política de reintegración es un caso de éxito en desarrollo social." Interview by Milena Sarralde D. *El Tiempo,* November 14, 2014, http://
www.eltiempo.com/multimedia/especiales/debates-de-paz-entrevista-con
-alejandro-der/14834955.

Einstein, Mara. *Black Ops Advertising: Native Ads, Content Marketing and the
Covert World of the Digital Sell.* Berkeley: OR Books, 2016.

Ejército Nacional de Colombia. *FARC: Guerrilla, infamia y dolor.* Bogotá: Ejército Nacional de Colombia, Dirección de Inteligencia, 2012.

El Espectador, Redacción General. "Avianca 203, la historia que nunca nos contaron." November 27, 2016. http://www.elespectador.com/noticias/nacional/avianca-203-historia-nunca-nos-contaron-articulo-667717.

El Espectador, Redacción Política. "La cuestionable estrategia de campaña del NO." October 6, 2016. http://www.elespectador.com/noticias/politica/cuestionable-estrategia-de-campana-del-no-articulo-658862.

El Tiempo, Redacción General. "Colombia, el país más desigual de A. Latina en el reparto de la tierra." November 29, 2016. http://www.eltiempo.com/vida/ciencia/concentracion-de-la-tierra-en-america-latina-oxfam-52376.

El Tiempo, Redacción. "Ordenan liberar a Francisco Santos." May 20, 1991. http://www.eltiempo.com/archivo/documento/MAM-86595.

Entel, Nicolás, dir. *Sins of My Father*. Film, 94 minutes. Red Creek Productions, 2009.

Ewen, Stuart. *PR! A Social History of Spin*. New York: Basic Books, 1996.

Fattal, Alexander L., dir. *Dreams from the Mountain*. Break the Frame Films and Casa Tarantula, n.d.

Fattal, Alex. "Facebook: Corporate Hackers, a Billion Users, and the Geopolitics of the 'Social Graph.'" *Anthropological Quarterly* 85, no. 3 (2012): 927–56.

Fattal, Alex. "Hostile Remixes on YouTube: A New Constraint on Pro-FARC Counterpublics in Colombia." *American Ethnologist* 41, no. 2 (2014): 320–335.

Fattal, Alex. "Interview with Alias Sergio Marín, Leader of the Commission for Propaganda and Communication in the FARC's Peace Delegation and Commander of the Antonio Nariño Front." https://www.academia.edu/31226866/Interview_with_alias_Sergio_Mar%C3%ADn_leader_of_the_commission_for_propaganda_and_communication_in_the_FARCs_Peace_Delegation_and_commander_of_the_Antonio_Nari%C3%B1o_Front, accessed May 22, 2017.

Fattal, Alexander L. "Narco-novelas as Faux Historical Memory: Resignifying the M19's Acts of 'Armed Propaganda' and the Foreclosure Left Politics in Colombia," Unpublished manuscript, n.d.

Fattal, Alexander L. *Shooting Cameras for Peace: Youth, Photography, and the Colombian Armed Conflict*. Cambridge, MA: Harvard University Press, forthcoming.

Fattal, Alexander L. "Uploading the News after Coming Down from the Mountain: The FARC's Uncanny Experiment with Online Television, in Cuba, 2012–2016." *International Journal of Communication* 11 (2017): 3832–56.

Fattal, Alex, and Juan Camilo Hoyos. *Hacia una reforma del DDR para la paz: Propuestas desde la academia y las experiencias actuales de desmovilización*. 2013. https://www.academia.edu/7090339/Hacia_una_reforma_del_DDR_para_la_paz_Propuestas_desde_la_academia_y_las_experiencias_actuales_de_desmovilizaci%C3%B3n.

Ferry, Elizabeth and Stephen Ferry. *La Batea: Impresiones del oro en Colombia / La Batea: Impressions of Gold in Colombia.* Bogotá: Icono, 2017.

Ferry, Stephen. *Violentology: A Manual of the Colombian Conflict.* Bogotá: Ícono, 2012.

Fineman, Mark, Robin Wrights, and Doyle McManus. "Preparing for War, Stumbling to Peace." *Los Angeles Times,* July 18, 2003. http://articles.latimes .com/2003/jul/18/nation/na-postwar18/6.

Fletcher, Robert. "'The Only Risk Is Wanting to Stay': Mediating Risk in Colombian Tourism Development." *RASAALA: Recreation and Society in Africa, Asia, and Latin America* 1, no. 2 (2011).

Forbes, Bruce David. *Christmas: A Candid History.* Berkeley: University of California Press, 2007.

Foster, Robert J. *Coca-Globalization: Following Soft Drinks from New York to New Guinea.* London: Palgrave Macmillan, 2008.

Foster, Robert. "Things to Do with Brands." *HAU: Journal of Ethnographic Theory* 3, no. 1 (2013): 44–63.

Foster, Robert J. "The Work of the New Economy: Consumers, Brands, and Value Creation." *Cultural Anthropology* 22, no. 4 (2007): 707–31.

Fulbright, William J. *The Pentagon Propaganda Machine.* New York: Liveright, 1970.

Fundación Ideas para la Paz. *Retorno a la legalidad o reincidencia de excombatientes en Colombia: Dimensión del fenómeno y factores de riesgo.* N.p.: Informes FIP, 2014.

García Márquez, Gabriel. *News of a Kidnapping.* Translated by Edith Grossman. New York: Alfred A. Knopf, 1997.

García Márquez, Gabriel. *Noticias de un secuestro.* New York: Penguin, 1995.

Genosko, Gary. *Baudrillard and Signs: Signification Ablaze.* London: Routledge, 1994.

Gentry, John A., and David B. Spencer. "Colombia's FARC: A Portrait of Insurgent Intelligence." *Intelligence and National Security* 25, no. 4 (2010): 453–78.

Gershon, Ilana. "'I Am Not a Businessman, I'm a Business, Man': Typing the neoliberal self into a branded existence." *HAU: Journal of Ethnographic Theory* 6, no. 3 (2016): 223–46.

Gill, Lesley. *A Century of Violence in a Red City: Popular Struggle, Counterinsurgency, and Human Rights in Colombia.* Durham, NC: Duke University Press, 2016.

Gill, Lesley. *The School of the Americas: Military Training and Political Violence in the Americas.* Durham, NC: Duke University Press, 2004.

Gluckman, Max. "Les rites de passage." In *Essays on the Ritual of Social Relations.* Manchester: Manchester University Press, 1962.

Gordillo, Claudio, and Bruno Federico, dirs. *Apuntando al corazón.* Film, 53 minutes. Bogotá: La Danza Inmóvil, 2013. Posted April 4, 2014. https://www .youtube.com/watch?v=LbuXjhEDUYY.

Gow, David, and Joanne Rappaport. "The Indigenous Public Voice: The Multiple Idioms of Modernity in Native Cauca." In *Indigenous Movements, Self-Representation, and the State in Latin America*, edited by Kay B. Warren and Jean E. Jackson. Austin: University of Texas Press, 2002.

Graan, Andrew. "Counterfeiting the Nation? Skopje 2014 and the Politics of Nation Branding in Macedonia." *Cultural Anthropology* 28, no. 1 (2013): 161–79.

Grandin, Greg. *Empire's Workshop: Latin America, the United States, and the Rise of the New Imperialism*. New York: Metropolitan Books, 2006.

Gregory, Derek. "'The Rush to the Intimate': Counterinsurgency and the Cultural Turn." *Radical Philosophy* 150 (2008): 8–23.

Guevara, Ernesto "Che." *Socialism and Man in Cuba*. [Translated by Margarita Zimmerman.] Atlanta: Pathfinder, 1989.

Guignon, Charles, ed. *The Good Life: Readings in Philosophy*. Indianapolis: Hackett, 1999.

Gusterson, Hugh. *Drone: Remote Control Warfare*. Cambridge, MA: MIT Press, 2016.

Gutiérrez Sanín, Francisco. "Colombia: The Re-structuring of Violence." In *Economic Liberalization and Political Violence: Utopia or Dystopia?*, edited by Francisco Gutiérrez Sanín and Gerd Schönwälder. London: Pluto, 2010.

Han, Clara. *Life in Debt: Times of Care and Violence in Neoliberal Chile*. Berkeley: University of California Press, 2012.

Han, Clara. "The Work of Indebtedness: The Traumatic Present of Late Capitalist Chile." *Culture, Medicine and Psychiatry* 28, no. 2 (2004): 169–87.

Helmus, Todd C., Christopher Paul, and Russell W. Glenn. *Enlisting Madison Avenue: The Marketing Approach to Earning Popular Support in Theaters of Operation*. Santa Monica, CA: RAND Corporation, 2007.

Herran, María Teresa. *La industria de los medios masivos de comunicación en Colombia*. Bogotá: FESCOL, 1991.

Hewitt, Virginia. *Beauty and the Banknote: Images of Women on Paper Money*. London: British Museum Press, 1994.

Himpe, Tom. *Advertising Is Dead: Long Live Advertising!* London: Thames & Hudson, 2006.

Hoffman, Danny. "Violent Events as Narrative Blocs: The Disarmament at Bo, Sierra Leone." *Anthropological Quarterly* 78, no. 2 (2005): 328–53.

Hoyos García, Juan Felipe. "Capitales para la guerra y el testimonio en un contexto transicional: Etnografía de la producción narrativa de desmovilizados." Master's thesis, Universidad Nacional de Colombia, 2011.

Human Rights Watch. *Colombia: Top Brass Linked to Extrajudicial Executions: Generals, Colonels Implicated in "False Positive" Killing*. 2015. https://www.hrw.org/news/2015/06/24/colombia-top-brass-linked-extrajudicial-executions.

Human Rights Watch. *Smoke and Mirrors: Colombia's Demobilization of Paramilitary Groups*. New York: Human Rights Watch, 2005.

Human Rights Watch. *The Ties That Bind: Colombia and Military-Paramilitary Links.* 2000. http://www.hrw.org/reports/2000/colombia/.

Humphreys, Macartan, and Jeremy M. Weinstein. "Demobilization and Reintegration." *Journal of Conflict Resolution* 51, no. 4 (2007): 531–67.

Huntington, Samuel P. *The Third Wave: Democratization in the Late Twentieth Century.* Norman: University of Oklahoma Press, 1991.

Idler, Annete. "Espacios invisibilizados: Actores violentos–no estatales en las zonas fronterizas de Colombia." In *Las agendas de lo indígena en la larga era de globalización,* edited by Römy Kohler and Anna Ebert. Berlin: Gebr. Mann Verlag, 2015.

Iguarán, Agustín. "En el Caribe, 40 guerrilleros de FARC y ELN se entregaron." *El Heraldo* (Barranquilla), July 10, 2012. http://www.elheraldo.co/region/en-el-caribe-40-guerrilleros-de-farc-y-eln-se-entregaron-74226.

Immerwahr, Daniel. *Thinking Small: The United States and the Lure of Community Development.* Cambridge, MA: Harvard University Press, 2015.

Interbrand. "2016 Ranking, Coca-Cola." Accessed May 6, 2017. http://interbrand.com/best-brands/best-global-brands/2016/ranking/cocacola/.

Jacobs, Andrew, and Matt Richtel. "She Took On Colombia's Soda Industry. Then She Was Silenced." *New York Times,* November 13, 2017.

Jansson, Oscar. "The Cursed Leaf: An Anthropology of the Political Economy of Cocaine Production in Southern Colombia." PhD diss., Uppsala Universitet, 2008.

Jauregui, Beatrice. "Bluing Green in the Maldives: Countering Citizen Insurgency by 'Civil'-izing National Security." In *Anthropology and Global Counterinsurgency.* Chicago: University of Chicago Press, 2010.

Jimeno, Ramón. *Noche de lobos.* Bogotá: Editorial Presencia, 1989.

Judt, Tony. *Postwar: A History of Europe since 1945.* New York: Penguin Books, 2005.

Jünger, Ernst. *Der Kampf als inneres Erlebnis.* Berlin: E. S. Mittler & Sohn, 1922.

Jünger, Ernst. "Total Mobilization." In *The Heidegger Controversy: A Critical Reader,* edited by Richard Wolin. Cambridge, MA: MIT Press, 1983.

Jusionyte, Ieva. *Savage Frontier: Making News and Security on the Argentine Border.* Berkeley: University of California Press, 2015.

Kaldor, Mary. *New and Old Wars: Organized Violence in a Global Era.* 3rd ed. Stanford, CA: Stanford University Press, 2012.

Kaneva, Nadia. *Branding Post-communist Nations: Marketizing National Identities in the "New" Europe.* New York: Routledge, 2014.

Kaplan, Oliver, and Enzo Nussio. "Community Counts: The Social Reintegration of Ex-combatants in Colombia." *Conflict Management and Peace Science,* 2015.

Kaplan, Oliver, and Enzo Nussio. "Explaining Recidivism of Ex-combatants in Colombia." *Journal of Conflict Resolution,* May 2016.

Karl, Robert A. *The Forgotten Peace: Reform, Violence, and the Making of Contemporary Colombia*. Berkeley: University of California Press, 2017.

Karl, Robert A. "State Formation, Violence, and Cold War in Colombia, 1957–1966." PhD diss., Harvard University, 2009.

Kenez, Peter. *The Birth of the Propaganda State: Soviet Methods of Mass Mobilization, 1917–1929*. Cambridge: Cambridge University Press, 1985.

KienyKe. "El Sastre de las FARC entra a las pasarelas." May 20, 2012. http://www.kienyke.com/historias/el-sastre-de-las-farc-entra-a-las-pasarelas/.

Klein, Naomi. *No Logo*. New York: Picador, 2000.

Klein, Naomi. *The Shock Doctrine: The Rise of Disaster Capitalism*. New York: Metropolitan Books, 2007.

Kuntsman, Adi, and Rebecca L. Stein. *Digital Militarism: Israel's Occupation in the Social Media Age*. Stanford, CA: Stanford University Press, 2015.

Langlois, Roméo, dir. *Caught in the Crossfire*. Film, 28 minutes. Paris: France 24, released June 21, 2012. https://www.youtube.com/watch?v=5iZfvDfhHg4.

Lepore, Jill. "The Prism: Privacy in an Age of Publicity." *New Yorker*, June 24, 2013.

Lobo-Guerrero, Catalina. "Bailando cumbia con las FARC." *La Silla Vacía*, September 25, 2016. http://lasillavacia.com/historia/bailando-cumbia-con-las-farc-58080.

López, Sigifredo. *Sigifredo: El triunfo de la esperanza*. Bogotá: Planeta, 2011.

López de la Roche, Fabio. *Las ficciones del poder: Patriotismo, medios de comunicación y reorientación afectiva de los colombianos bajo Uribe Velez*. Bogotá: Universidad Nacional de Colombia, IEPRI, 2014.

Lowe/SSP3. "Lowe-mazda." YouTube, May 19, 2010. https://www.youtube.com/watch?v=kiT-wzngrNE.

Mahmud, Lilith. *The Brotherhood of Freemason Sisters: Gender, Secrecy, and Fraternity in Italian Masonic Lodges*. Chicago: University of Chicago Press, 2014.

Mally, Lynn. "Shock Workers on the Cultural Front: Agitprop Brigades in the First Five-Year Plan." *Russian History / Histoire Russe* 23, no. 1 (1996): 263–75.

Marcuse, Herbert. *One-Dimensional Man: Studies in the Ideology of Advanced Industrial Society*. Boston: Beacon, 1991.

Marwick, Alice. *Status Update: Celebrity, Publicity, and Branding in the Social Media Age*. New Haven, CT: Yale University Press, 2013.

Masco, Joseph. "Counterinsurgency, the Spook, and Blowback." In *Anthropology and Global Counterinsurgency*, edited by John D. Kelly, Beatrice Jauregui, Sean T. Mitchell, and Jeremy Walton. Chicago: University of Chicago Press, 2010.

Masco, Joseph. *The Theater of Operations: National Security Affect from the Cold War to the War on Terror*. Durham, NC: Duke University Press, 2014.

Maslow, Abraham H. "A Theory of Human Motivation." *Psychological Review* 50, no. 4 (1943): 370–96.

Mauss, Marcel. *The Gift: Forms and Functions of Exchange in Archaic Societies.* New York: W. W. Norton, 1967.

Maya, Maureén, and Gustavo Petro. *Prohibido olvidar: Dos miradas sobre la toma del Palacio de Justicia.* Bogotá: Editorial Pisando Calles, 2006.

Mazzarella, William. "Branding the Mahatma: The Untimely Provocation of Gandhian Publicity." *Cultural Anthropology* 25, no. 1 (2010): 1–39.

Mazzarella, William. *The Mana of Mass Society.* Chicago: University of Chicago Press, 2017.

Mazzarella, William, "Sense Out of Sense: Notes on the Affect/Ethics Impasse." *Cultural Anthropology* 32, no. 2 (2017): 199–208.

Mazzarella, William. *Shoveling Smoke: Advertising and Globalization in Contemporary India.* Durham, NC: Duke University Press, 2003.

McCandless, Brit. "Advertising to Sell Peace, Not Products." *60 Minutes*, December 11, 2016. http://www.cbsnews.com/news/60-minutes-colombia-advertising -to-sell-peace-not-products/.

McDonough, Tom. *"The Beautiful Language of My Century": Reinventing the Language of Contestation in Postwar France, 1945–1968.* Cambridge, MA: MIT Press, 2007.

McFate, Montgomery. "The Military Utility of Understanding Adversary Culture." *Joint Forces Quarterly* 38 (2005): 42–48.

Medina Arbeláez, Camila. *No porque seas paraco o seas guerrillero tienes que ser un animal: Procesos de socialización en FARC-EP, ELN y grupos paramilitares (1996–2006).* Bogotá: Universidad de Los Andes, Facultad de Ciencias Sociales, Departamento de Ciencias Políticas, 2009.

Medina Gallego, Carlos. *FARC-EP, flujos y reflujos: La guerra en las regiones.* Bogotá: Universidad Nacional de Colombia, 2011.

Meléndez, José. "Corte IDH condena a Colombia por el caso del Palacio de Justicia." *El Tiempo*, December 10, 2014. http://www.eltiempo.com/archivo/ documento/CMS-14955458.

Melley, Timothy. *The Covert Sphere: Secrecy, Fiction, and the National Security State.* Ithaca, NY: Cornell University Press, 2012.

Ministerio de Defensa Nacional. *Política de consolidación de la seguridad democrática.* Bogotá: Ministerio de Defensa Nacional, 2007.

Mitchell, W. J. T. *Cloning Terror: The War of Images, 9/11 to the Present.* Chicago: University of Chicago Press, 2011.

Molano, Alfredo. *Ahí les dejo esos fierros.* Buenos Aires: Aguilar, 2009.

Muggah, Robert, ed. *Security and Post-conflict Reconstruction: Dealing with Fighters in the Aftermath of War.* London: Routledge, 2009.

Muggah, Robert, and Chris O'Donnell. "Next Generation Disarmament, Demobilization and Reintegration." *Stability: International Journal of Security & Development* 4 (2015).

Nakassis, Constantine V. "Brands and Their Surfeits." *Cultural Anthropology* 28, no. 1 (2016): 111–26.

Nussio, Enzo, ed. "Desarme, desmovilización y reintegración de excombatientes: Políticas y actores del postconflicto." *Colombia Internacional* 77 (2013).

Nussio, Enzo. *La vida después de la desmovilización: Percepciones, emociones y estrategias de exparamilitares en Colombia.* Bogotá: Ediciones Uniandes, 2012.

O'Neill, Kevin Lewis. "Narcotecture." *Society and Space* 34, no. 4 (2016): 672–88.

Oppenheim, Ben, Abbey Steele, Juan F. Vargas, and Michael Weintraub. "True Believers, Deserters, and Traitors: Who Leaves Insurgent Groups and Why." *Journal of Conflict Resolution* 59, no. 5 (2015): 794–823.

Orozco, Iván. "La postguerra colombiana: Divagaciones sobre la venganza, la justicia y la reconciliación." Kellogg Institute, Working Paper 36, May 2003.

Paley, Julia. *Marketing Democracy: Power and Social Movements in Post-dictatorship Chile.* Berkeley: University of California Press, 2001.

Pandolfi, Mariella. "Humanitarianism and Its Discontents." In *Forces of Compassion: Humanitarianism between Ethics and Politics*, edited by Peter Redfield and Erica Bornstein. Santa Fe, NM: School for Advanced Research, 2011.

Pardo Pedraza, Diana. "When Landmines Do Not Explode: Peasant Life in the Colombian War." PhD diss., University of California, Davis, in process.

Peralta G., Andrés, ed. *La vida no da tregua: Memorias de desmovilizados.* Bogotá: Secretaría de Gobierno Distrital, Alcaldía Mayor de Bogotá DC, 2011.

Pérez, Federico. "Urbanism as Warfare: Planning, Property, and Displacement in Bogotá." PhD diss., Harvard University, 2014.

Pizarro Leongómez, Eduardo. *Las Farc (1949–2011): De guerrilla campesina a máquina de guerra.* Bogotá: Grupo Editorial Norma, 2011.

Porch, Douglas, and Jorge Delgado. "'Masters of Today': Military Intelligence and Counterinsurgency in Colombia, 1990–2009." *Small Wars and Insurgencies* 21, no. 2 (2010): 277–302.

Presidencia de la República de Colombia and Ministerio de Defensa Nacional. *Política de defensa y seguridad democrática.* Bogotá: Ministerio de Defensa, 2003.

Price, David H. *Weaponizing Anthropology: Social Science in Service of the Militarized State.* Petrolia, CA: CounterPunch, 2011.

Priest, Dana. "Covert Action in Colombia: U.S. Intelligence, GPS Bomb Kits Help Latin American Nation Cripple Rebel Forces." *Washington Post*, December 21, 2013.

Prieto Sanabria, Juan Diego. *Guerras, paces y vidas entrelazadas: Coexistencia y relaciones locales entre víctimas, excombatientes y comunidades en Colombia.* Bogotá: Universidad de los Andes, 2012.

Procuraduría General de la Nación. *Seguimiento a Políticas Públicas en Materia de Desmovilización y Reinserción: Tomo 2.* Bogotá: Procuraduría General de la Nación, 2006.

Ramírez, Juliana. "El No ha sido la campaña más barata y más efectiva de la historia." *La República*, October 5, 2016. http://www.larepublica.co/el-no-ha-sido-la-campa%C3%B1a-m%C3%A1s-barata-y-m%C3%A1s-efectiva-de-la-historia_427891.

Ramírez, María Clemencia. *Between the Guerrillas and the State: The Cocalero Movement, Citizenship, and Identity in the Colombian Amazon.* Durham, NC: Duke University Press, 2011.

Rappaport, Joanne. *Intercultural Utopias: Public Intellectuals, Cultural Experimentation, and Ethnic Pluralism in Colombia.* Durham, NC: Duke University Press, 2005.

Reichman, Daniel R. *The Broken Village: Coffee, Migration, and Globalization in Honduras.* Ithaca, NY: ILR Press, 2011.

Ricks, Thomas E. "The Lesson of Colombia's Demobilization of FARC Can Help Us Work against ISIS." *Foreign Policy*, January 28, 2016. http://foreignpolicy.com/2016/01/28/the-lesson-of-colombias-demobilization-of-farc-can-help-us-work-against-isis/.

Roberts, Kevin. *Lovemarks: The Future beyond Brands.* New York: PowerHouse Books, 2004.

Roitman, Janet. "The Ethics of Illegality in the Chad Basin." In *Law and Disorder in the Postcolony*, edited by Jean Comaroff and John L. Comaroff. Chicago: University of Chicago Press, 2006.

Romero, Mauricio, ed. *Parapolítica: La ruta de la expansión paramilitar y los acuerdos políticos.* Bogotá: Corporación Nuevo Arco Iris, 2007.

Romero Ospina, Roberto. *Unión Patriótica: Expedientes contra el olvido.* Bogotá: Alcaldía Mayor de Bogotá DC, 2012.

Ronderos, María Teresa. *Guerras recicladas: Una historia periodística del paramilitarismo en Colombia.* Bogotá: Aguilar, 2015.

Ross, Scott. "Encouraging Rebel Demobilization by Radio in Uganda and D.R. Congo: The Case of 'Come Home' Messaging." *African Studies Review* 59, no. 1 (2016): 33–55.

Ruiz Novoa, Alberto. *Enseñanzas de la campaña de Corea: Aplicables al Ejército de Colombia.* Bogotá: Antares, 1956.

Sánchez, Gonzalo. "Raíces históricas de la amnistía, o las etapas de la guerra en

Colombia." In *Ensayos de historia social y política del siglo XX*. Bogotá: El Áncora Editores, 1984.

Santos, Bonaventura de Sousa, and Mauricio García Villegas, eds. *El caleidoscopio de las justicias en Colombia: Análisis socio-jurídico*. 2 vols. Bogotá: Siglo del Hombre Editores, 2001.

Sawchuck, Kim. "Semiotics, Cybernetics, and the Ecstasy of Marketing." In *Baudrillard: A Critical Reader*, edited by Douglas Kellner. Oxford: Blackwell, 1994.

Schuster, Caroline E. *Social Collateral: Women and Microfinance in Paraguay's Smuggling Economy*. Berkeley: University of California Press, 2015.

Seipp, Adam R. *The Ordeal of Peace: Demobilization and the Urban Experience in Britain and Germany, 1917–1921*. Farnham, UK: Ashgate, 2009.

Semana. "La ruta de la espada." December 29, 1997. http://www.semana.com/imprimir/34708.

Serazio, Michael. *Your Ad Here: The Cool Sell of Guerrilla Marketing*. New York: NYU Press, 2013.

Spencer, Denise. *Demobilization and Reintegration in Central America*. Bonn, Germany: BICC, 1997. http://reliefweb.int/sites/reliefweb.int/files/resources/D4EA83D23A60E77EC12574410047F9AF-bicc_sep1997.pdf.

Spivak, Gayatri Chakravorty. "Cultural Talks in the Hot Peace: Revisiting the 'global village." In *Cosmopolitics: Thinking and Feeling beyond the Nation*, edited by Pheng Cheah and Bruce Robbins, 329–48. Minneapolis: University of Minnesota Press, 1998).

Stahl, Roger. *Militainment, Inc.: War, Media, and Popular Culture*. New York: Routledge, 2010.

Steele, Abbey. *Democracy and Displacement in Colombia's Civil War*. Ithaca, NY: Cornell University Press.

Steyerl, Hito. "Proxy Politics: Signal and Noise." *e-flux Journal* 60 (2014): 12.

Stole, Inger L. *Advertising at War: Business, Consumers, and Government in the 1940s*. Urbana: University of Illinois Press, 2012.

Stone, Nomi. "Living the Laughscream: Human Technology and Affective Maneuvers in the Iraq War." *Cultural Anthropology* 32, no. 1 (2017): 149–74.

Stricker, Gabriel. *Mao in the Boardroom: Marketing Genius from the Mind of the Master Guerilla*. New York: St. Martin's Griffin, 2003.

Sullivan, Christopher M. "The (In)effectiveness of Torture for Combating Insurgency." *Journal of Peace Research* 51, no. 3 (2014): 388–404.

Superintendencia Financiera de Colombia. *Informe sobre sector financiero: Tarjetas de crédito en Colombia*. 2015. https://www.superfinanciera.gov.co/jsp/loader.jsf?lServicio=Publicaciones&lTipo=publicaciones&lFuncion=loadContenidoPublicacion&id=60952.

Tate, Winifred. *Counting the Dead: The Culture and Politics of Human Rights Activism in Colombia*. Berkeley: University of California Press, 2007.

Tate, Winifred. *Drugs, Thugs, and Diplomats: U.S. Policymaking in Colombia.* Stanford, CA: Stanford University Press, 2015.

Tate, Winifred. "From Greed to Grievance: The Shifting Political Profile of the Colombian Paramilitaries." In *Colombia: Building Peace in a Time of War*, edited by Virginia Bouvier. Washington, DC: United States Institute of Peace Press, 2009.

Taussig, Michael T. *Beauty and the Beast.* Chicago: University of Chicago Press, 2012.

Taussig, Michael. *Law in a Lawless Land: Diary of a Limpieza in Colombia.* Chicago: University of Chicago Press, 2003.

Theidon, Kimberly. *Intimate Enemies: Violence and Reconciliation in Peru.* Philadelphia: University of Pennsylvania Press, 2012.

Theidon, Kimberly. "Reconstructing Masculinities: The Disarmament, Demobilization, and Reintegration of Former Combatants in Colombia." *Human Rights Quarterly* 31, no. 1 (2009): 1–34.

Theidon, Kimberly. "Transitional Subjects: The Disarmament, Demobilization and Reintegration of Former Combatants in Colombia." *International Journal of Transitional Justice* 1, no. 1 (2007): 66–90. doi:10.1093/ijtj/ijm011.

Thomas, Kedron. *Regulating Style: Intellectual Property Law and the Business of Fashion in Guatemala.* Berkeley: University of California Press, 2016.

Thorsell, Stefan. "¿Hacia una reintegración económica centrada en las personas? Análisis de la estrategia de reintegración económica de combatientes desmovilizados en Colombia." *Colombia Internacional*, no. 77 (2013), 177–215.

Tilly, Charles. *The Formation of National States in Western Europe.* Princeton, NJ: Princeton University Press, 1975.

Trejos, Luis Fernando. "Uso de la internet por parte de las FARC-EP: Nuevo escenario de confrontación o último espacio de difusión política." *Revista Encrucijada Americana* 5, no. 1 (2012): 25–50.

Trejos, Luis Fernando. "Las FARC-EP en Europa y Centroamérica. Una mirada desde la categoría de actor no estatal." *Ópera* 13 (2013): 109–21.

Troyan, Brett. *Cauca's Indigenous Movement in Southwestern Colombia: Land, Violence, and Ethnic Identity.* Lanham, MD: Lexington, 2015.

Tucker, Patrick. "How US Special Forces Helped Take Down Joseph Kony's Army with Tailored Messages." *Defense One*, October 17, 2017. http://www.defenseone.com/technology/2017/10/how-4-green-berets-took-down-joseph-konys-army-tailored-messages/141851/

Turner, Victor. "Betwixt and Between: The Liminal Period in *Rites of Passage*." In *Reader in Comparative Religion: An Anthropological Approach*, 4th ed., edited by William A. Lessa and Evon Z. Vogt. New York: Harper and Row, 1979.

Turow, Joseph. *The Daily You: How the New Advertising Industry Is Defining Your Identity and Your Worth.* New Haven, CT: Yale University Press, 2013.

Twitchell, James B. *Branded Nation: The Marketing of Megachurch, College, Inc., and Museumworld.* New York: Simon & Schuster, 2004.

UN Human Rights Council. *Statement by Professor Philip Alston, UN Special Rapporteur on Extrajudicial Killings—Mission to Colombia.* 2009. http://www.unhchr.ch/huricane/huricane.nsf/0/C6390E2F247BF1A7C12575D900 7732FD?opendocument.

United Nations. "Integrated Disarmament, Demobilization and Reintegration Standards: Operational Guide to the Integrated Disarmament, Demobilization and Reintegration Standards." 2006. http://unddr.org/iddrs-framework .aspx.

Universidad Nacional de Colombia. "Caracterización comunidad FARC-EP: Resultados generales." Censo Socioeconómico UN-CNR 2017, July 6, 2017. http://www.reintegracion.gov.co/es/sala-de-prensa/SiteAssets/Presentaci %C3%B3n%20rueda%20de%20prensa%20Julio%206%202017.pdf.

Uribe, María V. "Dismembering and Expelling: Semantics of Political Terror in Colombia." *Public Culture* 16, no. 1 (2004): 79–96.

Valencia Tovar, Álvaro, and Jairo Sandoval Franky. *Colombia en la Guerra de Corea: La historia secreta.* Bogotá: Planeta, 2001.

Van Gennep, Arnold. *The Rites of Passage.* Chicago: University of Chicago Press, 1960.

Verdad Abierta. "Muerte a Secuestradores MAS: Los orígenes del paramilitarismo." September 20, 2011. http://www.verdadabierta.com/component/ content/article/11-periodo-1/3556-muerte-a-secuestradores-mas-los-origenes -del-paramilitarismo-.

Vidart-Delgado, María L. "Cyborg Political Machines: Political Brokering and Modern Political Campaigning in Colombia." *HAU: Journal of Ethnographic Theory* 7, no. 2 (2017): 255–77.

Vidart-Delgado, María Lucia. "The Pragmatics of Hope: Class, Elections, and Political Management in Contemporary Colombia." PhD diss., Rice University, 2013. Proquest 3577588.

Villa, Santiago. "El peligro de cobrar recompensas." *El Espectador,* February 11, 2011. http://www.elespectador.com/opinion/columna-404247-el -peligro-de-cobrar-recompensas.

Villamizar Herrera, Darío. *Aquel 19 será.* Bogotá: Planeta, 1995.

Villamizar Herrera, Darío. *Las guerrillas en Colombia: Una historia desde los orígenes hasta los confines.* Bogotá: Random House, 2017.

Villamizar Herrera, Darío. *Jaime Bateman: Biografía de un revolucionario.* Bogotá: Planeta, 2002.

Villamizar Herrera, Darío, ed. *Jaime Bateman: Profeta de la paz.* Bogotá: Corporación Compañía Nacional para la Paz, 1995.

Virilio, Paul. *Desert Screen: War at the Speed of Light.* New York: Continuum, 2005.

Wedeen, Lisa. *Ambiguities of Domination: Politics, Rhetoric, and Symbols in Contemporary Syria*. Chicago: University of Chicago Press, 1999.

Williams, Raymond. "Film in the Dramatic Tradition." In *The Raymond Williams Reader*, edited by John Higgins. Oxford: Blackwell, 2001.

Wolin, Richard. "Introduction: Ernst Jünger." In *The Heidegger Controversy: A Critical Reader*, edited by Richard Wolin. Cambridge, MA: MIT Press, 1983.

Wolin, Richard. *Walter Benjamin: An Aesthetics of Redemption*. Berkeley: University of California Press, 1994.

World Organisation Against Torture. *State Violence in Colombia: An Alternative Report to the United Nations Committee against Torture*. Geneva: World Organisation Against Torture, 2004. http://www.omct.org/files/2004/06/2421/stateviolence_colombia_04_eng.pdf.

Wyss, Jim. "He Murdered 300. Now Popeye the Assassin Is a Colombian Media Star." *Miami Herald*, November 11, 2016. http://www.miamiherald.com/news/nation-world/world/americas/colombia/article114199558.html.

Zeiderman, Austin. *Endangered City: The Politics of Security and Risk in Bogotá*. Durham, NC: Duke University Press, 2016.

Zimbalist, Jeff, and Michael Zimbalist, dirs. *The Two Escobars*. Film, 100 minutes. All Rise Films, 2010.

Zyck, Steven A. "Former Combatant Reintegration and Fragmentation in Contemporary Afghanistan." *Conflict, Security & Development* 9, no. 1 (2009): 111–31.

Index

Page numbers in *italics* indicate figures.

ACR. *See* Colombian Agency for Reintegration (ACR)

Adorno, Theodor, 149

affect, as form of infrastructure, 14

affective total mobilization, 12

Afghanistan, 205–6, 209

agitprop, 42–43

Alternativa (magazine), 47–48, *48*

ANNCOL (New Colombian News Agency), 20

antiguerrilla warfare. *See* counterinsurgency strategy

apertura (economic "opening"), 2. *See also* neoliberalism

Arenas, Jacobo, 5, 44, 89

"armed neoliberalism," 10

AUC (United Self-Defense Forces of Colombia), 6–7, 97

Bateman, Jaime, 43–45, 48, 49, 50

Baudrillard, Jean, 216

Benjamin, Walter, 188

Berlant, Lauren, 166

Bernays, Edward, 188

Betancourt, Íngrid, 63, 67, 101, 153

Betancur, Belisario, 51

black propaganda, 257n29

blindar, 109

blowback, 151

Bolívar, Simon, sword of, 44, 46–48, *48*

borders: Ecuador-Colombia, 89, 92; in Latin America, 268n13; Venezuela-Colombia, 96, 131, 145

boundary between peace and war, 14–15, 220–21, 240, 245

branding: as camouflage, 15–16; demobilization program and, 82–83; Escobar and, 53–54; of FARC, 20–22, 229, 245; governance and, 108–9, 127, 215–21; lovemarks and, 237; of Lowe/SSP3, 86; of military, 85, 88, 108, 154; of PAHD, 108; performativity and, 216; postconflict state and, 109, 210, 215–21; reforms and, 2; tourism campaigns and, 109. *See also* brand value; brand warfare

brand value, 16–17, 149

brand warfare: after peace accord of 2016, 220–21; definition of, 79–80; FARC and, 229, 245; history of, 67–68; intimate mode of, 237–38; by military, 208; overview, 11–22; of PAHD, 245

Bush, George H. W., 12

Bush, George W., 14, 205

Caguán peace talks (1999–2002), 2, 8–9, *9*, 61, 63

Cali cartel, 6

Cano, Alfonso, 88–89

Cano, Guillermo, 59

capitalism: as cure for terrorism, 179; ethical, 186–87; late, xi, 13, 234; marketing and, 17, 216; savage, 172; war and, 15–16. *See also* economic reintegration

capture compared to demobilization of rebels, 143

Caribbean Bloc of FARC. *See* Martín Caballero Bloc of FARC

Caro, Antonio, 22, *22*

Cartagena Contribution to Disarmament, Demobilization and Reintegration, 209

Catatumbo: AUC in, 97, 261n3; flight to, 95; impact of event in, 100–101; overview of, 92; staging of event in, 95–96, 98–100, *98*; Tibú–La Gabarra corridor of, 96–97

Cauca Department, 92

Center for National Memory, 3

Central Intelligence Agency (CIA), 6, 153, 271n10

Cesar Department, 134, 137

Chamayou, Grégoire, 15

Chance brand, 180–83, *182*, 186, 189

Chávez, Hugo, 9, 143–44

Chile, advertising strategies in, 281n32

Christmas: corporatization of, 267n4; in insurgency, 134–35

Christmas campaigns: awards won by, 88, 90; design of, 105–6; Operation Christmas, 83, 84–88; Sokoloff on, 82; as stagecraft-cum-statecraft, 107–8; success of, 102; "Your family is still waiting for you," *94*. *See also* Operation Rivers of Light; "You Are My Child" campaign

CIA (Central Intelligence Agency), 6, 153, 271n10

"cleansing" (*limpieza*), 170, 176

CNN, 13

Coca-Cola Femsa, 168–69

cocaine, 4–5, 55

Cold War, 14, 206

collectivist economy, as vision of FARC, 238

Colombian Agency for Reintegration (ACR): ARN (Agency for Reincorporation and Normalization), 238; leadership of, 276n24; mission statement and objective of, 167; model of, 179, 195, 196–97; role of, 23, 79; South-South Tour of, 210–15, *213*, *214*, *215*; success stories of, 189–94

Colombian armed conflicts: in Catatumbo region, 97–98; main actors in, 3–7; material foundation of, 140; mediatization of, 41, 67–68; as recombinatory

system, 7–8; urbanization of, 186; US and, 205–6

Colombian nation-state, branding of, 22–23, *22*

Colombian Peace Accord of 2016, plebiscite, xii, 238–40. *See also* peace agreement of 2016 with FARC

Come Back and Play campaign, 90–91

commanders, midlevel, targeting of, 126, 127, 132, 134, 135–37, 145–48

commodity fetishism, 188–89

Communal Action Board, 192

Communal Social Economies (ECOMUN), 234–35, 238

Communist Party, 4, 61

Communist Youth League (JUCO), 42–43, 44

community organizations, 28, 177, 178

Constitutional Assembly of 1991, 57–58

consumerism: citizenship and, 17; counterinsurgency and, 181–83, 185, 187–88; ethical fashion and, 186–87; terrorism and, 183; war drama and, *184*, 185

Cooperating for Good Living, 177, 178

Corinto Accords with M19, 50–51

corporatization of Christmas, 267n4

counterinsurgency strategy: consumerism as, 181–83, 185, 187–88; demobilization as, 8, 151–54, 234; intimacy as, 236–38; marketing and, xii, 221, 241–42; network approach in, 207; press favorable to, 153; value of former rebels in, 19; as "winning hearts and minds," 84. *See also* humanitarian counterinsurgency

crimes against humanity, 146, 148

criminal gangs (*bacrim*), 7

Cuba: negotiations in (2012–2016), 30, 61, 144, 218, 233; US and, 219

Cuban Revolution, 4

cultural differences and implementation of demobilization model, 210–15

currency, as medium of propaganda, 104–5, *104*

Curtis, Adam, 188

Dávila, Arlene, 166

DDR. *See* disarmament, demobilization, and reintegration (DDR)

Dean, Jodi, 126

death threats, 177–78, 194

decision making, messages to influence, 80–81

demobilization: after death of Cano, 89; branding and, 82–83; as counterinsurgency strategy, 8, 151–54, 234; cultural differences and implementation of, 210–15; evolution of meaning of, 256n23; military pressure and, 83; of paramilitaries, 2–3, 24, 240; skepticism about, 97–98, 101; Sokoloff on, 81; transmission of message about, 87. *See also* disarmament, demobilization, and reintegration (DDR); individual demobilization

demobilized. *See* former rebels

democratic left in Colombia, 30, 31

Democratic Security policy, 10–11, *11*, 17. *See also* Program for Humanitarian Attention to the Demobilized (PAHD)

Denmark, Fighters and Lovers collective in, 21–22

Der Derian, James, 13

Derrida, Jacques, 219–20

"Deserter" (song), 84

desertion: conflation of demobilization and, 207; from FARC, xiii, 164–65, 191–92; FARC policy on, 237. *See also* demobilization; individual demobilization

de Soto, Hernando, 179

Diesel advertisement, 185–86, *185*

disarmament, demobilization, and reintegration (DDR): agencies dealing with, 23; as designed for failure, 197; quantitative studies of, 167–68; as ritual, 216–17; statistics on, 281n2; success of, 212; trajectory of, 138–39; UN perspective, 8

displaced, relationships between demobilized and, 174

displacement crisis, 24

dissident fronts, 282n7

Dreams from the Mountain (provisional title for documentary, installation, and transmedia project), 32

drone warfare, 15, 206, 207

drug trafficking, 4–5, 55, 97, 164

Duffield, Mark, 129

ECOMUN (Communal Social Economies), 234–35, 238

economic reintegration: Boris and Tanja on, 237–38; Chance brand, 180–83, *182*, 186, 189; as political, 179; project for, 212; resource management problems and, 171–74; through entrepreneurship, 163, 164, 167–68, 170–74, 179–80, 190–93, 196–97. *See also* Colombian Agency for Reintegration (ACR)

economic rewards for information, 25, 104, 139, 150

Ecuador-Colombia border, 89, 92

Eder, Alejandro, 212, 213

ELN. *See* National Liberation Army (ELN)

entrepreneurs, transformation of guerrillas into, 163, 164, 167–68, 170–74, 179–80, 190–93, 196–97

EPL (Popular Liberation Army), 4

Escobar, Pablo: bombings by, 57, 59; branding and, 53–54; hunt for and killing of, 58–59; kidnapping of journalists by, 55–57; media spectacle and, 52–53, 59; release of hostages by, 58; rise of, 53, 54–55; violence of, 54, 59

ethical capitalism, 186–87

ethics of research, 25–29

ethnography, embedded, structural challenge of, 128

Euskadi Ta Askatasuna (ETA), 91

ex-combatants. *See* former rebels

extortion charges, 163

Extraditables, 54, 56, 57, 59

FAC (Colombian air force), 269n22

Facebook: campaign against FARC on, 66; profiles of guerrillas on, 132, 148

fact and fiction, indistinction between, 14

Fals Borda, Orlando, 48

false positives scandal, 142

family: of deserters, 151; exploitation of, 149; in Operation Rivers of Light, 92, 93–94; reunions with, 235–36; *sacando adelante a la familia*, 196; targeting of, 132–33, 134; in video appeals, 146–47; as weak spot, 147

FARC. *See* Revolutionary Armed Forces of Colombia (FARC)

fashionista peace initiative, 181–83, *182*, 186

Fayad, Álvaro, 46

Feel Like a Woman Again campaign, *241*, 242–43, 245
fieldwork, 29–30
Fighters and Lovers, 21–22
First International Congress of Disarmament, Demobilization and Reintegration, 208–9
flood-relief kits, 96–97, 99
focus groups, 91
foreign direct investment, 22, 109, 207
former rebels: Chance brand and, 180, 181, 182, 186, 187–88, 189; Ciro, 180, 189–94; Claudia, 155–61; collaboration with military, 28, 126, 127, 139, 150; control of access to, 213; in counterinsurgency strategy, 19; as entrepreneurs, 163, 164, 167–68, 170–74, 179–80, 190–93, 196–97; expenditure on, 218; female, 242–44; good life for, 194–96; graduation ceremony for, 212, *213*; intelligence provided by, 126, 127, 150; liminal stage of, 216–17; obstacles faced by, 165–67, 168, 196–97, 238; Operation Rivers of Light and, 107; organizations launched by, 178; at press conference, 143; protection for, 28–29; relationships with, 27–29; reward money owed to, 139; *SoHo* and, 183, *184*, 185; targeting of, 255n21; trajectory for, 138–39; transactions between military and, 140; in urban settlements, 164; urban war and, 186. *See also* intelligence
Foster, Robert, 237
FUDRA, 85

Gálan, Luis Carlos, 264n37
García Márquez, Gabriel, 48, 54, 56–57, 58, 270n27
Gaviria, César, 56, 57, 59, 60
Gill, Lesley, 168–69
Global War on Terror, 14, 206
González Pacheco, Fernando, 50
good life: deferred, 166, 194–97; maintenance of, 165–66; narcoparamilitary vision of, 178; obstacles to, 167
governance and branding, 108–9, 127, 215–21
Granda, Rodrigo, 153, 219
Grandin, Greg, 205

guerrilla fighters, targeting of, 87, 90. *See also* Operation Genuine
guerrilla marketing, 15–16
guerrilla warfare: military-civilian ambivalence in, 186; US and, 205. *See also* Colombian armed conflicts
Guevara, Che, 3, 15, 149
Gulf War of 1991, 12–13
Gutiérrez Sanin, Francisco, 6

halfway houses for demobilized, 150–51
Harvey, David, 10
Hernández-Mora, Salud, 183
High Presidential Advisory for Social and Economic Reintegration, 170. *See also* Colombian Agency for Reintegration (ACR)
Himpe, Tom, 15
Horkheimer, Max, 149
Hoyos García, Juan Felipe, 93
human intelligence (HUMINT), 125–26
humanitarian aid, 95, 99–100
humanitarian counterinsurgency, 17–18, 108, 127, 148–54
Human Terrain Systems project, 26, 268–69n20

individual demobilization: in Afghanistan, 209; in Africa, 208; alleged FARC members and, 150; as charade, 240; of Ciro, 192; effect of peace process on, 144; as failed ritual, 217; family targeted in, 132–33, 134; as form of lipstick, 245; as front in war, 150–51; gender and, 241–45, *241*; Granda on, 153; intelligence emphasis of, 151–54; Jaramillo on, 18–19; legal gray zone of, 147–48; midlevel commanders targeted for, 126, 127, 132, 134, 135–37, 145–48; moral spiderweb of, 152, 154; PAHD and, 256n25; peace agreements and, 207; as performing postconflictness, 2; as prioritized, 141–42; reactions to, 195; return of prodigal son theme of, 93, *94*; staff for, 25; time period for and numbers of, xiii; in 2008, 101; video appeals for, 145–48. *See also* Colombian Agency for Reintegration (ACR); former rebels; Program for Humani-

tarian Attention to the Demobilized
(PAHD)
inequality in Colombia, 194
intelligence: economic rewards for, 25, 104,
139, 150; as focus of individual demobilization, 151–54, 169, 207. *See also* former rebels: collaboration with military;
Regional Military Intelligence unit
(RIME)
intelligence agents, 125–26
international audience, targeting of, 87–88,
90, 107–8
International Organization of Migration
(OIM/IOM), 211
Interpublic Group (IPG), 80
intimacy, transformation of, into battleground, 236–38
Invisible Children, 208
ISIS, 208

Jairo Velásquez, John "Popeye," 264n31
James (government agent), 142, 232–35,
238
Jaramillo, Sergio: and democratic security
doctrine, 17; on Directive 300-28, 142; as
high commissioner for peace, 233; James
and, 232; Lowe/SSP3 and, 82; Operation
Rivers of Light and, *103*; role of, 18–19
Jojoy, Mono, 18, 89
José (intelligence officer), 130, 141
journalists: borders in Latin America and,
268n13; David (former rebel) and, 236;
embedded, 128; kidnappings of, 55–57;
Operation Rivers of Light campaign
and, 100, 107–8; at tenth guerrilla conference, 229
Juan Carlos (anthropologist), 101, 240
Juan Pablo (account manager), 17–18, 82–
83, 95, 107–8
JUCO (Communist Youth League), 42–
43, 44
Julián (bloc leader), 146–47
Jünger, Ernst, "Total Mobilization," 11–12
Justice and Peace Law of 2005, 146, 148

Kaldor, Mary, 129
Kenez, Peter, 42
kidnappings: by Escobar, 55–57; by FARC,
62–67; by M19, 49, 50

Knight, Phil, 17
Kony, Joseph, 208

Langlois, Roméo, 27
Lara Bonilla, Rodrigo, 55
late capitalism, xi, 13, 234
La Violencia, 4
Lenin, Vladimir, 42
liberation theology, 3–4
light, transformation of rebel territory
with, 84–85, 86, 91. *See also* Operation
Rivers of Light
loan sharks (*la gota a gota*), 171
Logan, Lara, x
Londoño, Fernando, 130
López, Sigifredo, 64–65, 66
Lord's Resistance Army (LRA), 208
Los Pepes, 58
love: brand value and, 149; as target of war,
236–37. *See also* family
lovemarks, 237
Lowe and Partners, 80
Lowe/SSP3: account with Ministry of Defense, 82–83; as "attacking the heart,"
xi, 83–84; focus groups of, 91; headquarters of, 17, 79; as hybrid, 80;
merger to become MullenLowe SSP3,
253n2; as playing long game, 81–82; political message of, 91–92; research of,
82; role of, in plebiscite, xii; Yes campaign (plebiscite on peace accord) and,
239–40. *See also* Program for Humanitarian Attention to the Demobilized
(PAHD); Sokoloff, Miguel; *and specific
campaigns*

Machista-Leninista, 282–83n12
malls in Colombia, 166
Mancuso, Salvatore, 97
Mao Zedong, 15
Marcela (communications manager): Afghan program and, 209; career of, 108;
Operation Rivers of Light and, 88–89,
91–93, 96–100, 102–4, *103*, 107–8; relationship with, 27; role of, 24–25, 127
Marín, Sergio, 61, 221
marketing: belief in power of, xi; capitalism and, 17, 216; coevolution of warfare and, 14–15; consumer marketing,

marketing (*continued*)
20, 80, 83, 140, 221; counterinsurgency
and, xii, 221, 241–42; creation of surplus value and, 16, 186, 216, 236–37; as
meaning-making system, 17; as mes-
sage, 13–14; as producer of "structure
of feeling," 80; rise of global middle
class and, 15. *See also* branding; con-
sumerism; Lowe/SSP3
Márquez, Iván, 144, 233
Martín Caballero Bloc of FARC, 131, 143,
144
Marulanda, Manuel, 9, 89
Marx, Karl, 189
Marxism, 3–4, 219–20
MAS (Death to Kidnappers), 265n38
Masco, Joseph, 14, 151
Maslow, Abraham, on "hierarchy of
needs," 83
mass distraction, tactics of, 17, 52
Mauss, Marcel, 99
Mazda advertisement, 80–81
Mazzarella, William, 267n7
McCann-Erickson, 10
Medellín cartel, 54. *See also* Escobar,
Pablo; Extraditables
media, manipulation of, 107–8. *See also*
journalists
Mercado, José Raquel, 49
Meta Department, 211
microcredit schemes, 179
"militainment," 12–13
militarism: branding and, 16–18; convergence of humanitarianism and, 99; convergence of marketing and, 3, 14–15;
rebranded, 20
militarization of social life, 148–54
military: bounties on guerillas and, 142;
brand warfare by, 208; conflict between
agencies of, 136, 140–41; exchanges between US and Colombia, 206–7; FARC
and, 150–52; humanitarian aid of, 99;
pressure by, and demobilization, 83; refashioning of image of, 85, 88, 108, 154;
transactions between former rebels
and, 140. *See also* former rebels: collaboration with military
military-industrial-media-entertainment
(MIME) complex, 13

Military Operations Other than War
(MOOTWs), 206–7
Ministry of Defense: contract with Lowe/
SSP3, 82–83; corruption in, 139; Direc-
tive 300-28, 141–43; as equated with
Santa Claus, 85; false positive scan-
dal in, 142; institutional campaigns
of, 10; on transactions between military and former rebels, 140. *See also*
Program for Humanitarian Attention to the Demobilized (PAHD);
propaganda
Mitchell, W. J. T., 56
Mittroti, Joshua, 187, *187*
Molano, Alfredo, 183
monetary values, 29
money laundering, 169–70, 176–77
Montoya, Marina, 57
MOOTWs (Military Operations Other
than War), 206–7
Mora Rangel, Jorge Enrique, 212–13
Movement of the 19th of April (M19): advertising campaigns of, 46, *47*, 48–49;
from agitprop to armed propaganda,
43–53; Corinto Accords with, 50–51;
origins of, 4; siege of Palace of Justice
by, 51–52; theft of Bolívar sword by, 44,
46–48, *48*
Mujahid, Abdul Hakim, *213, 215*
MullenLowe SSP3, 253n2. *See also* Lowe/
SSP3

Naranjo, Óscar, 278n13
narcoparamilitaries: community-based
organizations and, 28, 177, 178; former
rebels and, 169–70; murders by, 164;
recruitment by, 175–76
Narcotic Affairs Section (NAS, US), 24
national audience, targeting of, 90
National Commission for Reparation and
Reconciliation (CNRR), 3
National Front (Frente Nacional), 4
National Liberation Army (ELN): advantage of, 8; FARC and, 97; Marxism of,
3–4; PAHD and, 19, 95, 98
national mood, targeting of, 87–88
nation branding and tourism campaigns,
109
Navarro Wolff, Antonio, 213

negotiations. *See* Caguán peace talks (1999–2002); Cuba: negotiations in (2012–2016)

neoliberalism: *apertura*, 2; armed, 10; in Colombia, 165; in decision to join FARC, 6; political violence and, 168–69; reforms and, 1–2; reintegration and, 217

neoparamilitaries, 7

Network of Concerned Anthropologists, 26

New Colombian News Agency (ANNCOL), 20

Nicolás (intelligence officer): bombing of FARC and, 140–41; career of, 129–30; on Directive 300-28, 142–43; on law, 147–48; relationship with, 26, 127–28; role of, 25, 125–26, 127, 128–29; Uribe and, 145; on winning trust, 139

Nieves Ochoa, Martha, 265n38

No campaign (plebiscite on peace accord), xii–xiii, 239, 240

Northrop Grumman, kidnapping of contractors from, 63, 67

Nudo de Paramillo, 92

Omega Task Force, 89

Operation Check (Operación Jaque), 67

Operation Christmas, 83, 84–88, 108

Operation Desert Storm, 12–13

Operation Genuine: elements of, 139; outcome of, 137–38, 143; overview of, 131–37; PowerPoint on, 130

Operation Rivers of Light: as brand warfare, 19–20; coherence of, 105–6; counterfeit bill during, 104–5, *104*; impact of, 100–101; launching of, 95, 98; leaflets for, 104, *105*; origins and development of, 88–95, 105–6; staging of events of, *19*, 98–100, *98*, 102–4, 106–7; at Tres Esquinas air force base, 102

Osorio, Nelson, 45–46

Ospina, Lucas, 32, *40*, *78*, 124, 162, *204*, *228*

Otero, Luis, 44, 52

ownership society vs. "owership" society, 179

Pablo (FARC leader), 131–32, 135–38, 139, 144, 150

Pachón, Maruja, 56, 57, 58

PAHD. *See* Program for Humanitarian Attention to the Demobilized (PAHD)

Pandolfi, Mariella, 99

paramilitaries: in Catatumbo region, 97–98; demobilization of, 2–3, 24, 240; extortion charges of, 163; MAS, 265n38; neo-paramilitaries, 7; remobilization by, 164; response to guerrilla threat by, 6–7; use of torture by, 152. *See also* narcoparamilitaries

Pardo, Rafael, 107

parodies of PAHD marketing, 109, *110*

participatory photography project, Shooting Cameras for Peace (*Disparando Cámaras para la Paz*), 23

Pastrana, Andrés, 2, 8–9, *9*, 63

Patriotic Union (UP), 5, 50

peace, boundary between war and, 14–15, 220–21, 240, 245

peace agreement of 2016 with FARC: approval of, 207–8; FARC members and, 229, 231; negotiations over, 143–45, 183, 185, 218, 221, 233–35; plans for postconflict state and, 238; *60 Minutes* and, x, xii. *See also* Caguán peace talks (1999–2002); Cuba: negotiations in (2012–2016)

peace through consumption, 181–83, 185

Pérez, Álvaro, 180, 187, *187*

Petro, Gustavo, 263n26

Pineda, Alexandra, 50

Pinzón, Juan Carlos, *19*, 92, *98*, 181

Pizarro, Carlos, 46–47

Plan Colombia, 9–10, 24

Plan Lazo, 206

Popular Liberation Army (EPL), 4

postconflict state: branding and, 109, 210, 215–21; demobilization in, 8; PAHD and, 1; in peace agreement, 238; rise of, 2–3. *See also* Program for Humanitarian Attention to the Demobilized (PAHD)

predatory lending, 172

"pre-post conflict," 2–3, 219

pre-postconflict state, origins of, 8–9

Priest, Dana, 153, 271n10

private sector, appeals to, to hire former guerrillas, 168, 169 private security industry, 275n15

prodigal sons, call for return of, 93, *94*

Program for Humanitarian Attention to the Demobilized (PAHD): access to, 23–27; as alternative to torture, 152, 153; brand of, 108; brand warfare of, 245; defensive posture of, 109–10; during negotiations, 218–19; formats and props of, 81–82; impact of, 19, 208; international coverage of, 87–88, 90, 107–8; Lowe/SSP3 and, 79; as model, 207–8, 210–15; overview of, 1, 79–80; Pablo on, 17; parodies of marketing of, 109, *110*; as remobilizing demobilized guerrillas, 8; slogan and logo of, 20, 83; strategic area team of, 125–26, 127, 151; units of, 25; US and, 205; virtuous circle and, 10–11. *See also* intelligence; propaganda; *and specific campaigns*

propaganda: against FARC, 61, 66; agitation and, 42; Café Estereo, 20–21; currency used as, 104–5, *104*; of FARC, 61–62, 63–66; of Ministry of Defense, 10; Pentagon budget for, 258n38; Rendon and, 10. *See also* Program for Humanitarian Attention to the Demobilized (PAHD); *and specific campaigns*

propaganda armada, 43, 50, 52, 53, 60

proyectos productivos, 168

publicity and secrecy, 126–27

publics and Operation Christmas campaign, 86–87

Quintero, Nydia, 56, 57, 63

Quintín Lame Armed Movement, 4

radio, transmission of message by, 86, 87, 91

Rand Corporation, *Enlisting Madison Avenue*, 16

rapid-response propaganda unit, 88–89

RCN Television, 103

Reagan, Ronald, anticommunist crusade of, 205

rearmament. *See* remobilization

rebel territory, transformation of, with light, 84–85, 86, 91

rebusque, 196

recidivism. *See* remobilization

recombinatory circulation, 66

reforms: neoliberalism and, 1–2; of security sector, 129

Regional Military Intelligence unit (RIME): FARC member and, 138, 140–41; FARC regional meeting and, 131; research on FARC family by, 132, 134; view of peace talks in, 145

reintegration: graduation ceremony from program of, 212, *213*; negotiations over model for, 234–35; neoliberalism and, 217. *See also* Colombian Agency for Reintegration (ACR); economic reintegration

remobilization: as military informants, 169, 207; as paramilitaries, 164; road to good life and, 195; statistics on, 167; urban precarity and, 169

Rendon, John, 10

Restrepo, Luis Carlos, 272n14

Revolutionary Armed Forces of Colombia (FARC): blocs of, 131; bombing of, 140–41; branding of, 21–22, 245; brand warfare and, 245; Christmas inside, 134–35; cocaine and, 4–5; as commitment for life, 83; criticism of, 30–31; desertion policy of, 151, 237; desertions from, xiii, 164–65, 191–92; disposition and vision of, 43, 238; ELN and, 97; Facebook campaign against, 66; family policy, 244–45; gender in, 242–45; ideology of, 4–5, 31; kidnappings by, 62–67; Langlois and, 27; Marxism of, 3–4; media initiatives of, 20–21; negotiations between government and, 143–45, 183, 185, 218, 221; political isolation of, 66–67; propaganda and, 61–62, 63–66; rebranding of, 221; recruitment by, 5–6; secretariat of, 153; tenth guerrilla conference, 229, *230*, 231–32, *231*, *232*, 235–36; transitional camps of, 282n7; in 2008, 101; Uribe Accords with, 50. *See also* peace agreement of 2016 with FARC

Reyes, Raul, 89, 106

Reyes Echandía, Alfonso, 51

Ríos, Iván, 89

rite of passage, demobilization as, 216

Roberts, Kevin, 237

sacando adelante a la familia (pushing the family forward), 196

Samper, Ernesto, 6

Samper, Francisco, *103*, 106

Santos, Francisco "Pacho," 56, 57, 58

Santos, Juan Manuel: on death of Cano, 89; democratic security doctrine of, 17; Jaramillo and, 18; on negotiations with FARC, 144–45; Nobel Peace Prize for, 233; Operation Rivers of Light and, 19, *19*, 20, 102–3, *103*, 106–7

Santos Calderón, Enrique, 48

savage capitalism, 172

School of the Americas, Fort Benning, 271n6

security sector reform, 129

security state: affective infrastructure of, 14; targeting as connecting marketing nation and, 15

shielding, as defensive posture, 109–10

Shining Path, 179

Sierra Nevada de Santa Marta, 131, 134

sign systems, 216

SINALTRAINAL, 168–69

60 Minutes, x–xi, xii

soccer, national redemption through, 60

soccer campaign, "Come Back and Play," 90–91

social life, militarization of, 148–54

SoHo (magazine), 183, *184*, 185–86, *185*

Sokoloff, Miguel, x, xi, 81, 82, 90

Somalia, DDR policy in, 279n19

South-South Tour, 210–15, *213*, *214*, *215*. *See also* Colombian Agency for Reintegration (ACR)

Soviet Union, agitprop in, 42

Stahl, Roger, on "militainment," 12

state: anxiety over sovereignty of, 86; branding and, 108–9; demobilized as prodigal sons theme of, 93, *94*; legitimacy crisis in, 6, 153–54; M19 takeover of Palace of Justice and, 52; marketing campaigns of, 41; modernizing project of, 7; pre-postconflict, origins of, 8–9; self-defense function of, 104–5; sovereignty of, 59–60; structural dysfunction within, 218. *See also* postconflict state

State, US Department of, 209

stigma, 166, 168, 217

Stockholm Initiative, 209

strategic area unit of PAHD, 25, 151

Sweden, activism in, 20–21, 30

symbols, focus on, 92

targeting: as connecting marketing nation and security state, 15; of family in demobilization efforts, 132–33, 134; by FARC, 221; of former rebels, 255n21; of guerrilla fighters, 87, 90; of international audience, 90, 107–8; of national audience, 87–88, 90; by No campaign (plebiscite on peace accord), 239; of nodal individuals in enemy network, 207; by Operation Christmas campaign, 86–87. *See also* commanders, midlevel, targeting of

Tate, Winifred, 128

Taussig, Michael, 6, 183

television: saturation of, 55–56; transmission of message by, 86, 87. *See also specific campaigns*

terrorism, 206

theft: of Bolívar sword, 44, 46–48, *48*; embezzlement and, 173–74; reprisals and, 194

Theidon, Kimberly, 3

This American Life, xi

Tilly, Charles, 7

Timochenko, 96, 229, 231

torture, 152, 153

total mobilization, 11–12, 14, 15–16, 19–20, 245

tourism campaigns, 109

transitional justice laws, 148

Tres Esquinas air force base, 102, 106

Turbay, Diana, 56, 57

Turbay, Julio César, 56

unionists, assassinations of, 168–69

United Nations: DDR policy of, 8, 209; DDR programs of, 280n27

United Self-Defense Forces of Colombia (AUC), 6–7, 97, 261n3

United States (US): militainment in, 12–13; MIME complex in, 13; Narcotic Affairs Section, 24; PAHD and, 205; Pentagon budget for propaganda, 258n38; Plan Colombia and, 9–10; professionals paid by, 269n23; rapprochement between Cuba and, 219; relations between Colombia and, 205–7; School of the

United States (US) (*continued*)
  Americas, Fort Benning, 271n6; Viet-
    nam War and, 12. *See also* Central In-
    telligence Agency (CIA)
urban guerrilla, 43, 44–45
urbanization of Colombian conflict, 186
Uribe Accords with FARC, 50
Uribe Velez, Álvaro: attacks on J. San-
    tos by, 268n9; AUC and, 6; demobiliza-
    tion policy of, 24; election of, 10; First
    International Congress of Disarma-
    ment, Demobilization and Reintegra-
    tion and, 208–9; militaristic populism
    of, 20; Nicolás and, 145; No campaign
    (plebiscite on peace accord) led by, xii;
    PAHD and, 8; peace talks and, 144
USAID and ACR, 197

Valle de Cauca departmental assembly,
    kidnapping of members of, 63–66
Van Gennep, Arnold, 216
Vargas Lleras, Germán, 107
Venezuela-Colombia border, 96, 131, 145.
    See also Catatumbo
victims, compensation for, 3, 218
Vidales, Luis, 262n10
video appeals to demobilize, 145–48
Vietnam syndrome, 12

Villamizar, Beatriz, 56, 57
Villamizar Herrera, Darío, 49
Virilio, Paul, 13
virtuous circle, 10–11, *11*
visual impact, primacy of, 105–6

Waldman, Matt, 209
war: boundary between peace and, 14–15,
    220–21, 240, 245; as business, 68; capi-
    talism and, 15–16; drone warfare, 15,
    206, 207; as global and unbounded in
    time, 206–7; mythos of, 13; political
    economy of, 140; sex and, 183, *184*, 185;
    zero-sum logic of, 30. *See also* Colom-
    bian armed conflicts
Wardynski, Casey, 13
war tours, 279n21
welfare for displaced and demobilized per-
    sons, 2
Williams, Raymond, 80
women: demobilized, 242–44; as guerril-
    las, 94, 155–61
world fairs, 188
World War II, provisioning for, 12

Yes campaign (plebiscite on peace accord),
    xii, 239–40
"You Are My Child" campaign, ix–xi, *x*, 93